For Sarah, Guy, & Eliza
I hope this gives
you pleasure!
Sylvia ♡

The Kitchen Garden

Also by Sylvia Thompson

Economy Gastronomy
The Budget Gourmet
Feasts and Friends
The Birthday Cake Book

THE
KITCHEN
GARDEN

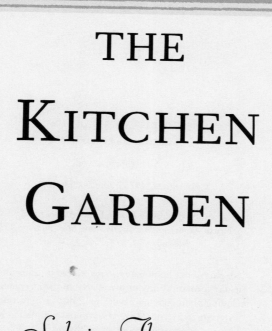

Sylvia Thompson

BANTAM BOOKS
NEW YORK TORONTO LONDON SYDNEY AUCKLAND

THE KITCHEN GARDEN
A Bantam Book/April 1995

All rights reserved.

Book design by Maura Fadden Rosenthal
North American Hardiness Zone Map on page 333
drawn by GDS/Jeffrey L. Ward

Library of Congress Cataloging-in-Publication Data
Thompson, Sylvia Vaughn Sheekman.
The kitchen garden. Sylvia Thompson.
p.   cm.
Includes bibliographical references (p.   ) and index.
ISBN 0-553-08138-1
1. Vegetable gardening.   2. Biointensive gardening.   3. Edible
landscaping.   4. Vegetable gardening—United States.
5. Biointensive gardening—United States.   6. Edible landscaping—
United States.   I. Title.
SB324.3T48 1995
635—dc20   94-32114
CIP

Published simultaneously in the United States and Canada

Bantam Books are published by Bantam Books, a division of Bantam
Doubleday Dell Publishing Group, Inc. Its trademark, consisting of the
words "Bantam Books" and the portrayal of a rooster, is Registered in
U.S. Patent and Trademark Office and in other countries. Marca
Registrada. Bantam Books, 1540 Broadway, New York, New York 10036.

PRINTED IN THE UNITED STATES OF AMERICA

FFG   0 9 8 7 6 5 4 3 2 1

For Great Gloria—
my inspiration,
my cherished friend

Contents

Acknowledgments

As vastly different as people who love a garden may be, I've found they have two qualities in common—generosity and a gift for friendship.

Ring up a seedsman with a question, and by the time you've put down the phone, you have a new friend. Sam Benowitz, Jan Blüm, Peter and Susan Borchard, Gail Haggard, Kate and Fairman Jayne, Tovah Martin, Michael McConkey, Jeff McCormack, and Shepherd and Ellen Ogden have become friends by long distance. They have been particularly generous answering questions and often sending seeds for me to try. Some, like the Ogdens (The Cook's Garden) and Jan Blüm (Seeds Blüm), continue offering seeds of unique plants, even when it may be unprofitable, so we can grow and taste them.

In other consultations, Suzanne Ashforth, Rosalind Creasy, Professor Darleen Demason, Craig and Sue Dremann, Glenn Drowns, George Gleckler, the pseudonymous J. L. Hudson, Sakae Komatsu, Roger Lemstrom, Professor Albert Paulus, Conrad Richter, and Howard Shapiro also generously gave time to answering questions.

I've imposed on the good nature of a number of people, asking them to read my work for errors and omissions. Diana Kennedy, Mexico's national culinary treasure, has graciously shared her knowledge. David and Lynn Ronniger (Ronniger's Seed Potatoes) approved my entry on potatoes. Charles E. Voigt, Vegetable Specialist at the University of Illinois at Urbana-Champaign, did the same for my entry on gardening in winter. Three remarkable people read the entire manuscript. Wendy Krupnick, former assistant to Rosalind Creasy (Creasy's *Cooking from the Garden* is dedicated to her) and now Senior Horticultural Advisor to Renee Shepherd, brought to bear formidable growing experience. John Gale, President of Stokes Seeds, gave me a crash course on gardening in the Northeast and astonished me with his overall knowledge. Joseph Seals, Director of Product Development at Park Seeds, contributed much about gardening in the South and solved many horticultural puzzles. They, too, have become friends.

People in the book world have also been wonderfully generous. Bantam's Managing Editor Chris Fortunato and Art Director Jim Plumeri did everything short of handsprings to make this book shine. Copy editor Chris Benton brilliantly gave order to an appallingly complex manuscript. Designer Maura Fadden Rosenthal shaped my words in this elegant form. Faith Echtermeyer gave me a delightful book cover—and more friends. Ann Cutting shared her bower of a garden. Jennifer Webb, Lauren Janis, and Carolyn Larson were always calm and efficient when I was frazzled.

It was Jack Shoemaker at North Point Press who first gave me the opportunity to write this book. When North Point's light was extinguished, Frances McCullough took on the project. My dear friend and editor dazzles. She has given me unstintingly of her energy and gifts.

Susan Lescher, two shimmering words in the language.

Yes, I am blessed. Diane Bridgford, dear friend of long standing, compiled the pH table, the list of sources, and was my saving grace. Hildegard Manley has always faced me in the right direction. Moreover, she spent endless scholarly hours compiling the charts in The Gardener's Notebook. Lynnda Hart is there when I need her—and I've needed her lots. Dolores Sizer has been adorable helping tirelessly in the garden and in my study.

My mother could not have been more generous and marvelous. It was she who first set me on the garden path. My children have ever given me their sweet support. My husband? His boundless selflessness and loving kindness—not to mention his counsel and judgment—have turned him into nothing less than an angel.

Most of these people know I am in their debt because I've told them. To those whom I have not had the pleasure of telling, I thank you with a full heart.

And I am grateful to Sam, my big black dog, who was at my side in and out of the garden all the years I worked on this book.

Sylvia Thompson
The Chimney House
Idyllwild

Introduction

When I was in the ninth grade, my parents bought an old house on a half-acre close to the Pacific Ocean. My friends spent weekends at the beach, I in my mother's garden. The garden had been exquisitely landscaped and tended for 40 years by the former owner, a venerable horticulturist. It was my mother's first garden, and she threw herself into restoring it with characteristic creativity and verve. She threw me, grumbling and tearful, into her garden, too. I *hated* watering, weeding, mulching, hoeing, pruning, and being responsible for eccentricities like mounding ice cubes at the base of the lilac bush (lilacs do not flower in the subtropical parts of southern California).

After I married, my husband and I rented a house in Berkeley overlooking San Francisco Bay. One spring day I impulsively bought a few small tomato plants at the market. When I got them home, I panicked. Behind our house was a terraced garden smothered in weeds. I realized I would have to not only plant these little tomatoes but first clear a place for them. It crossed my mind to give them away, but I hadn't the heart.

I borrowed a shovel and hoe from a neighbor, who lugged over a sack of manure for me to use. As I watered and weeded and cultivated and dug and planted and patted and watered again, I was astonished to find myself responding to the rhythms of my toil. More than that, I realized I knew what I was doing. More than that, *I loved it!* It was dark by the time I finished, and after I poured myself a glass of wine I called my mother. She wept. That summer, like a sculptor freeing a shape from the marble, I pulled every weed on that slope and uncovered a kindred spirit's garden from long ago.

In the years since, I've been lucky in having delicious gardens to work in. A cottage garden by the Thames that had no hoses ("What do we do for water?" I asked, and the gardener replied, "Why, it rains!"). Returning to Berkeley, we had a stately old garden where the azaleas liked to be moved biannually. Then to a hilltop on the island of Belvedere in San Francisco Bay, where the wind killed everything but the native plants. Then to a small Mill Valley garden where I joined the Marin County Chrysanthemum Society but never went to a meeting because the deer kept eating all my flowers. And then to a balmy canyon in sight of the sea in Malibu where for

16 years my husband and I created a terraced garden of flowers, vegetables, herbs, and fruits in a grove of eucalyptus.

In the kitchen, in the garden, books have always been my teachers, and I read and experimented endlessly. But in those days the books I read had no list of resources. All my plants came from the local nursery. Then one day a friend who was a great gardener showed me her collection of thymes.

"Where on earth did you find them?" I asked, amazed.

"From a mail-order nursery."

"And how'd you know where to write?" says I.

"From *Horticulture*."

"What's that?"

"A magazine."

Thus I discovered catalogs, and my world opened wide.

What's so exciting about having a kitchen garden these days is that it transports you to places you never thought you'd go. It used to be that unless you traveled to Turkey, you could live and die without enjoying roasted small black chick-peas. Now, without the expense of a trip to Japan, you can sip minty/meaty perilla tea and feel yourself in the cool of a Kyoto temple garden. And it takes only a little imagination to feel the hot dry air of the Hopi Indian Reservation in Arizona as you munch on the crisp sweet flesh of a Hopi yellow-meated watermelon.

From the beginning, instinct led me to design our gardens in what has come to be called *edible landscaping*—vegetables, herbs, and fruits mixed decoratively into the border with flowers. In every aspect of my life I have catholic tastes. I'm eager to see every flower and savor every edible thing there is.

Partly because we lived in radical Berkeley and partly just out of common sense I gardened organically from the start. It was in Malibu that I discovered the French intensive method of growing plants close together, which suited my desire to grow just a sampling for the pleasure of a taste of something new. Once, midsummer, a friend asked what I was growing. Curious, I added it up. We both were surprised: 136 sorts of vegetables, herbs, edible flowers, and annual fruits. For example, I was growing 2 square feet each of 22 kinds of beans. In one area of 50 square feet that were on their leaves rotation were 10 square feet of spinach, 6 square feet each of chard, corn salad, and orach, 5 square feet each of New Zealand spinach and Good-King-Henry, 3 square feet each of celery and celeriac, 1 square foot each of curled peppergrass, miner's lettuce, Johnny-jump-ups, nasturtiums, and golden and green purslanes.

For space, by the house we have about 850 square feet that gets six to eight hours of sun each day and another 250 square feet that receives half-day sun. Some parts of the beds are taken up with perennials and shrubs, and it is in these beds that I squeeze and rotate our annual growings. In the past, when I've felt ambitious, I've gardened on 1,000 square feet more of full sun on the slopes of our small orchard, among the trees—some enormous, some minuscule. But these days I stick to the beds around the house.

How do I choose what to grow? By flavor, first and foremost. I am a cook, and the more I cook, the simpler I cook, and the simpler I cook, the more I depend on the finest flavors around. Since we live in droughty southern California, the second consideration must be drought tolerance. Were water not a problem, the second most important quality would be beauty. Color and form matter enormously to me—in the garden, on the plate, in a jug or vase or basket.

Another wonderful thing about a kitchen garden is that all of it needn't stay outside. "In a jug or vase or basket" means that when I snip the stalks of flowers from the nebuka onions so I can harvest the onions longer, instead of throwing them onto the compost heap, I tuck the stalks into a copper jug and set them on the kitchen table. Trimmings of all sorts can be cheering in a jug—from the top leaves of brussels sprouts to feathery branches of fennel to seedpods of brassicas. Through winter, an autumn arrangement of dried corn tassels delights me. That's why I keep a few pumpkins and winter squashes in the cool entry hall, rather than stash them away in the cellar. Because I grew them. They are part of me. When the earth is bare outside, the fruits of summer are close by.

I have learned much through these years in the garden. I have so much more to learn. I would be glad to hear from you—tell me what you know that I don't. That's another aspect of gardening I love—sharing the wealth and the joy.

How to Use This Book

At heart, this book was inspired by a wish to taste food that isn't ever going to be in the market. That's why so many of these pages are devoted to the unusual and rare. Anything you grow will taste better than anything you can buy, and if you're keen on growing just plain cantaloupe, the information's here. But the same information applies to growing a perfumed orange-fleshed French Charentais melon, which you can't buy for love or money—it wouldn't survive the journey to market.

Each vegetable, fruit, herb, and edible flower has its own entry in which I tell you how it tastes, what it needs to grow, perhaps a little lore, my experience with it, some recommended cultivars—both open pollinated (OP) and hybrid—and how the plant fits into the landscape.

At the beginning of each entry, I've given just as much information about growing something as you need to know to decide whether or not you want to. If the information isn't under the title, look back to the umbrella title and there it will be for all plants that follow.

Once you've decided you'd like to have a particular plant in your garden, consult The Gardener's Notebook for the growing information. There, in user-friendly charts, you'll find what you need to know about planning where the plant can go in the landscape, sowing and germinating the seeds, transplanting the seedlings, growing, and finally harvesting the crop. These charts combine the best features of those I've found invaluable over the years.

Each entry also notes the suitable size for the plant in a container, which is sometimes the only way we can accommodate a sun-loving plant when there is no sunny ground, only a sunny patch that's decked or paved.

My recommendations of cultivars complete the entry. When there is none, it's because all offerings are generic—no named cultivars are in catalogs thus far.

From time to time you'll want to dip into The Gardener's Notebook and read about other aspects of gardening, everything from blanching chicories to putting rodents in perspective to the weights of floating row covers. The Notebook is part glossary, part technical material, part good old-fashioned know-how and common sense.

Also in The Gardener's Notebook are three maps. The first is the widely accepted USDA Hardiness Zones, which tells you the approximate annual average minimum temperatures within 10 degrees of where you live. The second is a map that gives the last date you can expect a killing frost in spring within probability of 10 percent and with a leeway of 10 days. The third map gives you the first date you can expect a killing frost in autumn, with the same application as the spring map. If your dates are April 5–15, chances are that in 9 out of 10 years, you won't have a killing frost after April 15. Likewise, if your dates are October 5–15, the map will tell you that 9 out of 10 years there won't be a killing frost before October 5. Therefore, you have reasonable assurance that your growing season is the time in between.

As I mention occasionally, *Hortus Third* (subtitled *A Concise Dictionary of Plants Cultivated in the United States and Canada*) is my primary reference for botanical information. Since a number of the plants in this book are new to this country, they're not yet listed in *Hortus*. I then consult other reliable sources, but sometimes the information regarding plant type, hardiness, origin, and such just isn't available. When cross-references are included, they're by section rather than page number.

All entries are alphabetical. You should be able to find what you're looking for easily—with this in mind: When presented with the problem of ordering the myriad greens we can grow in the kitchen garden, I decided to gather them in four groups. This way, plants in a group are interchangeable in preparation, and you can cruise through the section for inspiration and ideas. You'll quickly get used to the logic of these groups:

Asian Greens are the mild sweet leaves common to Asian cooking.

Mustard Greens are the peppery leaves beloved in Asia and America's Deep South.

Potherbs are the fresh young things that mostly pop up in spring—some are sweet and some are hot, and all are underappreciated. They can go into the pot, or they can go in salads.

Salad Greens include common and not-so-common leaves for salads.

Other entries are also not botanical but descriptive: Beans for Frying, Savory Cabbages, Cooking and Slicing Onions, and so forth.

Although I garden on a mile-high mountain, in writing my cooking/gardening column for newspapers in the mid-Atlantic region, the Midwest, Northwest, and multi-climate southern California, I've had ample experience familiarizing myself with gardening in those areas as well. Finally, I've consulted experts from the temperate West, the intemperate Northeast, and the sultry South to guide me. So this is a book for the whole marvelous country. Happy gardening!

The Kitchen Garden

IN
THE
GARDEN

ADZUKI BEANS. *See Beans for Drying.*

AMARANTH. *See Potherbs.*

AMBROSIA. *See Salad Greens.*

ARTICHOKE (GLOBE) AND CARDOON
Cynara spp.

ARTICHOKE *C. Scolymus*

CARDOON *C. cardunculus*

Half-hardy perennials in the Sunflower family, native to southern Europe . . . grows in 10-gallon containers. Artichokes and cardoons need a sunny site and deep, rich humusy soil kept constantly moist.

No vegetable plants are more elegant than these blue-green or silvery green fountains with their thistlelike blooms. Cardoons were eaten by the Greeks. The Romans enjoyed artichokes so much they preserved them for serving out of season. I find the two plants indistinguishable, they're that closely related. With artichokes, it's the bud we eat—with cardoons, the fleshy stalks. Buds on cardoons are prickly and much smaller than artichoke buds. Artichokes can grow to 5 feet and cardoons to 8 or more, but that's in places like Watsonville, California, Artichoke Capital of the World. In the hot, dry mountains, our artichokes struggle to knee height, and the flesh of their buds is on the dry side. But our cardoons are magnificent—their stems as thick as my wrist. Artichokes and cardoons are survivors.

Artichoke seeds are variable—up to two-thirds may deviate from form. You're safest with root cuttings. But if you want to taste an unusual cultivar, you must try your luck with seeds. In Europe, cultivars are named Venice, Tuscany, and Provence violet, Breton, and Roman. Here we can taste the small, pointy, purple Italian Violetto (of unknown parentage). For the sensuous experience of popping artichokes the size of a walnut into your mouth, you must try to grow them. If you sow them indoors in spring, then harden them off and plant them outdoors under row covers six to eight weeks later, you may have Violetto buds to eat the first year—as you may from the large Green Globe Improved. Imperial Star is another cultivar bred to give buds the first summer from spring-sown seeds. Otherwise you have to wait until the second year (and each year thereafter) for the harvest.

Once established, mulch plants deeply with straw or something similar, but make a barrier or set traps for slugs and snails (see The Gardener's Notebook)—they love hiding beneath mulch by day and then gliding up to nibble on all that succulence at night. Aphids and/or ants will probably be a problem. Once a week or so, holding the pested frond by its tip so the force of the water won't break it, use a strong spray the length of each frond, front and back and down the center, to drown them. Gophers—which I entertain royally in my garden—are fond of artichokes and cardoons. To foil them, in late winter dig up established plants and replant them encased in 1-inch-gauge chicken wire cages.

An artichoke plant grown for its buds is regal and all green. Once it starts to come awake in spring, you'll see a voluptuous swelling in the stalk of this magnificent plant, with great fronds of leaves over it lying smooth as feathers over a bird's breast. Press the spot gently with your hand and you'll feel something tiny and firm. A baby artichoke.

Up to about the size of a plum, you'll be able to eat the whole bud—no fuzzy choke will have formed. Cut the stem off with a knife at its base. You can pare and cook the stem—its flavor and texture is much the same as the heart's.

But let the cardoon open its buds to royal blue and you have a plant that lifts your spirits each time you look at it. At some point, though, you'll want to keep the buds from flowering and prepare cardoon stalks for eating. To keep them sweet, juicy, and tender, it's traditional to blanch the stalks (see The Gardener's Notebook). It makes a clumsy-looking arrangement, so think about that when you place the plant in the border. Set it well in the back and you can camouflage it with a tall distracting annual such as cleome.

The first cardoon harvest will be about four months after sowing. After that, where it's temperate, you can harvest cardoons in late winter and early spring. Harvest by cutting the stalk off flush with the ground.

When the plants are grown for flowers instead of buds or stalks, they can manage with just enough water to keep from drooping. Artichokes and cardoons are an incomparable focal point in the border.

Recommended: Violetto and Imperial Star artichokes—cardoons are thus far generic. I'm told named cultivars of cardoons appear in catalogs from time to time; I've never seen them and have always grown the generic.

ARUGULA. *See Salad Greens.*

Asian Greens: Mild and Sweet

Unless otherwise specified, give plants at least six hours of sun—although shade in the heat of a hot summer day is a good idea since most of these greens hate heat. Soil must be well drained, fertile, humusy, and moisture retentive.

In this group are leaves with a mild flavor, usually cabbagey. Nippy-tasting leaves are gathered in Mustard Greens.

An enthralling array of mild and bitter, crunchy and silky, pale and dark mustards is grown and prepared in the Orient. Between the confusion of classifying brassicas—these are nearly all mustards—and the confusion of transliterating Japanese, Chinese, and Korean words, names of cultivars can get screwy. One man's tsai tai can be another's tah tsai and still another's taisai, and they can be the same plant or three different ones, probably the latter.

Regardless of what we call them, these greens will grow for us with dazzling speed and generosity. Of all vegetables in the garden, they are the most carefree. Knowing what we know about the protective value of brassicas against human disease, we ought to put some of these greens and flowers and stalks and shoots on our table every day.

For the finest greens, observe the four-year rotation cycle (see The Gardener's Notebook). If your soil isn't splendid, before sowing dig in an inch of sphagnum peat moss or redwood soil amendment and as much compost and/or aged manure as you can spare. Then sprinkle with blood meal, bonemeal, and kelp meal or wood ashes and dig them in. Give abundant water. When the seedlings have two leaves, begin weekly treats of half-strength manure tea or fish or kelp emulsion. Mulch and inspect regularly for slugs. If aphids or flea beetles are in the garden, protect the plants by wrapping with insect-weight floating row covers from sowing to harvest. As with lettuces, the faster greens grow, the better their protection against pests and the finer the quality of their leaves.

CHINESE CABBAGES   *Brassica Rapa*, Pekinensis Group

Half-hardy biennials in the Mustard family, native to China . . . aka
bok choy, pe-tsai, celery cabbage, Napa, wong bok, Michi-
hili . . . grows in 5-gallon containers.

These cabbages have been cultivated in China since the fifth century.
Thought to be a cross between the South's pak choi cabbage and the
North's turnip, the tender leaves of Chinese cabbages are thinner than
those of European cabbages, as though they were a blend of lettuce and silk. The
flavors are milder and sweeter, with a delicate aftertaste of mustard, but the leaves
must be picked young. The midribs, instead of being thick and firm, are thin, broad,
and succulently crunchy. Chinese cabbage comes in three shapes, two firm-headed
and one loose-headed. Most of us are familiar with the firm-headed forms.

The firm-headed forms of Chinese cabbage are particularly suited to northern
climates. Toward the south, heads develop more loosely, probably in response to
the heat—Chinese cabbages hate heat. The ruffly loose-headed form of Chinese
cabbage resembles some of the mustards and the rosette pak chois—a big blowsy
rose. There are a number of Chinese cabbages in this shape, and it's the more con-

Sowing Half-hardy and Hardy Vegetables in Autumn and Winter

If you garden where there's little or no frost, by and large you can sow seeds
of half-hardy and hardy vegetables from fall through winter. If summers are
very hot, this is the preferred sowing time, since spring-sown seeds would
quickly hit a wall of summer heat and prematurely succumb.

Seeds of some plants in some climates may not prosper in the dead of
winter—sowing is through October and then starting again in January. But
you won't know until you try.

fusing because there are crosses between them. To the Western eye, they all bear a close resemblance, and they're all delicious.

Firm-headed cabbages are very long keeping—Napa more than Michihili. Store the whole plant without wrapping, including root and outer leaves, at around 34°F. Plants must be dry at all times. They can keep for months, almost as long as European cabbages.

Napa. This firm-headed Chinese cabbage has finely pleated leaves of pale to white-green tightly furled into a chunky barrel—like a big European eggplant. Quick to mature (from 45 days after transplanting) and fairly slow to bolt, this is the type to sow in earliest spring.

Michihili. This firm-headed Chinese cabbage is a long, narrow cylinder shaped like a head of bunching celery. These heads are slower growing (upward of 70 days after transplanting) and quicker to bolt, but they are the ones to grow for autumn. Sowing about 3 months before autumn's first expected frost will provide nourishing leaves until then.

For an especially luminous white center, blanch these cabbages (see The Gardener's Notebook).

Loose-headed Chinese cabbage is easier to grow than the firm-headed forms. It matures earlier and is more resistant to heat, cold, bolting, and disease. Sow from early spring through early autumn—best transplant seedlings from soil blocks or paper pots. In fact the earliest harvests of Chinese cabbage come from loose-headed types. Give them a layer of floating row cover if there's frost. But don't worry—cold sweetens their flavor. Any frostbitten outer leaves can go in the compost. Loose heads don't keep as well as firm heads do and should be eaten right away. In cool climates you can sow loose-headed Chinese cabbage successively, harvesting two crops in spring and two or three in autumn. In the border, since they're not too tall, sow them among primroses in spring and among petunias in autumn.

As with all the brassicas, you can sow seeds extra thickly and pick small leaves forever. For beautiful, crisp, firm Chinese cabbages, it's safest to sow in place, because if seedlings are too old when transplanted, plants tend to bolt. If you're going to transplant, best sow seedlings into soil blocks or paper pots.

Should timing and climate make it necessary to grow Chinese cabbage in hot weather, select tropical cultivars, mulch deeply, and wave the hose in the air for a cooling shower from time to time.

Chinese cabbage is susceptible to more pests and diseases than most brassicas. If yours is a cool, wet climate, ask your county farm adviser or university extension whether Chinese cabbages are susceptible to disease—there are disease-resistant cultivars.

Harvest from seedling to young leaf stages (at which time you'd take the whole plant)—the mature leaf is devilishly tough when cooked, although acceptable raw in salads.

Recommended: Flavor in these cabbages is similar, so choose other traits that are important to you. The easiest and among the most delightful I've found is the open-pollinated South China Earliest. For very hot weather: Napa hybrids Tropical Pride for summer sowing and Tropical 50 for sowing in spring. Barrel-shaped Napa or wong bok: WR-70 and China Express are considered superior hybrids—they resist frost, disease, and bolting. Long, narrow cylinder-shaped Michihili: the open-pollinated Michihili or hybrids Jade Pagoda (for both spring and fall sowings) and Monument get high marks. Loose-headed: look for the Santo cultivars (Shanto, Santoh, Shandong, and Shantung), as well as Tokyo Bekana and Chin-Tau. Their leaves can be big, round, and smooth or medium-sized, toothed, and frilled. Tokyo Bekana can be sown the year around and is easy to grow.

China Pride is slow to bolt and tolerant to many diseases, including downy mildew, bacterial soft rot, and tip burn. Summertime II is resistant to alternaria, downy mildew, and white spot. But all are susceptible to black rot.

CHINESE KALE   *Brassica oleracea,* Alboglabra Group

Half-hardy annual in the Mustard family, probably native to Asia . . . aka Chinese broccoli, white flowering broccoli, gai lon . . . grows in 5-gallon containers. To grow this generous plant, observe the 4-year rotation plan (see The Gardener's Notebook); provide about 6 hours of sun, rich, moisture-retentive, well-drained soil with lots of compost and/or aged manure, abundant water, and weekly treats of manure tea or liquid fish or kelp.

One of the easiest of brassicas to grow, this plant is interesting—some have a frosty look, as though dipped in wax. The flowers are white or yellow, and, according to the cultivar, leaves are wrinkled or smooth, shiny or matte, round or pointed.

The leaves of this large amiable plant taste very much like other kales, mild and cabbagey. The stalks, if picked no thicker than your little finger, are tender skinned, sweet on the inside, and crunchy. Allowed to send up flowers, the buds look like broccoli buds, but they're fewer and looser.

Every part may be harvested and sliced into salads or stir-fries. It's best to cut the stalks when the buds are just about to open. Once the buds open to small white flowers, the flavor is far stronger and the texture tougher than those of other flowering brassicas. Cut the first tender stalk several inches above the ground, leaving nodes from which more sprouts will come. Chinese kales tolerate more heat than most Asian greens, but still they prefer—and are most palatable in—cool weather. But because they're so easygoing, you can harvest from early summer to early winter with one spring sowing. After three cuttings the shoots get very skinny.

In temperate climates, sow seeds indoors in soil blocks early in February. Two weeks later, move them into the cold frame to harden. Two to three weeks later, into the ground they go, protected with a layer or two of floating row covers. The seedlings can take frost, but if they're hit by a hard frost, all you have to do is rinse off the leaves and let the air dry them. If the ground isn't workable in March, push this process forward until it is.

Mulch deeply. If the plants show a tendency to lop over from the wind or their weight, earth up around the base for support. And if any insects threaten, cover the plants with insect-weight floating row covers. Chinese kale is susceptible to the fungi of downy mildew. Since no disease-resistant cultivars are offered, I'm careful not to water the plants overhead in the afternoon, and I set them where they can get good air circulation.

Recommended: Start with generic White Flower/Pointed Leaf. Green Lance is a delicious hybrid.

FLOWERING BRASSICAS

Grows in 5-gallon containers.

These are nonheading leafy cabbages prized especially for their flowering shoots. The leaves are harvested while the plant matures, but then, when it bolts, the real harvest begins. Generally the shoots are mild and sweet, especially good in stir-fries. These cabbages are considered a bit more difficult to grow than pak choi, since their urge is to bolt, bolt, bolt (see Flowering Pak Choi for an alternative crop). It's easiest to germinate seeds and then transplant the seedlings at the right time.

CHOY SUM   *B. parachinensis*

Tender annuals in the Mustard family, native to eastern Asia . . . aka false pak choi, flowering white cabbage.

This is one of China's favorite vegetables. Plants can have various growth habits, from spreading to upright, from ankle to knee high. Leaves are generally oval and pinked, but the flowering shoot is what's harvested. So in effect, you won't be sure what plant you're getting, but you can be sure the leaves and shoots will be delectable. These are not frost hardy and need heat to germinate, so sow them midsummer, the last crop about 6 weeks before the first expected frost of autumn.

The choy sums can grow vigorously and a bit lanky, so set them among perky plants with clean lines such as tall marigolds. When you harvest, always leave a few shoots on the plant so that more will come.

Recommended: Long White Petiole and Short White Petiole are equally easy and good—in a cabbage patch, I find them indistinguishable. Not to be confused with the Long White Petiole and Short White Petiole forms of pak choi.

PURPLE-FLOWERED CHOY SUM   *B. parachinensis*

Aka hon tsai tai, tsai shim, flowering purple pak choi.

Read this as purple choy sum with flowers—the turniplike leaves are purple with dark red veins, the flowers yellow. When the plant goes to seed, up come purple-red shoots—long and slender—tipped with golden flowers and buds of green. The colors are beautiful.

Although called flowering purple pak choi, this is not a true pak choi.

GARLAND CHRYSANTHEMUM   *Chrysanthemum coronarium*

Half-hardy annual in the Sunflower family, native to the Mediterranean region . . . aka edible chrysanthemum, shungiku, chop suey greens, crown daisy . . . grows in 5-gallon containers. These chrysanthemums grow best in temperate climates in cool weather. For the lushest leaves, grow on light fertile soil in high shade where it's warm or in a sunny spot where it's cool. Protect from drenching rain.

This is a wonderful green to eat! The flavor of the leaves and stems is slightly musky, slightly lemony, slightly herbal. Two types of edible chrysanthemums, large and small, are offered in the Asian catalogs. Get the large leaves.

Don't expect these daisies either to be as perky as summer's daisies or as elegant as autumn's chrysanthemums. The plants have a wistful, ungainly quality. That's because they're cultivated for their leaves, and no breeder has bothered to make the plants appealing.

The fleshy leaves and tender stalks are wonderfully tasty in salads, stir-fries, tempura, and soup. Pick just before using, because they wilt rapidly. The yellow flower petals—if you let the plant hang around that long—add a delightful touch to everything you can think of.

To harvest older leaves, grow a number of plants. That way you can cut the leafy stalks about halfway down rather than commit the indiscretion of plucking all the leaves from one or two plants and having their stalks look nude. More leaves will sprout from the sides of the cut stalks. The plants grow about a foot tall and then, when the weather warms, send up flowering stalks of another foot or so. At that point the leaves and stalks are past their prime. The rule of thumb is to harvest no more leaves after a flower bud has formed. I've taken leaves when the plants were in full bloom, but they were barely tender.

Recommended: The large-leaved forms are easiest and most satisfying all around. Generic.

KOMATSUNA

B. Rapa, Perviridis Group

Hardy (to −14°F) annual or biennial in the Mustard family, probably native to Asia . . . aka spinach mustard . . . grows in 5-gallon containers.

Komatsuna is a fast-growing, wonderfully hardy, large and productive sort of green with a flavor somewhere between mustard, cabbage, and spinach. For a species called *spinach mustard*, there's not a drop of spinach in its veins. Discovered near Tokyo, the thick, dark green leaves are favorites in Japan and Korea but little known in China. The juicy young leaves and stalks are marvelous in salads. As with all mustards, the flavor gets nippier as the leaves mature. Field mice and other small rodents seem to prefer thinner leaves like bok choy—they've left my komatsunas alone.

You can sow seeds directly in the ground as soon as the soil can be worked in spring and every few weeks through summer and autumn. But, as you'll hear me say again and again, I find it infinitely surer to germinate seeds in a pot or flat and then transplant them. If it's cold, shelter seedlings with floating row covers or cloches or a cold frame to hasten growth. Tokyo komatsuna is an old favorite in Japan and ready in 30 days. Harvest mature leaves from the outside, leaving an inch or so of stem so leaves will come again. And when they bolt, toss tender stems and buds into stir-fries. In the border you might set off the lush dark green of komatsuna with the sunny-green finely cut leaves of Chinese celery.

Part of the field mustard clan, komatsuna crosses with everything that blows its way, so there are komatsuna–komatsuna greens (Savanna hybrid), komatsuna–turnip greens (All Top and Big Top), komatsuna–pak choi greens (Green Boy), komatsuna–Chinese cabbage greens, and now a komatsuna–European cabbage green (Senposai). Leaves can be turnipy coarse and/or glossy smooth. Stems can be thin and bare or ruffled with greens to the base. Since they're such happy campers, no harm in trying whatever turns up in catalogs. I'm crazy about it, and intend always to have some in the garden.

Recommended: I've loved every aspect of komatsuna I've grown. They're delicious and a cinch.

MIZUNA

B. Rapa var. *nipposinica*

Hardy annual or biennial in the Mustard family, probably native to China . . . grows in 5-gallon containers. More tolerant of heat than common mustards.

Mizunas are some of the most decorative leaves in the garden. The plant is a small explosion of a rounded bush tipped with a hundred miniature staghorn ferns. Cold- and heat-tolerant mizuna is a favorite green in Japan—and in my house. It grows easily and without pests (except for the horrid slug). The leaves are dark green; the stalks are slender, pale, and juicy. The flavor is mustardy but delicate. I love mizuna in a wild salad. Sow mizuna several times during the season for mizuna sprouts for salads. Pick mizuna leaves frequently in a cut-and-come-again way to encourage new growth, picking from the outside.

Mizunas are fairly hardy and can be sown in autumn and then sheltered over winter, when they will produce leaves until the following spring. But do watch the flow of air—mildew can be a problem—and water only in the morning.

Mizuna is one of those plants to perch at the edge of garden steps or beside a path so it can float all by itself, perhaps softened around the base with the small enchanting faces of toadflax. The basic open-pollinated mizuna is easy and widely adapted—no need to look further.

PAK CHOI   *Brassica Rapa* var. Chinensis Group

Half-hardy biennials in the Mustard family, native to Europe . . . aka celery mustard, Chinese mustard, mustard cabbage, Chinese white cabbage, white stalked cabbage, spoon cabbage . . . grows in 3-gallon containers. For superb pak choi, plan so most growth takes place when the air temperature is in the 60s (some cultivars tolerate more heat). To outwit pests, grow the plants fast and strong—or under floating row covers if you must.

Pak choi cabbages have been cultivated in China since the fifth century. Some are so delectable, bugs of the field prefer them to Western brassicas, and farmers offer a catch crop of pak choi to lure insects away from the cauliflower and broccoli. Unlike other mustards, their green leaves don't form tightly furled heads. Pak chois are bunches of fleshy stalks, like celery, with broad smooth or ruffled leaves like chard. Whether just a few inches high or two feet tall, all are beautiful additions to the garden. And with a hint of mustard in their flavor, all are delectable raw in salads or cooked in stir-fries.

According to their appearance, pak chois are loosely gathered into four forms.

Probably the easiest to grow, the hardiest and among the most aesthetic and flavorful is the green leaf stalk type, sown from spring through fall. Although tasty when harvested at 8 to 10 inches, often it's offered as "baby" pak choi, and you're instructed to harvest it at 6 inches. The leaves are a much brighter, lighter green than on most Chinese cabbages. Evergreen Y. H. Enterprises seedsmen call these Ching-Chiang pak chois and divide them into Long Green Petiole and Short Green Petiole—both handsome and delicious. The old Shanghai and the new hybrid Mei Qing cultivars are also recommended.

The white stalk type has dark green leaves that curl outward on tender, pure white stalks a foot tall. Very productive, very mild. Evergreen's short white petiole pak choi tolerates severe heat and bad weather and may be sown from July to September—it originated in Southern China.

The true babies are the squat or Canton types—they can be harvested at just a few inches. In addition to their tender size, these pak chois are prized for their delicate flavor and for their tolerance of warm weather. Sow them midsummer and harvest before cold weather. Evergreen's Canton Short White (aka Short White Petiole) is lovely.

Possibly the best flavor of all is in the thinnish cupped soupspoon or spoon-shaped dark green leaves on long crisp stalks, themselves somewhat spoon shaped. These heads are best harvested around 10 inches tall. Evergreen offers these as Long White Petiole Pok Choy and Short White Petiole Pok Choy, to confuse matters.

Unlike European cabbages, pak chois grow quickly, averaging six weeks to maturity. Harvesting may begin within a couple of weeks of sowing. At this stage the Chinese call the large seedlings chicken feathers. In two more weeks miniature heads have formed, and they can be used as baby pak choi—the pert little bundles are a delight. When they mature, you can harvest individual stalks or the whole bunch cut at the base, and more shoots will sprout in their place.

Ideally the biennial pak choi's bright yellow flowers won't come up from the center of the plant until the second year. But there are two tricky aspects to growing pak choi (which some consider easier to grow than Chinese cabbage). Pak choi doesn't like being transplanted, and although it is a cool-weather crop, it bolts when subjected to too much cold in its formative stages and also tends to bolt when it's hot. Sow any pak choi in chilly spring for chicken feathers and baby pak choi. But to harvest mature plants in summer, sow cold-hardy cultivars such as Mei Qing, Chinese White Pak, the Tai Sai group, and Joi Choi in early spring indoors in soil blocks or paper pots, harden off, set in the garden, then protect them with floating row covers until it's warm. You can sow another crop directly in the ground in early summer for fall and another in fall to winter over (under cover).

I like to set these lovely cabbages among ruby chards or beets for the warmth of the deep greens and reds.

Should your pak choi bolt before you'd intended, it's an inconvenience, but you can harvest the flowering shoots just as for choy sum. If you'd rather have leaves, just keep nipping out the flower stalks, and you'll forestall the demise for a while.

Pak choi is easy to grow late in the fall in a cold frame or sheltered spot in a temperate climate—they love cool weather.

As a Japanese seedsman said to me about growing pak choi, "Just throw out the seeds and don't worry about them!"

Recommended: Short Green Petiole and Mei Qing are superior green leaf stalk types that grow easily. Hybrid Joi Choi is the surest white stalk type, but Prize Choy is worth growing, too. Canton Dwarf and Canton Short White are very reliable Canton types. Long White Petiole Pok Choy and Short White Petiole Pok Choy are the easiest soupspoons. For cold hardiness, try Mei Qing, Chinese White Pak, the Tai Sai group, and Joi Choi.

FLOWERING PAK CHOI

Many Chinese who find choy sums too tricky to grow sow medium-size pak chois, let them bolt, and harvest the shoots—although they're not considered as choice as the bred-for-flavor choy sums.

Recommended: Hybrid Mei Qing, though not quick to flower, is of superb quality.

ROSETTE PAK CHOI   *B. Rapa* var. *rosularis*

Hardy biennial in the Mustard family . . . aka tatsoi, tah tsai, Chinese flat cabbage, flat black cabbage . . . grows in 3-gallon containers.

Thought to be very ancient, this pak choi has deep green to black spinachy leaves forming an exquisite rosette, a little like a large version of the best African violets you ever managed to grow. The thick roundish leaves—sometimes crinkled or puckered—lie close to the ground, although in warm weather they can rise to 8 or 10 inches. And some spread themselves 1 ½ feet across. Rosette pak choi is extremely cold tolerant, one of the rare vegetables that continues to grow through short cold days. You can pluck leaves from under the snow.

Rosette pak chois are more pronounced in flavor than most, and the Chinese feel that the smaller the leaf, the richer the flavor. You can harvest leaves individually from the seedling stage on—they're uncommonly nourishing. Weave a couple of rosette pak chois with three white ornamental kales and white alyssum sprinkled throughout the border. Start with generic Chinese flat cabbage, aesthetic and easy.

TENDERGREEN   *Brassica Rapa,* Perviridis Group

Half-hardy annual or biennial in the Mustard family, probably native to Asia . . . grows in 5-gallon containers.

ppealing name for an appealing plant with an appealing mild spinach-mustard flavor. Smaller than mustard, a little larger than spinach, the leaves are large, thick, shiny dark green, rounded, with pale green midribs. They bunch together in a casual crisp way like a scarf tucked into a breast pocket.

Sow in early spring and again from late summer through autumn. Tolerant to heat, cold, and drought, nutritious and ready in a month or so. Tendergreen is similar to marvelous komatsuna. Harvest from seedlings to mature leaves, taking older ones from the outside.

Asparagus

Asparagus officinalis

Usually winter-hardy perennial in the Lily family, native to Europe, Asia, and North Africa . . . grows in half-barrels. It's important to grow a strain of asparagus that has been developed for your climate. And it's important to give asparagus a rest from picking each year. For years of superb spears, prepare the richest possible bed for them in full sun. Once established, asparagus is surprisingly drought tolerant and undemanding, and the bed will last for years. In early autumn, spread a couple of inches of well-rotted manure or compost over the bed—it will work its way down over winter, feeding the roots. Do this again in very early spring and then again when the harvest is over.

Whether as skinny as a flower stem or as thick as a corn stalk, the spears of asparagus we love buttering are in fact shoots. Left alone, they'll open into a green tracery of leaves as thin as needles—ferny plants that make a tall, thick, bright green hedge. The Romans cultivated asparagus for centuries, using the seeds of wild plants. Our asparagus seeds have been tinkered with, but we grow the plants much the same way as the ancients.

Because you can't harvest too many shoots for a year or two after planting, the *first* thing I'd do in a new garden is plant asparagus. Even two-year-old crowns won't change this. When the well-established plants are lifted from the field, proportionately so many more roots are lost that it takes the plants longer to recover than one-year-olds with skimpier root systems. Once it's planted, *that* chore is taken care of for 15 or 20 years, and there's less fussing with asparagus than with most perennials. But planting is a chore. Since it will be in place for so long, the best thing is to feed the soil, not the plant; in fact the earth for asparagus must be excellent.

Asparagus plants are sexed. The male plants produce the succulent shoots we eat, and they also live longer than the females, whose shoots are stringy because their energy goes into making bright red berries. (These are the seed berries that fall to earth and produce new plants, which are rarely of the quality of the parent.) Once, all cultivars included a balance of male and female, and what made one superior was disease resistance. Today, botanists have given us almost all male cultivars, which produce up to four times the harvest.

Because the roots must be given a chance to become strongly established, asparagus spears may not be harvested until the third year after planting. Don't be alarmed, as we were, if the spears come up at a vastly different rate. Is it better to fund the patch with seeds or crowns? Crowns are roots with the bud of the stem attached, and they're pulled up from the field when they're dormant after growing for usually one year.

Time was, starting with seeds added an additional year's wait for the first harvest. Today's all-male cultivars are so vigorous, the seeds play catch-up with the crowns and come out even. Seeds are at least 50 percent cheaper than crowns, so sowing seeds makes sense. If you wish to start with crowns, unless the nurseryman is a trusted friend, order from ¼ to ½ again as many as you'll need. Compost the skimpy ones and plant a superbly strong bed for yourself.

You can plant asparagus in rows or decoratively in beds—they're fine mixed with tall flowers at the back of the border. Any number of combinations of depth and breadth will work for preparing the soil. What I did was to dig a foot down and a foot wide and set this soil beside the row. I shoveled in about 3 inches of compost, well-rotted manure, and bonemeal according to the package and dug this into the earth at the bottom. Since asparagus must have perfect drainage, in heavy clay, dig about 15 to 20 inches down, add sand or gravel to the bottom 12 inches, then proceed as described. It's crucial that the asparagus roots stay moist, so I kept them in a plastic bag under a damp towel. I gave them each about 2 ½ square feet—a foot apart in rows 2 ½ feet apart. I carefully spread out the roots of each crown, then covered them with about 2 inches of soil mixed with compost and watered them all well.

For a week or two, I kept the soil moist while the crowns caught their breath. As time advanced and the spears appeared, I kept them covered with 2 inches of soil/compost and watered. I stopped adding soil when, after watering, each trench was 4 inches higher than the surrounding soil. From there the spears just kept growing. (It's an odd feeling, heaping earth over a pretty shoot until it disappears.) More came up after that, which I left alone.

Stalks appear according to their own sweet rhythm, some weeks after the first flush. And they emerge enchantingly, small violet bullet-shaped heads peeping slowly, demurely, out of the ground.

Do not hoe (you'll damage tender roots), but keep weeds out of the bed. You'll have to hand-pull them in early spring, but once the soil is warm, it's past picking season, and all the shoots are up, top with manure or compost to keep out weeds.

Then, not in the year of planting or the year after that but the year after *that,* when stalks are 4 to 6 inches tall and less than an inch thick and the buds are still tight—and moments before you plan to cook them—snap off the spears at ground level. Using a knife can damage shoots beneath the soil and spread fusarium wilt. Harvest for two weeks, then let the spears turn into fernlike plants over the summer, storing up the wherewithal for next year. At any stage of growth, cutting down the spears on the plants for too long can permanently reduce the vigor of the plants and ruin future yields. Next year you can harvest for four weeks and ever after for about six weeks. After the fifth year, if you forget how long you've been picking, the sign to stop is when you notice lots of spears popping up that aren't much more than ⅜ inch wide.

As lovely as they are, don't make a habit of cutting the ferns for floral bouquets. The plants need all the support they can get. Should a female plant slip through and produce red berries, cut off the frond just below the berries. Don't routinely cut the stalks back as winter approaches (some people tell you to). As the ferns fall, they'll form a natural mulch that helps protect the crowns.

If by mid-January the winter hasn't taken the stalks all the way down, cut them to a few inches above the soil, because new spears will soon be coming up, and they need space and light. Chop the spears all the way down with your pruning shears, cutting into small pieces, making mulch.

Fill in the empty space around the edges of the patch with annuals that like filtered sun and are fairly drought tolerant (remember once established, asparagus doesn't require much water). In fact, the annuals are what's called a living mulch. Nasturtiums frolic happily in the patch, as does arugula, spinach, and chervil.

Keep an eye out for slugs and control serious infestations of asparagus beetles and their larvae with 1 percent Rotenone (an extract from roots of a South American plant—follow label directions carefully).

Recommended: UC 157 is a predominantly male hybrid of exceptional flavor and vigor with large, bright-green spears that tends to send up several (instead of one) at a time. UC 157 is recommended for all asparagus-producing regions—California, the Northwest, and mild areas such as nonhumid parts of the South and the Southwest. Already there is UC 157 F1 and UC 157 F2. Mostly male purple-tipped Jersey Giant, a hybrid some call Syn 4-56, is especially cold tolerant and good in heavy soils—highly recommended for the Northeast, Mid-Atlantic, Midwest, and Great Plains areas. Stokes Seeds offers Viking KB3, a male/female cultivar that is considered the most stable open-pollinated asparagus in the world, particularly tolerant of both excessive heat and cold. It's difficult to grow asparagus where it's hot, humid, and frost free. California 500 can do without frost, which asparagus normally wants, but the strain can't take great summer heat. Each of these cultivars has a particular level of resistance to disease. Before you choose, ask your county farm adviser or university extension agent what asparagus diseases are a problem in your area and which cultivar he or she recommends. Nourse Farms offers Jersey Centennial, and Johnny's Selected Seeds offers Jersey Knight. You can be sure there will be improved versions of all of these each year.

Beans and Legumes

The Pea Family

Dwarf and bush beans grow in 5-gallon containers, pole and runner beans in half-barrels (with support). Beans appreciate sun and soil rich in organic matter. If you can't give them good soil, or if your soil hasn't grown legumes in that spot within a few years, inoculating the seeds will give the plants a boost (see The Gardener's Notebook). Wait to sow until the soil is warm—until the hardwood trees are in leaf. In cold soil, many beans molder, and the ones that survive to germinate will likely never amount to much, having struggled from the start. Some cultivars are healthy come what may. But most beans aren't of a mind to limp along valiantly and produce even so. Vigorous plants provide the richest harvest, so keep 'em healthy.

Given a choice of companies that sell open-pollinated seeds, please support the people who are striving to maintain genetic diversity, particularly in beans; see Sources at the back of the book.

Ancient and sustaining as they are, beans have come to have deep significance all over the world. There were Greeks and Romans who believed beans held the souls of the dead.

Beans, like peas, improve any soil on which they grow. Whichever bean you choose from the enticing number that follow, you will be rewarded with beauty in the garden, fine eating, *and* soil better than you found it.

But don't think that if one season of beans in a patch is good for the soil, two seasons will be twice as good. Because Mother Nature wants you to rotate her crops, she's worked it so that too much nitrogen in the soil actually slows legumes down. Keep your beans moving.

Over friable soil, spread a veil of steamed bonemeal and a couple of inches of manure and dig it in. To sow bean seeds, have the soil moist but not soggy at least a couple of inches down. Some people soak the bean seeds first. I don't, since the seeds may split.

Beans are a natural in the mixed border. All bean vines, whether bush or pole, are gay and vibrant, their sweet pea-like flowers blooming in white or butter or butter-white to red to purple, so don't hesitate to rotate them through your flower beds.

Because bean seeds easily rot in soil that's colder than it ought to be, nonorganic gardeners ensure theirs will sprout by sowing seeds that have been treated with a fungicide and perhaps an insecticide as well. Untreated seeds are better because no fungicides or insecticides will be mixed into the soil. Organic gardeners are patient and wait a couple of weeks until the soil has warmed to 65°F, then plant untreated seeds.

If your soil is alkaline or salty, grow limas and tepary beans, particularly the native American cultivars offered by Native Seeds/SEARCH. If your summers are scorching and humid, grow yard-long or winged beans for their pods. A black-seeded soybean such as the Japanese Kuroname is worth a try for drying.

If water is scarce for green or dried beans, grow cowpeas. For dried beans, grow chick-peas and tepary beans.

In moisture-retentive soil, you can grow common bush snap beans and water just twice: first at the time when the flower buds look as though they'll be in full bloom in about a week; second a week after they've fully bloomed. Mark your calendar. If you have more than minimal water, water deeply when the soil is dry 2 inches down.

Pollywogging—a few beans developing at the top of the pod while the lower half withers to a tail—is a symptom of too little water.

If there are hungry birds and critters, shelter bean seedlings from birds with insect-weight floating row covers until the leaves are past the tempting young succulent stage. Against small hungry rodents and animals, a shelter of ½-inch chicken

Sorting Out the Beans

In terms of eating, beans are classed according to the age of their seeds, and there are three stages: snap, shell, and dried. Snap beans are cultivated for their tender pods, which are harvested when the seeds inside are so immature as to be inconspicuous—snap/green/string beans. The test is that you should be able to snap the pod in half without a thread of a string attached to either side. Shell beans are pods cultivated to be harvested when the seeds are more mature than this. By now the pod is leathery and inedible, and it is the shelled seeds inside that are eaten. Shell beans harvested while the seeds are still green and succulent are termed *fresh shelled*, as in fresh lima beans. A week or two later the seeds are at the ephemeral moment between succulent and flinty, when they still taste green but they're wonderfully meaty, and that's a shell or—affectionately—shelly bean. Fresh shelled and shelly beans are usually lumped into one classification in seed catalogs. Finally, the seeds reach the rock-hard, fully matured, and ready-to-sow-or-store stage, when you must cook them for an hour or more before eating, and that's a dried bean—also called a *field* bean.

Although breeders have worked hard to give us melt-in-the-mouth snap beans and plump meaty shelly beans and intensely rich dried beans, the pods of nearly any shell or dried bean can be eaten young, and conversely, any snap bean can be left on the vine to become a shell or dried bean.

In terms of growing, there are three sorts of beans, classed according to vine length. Closest to the wild are the vines that grow from 5 to 20 feet long—pole beans and runner beans. These need support to produce their best. (Although runner beans need more cool weather than most pole beans, they're in this class.) Bush beans, growing less than 2 feet tall, are self-supporting. Half-runners, not too common, are in between and can use tall pea sticks for support.

wire sunk an inch or so in the ground is the only reliable deterrent. Make it even more foolproof by weighting it down with a rock. In some gardens, critters won't cross a 3-inch-wide circle of blood meal. In mine, they do.

Spray bean vines with a kelp solution four times during their season to increase bean yields. Spray the first time when the first true leaves appear. Spray the second time when the first pods are babies. Divide the expected harvest time remaining by three and you'll have the intervals for the remaining two sprays. For example, bush beans have an expected harvest time of 21 days; 21 divided by 3 equals 7. The third spraying is 7 days after the second, and the fourth 7 days after that.

When the vines are established, for optimal growth spread a few inches of a material that will decompose slowly but steadily over the season, such as compost, rotting straw, shredded newspaper, or well-aged manure. But don't overdo it: If the plant receives a surfeit of nitrogen, flowering will be slowed.

Beans and Legumes for Drying

There are always beans we can't buy at the market that we want to taste. When you *do* find unusual dried beans at a market, reserve a handful before you cook them. If you're crazy about them, sow the seeds in their season. But before the pods dry, do pick and cook a few as snap beans to get a sense of each type's distinctive flavor in the fresh stage.

To harvest and thresh dried beans, when you see the pods are drying on the plant, start checking daily. You must catch the stage when the seeds rattle in their cages but before the bone-dry pods split open and spill your beans all over the ground. Gently pull up the plants and hang them upside down over a sheet in a cool, dark, dry place for a month or so to dry the beans thoroughly.

Threshing the seeds—an ancient task—is easy. Take a bunch of plants by the roots and gently but firmly thwack them against the inside of a large, tall clean container. The seeds drop to the bottom, and so does the chaff, of course, but afterward you can lay it all out on a sheet and use the low cycle of a hair dryer—or plenty of huffing and puffing—to speed the chaff on its way across the garden.

Store dried beans in tightly covered jars. Should you see the tiny holes of weevils—which I never have—freeze the beans for two to three days.

Here are a few beans for drying that are especially rewarding to grow and cook. Unless noted, they are bush beans.

Adzuki Beans (Vigna angularis). The taste of these tiny beans is beany, strong, and sweet all at once. Their flavor and rich burned color have made them very special in the Orient. For nearly 1,800 years the Chinese have served adzuki beans on celebratory occasions—their redness is thought to bring good fortune. The Japanese sprinkle the beans around the house on New Year's Day to fend off evil spirits. In both countries a thick, sweet, red grainy paste flavors endless sweets.

Being day-length sensitive, the plants won't start forming flowers until midsummer in the North. If you can grow them, their primrose-yellow blossoms are especially pretty and an unusual color for bean flowers.

Black Beans, Common (Phaseolus vulgaris). Midnight Black Turtle Soup is a superior small bean for the North—a vigorous, prolific, upright bush. From Oaxaca, drought-tolerant Mitla Black is a smaller bush that produces smaller seeds. Black turtle is a disease-and-heat-resistant bean that's been making soup from Santa Fe to Santiago for 150 years.

Chick-Peas (Cicer arietinum). In prehistory there is evidence that wild types of chick-peas (together with lentils and other unnamed beans) were harvested and cooked in regions as far apart as the Near East, Central America, and Europe. The plant is delightful in the garden. From a distance you might mistake it for a small wild rose. The sweet pea-like flowers are white or lavender. I grew chick-peas with purslane, which repeated the delicate line but was fleshy rather than fine. These beans are happiest where it's hot and dry—southwestern Native Americans traditionally grow them in winter, interplanted with wheat. In light loamy soil, chick-peas can be dry farmed (not irrigated if there are rains).

The most important legume grown in India, chick-peas come in different colors. In addition to the large rosy-beige beans we're familiar with, there are velvety black chick-peas so shiny it's almost a shame to cover them with soil or drown them with water in a pot—the black kabouli are said to bring on thunderstorms when their plants flower.

Kala chanas or channas or grams are small and brown. The J. L. Hudson catalog says they're good in dry areas with short seasons, but not along the cool, foggy coast. Their flavor is nuttier than that of the larger bean.

Cowpea Relatives (Vigna spp.). There are several tiny beans that grow easily under trying conditions, all related to cowpeas. Moth beans (*Vigna aconitifolia*) resemble brownish grains of barley, and they're tasty. Beloved in India, the plants form sprawling mats and flourish in miserably hot weather on little water. The seeds of mung beans (*Vigna radiata*) are as drab as moth beans. The plants need long summers, but they're very tolerant of heat and humidity. Mungs are usually sprouted in this country, but they're pleasant when cooked. Rice beans (*Vigna umbellata*) are reddish and also flavorful. Their young leaves are especially good stir-fried or steamed. Grayish urd beans (*Vigna Mungo*) mature faster and are more productive than mung beans. Another bean dear to Indian hearts.

Kidney Beans, Common (Phaseolus vulgaris). For red beans, Montcalm is early and productive, and the bushes hold themselves above the mud—an important trait when beans are supposed to be drying in their pods. It's especially suited to the Pacific Northwest. California Red Kidney is hardier, with pale red beans. For a big, fat, meaty classic white kidney bean, grow a cannellini.

Lentils (Lens culinaris). By the time Jacob sold his birthright for a mess of them, lentils had been around for thousands of years—they were cultivated centuries before the invention of the wheel. The ferny plants don't need pollination, they produce over a long period, and the pods of tiny seeds shell easily. Where days are hot, set them so they'll have respite from the sun for a couple of hours—combine with impatiens for a delicate effect. Tarahumara Pinks are Mexican and delicious.

Tepary Beans (Phaseolus acutifolius var. *latifolius).* These have been cultivated in the Southwest for thousands of years. Plants are tolerant of drought, heat, alkaline soil, and blight. So acclimated to adversity are they that if teparies are given rich soil and watered before the plants show signs of stress, production declines. Plants are broad-leaved semibushes—they send out runners that don't need staking. Plant for plant, yields are four times those of the common kidney bean. Tuck pots of tender sages among them for color.

Caution: The beans can carry bean mosaic virus. If you're planning to save seeds of any other beans in your garden, sow only teparies declared virus free and don't grow them around other teparies, which might infect them.

Delicious tepary beans come in white, yellow, gold, tan, brown, orange, pale green, speckled black, and speckled blue—and you can grow seeds from the Hopi and Papago Indians, and the Mexican site of ancient Mitla, and from Morocco. Which is a forceful reminder that in a handful of seeds in your garden you can summon to life lost civilizations—or bring remote ones near. Where else in your daily life can you revive the past or pull close a vivid but hopelessly distant present? In the kitchen, but there everything to be cooked is dead or dying. In the ground, in the garden, it's alive.

Yankee Beans, Common (Phaseolus vulgaris). Maine Yellow Eye and Sulphur Yellow—both of which cook white—are bean-pot beans. Soldier is a white kidney bean that's somewhat larger and good for thick soups. Vermont Cranberry is also wonderful at the shelly stage in succotash. Seafarer, a fine navy bean, resists anthracnose, blight, and bean mosaic virus. Noble American traditions.

BUTTER/SIEVA BEANS, POLE   *Phaseolus lunatus*

> *Tender annual native to tropical South America . . . aka civet bean, sewee bean, Carolina bean. If you want to grow limas but don't have a long enough season, grow butter beans instead. Best suited to the South, butter bean plants take up less room in the garden than limas—that's because the vines are less vigorous. However, the pods aren't as easy to shell as limas. As with snap beans, pole butter beans have better flavor and greater yield than bush cultivars. Supports for these beans must be sturdy. Culture and harvest as for limas.*

Butter beans are confused with lima beans all over the place, which is all right culinarily but not botanically. Usually I'm a pragmatist, but I do feel every individual in the plant kingdom deserves pride of place. Henderson's Bush Lima is no lima, for example; it's a butter bean. And by and large, butter peas are butter beans.

What makes it more confusing is that southerners separate butter beans and sieva beans—pronounced *sivvy* and named after the Sewee Indians of the Carolina Lowcountry. Sievas are regarded as the smallest of the lima beans.

Butter bean seeds come in plain white or speckled in combinations of purple/brown/buff/reddish. Cooked as dried beans, they turn either light or dark.

Problems with butter beans are caused mostly by fungus or bacteria. So far there are no resistant cultivars, but if you practice crop rotation, keep the plants healthy, and stay away from the patch when plants are wet, you can keep trouble from spreading. If plants become affected, remove and destroy them immediately, *then wash your hands and any tools that touched the vines* in a solution of one part chlorine bleach to four parts water.

The pale blossoms of breadseed poppies are lovely at their feet.

Recommended: For superb eating in all stages, easygoing Carolina Sieva.

DWARF BUTTER/SIEVA BEANS   *P. lunatus* var. *lunonanus*

Tender annual. Culture and harvest is the same as for pole butter beans. These are the bush cultivars. Grow pole types when you can.

Recommended: Easy and the most prolific, the striking purple-speckled Jackson Wonder. For flavor and hot, humid weather, carmine-speckled Dixie Speckled Butter-Pea. For canning and freezing (also easy picking), light green Henderson. For short seasons and against downy mildew, Eastland. And Geneva will germinate in April in upstate New York.

COWPEAS/SOUTHERN PEAS   *Vigna unguiculata*

Tender annual, native to central Asia . . . aka crowder peas. Kept free of weeds, cowpeas are one of the most productive and trouble-free legumes. Cowpeas produce beans when it's too hot and/or too dry for snap beans and limas. They must be sown in warm soil, and they need at least 65 warm days and nights to reach the snap bean stage, then another month to mature to the dry stage. Shelly beans can be harvested in between. Bearing in mind their need for warmth, culture is the same as for snap beans.

Cowpeas are even rarer in seed catalogs—where they're sometimes listed under "Peas"—than fava beans. They migrated from their native Asia to Africa, then found their way from Africa to the American South. There these tropical plants are possessively called *southern peas.* Their flavor is rounder and fuller than that of most other beans, with a bit of a silvery aftertaste.

The shiny leaves resemble those of snap beans (dark and heart shaped), as do the long (up to 12 inches) narrow pods, which generally grow in pairs. Some pods dangle from the plants; some are perched on top. They can be beautiful. For example, Pinkeye Purple Hull has deep purple pods often splashed with shades of green or magenta that make them look tie-dyed—and the creamy beans inside have purple eyes. "Cream" cowpeas have creamy white seeds and generally no eye markings. Mississippi Purple has warm purply red pods at the fresh bean stage, then the color deepens to dark purple when the pods are dry. "Crowders" are jammed so tightly in the pods that the rounded corners have become squarish.

Cowpea plants range from short erect to tall floppy bushes to sprawling mini-vines. Most flowers are yellow-white, some blushed with purple. Cowpeas are particularly beneficial to the soil, and all can find a place in the mixed border in the manner of dwarf peas and bush snap beans. Cultivars with long vines, however, are as happy as cows among corn. Sow corn seeds half again as far apart as usual and tuck in a cowpea vine about 6 inches from each stalk. The vines will clamber up the stalks.

A few bugs are attracted to them, but cowpeas are self-fertile, so they can spend their whole lives under an insect-weight floating row cover if need be.

Recommended: Creams are all tasty, but Zipper Cream is most easily hulled and therefore the place to start. For best flavor in crowders, White Acre is superb eaten fresh. For shellies, small tender Lady is delicious. Pinkeye Purple Hull is early and productive. Big Boy has green hulls and is good for eating fresh as well as for canning and freezing. Colossus has brown extra-large seeds with pale pods blushed with red. Sunapee has been developed as a cowpea for the North.

BLACK-EYED PEAS   *V. unguiculata* subsp. *unguiculata*
   Tender annual native to Central Africa.

Some seed catalogs place black-eyed peas with cowpeas, but in fact black-eyes are a separate subspecies. Native Seeds/SEARCH offers thirteen fascinating cultivars under the heading "Black-Eyed Peas," and it's conceivable the resourceful people who have grown them for centuries haven't a clue about which subspecies their beans belong to. It doesn't matter.

A true black-eyed pea is California No. 5. They're vigorous bushy plants, almost trouble free, and really delicious. Mix them with golden gloriosa daisies.

Black-eyed peas are equally—uncommonly—flavorful at the snap, shelly, and dried stages.

Recommended: For flavor, ease, and everything else, California No. 5 Black Eye. And for a taste of fruit that grew beside the Rio Mayo, small white beans with chocolate-brown eyes—Sonoran Yori Muni.

My Favorite Garden Vegetables

What are my criteria? Flavor, of course, must be the best. Then the beauty of the vegetable and of the plant in the garden—is it among the handsomest of its kind? Next rarity—no point in growing something I can buy. Productivity comes next—does it give good reward for my investment of time and energy and expense and space? Finally, fulfillment of expectations—is it what I'd hoped for? With these in mind, here they are:

Arugula: Rustic; *Asian green:* mizuna; *bean:* Violet Podded Stringless purple pod pole; *cabbage:* Promasa baby savoy; *carrot:* Planet baby round; *chard:* Charlotte ruby; *corn:* Mandan Bride sweet; *eggplant:* Pingtung Long; *garlic:* green garlic (any cultivar); *kale:* Red Russian; *lettuce:* Royal Oak Leaf; *onion:* Cipollini Italian buttons; *pepper:* Sweet Pickle (small multicolor); *potato:* All Blue; *summer squash:* Ronde de Nice round zucchini; *tomato:* Costoluto Genovese; *winter squash:* kabocha.

YARD-LONG BEANS

V. unguiculata subsp. *sesquipedalis*

Tender annual, native to southern Asia . . . aka asparagus bean, long horn bean, dow guak. These fussy beans are not the best ones to grow where summers are cool, but try them anyway, giving them a microclimate that will make them think their days and nights are warm—a south wall, a sheltered spot, or beneath a cloche tunnel. They also need warmth for a couple of months in autumn; they're day-length sensitive, like onions. In the North they won't be moved to start making flowers until midsummer. In fact, above the 35th parallel, they won't mature. But if you can grow them, even the leaves and stems of these beans are edible. Fertile soil and ample moisture are wanted for highest yields, although they can get by on skimpy soil and water if need be. However, vines do need support. Grow as snap pole beans.

To my mind, yard-longs are *the* beans. Picked at their *moment suprême,* pods are velvety tender, sweet beany, stringless. And there's something crazily extravagant about having a bean a foot or more long for your pot! They may grow a yard long in China, but 16 inches is about the limit of edibility here.

Flowers are usually light blue, and if you can, grow them against an airy fence or trellis and get ready for a dazzling sheet of green that rivals Niagara. If, in seasons past, yours haven't been that dramatic, try interplanting yard-longs among closely planted (12 inches) tall corn for support, as they do in China.

There are pale and deep green cultivars and purple too, although the latter hasn't yet been offered in this hemisphere.

Recommended: The Taiwanese Kaohsiung Asparagus Bean.

FAVA BEANS   *Vicia Faba*

Half-hardy annual, native to North Africa and southwest Asia . . . aka broad beans, horse beans, English beans, European beans, Windsor beans, field beans, tick beans. These beans prosper only while days and nights are cool and the air is moist. In the period between when you can first work the soil and when daytime temperatures reach 65–70°F, sow the seeds. Usually that's around the time in March when the crocuses bloom or you plant peas. If you don't have 10 weeks of cool weather in spring, but your winter days stay above 15°F, sow seeds of an overwintering cultivar from October to mid-November—you'll have fava beans the following spring for certain before hot weather hits. If your spring is short, your summers hot, and your winters frozen, sow a heat-tolerant cultivar such as Loreta as early in spring as you can and take your chances. Otherwise, grow as snap beans.

These beans aren't beans, really. They're vetches—vetches are the kids that scramble over a farmer's field, making hay and sweet pasture. You can see that they're not beans by the leaves—a matte finish instead of shiny, and rounder than those of beans.

Favas are thought to have first appeared on this planet in North Africa and southwest Asia. A type of fava bean has been found by Swiss lake dwellings of the

Bronze Age. Between 3000 and 2000 B.C. they appeared on Chinese and Egyptian tables, then Greek and Roman.

Favas are possibly the meatiest and richest of legumes. Very young pods may be cooked and eaten as snap beans. After that the seeds may be eaten at the fresh shell stage—pick overwintered pods when the roses first bloom. After that, harvest as shelly and then dried beans, which can be spectacular. The young leaves make tasty greens. In the world of legumes, mature fava beans are second in protein content only to soybeans (between 25 and 30 percent).

As for the plants, the flowers—white blotched with dark purple or violet—are fragrant and lovely. The handsome vines—usually knee high, but some can reach your shoulder—tolerate cold, wet, heavy soil and spring frosts. I've seen the vines glazed with ice in the morning and perky by afternoon. They're fetching in the early spring border, with pink and plum English daisies at their feet. When spent, chopped vines quickly decompose so the crop that follows does especially well. Green fava bean plants returned to the soil add dozens of times more nitrogen than would the same amount of manure.

Past the snap stage, the seeds must be shelled to be eaten—like limas. But the big, heavy, plush pods are much easier to deal with. As favas mature, the seeds develop a jacket that can be thick and bitter to some palates. There is still the heavenly morsel beneath, and there are those who invariably peel off the jacket. Others have no problem with the jacket, feeling it adds to the lusty gustatory experience. As a rule of thumb, favas-cum-jacket are quite acceptable when eaten hot, because heat lightens and tenderizes the skin. To serve them cool in a salad, peel them.

Choose a cultivar developed for this country. And choose one with large seeds that have been developed for the table, not the small seeds intended for green manure.

If there is rain, you won't need to water until plants begin to flower. When at least four flower clusters have set, hasten the crop along and deprive blackflies and aphids of hiding places by pinching off the tips of the plants. Cook them as greens.

Provide pea sticks to support the vines as they grow and mulch from seedling stage with straw or leaves or even pine needles to help keep moisture in and frost out.

For the South, the Porter & Son seed catalog says, "After spring harvest, cut plants back to one inch for regrowth and fall production."

Recommended: For ease and for flavor when eaten fresh, spring-sown Giant White Windsor. For the Northwest, productive dwarf Toto and for size, Aprovecho Select. For autumn sowing/overwintering, Aquadulce Claudia. At the small end, the new Talias are half-inch size, pale lime-green and delicious.

LIMA BEANS, POLE   *Phaseolus limensis*

Tender annual native to tropical South America. Limas can be more temperamental than butter beans in some climates (mine), but if you can grow these larger beans, their flavor and texture are matchless. And limas take less time in the picking and shelling, since fewer pods render more weight. Limas will not germinate in cold soil, so northern growers sow seeds in 3-inch paper pots indoors 2 weeks before setting them into the garden, which is 2 to 4 weeks after the last frost date. Pole limas produce their best when given 2 feet between plants—that's how fruitful they are.

Native Americans, North and South, have a few thousand years on us in raising lima beans. The beans have been found in Incan graves, and an extraordinary heritage of beans remains in this country: Pima Beige, Hopi Mottled Orange, and Calico Colorado Wild Horse beans. I've grown Hopi Mottled Orange, and they were not only gorgeous when dried—orange mottled with black—but also delicious when cooked.

Those who love limas say the finest-flavored beans are large and flat.

Dr. Martin, a unique pole cultivar, has white beans that are perhaps the largest of all limas, and many limaphiles place it at the top of their list. Because the beans are so large, they can be picked when immature à la baby limas. The vines are exceptionally vigorous and high yielding, growing 8 or more feet tall. Harvests have been from 1 ⅔ to 4 ¾ pounds of shelled beans per plant. Dr. Martin's flavor is nutlike and its texture is smooth and melting.

However, Dr. Martin is sensitive to high heat and can crop inconsistently. For that reason breeders have crossed it with Christmas, an Appalachian heirloom—large speckled seeds that produce under hot, humid, or droughty conditions. The result: light green-seeded Illinois, combines the size and heavy yields of Dr. Martin and Christmas's adaptability. Pods are easy to shell.

Generally, lima beans are pale green or white. Harvest as for shelly beans. Also see the entry on butter beans.

Recommended: Probably because of my dry climate, I've never been able to get any pole limas to grow well, but successful lima growers tell me two cultivars stand out: King of the Garden and Burpee's Best (developed from Burpee's superbly flavored Fordhook). Burpee's Tenderpod bush beans have astonishing flavor, so if you're in lima bean land, try Burpee's pole beans first. For large beans and yield, Dr.

Martin. For hot, droughty conditions, Illinois Giant. Christmas is another that is big, beautiful, and tasty.

LIMA BEANS, BUSH   *P. limensis* var. *limenanus*

Aka dwarf lima bean. These are dwarf versions, grown and harvested the same as bush butter beans and bush snap beans.

Bush beans tend to set their pods all at once, and if your bush lima plants blossom during a heat wave, you may get no pods at all. Pole limas—like pole snap beans—blossom over an extended period, and therefore your chances of getting beans, despite the weather, are better. If you live in a very hot climate and want lima beans for sure, grow a cultivar of each—and then some butter beans for insurance. Tuck pots of sages in their midst.

Recommended: For sweet flavor, growing in hot, humid conditions, and canning and freezing, greenish white Fordhook 242, an All-America winner. For cool summers, whitish Excel. For cold soil tolerance, Eastland. For disease resistance, Packer DM.

RUNNER BEANS   *Phaseolus coccineus*

Tender perennial, native to tropical America . . . aka Dutch case-knife. Runner beans are a glory in the garden and a rare heavy-fruiting veg-etable that doesn't need full sun. Although runner beans aren't happy in dry climates, Desiree will set more pods than most, and she made a brave effort in my garden. Grow and harvest as snap beans.

Dashing 10 to 12 feet up a trellis, across a latticed wall, or enfolding a child in a bean tepee, runner beans' profuse flowers provide beauty as well as richly flavored beans from July or August until frost.

If you have a hot, dry climate, a long growing season, and an overwhelming wish to grow scarlet runners, I suggest Tarahumara Bordal or Tecomari runners, varieties accustomed to challenging conditions. Give these beans center stage. Pick slender pods, no longer than 6 inches—4 is better. For cultivars with long, large pods, harvest for snap beans while pods can be bent from both ends without break-ing. Leave some pods to dry for beans for soup.

Park Seed offers Black Runner, a pole bean eaten as a snap bean but grown mostly for drying the sweet glossy black seeds. Also Pole Bean Mauve Runner—brilliant red flowers with very tasty mauve dried beans.

Because runners' blossoms must be pollinated by insects, sow sweet peas among the vines to doubly tempt the bees.

Recommended: Red Knight, Desiree, and Lady Di are among newer cultivars that offer fleshy and flavorful stringless pods. Strings can make traditional runners picked late inedible. For dry climates: see above. For disease resistance: Red Rum.

RUNNER BEANS, WHITE DUTCH   *P. coccineus* var. *albus*

Although the scarlet blossoms are scandalously beautiful, the white flowers of this subspecies are as delightful as sweet peas, and hummingbirds adore them. Introduced before 1825, Thomas' Famous White Dutch Runner Pole Beans can be harvested as snap beans (although they can have strings) or shellies or dried, large, pure white seeds. I had little luck with these beans in our dryness, but the few flowers and handful of pods that set were lovely. Remember: because they must be pollinated by insects (notably bees), it's a good idea to surround the runners with other blossoms tempting to the pollinators—sweet peas are traditional.

Recommended: If you don't mind strings, grow Thomas' Famous White Dutch Runner Pole Beans, picking them as young as you can. And there's Painted Lady, bicolored blossoms of salmon and white.

SHELL BEANS, COMMON   *P. vulgaris*

Whereas pliant snap beans are immature and dried beans are mature, shell beans are the middle stage of growth in the bean pod, between pliant snap and crackly dried. There are beans that have been developed specifically for harvesting at this stage. How do you tell when a shelly bean's a shelly bean? When the pods are at the shelling stage, their texture is silky/leathery but still a shade of green and the beans inside are plump and well defined, with small spaces between them.

The two main types of developed-to-be-shell-beans are French flageolets and horticulturals.

Flageolets are buttery, small, oval, white or pale green beans. At the fresh shell stage they're steamed and prepared in the manner of baby limas—whose flavor they call to mind. Dried, they're traditionally cooked with leg of lamb. These are super-special, and another must to grow, especially because you can't buy them.

One of the best things about *horticultural beans* is that their pods can be gorgeous. Taylor's Dwarf Horticultural is a bean from the early 1800s. Its pods are

How to Plant Limas

Important: Set the seed with the indented side down. This eye is where the root sprouts. Correctly oriented, the little plant is off to a smooth start. Topsy-turvy, it has to turn a somersault before it can start growing.

Even though bean seedlings are capable of lifting ¾ pound of earth, in soil that crusts over, set the seeds only three quarters into the soil to make emerging easier.

Lima bean plants, whether pole or bush, are vigorous indeed. If you set them too close, they don't pollinate well, leaves will proliferate instead of pods, and mildew can escalate from a nuisance to a serious problem. When you're planning where to put your vines, allow pole limas 2 feet between plants and bush limas 8 inches.

Seeds may be sown in paper pots early, then seedlings set in the ground when the soil is warm. Disturb roots as little as possible. However, if your season is very short, they will not mature.

carmine-splashed buff. French Horticulture pods are red and yellow. Pods of the Italian heirloom Borlotto are rose and cream.

Recommended: For ease and flavor in flageolets, I find it hard to choose between Flambeau, Chevrier Vert, and Vernel. For ease and best flavor in horticulturals, Tongue of Fire, with Borlotto and Taylor's Dwarf Horticultural close behind. The white kidney bean for cannellini is the shelly bean sine qua non.

SNAP BEANS, COMMON   *Phaseolus vulgaris*

Tender annual, native to tropical America . . . aka green beans, string beans. These beans are easy—nay, foolproof—to grow, so if you're a beginning gardener, start here. Keep the soil moist for the most succu-

lent young beans—this moisture without interruption promotes the formation of flowers and fruit. Pick faithfully and pick young—it will be a pleasure! The larger and more mature the seeds grow in the pods (the little nubbins are nascent seeds, remember), the closer the plant comes to thinking it has done its job, and the closer it comes to shutting down production of flowers. Some cultivars are so vigorous they must be picked daily. Most bush beans can be picked every other day, and most pole beans every three to four days or even weekly. Let the directions on the packet be your guide.

No pharaoh, ancient emperor, or medieval pope feasted on green beans or warmed his bones with a steaming bean soup. It wasn't until the 16th century that common beans arrived on the Continent and in England from the New World.

The flowers of these beans, unlike the dazzling blossoms of runners, don't require bees for pollination.

To judge the point of utmost tenderness and well-developed flavor, pick snap beans at about 80 percent of the length described in the catalog. Taste a bean before the seeds inside have begun to swell. If it's sweet and supple and tender, start picking.

Bush or pole? Most of us choose bush beans since they seem so much simpler—no hassle of erecting a tall support for long vines.

Bush beans certainly do fit into the mixed border gracefully, whereas it's a challenge to make a 5- or 6-foot-tall pole look fetching. But it *can* be done. To help you make an educated choice, here are some considerations.

Indeterminate vs. determinate. Determinate vines need no support, growing little more than a foot or so long. Bush beans are determinates. Indeterminate vines—climbing vines—go on and on. Pole beans are indeterminates. Left to sprawl on the ground, they'd be a haven for pests that would chomp on every leaf, flower, and pod. Pole beans' heritage is closer to the wild, and just as they have no gene that inhibits their growth, as determinates do, no gene inhibits their productivity. As long as their beans are picked continuously, their quality remains consistent. Indeterminate annual vines flower and fruit until either frost or exhaustion gets them. In between are the semideterminates, vines that grow 3 to 4 feet long and flower and fruit for a period in between the other two.

Flavor. As with pepper plants, the greater the surface of leaves on bean plants, the greater the exposure to sunlight, the finer the quality of fruit. Leaves on vining beans are larger and more prolific than leaves on bush bean plants. Like hundreds of small solar collectors, pole bean leaves soak up sunlight and transform it into a special form of illumination, that of brilliant taste.

In this country, two pole beans stand out for their flavor. Kentucky Wonder, unanimously regarded as meaty, rich, and beany, is as vigorous a vine as its fruit is tasty. Kentucky Wonders develop rapidly, and their beans may be used in the shelly stage as well. Introduced before 1864 as Texas Pole, it was renamed Kentucky Wonder in 1877 by a seedsman. Since then, the name has changed again a few times, and Old Homestead endures to this day. But White Seeded isn't a Kentucky Wonder. Be sure your seeds are brown.

Blue Lake Pole bean is the other American flavor favorite—probably a selection of Striped Creaseback, a bean first written about in 1822. Blue Lake Poles have straight, round stringless pods that are smooth, tender, and sweet. And don't let catalog descriptions convince you that bush Blue Lakes are as flavorful. At this point, only AAS winner Derby comes close.

Calvin Lamborn, the brilliant breeder who gave us Sugar Snap peas, set about creating the perfect pole bean by combining the richness and elegant form of Blue Lake with the meatiness and vigor of Kentucky Wonder. Up came Kentucky Blue. The plant is beautiful. But even though it was an All-America Selection, letters in gardening magazines bleat about disappointment in Kentucky Blue.

Texture as it affects flavor. Understanding a few terms can help you pick your beans—whether bush or pole, cultivars described as having little fiber, as being good for processing, or as being for "fresh market" will not only be tender but they'll have taste. Cultivars to avoid are those described as having a high level of fiber or as being good for shipping. These are the tough tasteless beans of commerce.

Stringlessness. More stringless bush cultivars seem to be available than stringless pole cultivars, and that's because we are being offered more European stringless beans—most American snap bean cultivars are pole beans with strings. But if you pick beans when very young—about 4 inches—nearly every cultivar will be stringless or have a mere thread of string. Kentucky Wonder is a good example of a bean that, when picked early, is essentially stringless. Over 7 inches, it gets stringy. However, the flavor develops as the pod grows. So, to taste a great old-fashioned bean in its prime, you just might have to—or grab someone else and have him or her—sit down and pull the bothersome strings off your beans.

Time from seed to harvest. Sown at the same time and all things being equal, bush beans will be ready to harvest one to two weeks earlier than pole beans.

Length of harvest. The classic determinate bush bean vines flower once or twice intensively, set fruit intensively, then call it a day. Harvest averages three weeks.

This is ideal if you plan to process most of your crop for dilly beans or the freezer.

You can lengthen the harvest with bush beans by choosing a more flexible determinate and picking every other day. Jumbo is a luscious flat Italian pod cross between Romano and Kentucky Wonder. Its vines may reach 15 to 16 inches, they might sag under the weight of the beans, but they will still not need support. When well cared for, Jumbos can be counted on to fruit for at least six weeks, and in Maine a May sowing has lasted till frost. Naturally, the more protracted fruiting is not as concentrated as from the classic bush bean.

Long indeterminate pole bean vines bloom and produce fruit lazily but steadily, so you can harvest a handful of beans from each plant now and again all season long. Particularly in warm climates, pole bean plants produce continuously from a long two months after sowing until frost. Their pattern, however, is to send up a splendid first crop, slow down production in the heat, then start up again in the cool of autumn.

In your garden, where it's *very* hot, bean flowers may fall off. For snap beans, grow a cowpea or yard-long beans.

Ease of harvest. To find beans on low vines, you must bend over and riffle through the bushes. However, cultivars have been developed for easy picking, with the pods perched right on top. Purple and yellow cultivars are easiest to see. For the most part, pole beans dangle in front of your face.

Productivity. Pole beans have been reckoned as being three to 10 times more productive than bush beans. However, if your growing season is four months or less and you sowed bush beans every couple of weeks, the sum of their harvest would be more.

Bearing in the heat. Many cultivars won't set fruit well if the air is hotter than 90°F just before and during flowering—the pods are filled irregularly if at all. Since the majority of bush beans flower and fruit in a rush, a coincidental heat spell can be disastrous. But since pole beans flower over a long time, chances are the heat will wane long enough to let some beans come through.

Use of space. If you grow them straight up, there's greater yield per square foot with pole beans. If you let a vine wander, then bush beans crowd more beans in a smaller space.

Once I was a bush bean person, feeling that the hassle of erecting bean poles was more than I wanted to deal with. But having raised a dozen plants on one aluminum carousel-sort-of-pole, realizing how infinitely more efficient the watering is, how much longer and more prolifically the beans bear, and how extra-flavorful these beans are, I'm sold. Which is not to say I don't grow any bush beans, because I do—many are marvelous.

Recommended: As a benchmark and for an easy introduction to snap beans, Burpee's strain of Kentucky Wonder. For best flavor, it's a toss-up between Kentucky Wonder and Blue Lake. More marvelous flavor is in the extra-long stringless pods of Fortex. Park's Landfrauen is a Swiss heirloom described in the catalog as "unequaled beany taste and aroma" in tender purple-speckled green pods. Blue Lake is tops for freezing and canning. For a superproductive tasty bean, Emerite. For cold, wet soil, Cascade Giant (an improved Oregon Giant, a Northwest heirloom). Earliest pole bean of quality so far is probably Northeaster. In warm, droughty or hot, humid climates, Rattlesnake will produce flavorful long, round purple-streaked pods on vines 10 feet long.

And for a thrilling taste of the fifth century, grow a remarkable long-season snap bean, New Mexico Cave beans—grown by the folks at Deep Diversity from seeds found by archaeologists in a clay pot sealed with pine pitch.

BUSH SNAP BEANS, COMMON   *P. vulgaris var. humilis*

For fall crops, select bush cultivars and time them so you'll be sure to harvest all the plant has to offer. Most contemporary bush bean cultivars have been bred to hold their beans well off the ground, a good thing because beans draped through the dirt easily form soft brown spots. Heritage bush beans may drag, and the moment you see this, put something clean and airy beneath them, such as a few inches of straw or shredded newspaper.

One of the loveliest moments of early summer comes when you discover that overnight there are green or purple or gold slender pods dangling temptingly among the sweet blossoms and brave small bushes, and you call out to the house, "We've got beans!" Then, for about a week, there are never enough beans to pile on the plate. For the rest of the summer, when you have to pick them every other day, the groans begin. Then comes frost, and a week later you wish like crazy there were fresh beans for your plate.

As for blanching and freezing the excess, I've never had good luck, even with varieties developed especially for freezing. So I make dilly beans with our extras.

Bush beans, with their low habit, heart-shaped leaves, and pealike flowers—and often colorful pods—are ideal for the front of the border. But near the end of their run the vines turn brownish. If you have beans to harvest in another part of the garden, then it's most aesthetic to pull the bushes before their end. Otherwise, grin and bear it until the last lovely bean has been plucked.

Recommended: For the ultimate in ease and flavor, two bush beans taste like pole beans—Burpee's Stringless Greenpod, introduced in 1894, and Espada, which has built-in disease resistance, including to anthracnose. State White Half Runner is another with excellent flavor. For short seasons—its seeds can germinate in cool soil—adaptable and disease-resistant Provider is superior, as is Black Valentine, introduced c. 1850. Early, stringless, and delectable as a slender snap bean, its black seeds are equally tasty in the shell and dried stages. For weather tolerance, disease resistance, and tenderness over an unusually long period, well-flavored Derby. For resistance to anthracnose: this is a seed-borne fungus that doesn't occur in the West, so use western-grown bean seeds, which includes most of them (inquire of the seedsman). For ease of picking (no small matter), Burpee's dark green, round, tender Topper and E Z Pick, a Blue Lake type. Slankette is a delicious, productive, adaptable bush bean.

FILET BEANS   *P. vulgaris*

> *Aka French beans, haricots verts. Grow as snap beans, but pick most cultivars of these extraordinarily fine beans every 24 to 48 hours, or they'll turn stringy and tough. They're ready a few days earlier than basic snap beans.*

If any form were to tempt you to grow beans, it would be this one. Imagine round pods the length of your middle finger and less than half as thick as ordinary snap beans. With them come delicate green bean flavor and no strings. They're the Wallis Simpsons of beans—they can never be too rich or too thin—and seedsmen are constantly improving strains to make them richer and thinner.

In 1987 nine sorts of filet beans were grown and tasted at the Rodale Research Center. For flavor, texture, and disease resistance, productive Aramis was ranked first, but only Thompson & Morgan and Garden City Seeds still offer it. Old favorites Fin des Bagnols and purple-splashed Triomphe de Farcy still hold their own because of their superb flavor. All must be harvested daily.

If your life is such that you can't be a slave to picking beans, then grow one of the faux filets. Astrelle, Marbel (brushed with violet), and Finaud have been developed from long skinny beans to be picked ultra-early as filets. You can let several days if not a week or more go between pickings. For something truly rare, grow just Dorabel, a productive yellow filet bush bean with superb flavor.

Recommended: For ease and resistance to anthracnose, Marbel. *For flavor, productivity, and disease resistance,* Aramis. Vernandon won a national taste test recently, so try that, too.

Supports for Pole and Runner Beans

If possible, set these beans on the north end of your garden, so their height won't shade other plants. Set supports before sowing seeds, so you won't compact the soil or dislodge the seeds. Teepees are festive and a fine place for small children to hide. Draw a 4-foot circle in the earth. You'll need ten 8- to 10-foot poles—anything at least an inch round and strong, and the rougher the better so tendrils can cling to the surface. Gather the poles together, about a foot from their tops, and secure loosely with stout twine. Have a friend help you set them around the circle, a foot apart and, on an angle, buried at least 1 foot deep. You'll be leaving a 2-foot opening for the door or for you to occasionally check the vines and the watering from underneath. When the teepee is in place, tie the stakes tightly at the top.

Arbors and trellises are also ideal supports for flying beans. No harm in mingling them with other vines, but be careful about those with prickers, such as roses, because they may thwart you when you go to pick beans.

ITALIAN BEANS   *P. vulgaris*

These lush, broad, flat pods are just the opposite of filet beans. You nibble filet beans—you sink your teeth into Italians. Romano is the traditional Italian strain, and improvements have been made on it, such as Harris's Romano 26, Primo and Roma II. Jumbo is long, flat, dark green, and marvelous.

There are blond Italians, too. Frima is a productive yellow Romano and a pole bean—hooray. Wax Romano is a bush bean. Heritage Annelinos have small flat pods that curve, as Shepherd Ogden says, "like a crescent moon." They come in both green and yellow—Italian heirlooms with rich Romano flavor.

Recommended: Easiest: Jumbo—with its Kentucky Wonder heritage, it might just be judged tastiest, too. But every Italian bean I've tasted is delicious. For earliest maturing, Park's Early Riser is extra-tender.

PURPLE POD BEANS   *P. vulgaris*

Unlike their green and gold sisters, purple-podded snap beans germinate well in coolish soil—an advantage when your season is short.

Certainly purple beans add a depth of color to the garden, and kids love to pick them. The ones I get most excited about are Territorial Seed Company's Violet Podded Stringless pole beans. They are vigorous, prolific, beautiful, delicious, meaty, and tender no matter how long they grow—remarkable. Yes, they turn green when cooked, but so do they all.

Recommended: Easiest and best: Violet Podded Stringless. For special beauty, look into Trionfo Violetto.

WAX BEANS   *P. vulgaris*

When I was a girl in my mother's garden, somehow golden snap beans caught my fancy more than anything else we grew. I've been searching for the great wax bean ever since. I haven't found it. Sungold, developed at Cornell University, has rich color and flavor—and strings. So do Frima and Wax Romano, with their meaty Italian texture. I haven't the temperament for strings. Dorabel is a stringless baby French wax bean with a baby taste, probably the best. Beurre de Rocquencourt grows well in cool climates. It's an old French cultivar, much regarded and full of flavor. A friend in the seed industry says that after testing "a whole lot of wax beans in our trials," Butter Crisp was the most flavorful.

Recommended: For ease, especially in cool summers, Beurre de Rocquencourt is a real beginner's bean. For flavor, Frima, Butter Crisp, and Dorabel. Long, slender bush bean Roc d'Or is a close second. For disease tolerance, Goldkist is resistant to anthracnose.

SOYBEANS   *Glycine Max*

Tender annual, native to Southeast Asia . . . aka soya bean, soja bean.
Soybeans tolerate great heat but not dry heat. They're better for the
North than limas. Grow as snap beans.

These upright bushes with short fuzzy pods dangling in clusters were cultivated in China and Japan before written records were kept. That's thousands of years of enjoying buttery, delicately flavored beans containing the most protein in the plant kingdom. It's a mystery to me why they're not common in our gardens.

I like to soften soybean bushes with a scattering of Iceland poppies in their midst. Harvest as other shellies and as dried beans.

Simmered in the pod, shelly soybeans can be popped out to eat—another bean whose flavor is reminiscent of limas.

Recommended: I've found Black Jet an easy bean to grow. For flavor at the shelly stage, Butterbeans are ready to eat in about 3 months. For flavor as in dried beans, Black Jet. For short seasons, sow Maple Arrow around June 1 and harvest richly flavored green shelly beans in mid- to late August.

Cornfield Beans— One of the Three Sisters

The synergism between tall cornstalks and climbing beans—with squash vines frolicking at their feet—is one of the most appealing in the garden. Native Americans called them the Three Sisters. Roots of the beans provide nitrogen to the soil, which nurtures the corn, which provides shade for the squashes.

For the corn, the roastin' ears heritage dent Hickory King is the perfect companion for beans such as Genuine Cornfield/Striped Creaseback/Scotia. Introduced before 1822, these beans are heat tolerant and tasty at the snap and shelly stages. Alabama No. 1 Purple Pod has purple-tinged silvery pods, stringless when young.

Speaking of strings, these beans are traditionally strung on heavy thread to dry and called *leather britches.*

WINGED PEAS   *Lotus tetragonolobus*

Half-hardy annual native to southern Europe . . . aka asparagus pea.
These are easily grown, especially where summers are cool. You'll need
fertile, well-drained soil in full sun.

My introduction to these beans was the asparagus peas in the Thompson & Morgan catalog. I knew nothing about nothing. Nobody told me to sow the seeds around the rhubarb. The result was what the Japanese call a happy accident. The bloodred pealike blossoms, one of the deepest and most vibrant reds I've ever seen in the garden, bounced off the scarlet of the rhubarb, and the beans' smallish delicate leaves contrasted with rhubarb's elephant ears. Keep the pods picked at 1 inch, and the soil moist, and you can harvest for weeks. Pods *must* be picked small or they become so fibrous they're inedible. The baby winged pods have a silvery flavor reminiscent of artichoke—beats me why they're named after asparagus. Give 3 square feet to growing winged peas once, for amusement, and to expand your kitchen garden repertory. That many plants should give everyone in the family a taste.

BEETS, GARDEN   *Beta vulgaris*, Crassa Group

Hardy biennials in the Goosefoot family, native to the Canary and
Madeira islands, the Atlantic coast of Europe, the Mediterranean
region to southern Russia, Syria, and Iraq . . . aka red beet, yellow
beet, sugar beet, beetroot, mangel, mangel-wurzel, and man-
gold . . . grows in 3-gallon containers. Give beets the richest, fluffiest
soil, the fullest sun, lots of water, and no weeds.

Although in the first century the Roman gastronome Apicius gave recipes for what he called the *Beta* root, it wasn't until the 16th century that German gardeners took the long, straight, fleshy root and grew it short and plump. In Germany they've been mad about beets since, but how many people do you know—German or otherwise—who serve beets when entertaining guests?

I do. I pull my sugar babies no bigger than the tip of my thumb and serve them with cream and dill at dinner parties.

Beets are that rare root vegetable that can be easily transplanted, so you can start seeds of a first crop indoors in soil blocks early. Then sow in place until the weather is hot; sow again in autumn. In mild climates, Winter Keeper (aka Long Season) may be left in the ground, heaped with straw, and you can harvest beets until early spring. Let its green leaves fill spaces while annual flowers such as marigolds are coming along. Colors of the roots are most intense in cool weather. You may want walnut- or egg-size beets, or pull them tiny as I do.

Many people who never looked at a beet twice are captivated by the peppermint swirl inside Chioggia—it varies from cream to pale pink and bright red to cherry. What's more, the flavor is delicate, the root holds well in the ground, and the leaves, even after overwintering, are still cookable.

A robust relation of our refined little beets, older but lower on the social ladder, is the mangel. It's sweet and enormous—a hefty 8 pounds or more!

Until last year, beets wouldn't grow for me. The book said beets would tolerate shade and never mentioned heat. Then, in my pattern of crop rotation, last spring there was no place for my golden beets but in the full sun and loamy soil of my best bed. One summer morning I wondered about the patches of bright green leaves on slim crimson and gold stalks. Beets!

Recommended: For ease and flavor, I'm partial to the little guys—Little Ball or Little Mini or whatnot—and golden beets. And Dwergina. No gimmicks, just pure sweetness. For wintering over, Winter Keeper (aka Long Season). For bolt resistance, Sangria. To save space in the garden, carrot-shaped Formanova. For disease resistance, bloodred centers, and gusto, hybrid Big Red.

BEET GREENS   *B. vulgaris,* Crassa Group

Culture, of course, is the same as if you were growing the beets primarily for their roots.

Just as there are cultivars of turnips that produce finer greens than turnips, strains of beets such as Early Wonder Tall Top are especially prized for their leaves—their roots are still tasty, mind you, so do plan to cook them. Pick while sprightly.

Recommended: Most productive and easiest is Early Wonder. Green Top Bunching holds up in cool weather.

BLACK BEANS. *See Beans for Drying.*

BROAD-LEAF MUSTARDS. *See Mustard Greens.*

BROCCOLI, COMMON *Brassica oleracea,* Botrytis Group

Half-hardy biennial in the Mustard family, native to coastal western and southern Europe . . . grows in 5-gallon containers. Provide all broccolis with rich, well-drained soil with full sun, ample moisture, and a deep mulch in hot weather. One good dose of complete organic fertilizer at planting time should be enough for the season.

Common broccoli produces one large central head, and then, when it has been harvested, sprouts smaller heads along the sides of the stalk. The more side shoots there are, of course, the more desirable.

These plants are lovely in the border. About 2 feet tall, they have large ruffly gray-green leaves and bright blue-green or mauve heads with an aristocratic air about them. Mingle them among the pink and purple spires of larkspur or foxglove. Besides, broccoli's a challenge, and I like to show it off. Group five or six Green Valiants together—they love to be close to one another. Most broccoli cultivars do better when slightly crowded, although planted too close, the heads will be stunted. Since the leaves may get raggy, I set broccoli behind a bank of lower gray catmint, santolina, or sage.

Akin to purple beans, purple-heading broccolis turn green when cooked. When I grew Violet Queen, the sight of the rich purple florets always stopped me in my tracks when I went by. Flavors of all these broccolis are similar, nuances coming from the usual variables of site, climate, and care while growing.

Then there's Romanesco, the broccoli that looks as though it had come up from the ocean floor, a swirl of peaked water-green shells covering its dome. Heads of old-fashioned Romanescos average 6 to 7 inches, while the newer cultivar Minaret averages 4 to 5 inches. These seem not to have as long a period of harvest as the usual broccoli, although you can harvest them by florets instead of the whole head. And their flavor is not as refreshingly green as that of green broccoli. Actually, some regard these as cauliflowers.

Most broccoli aficionados agree that open-pollinated cultivars grow with disheartening irregularity, the heads are generally smaller, and their flavor isn't as sweet. So hybrids are often the best choice.

Broccoli is temperamental. You'll have best control over the vagaries of weather if you sow seeds indoors in spring and then transplant them with several sets of leaves at least 2 inches wide. If the leaves are smaller and the plant must endure several days of 40–50°F, it will respond by forming nascent buds. The moment warm weather hits, up they'll come, and that will be the end of your broccoli. So don't set the plants out too early.

In areas where spring comes and goes in a wink and hot summer brings broccoli-devouring bugs—where autumns are long and cool, and winters mild—start crops of Emperor in August for transplanting in September and enjoy them out of the cold frame from early winter on.

Set the seedlings in a cutworm collar when transplanting. A strong stream of water helps with aphids. But if you've been plagued by bugs in the past, swathe the plants in a floating row cover so nothing can get through.

Harvest the beautiful little central heads while still firm—cut cleanly with a knife on a slant so water will slide off and not rot the stalk. When harvesting side shoots, leave the base of the stalk with a couple of leaves, and more shoots will appear.

Broccoli, its sibling cauliflower, and cousins sprouting broccoli and Chinese broccoli (aka Chinese kale) all evolved from wild cabbage. Grow common and sprouting broccoli (which follows) together for a long, easy harvest.

Recommended: For earliness and flavor, Early Emerald hybrid. Paragon hybrid is sweet and tender. For side shoots, yields of Green Valiant and Shogun are unusually high. For cold weather, Green Valiant and Emperor hybrids are delicious through late fall and, under cover, a mild winter. For hot weather, Cruiser and hybrid Saga. For disease resistance, hybrids Everest, Eureka, and Umpquah.

Sprouting Broccoli   *B. oleracea*, Italica Group

Semihardy biennial in the Mustard family, native to coastal western and southern Europe . . . aka Italian Broccoli and asparagus broccoli . . . grows in 5-gallon containers. Grow as common broccoli, except harder-working sprouting broccolis want feeding again after the first harvest or in February, whichever comes first.

Sprouting broccoli forms a great many small heads on a leafy stalk. You can harvest a few shoots around the same time that you can harvest one big head of heading broccoli. It takes up to half again as long before all the shoots on sprouting broccoli have presented themselves, so this means a prolonged harvest, often over winter. Cut the sprouts with a few leaves at the point on the stalk where the skin starts getting tough—you can see it. Harvest all buds before they flower.

Sprouting broccoli comes in violet flowers and creamy white, and Purple Sprouting is hardy to −10°F. When you order seeds, make sure they are the true sprouting broccoli.

Recommended: Decicco is an old-time true sprouting broccoli of good quality.

BROCCOLI RAAB.   *See Mustard Greens.*

BRUSSELS SPROUTS   *Brassica oleracea*, Gemmifera Group

Hardy biennials in the Mustard family, native to coastal western and southern Europe . . . grows in 5-gallon containers. Brussels sprouts, like cabbages, need at least six hours of sun, plenty of moisture-retaining humus in the soil, especially aged manure (rabbit is perfect), ample water, and protection from pests.

If you've seen brussels sprouts only in plastic-covered pint baskets or frozen in a cardboard box, the plants will astonish you. The size of small children, they are mantled with tiny cabbages and hatted with enormous cabbage leaves. But the nutty leaf buds (for that's what brussels sprouts are, tiny buds of leaves), picked no bigger than the tip of your thumb after being sweetened by a couple of hard frosts, bear little resemblance to those green golf balls at the market.

Brussels sprouts are among the hardiest of the brassicas, and not fond of hot weather. Their idea of heaven is 65°F. Here on the mountain, where summers are hot and dry, my brussels sprouts have hardly been championship stuff. Still, I wouldn't miss the fun of sprouts for anything. They're one of the most interesting vegetables to grow.

Brussels sprouts come in two types, early and late—the labels are relative, because there's no cultivar that takes less than four months from seed to table. Early sorts generally are hardier and smaller, and their buds are larger and set closer together. The disadvantage of earlies is that the sprouts cling close to the stalks for dear life and you can lose part of the nubbins as you try to wrest them free. When water gets trapped between the tightly packed buds, it can lead to rot and disease. Later cultivars are taller, their sprouts grow farther apart on longer stems so harvesting is easier and water doesn't get trapped, and over time they've learned to deal gracefully with harsh weather, even hard frosts. Sprouts of later cultivars are also considered tastiest—flavor is related to maturity of the sprout at the first autumn frost.

Because each plant needs three to four square feet of space for several months, and because the plant looks like a visiting cousin of E.T., brussels sprouts can be hard to place in the garden. Hybrids have all but chased traditional sprouts out of seed catalogs—hybrids are more compact and more uniformly budded. Fine-tasting Rubine Red is an open-pollinated exception readily available from seedsmen. It's late, tall, with leaves and sprouts of deep crimson that look like miniature cabbages. Try tucking pots of small hardy roses in carmine, rose, fuchsia, and scarlet around Rubine Red.

Brussels sprouts like the soil to be firm—stomp around it after you set in the plant. And make sure the pH is up to snuff (see The Gardener's Notebook). If wind threatens, stake tall stalks to protect them from keeling over.

There's a golden rule among brussels-sproutsmen: no gathering until after two good frosts. As with cabbages, the cold makes sprouts sweeter. Mature late cultivars can stand 20°F, whether that's through November or all winter long. In balmy climates, transplants of late cultivars should go into the garden after the heat of summer for harvesting through winter and spring—but not so late that shorter days don't give the buds a chance to develop. But remember that without frosts, flavor won't be its best.

Pick tightly closed buds, just a few at a time, from the plant. Buds mature from the bottom up, and one plant can provide four or five pickings as you work your way up the plant. Remove the lower leaves as sprouts begin to develop so strength can go into the buds. If you know you'll want to harvest all the sprouts at once, cut off the leafy hat—the top 6 inches, the growing point—about six weeks before you'll want sprouts. Cook these top leaves as you would cabbage.

If a mean frost threatens to kill the plant, pull up the stalk with as much earth as comes with it, wrap in an airy sack in a bushel of soil, and set in a cold place to continue ripening. Trim off any remaining leaves. If it's cold enough, sprouts will keep for months this way.

Recommended: For overall ease and best flavor, Prince Marvel. Valiant hybrid is delicious, too. Oliver hybrid is the earliest. Red Rubine for color and variety. Roodnerf Late Supreme is holding its own in the Pacific Northwest. For overwintering and disease resistance, hybrids Oliver, Tardis, Widgeon, and, again, Prince Marvel. For an extended season, new hybrid Queen Marvel.

BUCK'S-HORN PLANTAIN.	*See Salad Greens.*

BUNCHING ONIONS.	*See Onions.*

BURDOCK, GREAT   *Arctium lappa*

Hardy biennial in the Sunflower family, native to Eurasia . . . aka edible burdock, gobo, cuckold, harlock, clotbur . . . grows in deep 3-gallon containers. Burdock roots must grow long and thin and straight. Sow in an out-of-the-way sunny spot with loose deep soil (not recently manured) so the roots can slip down, down, down. Don't let them lack for moisture.

Traditionally, the Chinese use all parts of great burdock as medicine. A thousand years ago the plant was introduced to Japan, and the Japanese discovered the root's delicate flavor—a hint of celery, a hint of potato, a certain silveriness. Autumn-sown seeds offer tender leaves and stalks for cooking as well as roots in spring.

Harvest the roots with your narrowest shovel, taking them when no more than ½ inch thick and 2 feet long (older, they're tough and bitter). With long bare stems and insignificant flowers, this is not a plant for the border. Place it where you won't mind if it returns. As with comfrey and Jerusalem artichoke, one niblet of root of this biennial starts a new plant. Fine with me.

Recommended: Takinogawa is the cultivar of choice.

BUTTER/SIEVA BEANS.	*See Beans and Legumes.*

CABBAGE   *Brassica oleracea*, Capitata Group

Half-hardy biennials in the Mustard family, native to coastal western and Southern Europe . . . grows in 5-gallon containers. One secret to magnificent cabbages is rabbit manure. Another is full sun. If there's shade to contend with, savoys will manage best. The supply of water

must never stop. Cabbages don't care what type of soil they're in as long
as there's humus to hold the moisture in the form of compost and/or
manure and the soil is well drained (poor drainage stunts growth dra-
matically). For best flavor, cabbages need to mature in cool weather—
but plants can deal with a number of days of heat as long as they have
plenty of water.

Looking at cannonball stacks of green and magenta cabbages at the market,
you'd certainly never guess the majesty of their birth. Savoy cabbages,
with their aura of wonderfully dimpled and crinkled leaves, give a hint.
Think of Rosa centifolia. This rose of a hundred petals is a source of attar of roses,
and its name is the cabbage rose. Like petals of their namesakes, cabbage leaves furl
from the center, around and around and around, until the heads are encircled in a
ruffled leafy bonnet. Small wonder that these roses of the vegetable patch are the
poetic homes of fairies. Or, in medieval tales, where babies come from.

Since a cabbage forms leaves from the inside out, outer leaves take the longest
to create, being the largest. The time it takes a cabbage to mature is the time it takes
to produce the number of leaves genetically predetermined. An early cabbage produces fewer leaves than a late cabbage, so the earlier the cultivar, the smaller the
head—and, of course, vice versa.

Quickly maturing cultivars are called *early* or *summer cabbages*—generally harvested mid-June through October. By and large, these are the tenderest and juiciest
cabbages. Being only 2 to 2 ½ pounds, earlies take less than a square foot of space,
although they need ideal growing conditions and don't hold their quality once
matured. Those moderately quick to mature are called *midseason, late, winter,* and,
in some cases, *storage cabbages*—they are generally harvested mid-October through
March. Savoy and kraut cabbages are here, too. Flavor is most developed in these
cabbages and they weigh from 3 to 15 pounds. To enhance sweetness, time some to
mature around autumn's first frosts. Slow-to-mature types are called *overwintering*
or *spring* cabbages. Sown in autumn, their not-yet-headed leaves provide greens in
early spring and the heads, harvested from the end of February through early June,
weigh about 2 pounds. These are a gamble. There must be plenty of rain or snow to
carry them over the bridge of winter, they can freeze or split or bolt. For my money,
there are a dozen marvelous greens that give leaves through winter and spring more
abundantly.

Shapes in cabbages can be an indication of when they'll mature. Cabbage leaves
wrap themselves into pointy, flat-topped, and round heads. Pointy-headed or conical cabbages are generally early, green, small, and luscious—and very susceptible to

bolting in late spring in parts of the North. Flat-headed cabbages, generally midseason types, were once prized because they stacked well at outdoor markets. Today these heirlooms are valuable for their heat resistance, keeping qualities, and hardiness. Round or ball-headed cabbages are today's standard for commercial green and red cabbages—they roll ever so nicely along production lines. Since they're invariably available at the market, grow something else.

And there's the core. From 1 to 4 inches long, it's the growing point of the cabbage. Some think that long-cored cabbages are more likely to split—something about too much growth to handle. Others believe that the smaller the core, the shorter the stalk, which makes standing in the field less stressful. In the kitchen it's clear that the less core, the more cabbage to eat.

Splitting is probably the most common cabbage problem—I've read half a dozen theories as to why a head will split open before it has matured. There are cultivars resistant to splitting, just as there are cultivars resistant to black rot and fusarium yellows. If disease becomes a problem with cabbages in your garden, disinfect all tools and equipment that come in contact with the plants, including germinating cell trays. Be sure any compost you use around cabbages has been thoroughly "cooked." Next year, choose a resistant cultivar.

Then, what color appeals to you? Cabbages come in all shades of green, from water-white to blue. Some longkeeping cultivars whiten with storage, but some have been bred to hold on to their green—often they have more layers of leaves. Hues in the reds are mostly in the spectrum of red wine colors, with cream core and ribs. Red cabbages fall into the midseason range.

You'll notice that red leaves in cabbages are generally thicker than green. Ravishing as they may be to look at, the flavor of red-leaved cabbages can't compare to that of the tender-leaved savoys and delicate earlies.

The first cabbage I grew was South China Earliest from Gleckler Seedmen. I was struck by the fact that the cabbages matured in just 45 days from transplanting—all other earlies took at least 2 weeks longer. I sowed the seeds indoors in March, set seedlings in the garden under floating row covers mid-April, and, in early June, when my calendar said 45 days were up, I harvested beautiful, small, roundish heads with tender delectable leaves. I was thrilled. And mystified that no other seedsman offered South China Earliest.

Last spring I was cruising through the cabbage section in Gleckler's and this time paid attention to the description of South China Earliest: heads were 10 by 4 ½ inches. They were pak choi cabbages! So what does this tell you? First, that maturity dates are invariably approximate—I was supposed to wait for the heads to elongate another 5 to 6 inches. Second, that what works works.

Although cabbage is a cool-season crop, in the temperate North you can dine on fresh homegrown cabbages almost any time of the year. In climates that are too cold or too hot at some point, you can (theoretically) bring cabbages out of cold storage. Cabbages are magnificent in the border—*if* you don't have to swathe them in floating row covers to keep out aphids. Apparently, though, the more aphids on your cabbage, the better-tasting the cultivar. Even infinitesimal creatures have a palate. And deer have been known to ignore indifferent cabbages and scarf down the ones that are delicious.

When you're choosing cabbages, know that the number of days given in a catalog indicates the time from transplanting of the seedling into the garden to maturity. Add 42 days when sown in early spring and about 35 days when sown in summer. You'll have much better control over their destiny if you start seeds in soil blocks or paper pots and then transplant them, rather than sow them direct.

Ideally the autumn before planting, dig manure into cabbage places. Use only robust straight-stemmed transplants and set them well into the ground to discourage a long, wobbly stem. Where aphids are a problem, wrap each plant in a layer of insect-weight floating row cover for the duration.

At planting time I reassure myself by mixing in a big bucket three rounded trowelfuls of wood ashes, three of aged rabbit or steer manure, one of bonemeal, and one of lime. Where I'll plant the seedling, I scoop out a shovelful of earth and drop in one heaped trowelful of the mixture. I return the soil on the shovel and mix. Then I make a hole with my dibber or trowel, set in the transplant, water, and pat it firm. Add a cutworm collar, a whole bunch of crumbled eggshells to keep out slugs, and cover with a square of floating row cover. Don't forget the mulch to keep weeds out and moisture in. Cabbages are shallow rooted, so don't cultivate around them too closely—stay beyond the outer leaves. If the virtues of a large and late cultivar appeal to you but you like your cabbages small and early, grow the large and late cultivar in half the recommended space and it should come as you like.

A cabbage is mature when it feels firm to the touch. There are no further guidelines. Once it's firm, you need to know whether your cultivar is one that can stand in the field or needs to be cut, lickety-split. A caution about numbers: Judging when a cabbage is mature can take a practiced hand. Beyond that, many cultivars can wait patiently in the field for *months*.

For long storage in a cold dark cellar, a cabbage must have food reserves. That's why cabbages for keeping must be harvested just before they're fully mature—firm, but not rock-solid. Fully mature cabbages have exhausted their food reserves and therefore spoil quickly. This is why early cabbages go past their prime so quickly—they have no reserves.

SAVOYS

Thickness of leaves plays a role in a cabbage's taste. Thinner leaves are generally the most flavorful. Savoy leaves, crimped and crinkled (as though you
scrunched them up in your hand then let go) are generally the thinnest of cabbage
leaves, and savoys are considered the finest flavored of cabbages. The lighter green
savoys are usually the best flavored, and savoys have very little cabbage aroma when
cooking. Savoys usually are the most cold-hardy, but once cut, they're not good
keepers. Savoys succeed on poorer soil than other cabbages. In fact, savoy is the easiest cabbage to grow—it's among the most vigorous of plants—and surely the most
exciting cabbage in the landscape. If you can grow just one cabbage, let it be savoy.

To harvest cabbages, cut with a clean sharp knife close to the base of the head.
If you can afford the space, leave the stalk in the ground, because new heads may
spring up around it. Since the new cabbages will be small, you can plant another crop
within 6 or 8 inches of the stalk without harm.

To store cabbages, trim off the stalk flush with the head. Remove large wrapper
leaves (you can boil them until tender). Make certain the leaves of the heads are bone
dry. Set in a box lined with dry straw or hay and keep in a dark dry place, ideally a
few degrees above freezing. The best storage cultivars keep until March.

And, on top of such interesting cultivars, good flavors, and crunchy textures, no
other vegetable except peppers has as high a concentration of vitamin C. Cabbage
has been nourishing man since prehistoric times.

Recommended: For ease, earliness, and fine summer eating, one early cabbage
stands head and shoulders above the others, and the delightful thing is that it was
introduced around 1840. Two- to 3-pound Early Jersey Wakefield has a conical
shape (once described as an upside-down ice cream cone), a small core, resistance to
frost and yellows (a fungus), holds in the field for a couple of weeks after maturity
without splitting, and is generally considered the most scrumptious of the earlies.
Golden Acre is also small and swift and tasty. Grenadier comes highly recommended.

For midseason/late savoys—OP Chieftain Savoy, with medium-light green
leaves. The Japanese hybrid savoys, Savoy Ace and Savoy King, are superbly flavored, handsome, and relatively early maturing. Small Promasa, a Dutch hybrid, is
even earlier. They've all grown superbly for me. *Late:* Tasty Centron can be harvested from softball to soccer ball size and won't split; Gourmet has short cores and
an especially beautiful wrapper.

For red cabbage, the Japanese hybrid Scarlett O'Hara is fetching, but the palm for flavor in red always goes to hybrid Ruby Ball, also a Japanese invention. Lasso and Red Acre are good open-pollinated reds.

For storage, introduced to this country around 1840, Premium Late Flat Dutch is excellent—and it makes heavenly sauerkraut. Its dense flat heads are more than a foot wide and weigh from 10 to 15 pounds. If autumn rain and weather are considerations, Safekeeper II is a hybrid with lots to recommend it.

For winter cabbages that are savoy/green crosses, the European January King is sweet, hardy, and as blue as a spruce. For rugged green overwinterers, use any cultivar recommended by Territorial Seed Company. All the preceding will stand in the field for weeks, if not months, patiently waiting to be harvested.

For heat resistance, Early Flat Dutch—good for southern and coastal gardens.

For yellows (fungus disease) resistance: earlies, heritage Early Jersey Wakefield and hybrids Puma and Regalia; midseason, hybrid Perfect Action; summer/fall hybrid Perfect Ball; for short-term storage, Multikeeper is yellows/black rot/black speck/thrips tolerant; for long-term storage, hybrid Albion (also resistant to thrips); and for red cabbage, Raven YR and Regal Red.

CARROTS   *Daucus Carota* var. *sativus*

Half-hardy biennial in the Parsley family, developed through cultivation . . . grows in 2- to 3-gallon containers.

You've seen Queen Anne's Lace in bloom—the creamy-green doilies are a lacework of hundreds of tiny stars. In the center is one star of rosy purple—stained by a drop of blood when Queen Anne pricked her finger. The aggressive roots are whitish, spindly, and have an acrid flavor. But flourishing in a meadow, the roots grow creamier, chunkier, and sweeter. Over the centuries, seeds from plants with the broadest, tastiest roots were sown and resown until what was once Queen Anne's Lace became known as carrot. Some were as large as a child's arm, sweet and tender. In 1853, in a catalog of French vegetables, *The Vegetable Garden,* 23 cultivars of carrots were listed.

At that time farmers around Nantes (eastern France, where three rivers meet—talk about fertile soil!) grew carrots to perfection. The fruits of those fields came into the vocabulary as the name of a shape of carrot. You'll find them in markets in France, but not here. Nantes tops are minuscule, and the roots crack easily when pulled from the soil (they have the ability to absorb more water, which makes them more succulent and thus more fragile). Mechanical harvesting of Nantes carrots is uneconomical.

Sorting out the carrots. Round carrots are not large carrots picked small and plump, but carrots bred to be 1 to 1 ½ inches round at maturity. They grow easily in most soils, are especially rewarding in containers, and all the cultivars I've grown have been delectable.

Finger carrots are just what they seem. They're about 2 ½ inches long and all sweetness. All are evenly cylindrical.

Amsterdams are called *baby Nantes.* Generally they're a luscious orange, almost coreless, and very sweet. In commerce, hybrid Amsterdams are grown twice as long, cut in half, pared appropriately, bagged, and labeled as baby carrots.

Berlicums have slim, tapered roots that look like Nantes. The color is vivid orange all the way through, the carrots have exceptional flavor, and they're superior keepers.

Chantenays can look like carrots for horses. Although they're usually picked much smaller, shoulders can reach 4 inches wide, tapering to 5 to 7 inches long, ending with a stumpy tip. Despite their unfashionable girth, old-fashioned Chantenays are flavorful and tender, excellent for juice. They'll easily grow in rocky and heavy clay soils and can be pulled from mucky soil. Chantenays are the carrots to carry you through winter. They'll keep serenely in the ground beneath a mulch of straw (from a few flakes to a whole bale, depending on how cold the winter) from early winter to spring. Chantenays are classified as intermediate carrots, and the huge ones mature in 20 to 24 weeks, although at 1 inch they're ready in half that time.

Danvers carrots are less straight than Nantes and less tapered than Chantenays but also blunt tipped. Around 6 ½ inches long, Danvers grow dependably in any soil.

Imperators are the slender, not terribly sweet 8- to 10-inch-long carrots at the market.

Nantes carrots are about 5 inches long, as thick as your middle finger, absolutely straight sided, and blunt tipped. Nantes are the finest carrots for eating and cooking fresh. Nantes will grow in any soil that will surrender a carrot without a fight, since the tops provide skimpy handles for pulling and the roots break easily. Obviously, Nantes aren't suitable for maturing in ground that will freeze at harvest time.

Each year brings more carroty delights from breeders. As of this writing, carrots are literally twice as sweet as they were in the 1960s. Then sugar content was 5–6 percent; now it's 11–12 percent. Not only are carrots sweeter, but their flavor has been refined through hybrids created with Nantes types. Their ancient characteristic qualities of an elusive soapy taste and overtones of bitterness are due to components called *terpenoids*—the elements that also make hops and orange peel bitter. Without terpenoids carrots wouldn't taste like carrots, so pinning them down to just the right level was the trick. Today's carrots offer superb flavor without a trace of suds or bitterness.

Breeders are also packing vitamin A into the roots. They began with deep-orange A-Plus, which contains twice the vitamin A of carrots in the 1960s. A-Plus has been replaced by Ingot and Juwarot, and they, in their turn, will give way to even more nutritious strains.

Carrots are sweetest when they mature in cool weather. Seedlings are hardy, so you can sow them early in spring. Sow carrots a week or two apart rather than count on a single sowing.

I grow mostly small round and finger carrots—small because the soil needn't be prepared all the way to China for them—and I grow them casually, their leaves feathery here and there through the borders. I never quite remember where I've put the carrots, and their ferny greens are such a lovely surprise. I'm not in danger of sowing over the carrot seeds because the white perlite mulch that keeps them moist while germinating tells me there's something underneath. By the time the greens are up, the mulch has blended with the soil, and the ferny tops take over keeping the soil cool.

Carrots are adaptable and will grow in any loose soil (if you don't push your luck by asking something long and thin to grow in something dense and stony).

Store-bought carrots (unless organic) are among the vegetables that may come with a considerable amount of pesticides—a very strong reason, in addition to incomparable flavor, to grow your own.

Carrot culture: To avoid making clods, work the soil when it's on the dry side. Loosen it with a cultivating fork 4, 8, or 12 inches deep, depending on the length of the carrot you're sowing and how energetic you feel. Toss out as many rocks as you can. To help retain moisture in sandy soil and to provide better drainage in clay soil, dig in well-rotted compost, about half and half with the earth. A couple of inches of well-rotted straw or decayed leaves worked into any soil is always welcome. As long as the humus is loose, its texture doesn't have to be fine. But remember, no manure within six months of sowing, and no fertilizer. The smart thing to do, if you can, is to work well-rotted manure into the soil a foot deep in the fall. In spring the carrot roots will dive down after it, thus growing wonderfully straight. Carrots are sensitive to nitrogen, and too much nitrogen makes them hairy. But don't spoil the fun for yourself. Just don't compact the soil of your carrot bed by walking on it.

I love germinating carrot seeds in a water bath because it takes only three days and you don't have to worry about the soil drying quite so much once sprouted seeds are planted. Starting carrot seeds in the ground comes with two headaches: They must never be allowed to dry out. That's true of all seeds, of course, but carrot seeds are especially vulnerable because they're so light and tiny. And they must be covered with something porous that won't crust over. The puny things can't break through crusted soil.

To sow, I run my finger in thoroughly moistened soil, making a trench a scant inch deep. I sprinkle in the seeds, then cover them with about ½ inch of perlite. Over that I strew a few shreds of something like rotting roots from the compost heap or strands of sphagnum moss or anything fine that will help hold moisture in—just enough to make a lace over the perlite. I cover the rows with a floating row cover, then water with a light mist until the bed is soaking. I keep an eye on the material and water as needed. It's a nuisance, because when you're starting carrots you can't leave home for more than a day until they germinate.

Sprouted seeds are planted the same way. Only some seeds, Kintoki for instance, seem rather gelatinous, and these must be set in the trench in a clump and then coaxed gently apart—not ideal. Some sprouted carrot seeds (Minicor) are easy to pick up with a moist toothpick and drop in place, just so.

It's never happened to me, but the carrot fly can be a problem—its larvae eat ugly holes in the root. The way to avoid attracting them is by not stirring up the soil, which releases that come-hither scent of carrots. That's why I don't mix radishes in with the carrots, which is a common practice (it's a traditional way to mark where the carrots are and to let the rough-and-tumble radishes break the soil for the effete carrot seeds). You can also avoid disturbing the soil by sowing so you won't have to thin. But this may not be possible with sprouted seeds. The floating row cover will keep the carrot fly out no matter what. But then, of course, you don't get to admire your little darlings as they grow.

The ferny tops of carrots are enchanting mixed with pansies. A light mulch of compost or small leaves keeps the soil cool and moist and helps prevent green carrot shoulders. But be careful not to let the mulch cover the carrots' crowns, from whence the leaves spring, or the crowns might rot. Harvest carrots while they're small, but be aware that there is more sugar in a mature carrot than in a young one.

Recommended: Easiest: Thumbelina. For extra vitamin A, Ingot, Juwarot, and A-Plus Hybrid. Best rounds: Orange-red Planet, but before Planet I was partial to Kundulus, and before that Paris Market. Thumbelina, an AAS winner, is now the rage. They can reach small-plum size. I grow them ½ inch apart and lift while still round. Thumbelina replaces Parmex in several catalogs, and Parmex was delicious. Finger: Although I've never found a frozen carrot I could tolerate, Suko is supposed to freeze well. Little Finger, 3 to 3 ½ inches long, and Lady Finger, 5 inches long, are other sweeties.

Amsterdam: Minicors are extra-early—they can be pulled at 3 inches.

Berlicum: Berlicummer. Falcon II is especially good for slicing. A carrot favored in both hot and cold climates.

Chantenay: Choose Royal or Imperial or whatever the current name is. Kinko, a cross between Chantenay and Nantes developed for the Japanese market, is a startling orange-red and is early, crunchy, and sweet. It may bolt prematurely in the South, however.

Danvers: Introduced before 1880, Danvers (aka Danvers Half Long) has a high vitamin A content and more fiber than Nantes sorts. It's especially valued for canning. Because it's open-pollinated, every seedsman has his strain, so when you find one you like, stay with it. The same is true of Chantenay.

Imperator: King Midas is wonderfully tasty, both when small and at full size.

Nantes: Scarlet Nantes has received highest marks in taste testings and is the standard for quality.

For disease resistance: Hybrid Klondike Nantes is tolerant to leaf blight and rusty root. Bolero is a blight-tolerant Nantes hybrid carrot for storage. Seminole has good tolerance to leaf diseases, including alternaria and leaf spot—it also has a Super Sweet gene for more sugar and vitamins. Choctaw is tolerant to alternaria, cavity spot, and cercospora. These two are Nantes × Imperator hybrids.

CAULIFLOWER
Brassica oleracea, Botrytis Group

Half-hardy biennial in the Mustard family, native to coastal western and southern Europe . . . grows in 5-gallon containers. Cauliflower is a prima donna. By comparison, every other member of the Mustard family is a dream. It hates heat, and with the exception of cultivars bred to withstand high temperatures, the curd factory essentially shuts down when the air hits 80° F. Cauliflower grows best within a breeze of the sea. After choosing just the right cultivars for your climate and season, select a bed in full sun. Enrich the soil with moisture-retaining humus, make sure it's the correct pH (see chart in The Gardener's Notebook), and calculate timing for early and late/main crops. It's crucial with cauliflower that there be nary a moment's stress from seedling to curd.

Splendid, elegant cauliflower is one of many choice mustards that scrambled up the social ladder from wild cabbage. Ancient Romans grew cauliflower, Arab botanists developed it in the Middle Ages, and by the time it was part of the royal table in the 17th century, cauliflower had been grown in French kitchen gardens for a couple of hundred years.

A light, silty loam that holds water fairly well is ideal. If you amend with compost, it must be well aged to avoid black rot. The cauliflower's root system can grow easily and shallowly, freeing up the plant's energy for making big leaves and curds.

Cultivars bred for Dutch and English farmers are not used to irrigation as ours are, so their roots tend to grow especially vigorously and deep. Some Dutch cauliflowers are Alpha Begum, Montano, Ravella, Vernon, White Rock, and the Walcherin series from Territorial. Purple Cape is English.

Cauliflower breeders have developed cultivars to mature in distinct seasons. Cultivars are sown in March in cool climates to mature in early summer before great heat. In the South, sow these late January and February for May and June harvest. These are the trickiest to time right and the ones most likely to button—i.e., produce tiny curds that never grow. Main-season or late cultivars are sown in June to mature in cooler autumn. Overwintering cauliflowers are sown in July for maturing from February or March to May in areas where the ground doesn't freeze hard— these are considered the easiest and the surest to grow because heat doesn't come anywhere near them, unless you live in a tropical part of the country. And if you do, still these are the ones to grow. The large ruffled blue leaves on this enormous flower make a marvelous centerpiece among orange and yellow calendulas. And cauliflowers around the gray-green tracework of golden yarrow are thrilling, too. For brightness, set snapdragons among these rather curious-looking plants.

If white doesn't excite you, cauliflower also comes in colors. Actually there's no agreement among seedsmen whether Violet Queen and Burgundy Queen and Purple Cape and Sicilian Purple and green Alverda are broccoli or cauliflower. The curds of these colorful types don't need to be covered from the sun as they grow. Their leaves are more like cauliflower's, and their flowers all turn green on cooking. But their heads are more the tight buds of broccoli than the curds of cauliflower, and they taste a bit more like broccoli—or is it cauliflower? These sorts also send up secondary stalks after the head has been harvested, in the manner of cauliflower and broccoli. And perhaps you've seen chartreuse broccoflower at the market.

The gold-swirled Romanesco types of broccoli, too, are now listed in the cauliflowers in some seed catalogs.

Growing your own head of absolutely gloriously gorgeous creamy or purple or golden curds will give you a thrill you'll long remember. And the flavor of your own fresh-from-the-garden cauliflower is infinitely sweeter than that of one from the market.

Plan it so seedlings are set in the ground at a time when they'll have eight weeks ahead of them with days between 65°F and 80°F (90°F for heat-tolerant cultivars) and nights above 50°F—night temperature of 50°F or below is a cause of buttoning.

You'll have much the best control if you sow seeds in soil blocks or flats. (Spring rains can compress the soil, which can cause irregular germination in direct seeding.) Transplant with care, setting the seedling in a cutworm collar a little deeper in

Mini-Cauliflowers

If, like me, you haven't room for more than one or two standard cauliflower plants at a time but wish for more, grow minis. Plants can be set on 6-inch centers (one fourth of the optimal standard spacing). Use the earliest and healthiest cultivars and the same culture, only crowd the plants. Harvest heads at around 3 ½ inches, taking two or three leaves along, too. Since they'll mature at the same time, sow as often as you'll eat baby cauliflower.

the soil than it was before. Firm the roots by carefully walking around the plant. Provide extra calcium—I sprinkle crushed eggshells copiously over the bed at planting time. (You could dig in a little lime instead.) Cover the seedlings immediately with a large sheet of floating row cover, sprinkling soil along all four sides so no insect can crawl under—this will save you enormous grief. Once the plants are strong and well established, mulch with straw or newspaper. When plants get taller, draw soil around their stems to keep them from being stressed by wind.

If, after a couple of tries, you've satisfied every requirement of this finicky plant and your cauliflowers aren't beautiful, have your soil tested, especially with an eye to magnesium, boron, and molybdenum. If there's a problem, foliar feed kelp solution monthly while the plants are growing, and water weekly with eggshell tea. That may do it. If not, consult your agricultural extension agent.

Harvest cauliflower when the heads are from 6 to 9 inches in diameter, depending on the cultivar, but while the curds are still tight. Cut the stalk a few inches above the ground—harvest in the morning with the dew upon it. Hold the head of cauliflower upside down or throw a towel over it—just protect the blanched head from the sun until you can get it indoors. Should a plant bolt, you'll find the flowers enchanting starry sprays, and you can cook them too.

Even if your plants button, leave them in place—it's possible that they'll produce a proper curd later in the season.

To get creamy white curds, be aware that a lot of sunlight turns them greige. See Blanching in The Gardener's Notebook.

Recommended: For ease, earliness, and quality, the AAS hybrid Snow Crown is the one to grow. Several seedsmen offer a mix of cultivars that, with a single June sowing, will give you cauliflower from August through November or beyond. I've loved Amazing, an open-pollinated, self-blanching cultivar. For main-season/late eating: The Danish open-pollinated Dominant (which tolerates some dry weather and is a good choice for arid climates), hybrid Ravella (slow to bolt), and OP White Rock for its vigor and exceptional flavor. For overwintering: Walcherin types—Fleurly, the Armado series, and Pinnacle—have been called "breeding master-pieces," and they're hardy to 10°F. For minis, use Snow Crown. For colorful tasty cauliflowers, green Alverda and purple hybrid Violet Queen. White Knight and White Bishop hybrids are tolerant of purple tinge.

CELERIAC
Apium graveolens var. *rapaceum*

Half-hardy biennial in the Parsley family, a widely distributed native . . . aka celery root, knob celery, turnip-rooted celery . . . grows in 3-gallon containers. Grow as celery.

Knobby-rooted, creamy-textured celeriac wants everything celery does, because they're very closely related. But large-hearted, exquisitely fla-vored celeriac—it's a creamy, nutty, earthy, yet refined celery taste—is considered easier to grow than trenching and self-blanching celeries. Stokes' Seeds' catalog goes so far as to say celeriac is easy. It must be me. I've tried five or six times to grow it with little success.

Because celeriac is slow to germinate, in cold climates start seed indoors very early in spring. Elsewhere you can start the seeds outdoors in the shade and trans-plant seedlings into the garden when it gets cool. Grow celeriac in a practical part of the garden—its celery stalks and leaves can look a little unkempt. The root is har-vested in autumn, when it reaches 2 to 3 inches in diameter.

Recommended: Easiest: the one you can get to grow for you. The old standard Giant Prague is still the cultivar of choice for several seedsmen. There's also open-pollinated Brilliant and Monarch—the latter has resistance to scab and is said not to discolor when cut.

CELERIES

Apium graveolens var. *dulce*

Half-hardy biennial in the Parsley family, a widely distributed native . . . grows in 3-gallon containers. All celeries need manure-enriched, moisture-retentive soil. Celeries grow best when the air is cooler than 75°F. Where summers are hot, they can have direct sun until early afternoon, then light shade is a good idea—and if you expect them to winter over, make it a spot that will be sheltered. If they're in a place where the turned-off hose can finish dripping, that's perfect.

Small white-flowered wild celery has been found in marshes from Swedish inlets to the islands of Tierra del Fuego to mountains above the Arabian Sea. Such celery was gathered by the ancients, but used only medicinally, although in Plutarch's time (A.D. 46?–120) the graceful leaves decorated funeral wreaths.

Happily, most critters aren't interested in celery. None of our celery has ever been so much as nibbled on. I can't speak for rabbits and deer, but celery's safe against raccoons, squirrels, ground squirrels, and chipmunks . . . so far. Although I read that celery can be struck by various diseases, such as fusarium wilt, we've had none. Disease-resistant cultivars are available.

In the coldest areas you can lift any celery before the ground freezes and either pot it up and bring it inside to grow in a bright corner or set it in the cold frame. Give celeries regular feeds of manure tea.

You can harvest celery in a cut-and-come-again way. Use a knife to take individual stalks and leafy tips, always leaving about two thirds of the bunch. If you cut all the stalks flush with the ground, more will sprout up in their place. Start a crop for winter in early summer.

CHINESE CELERY

The flavor of Chinese celery is considered stronger than European, and it's less of a hassle to grow. My Chinese Golden Medium Early celery *is* unusually flavorful, with a hint of anise in its round hollow stalks and large three-to-a-tip leaves. As with leaf celery, my plants didn't form a head, but rather sent up a large center stalk with more slender stalks on the side. Cut that stalk, and the side stalks will get larger for the next harvest. The plants are sweet next to dainty yellow mixed mimulus (monkey flowers).

I hadn't noticed Stokes Seeds' catalog's admonition not to set celery in the garden until after June 1 since cold nights will make the plants bolt. Stokes is so right. Chinese celery is responsive to long day length, which can cause it to bolt if stressed by sudden changes in temperature.

Recommended: Chinese Golden Medium Early.

LEAF CELERY, PAR-CEL, AND SMALLAGE

Aka cutting, green, or soup celery.

With stalks as thick as your little finger to as thin as a drinking straw—some cultivars are hollow—these celeries are warmly flavored, and the leaves are so lush and beautiful they'll make you weak. Think of them as an herb more than a vegetable. Close to the wild sort in habit, these celeries are undemanding to grow.

After my experiment with trenching celery I grew Thompson & Morgan's Par-Cel ("Looks like parsley—tastes like celery . . . can be grown as easily as Radishes . . .") in bright shade. Celery that is mostly leaves, it was probably first grown in the 18th century. The celery's crisply cut gathered leaves the color of pale daffodils were a joy all summer, both to look at and to eat. Then last year I sowed Solid Red celery, an English cultivar from Gleckler Seedmen, in soil blocks in spring and set out three plants in the garden. I now find the cultivar is a trenching celery, but not knowing that, I let them grow as they liked, and they're wonderful. The stalks aren't really red—they look like basic celery fallen into a vat of red wine. I'm proud of my plants. They're about a foot tall (with more water they'd be taller). You can't tell the leaves of Solid Red celery from flat-leaf parsley. I'm grateful for them, too. All winter I plucked leaves and dainty reddish stalks for salads, although I've noticed in their second spring, the stalks get slightly bitter.

In colder climates green-stemmed cultivars are hardiest, withstanding $-10°F$ with shelter. A Seed Saver notes that Par-Cel has been hardy to $-20°F$.

I'm going to try French Dinant, one of the best of the European leaf celeries. They really belong in the border, mixed with scarlet dahlias. Celery self-sows; I let it. Inexplicably, a plant of red celery has turned up 100 feet and a season away from where it grew last. Delicious surprise.

Smallage is defined as wild celery, but I've decided that it's the term for whatever leaf celery the seedsman can find. Don't send for smallage seeds, because you won't know what they are. Grow a self-described leaf celery instead. Or lovage; its appearance is much like leaf celery's, its flavor is spicier, and it's a perennial.

Recommended: Easy and delectable: Solid Red Celery, Par-Cel, Cutting Leaf, Dinant.

TRENCHING AND SELF-BLANCHING CELERY

Heft a pale sleek bunch of celery at the market and, could it speak to you, it might confess how much *trouble* it took for it to become so splendid. Celery like that has absorbed an enormous amount of time and water. For flavorful crisp, unstringy white stalks, celery must be planted in trenches—after taking three months just to grow big enough to be put into the trench! The Gardener's Notebook gives instructions for blanching.

Nowadays there are cultivars that need no shroud of earth. Called *self-blanching*, these are classed as early celery (all self-blanching celeries are early, but not all early celeries are self-blanching). Self-blanching types aren't hardy, and they're considered inferior in texture and flavor to the old-fashioned work-intensive trenching cultivars, which are classed as late celery. If you cover late celery with straw when frost comes, you'll have a few weeks' grace, and often the frost sweetens the flavor. When I tried growing trenching celery, after a month I couldn't bear the fussing, so I chopped up what stalks there were into a salad, and the following year I sowed leaf celery.

Recommended: Golden Self Blanching is what I began with. It's easy enough for a fussy plant. For some disease tolerance, Ventura and Matador.

CELTUCE   *Lactuca sativa* var. *asparagina*

Half-hardy annual in the Sunflower family, not known in the wild . . . aka stem lettuce, asparagus lettuce, Chinese lettuce . . . grows in 2-gallon containers. Celtuce tolerates both light frosts and temperatures over 80° F. Give moist, fertile soil with ample sunshine.

The Chinese are crazy about celtuce—they grow it commercially—so I was eager to try it in our garden. The first year, no seeds germinated. The second year, mice ate every seedling. The third year, I caged the seedlings with ½-inch chicken wire.

All summer the plants looked like romaine lettuce leaves loosely bunched—pretty with pansies and Johnny-jump-ups at their feet. But the flavor of the leaves I picked was thin. At summer's end the stem quickly mounted, and the plant looked like bolting lettuce. Which I have to believe it is. Harvest time is meant to be when the stalk is about 1 ½ feet tall and 1 ½ inches thick. Mine reached half that size. I suspect it's a matter of sun. The plants had bright shade in the morning and afternoon sun. Although culture for celtuce is supposed to be that of lettuce, lettuces beside my celtuce thrived while the celtuces looked as though they were in the wrong place.

No matter. The crisp juicy stalk is the object. Some say it tastes cucumbery, some like asparagus. The celtuce I've bought from the Chinese market tasted like neither but like mine: the stalk's heart has the texture of a succulent pared broccoli stalk with the flavor of lettuce.

Recommended: Generic from a seedsman that has good turnover in celtuce— seeds must be fresh.

CHARD   *Beta vulgaris,* Cicla Group

Hardy biennial in the Goosefoot family, native to the Atlantic coast of Europe from the Canary to the Madeira Islands, the Mediterranean region to southern Russia, Syria, and Iraq . . . aka beet Swiss chard, seakale beet . . . grows in 5-gallon containers. Give chard rich, moisture-retentive soil in a sunny but sheltered spot, ample water, and it will return the kindness with leaves through summer and winter.

With leaves that look like elephant ears of spinach but can taste as delicate as lettuce, with stalks and midribs that crunch like celery but have a hint of asparagus about them, chard is two vegetables in one. It asks for nothing but a few hours of sunshine, its share of water, and freedom from slugs and snails. Chard is so accommodating that it will tolerate some shade and dry and poor soil. The plant grows lush and elegant, a fountain of dark green. The most exciting are the ruby chards with shimmering scarlet stalks. I set Charlotte ruby chard beside Japanese flowering quince. With the afternoon sun behind them, the quince's hot pink blossoms bounced off the scarlet stalks, and stiff quince leaves nodded against floppy chard's. There is no more beautiful pair in the garden.

One more virtue? You'll have it for at least a couple of years. If you let it go to seed, there will be a nurseryful of babies next spring. Scoop them up and set them around the garden—there can never be too much chard.

To harvest, cut stalks with a knife from the outside first. You can also cut all the stalks at once down to 2 inches, and leaves will sprout from the crown.

Recommended: All are easy, adaptable, and flavorful, perhaps Argentata the most. For beauty, the ruby-stalked Charlotte. The hardiest: Swiss Chard of Geneva. Fordhook Giant and Lucullus are large and leafy with white stalks. Silverado is dwarf. Most cultivars are mostly green leaves, but for more stalk, grow Monstruoso.

CHICK-PEAS.   *See Beans for Drying.*

CHICORIES.   *See Salad Greens.*

CHINESE ARTICHOKES   *Stachys affinis*

Hardy perennial in the Mint family, native to China . . . aka Japanese artichoke, chorogi, knotroot, crosnes-du-Japon . . . grows in broad 3-gallon containers. These small tubers lie just beneath the soil and are easy to grow. They survive great heat and cold, although their leaves collapse in frost. They need full sun, light, rich sandy soil, and ample water. They take the summer to increase. They're not productive, so plant lots and give them good care for an ample crop.

Looking like ivory-whorled shells no bigger than the tip of your little finger, Chinese artichokes are crunchy with a sweet and delicate flavor, described by a Frenchwoman as a combination of artichoke heart and salsify, to which I would add a trace of Jerusalem artichoke.

Chinese artichoke plants are handsome in a far corner of the border. Standing knee high, the dark green leaves bear a family resemblance to mint, and the flowers are pale red. However, toward midsummer the plants tend to sprawl. I grew ours beside some bush beans, a perfect place.

Plant the largest tubers you have. Stick a finger in the ground; then set a tuber upright in the hole so the top is an inch below the surface. Cover and pat firmly. The soil can be surprisingly cool—41°F. The tubers increase in mint fashion. Underground runners spurt along, then stop according to some inner voice and form a tuber—which sends a runner, which forms a tuber, and so on.

Mulch with straw once all the leaves are up and keep weeds pulled. You can start harvesting after the leaves have died down. Dig tubers—feel around for them in the earth; then gently follow the threads to the next tuber. Dig just before you need them, since they rapidly dry out and lose their pearly sheen. Tubers may be left in the ground to winter over if protected with straw. However, if you must free up the bed, tubers can be buried in a bucket of sand that's kept moist, at about 36°F, should you have such a chilly spot!

Tubers left in the ground will likely sprout in spring and begin the cycle again.

CHINESE CABBAGE. *See Asian Greens.*

CHINESE KALE. *See Asian Greens.*

COLLARDS
Brassica oleracea, Acephala Group

Hardy biennial in the Mustard family, native to coastal western and southern Europe . . . aka cole, colewort, braschette . . . grows in 5-gallon containers. Even though it's one of the least demanding of vegetables and one of the most vigorous and productive, you'll have the best leaves if you grow collards as you do kale, cabbage, and all the other mustards.

You can tell collards and kales are closely related: they have in common their ease of culture, their hardiness, high yields, harvestability most of the year, and exceptional nutritive value. Collards are large nonheading rosettes of broad green or blue-green leaves that tolerate summer heat and dry spells better than kale, and they barely interest pests.

Compared with the kales, which are for the most part ravishing, the sight of collards in the garden is merely reassuring. It means you won't go hungry.

To many in the South, *greens* means "collards." The leaves of collards—essentially a primitive cabbage—resemble the coarse outer leaves of cabbages.

The flavor is, in fact, more cabbagey than kale. Taller cultivars—collards grow upright, from 1½ to 3 feet tall—look a bit like broccoli. Tuck sassy yellow marigolds here and there for color and mix in some corn salad for contrast of leaves—long, thin, and green against big, coarse, and blue.

Sow collards in early spring for summer greens and again in late summer for fall and early winter greens—don't forget that a touch of frost sweetens them. Aim strong sprays of water at any aphids that might come by. Or wrap the rosettes in insect-weight floating row covers, and you won't have to think about aphids.

Harvest as for kale.

Recommended: For ease, the old standard, Georgia, will produce juicy leaves even in marginal soil and weather—it's best for the spring sowing. Champion, an improved form of the old favorite Vates, can stand up to wintry weather better than most—sow it in fall. Morris Heading is another old favorite, different from other collards because its dark green leaves form a loose, heavy head. It is particularly slow to go to seed. Also for slow bolting, hybrid Flash.

COMMON OR LEAF MUSTARDS. *See Mustard Greens.*

CORN *Zea mays*

Tender annual in the Grass family, native to tropical America . . . aka Indian Corn, maize . . . 20 plants of a short cultivar will grow in half-barrels. Corn needs full sun, rich soil, and roots that are constantly moist until the plants are established. Dig in about 6 pounds of aged manure—chicken and rabbit are best—for every 10 feet of bed. Once plants are established, water deeply but infrequently—although the soil must never dry out around the plants—to encourage the development of strong roots.

For thousands of years, corn has been grown by native tribes from Canada to Chile. Olmecs and Mayans invested their corn plants with divinity. Mayans sowed corn along roadways so that travelers would not go hungry. Hopis believe that each color of corn represents a direction of the wind and that multicolored corn represents all plants, all birds, all butterflies.

The ancestor of these corn plants is *teosinte,* a primitive sort of popcorn with tiny ears that was probably first cultivated 7,000 years ago in the highlands of Mexico. But no one knows the wild origins of *teosinte.* Charles Darwin wondered—as have botanists since—why and how corn plants that flourished in the wild for aeons developed into a plant that couldn't reproduce itself if it was down to the last ear on the last stalk on earth.

Corn kernels are the plant's seeds. We eat corn on the cob when the seeds are immature—called the *milk stage* because the kernels spout a milky substance when pierced with a thumbnail. For popping, for grinding into meal, and for saving seeds we let the kernels dry in the husk to the point that they're hard as little rocks. Seeds of other plants have developed ingenious ways of reproducing their species. Some sprout wings or plumes that catch the wind and glide to earth. Some float on streams or ocean currents, never absorbing water, until deposited to germinate in silt or on beaches. Some stay in pods that dry until the papery shells twist and crack open, broadcasting their seeds to the soil. Some have gluey coats or tiny barbs that stick to fur and feathers and are thus transported to brave new lands. Some make themselves attractive to creatures who eat them, digest them, then eliminate them intact over the soil. But even should corn's husks and silk dry to dust, even should the ear fall to the ground with enough force to dislodge seeds from their cob, even should the seeds settle into the soil and germinate, seeds set so closely produce a tangle of plants in one spot that would all choke to death.

I used to think corn is corn, and there is in fact only one species, *Zea mays*. But there are several distinct subspecies—in terms of the kitchen, the differences between them being the degrees of starch the kernels contain. By all means, treat yourself to the excitement of growing and savoring each type.

There are hundreds of cultivars of corn from which to choose, and there isn't one offered in catalogs that won't make you whoop for joy when you taste it fresh from your garden—if the cultivar is right for your area. Some native cultivars mature in 2 months; some take 11. Some stalks grow 2 feet tall, some 20. The number of rows of kernels on the cob may vary from 4 to 36; the ears may be the size of a man's thumb or the length of his arm; and the kernels may be less than an eighth of an inch or a full inch square. Stalks, leaves, and husks may be green, gold, purple, red, brown, or multistriped. Silks may be green, salmon, or shades of red. Kernels may be hues of cream, yellow, brown, red, blue, purple, or a confetti of all of these colors.

One thing about husks: The tighter they are, the more protection they give against hungry birds and corn earworms. When the seed catalog talks about good "cover," that's what it means.

As with other crops, picking the right cultivars for your season and climate is the first step in growing *great* corn. If you live where summers are long and hot, you can take your pick of any cultivar and it will grow wonderfully. If you live anywhere else and you're growing corn for the first time—or haven't had sensational corn in the past—ask a fellow corn grower what's worked, or call the nearest university extension or county agricultural adviser.

Or, for guaranteed results, choose the corn according to Heat Units.

Can't you just go by the number of days to maturity noted after a cultivar in the catalog? Yes, but only if you live close to the cornfield where the corn grown for the catalog matured. Corn doesn't ripen by day length. It ripens by accumulation of heat. Each cultivar of corn matures when it has absorbed a particular amount of heat through the season—the amount inscribed on its genes. Breeders have given this amount the name *Heat Units (HU)*.

The number of Heat Units each cultivar requires is the average of a day's maximum and minimum temperatures minus 50°F (the base temperature—corn won't grow when it's cooler).

Now you can see that the 92 days listed in the catalog after the legendary cultivar Silver Queen are going to be 92 very different days in terms of heat when the corn is grown in sultry Natchez from when it's struggling in lofty Missoula.

Another element to factor in is your soil. Sandy, gravelly soil will germinate seeds in three to four days, while clay soil in the same climate can take 12 more days.

Cultivars termed *extra-early* (the fastest to mature) are listed in catalogs as between 53 and 62 days. These need about 1,350 HU. Main-season cultivars generally are said to mature between 80 and 90 days, which would be around 1,750 HU. Late cultivars with large lush cobs will need around 2,200 HU, and as much as 2,500.

To figure what you can grow, get the average day and nighttime temperatures in your area—from the last spring frost to the first autumn frost (ask the local newspaper). For example, if your days average 72°F and nights 58°F, add the 2 (130), divide in half (65), subtract the 50 (base temp), and you get 15. Each day gives you 15 Heat Units. Say your growing season is 150 days; 150 days times 15 HU gives you a total of 2,250 HU. Silver Queen is generally listed as needing 94 days to mature (although with gravelly soil, it could take less). A late cultivar, figure 2,200 HU. Your Silver Queen will probably squeak through.

Then to see how long a cultivar will take, for example, divide extra early Earlivee's need for 1,300 HU by your 15 and you get about 87. Earlivee is listed in Stokes as maturing in 57 days. Your Earlivee could well take a month longer to mature.

When you're thinking about growing corn whose kernels must dry on the stalk, you'll need to add another 900 HU or so to the milk stage given in catalogs.

By and large, the later-maturing the cultivar, the larger the ear. There is often just one ear of corn on a stalk, and it's usually at the top, but breeders are working on cultivars that will produce two or even more good ears. Look for this in the catalog description—otherwise it's a lot of energy for one ear of corn.

All these diverse corns are gifts from the wind—it pollinates them. Since the wind blows in a broad sweep, the thing to remember about plotting your corn is that stalks are grown most efficiently in blocks—minimum 4 feet square. If your block is a rectangle, set it at 90 degrees to the wind. That will be four plants in four rows, sixteen plants, producing from sixteen to thirty-two ears. In most cases they'll all ripen within a week of one another. That's a good reason to consider growing corn that will hold on the stalk without losing quality.

Then there's the corn your neighbors plant. The wind knows not of property lines. Tall deflectors such as a trellis of pole beans or raspberries or a stand of sunflowers or shrubs or a fence may make it possible to grow *your* corn while they grow *theirs*. Best inquire what they're growing.

Space. To keep your cultivars of corn pure, you'll need to isolate them. Purists say you'll need ¼ mile, 1,320 feet, between cultivars. But in the home garden, unless it's ferociously windy, for purity you can get away with a separation of 250 feet in all directions. There will be some cross-pollinating, but not enough to make a difference. Separate supersweets from everything else by at least 25 feet—their pollen will toughen all other corn to inedibility.

Time. Tassels of the first cultivar must finish shedding their pollen before silks of the second cultivar begin to emerge. Vagaries of weather and the accuracy of the seedsman's maturity dates can make isolating by time tricky. But as long as you're not working with rare cultivars whose seeds you want to save, you can plant two cultivars the same day if they have at least 12 (better 21) days' difference in maturing time between them—or you can plant cultivars with the same maturing date 12 days apart.

Hand-pollinating. If you haven't room to plant corn in blocks of four by four, or if you're hungry for an assortment of cultivars and you must plant them at the same time and close together—or if you want to grow from one to several stalks in a container—you can stand in for the wind and pollinate corn plants yourself. When *you* do it, you'll be assured of ears with all rows plumply filled, and none of your supersweet kernels will be tough. Pollinating corn by hand is easy and fun and takes little time.

The object is to get pollen from the tassels onto the silks in the ears—making sure each strand of silk receives a grain of pollen. If you're working with rare cultivars, consult Suzanne Ashworth's *Seed to Seed*. For just good-eating corn, mixed kernels in the ears aren't a problem, and you can be more casual.

Begin hand-pollinating when the tiny anthers dangling on the tassel branches turn gold and when the silks are thick at the tip of the husk. Make sure the plants have been well watered in the days before pollinating—stress shuts down their reproduction factories. Cut the silks evenly to 1 inch. Pollen is generally shed after the morning dew has evaporated and before noon, so do your pollinating then.

Select a few tassels from healthy plants. Gently bend each down and run your hands through it, dropping pollen into a paper bag. Pollinate the top ear of each stalk (the plant nourishes that ear first and abandons it last when stressed). Slowly sprinkle the bright yellow powder evenly over the silks (no need to pull back the husks)—½ teaspoon pollen per ear is ideal. If there's pollen to spare, pollinate the next ear down on the stalk.

Tassels produce pollen for up to a week, and silks remain receptive for up to 10 days, so for insurance you can pollinate on subsequent mornings. Cover those ears from which you want to save seed—and all ears on supersweet corn—with paper bags closed with clothespins.

Where to grow corn? I rotate tasty and productive Early Sunglow around the garden, since it grows only 4 to 4 ½ feet tall. I plant a 4-foot block at the back of the border and the afternoon sun shines over it. Sometimes I also sow the popcorn cultivar Tom Thumb—it grows only 3 ½ feet tall.

Taller stalks are harder to place in the border, although you can soften the edges of a block of 8-foot-high cornstalks with a buffer of airy 6-foot-tall cosmos—or combine them with tall sunflowers.

Some corn leaves are touched with color, which makes them appealing mixed with other plants. The Mandan Bride multicolored corn I grew last summer had red brushed down the leaves. You still must place them in a block, of course (or hand-pollinate).

Southern folklore warns us not to plant corn with a coat on—the air and ground must be warm. If your growing season is less than 60 days, start seeds indoors in paper pots. Some recommend soaking the seeds overnight, then sprouting them in paper towels (see The Gardener's Notebook). Set in soil blocks or paper pots and plant when 6 inches tall. If you sow larger seeds rather than smaller, you'll likely have crops earlier than later—but to preserve a well-rounded gene pool, sow a mix of seeds.

If your seeds are untreated (not dipped in fungicide), the soil must be 60°F. Treated seeds can take 50°F soil if it is sandy or gravelly. If you have enough, it's wise to plant 2 seeds in each space, then snip off the punier plant before the bigger one is 4 to 6 inches tall. If your summers are cold, grow the quickest-to-mature cultivars you can find, like Earlivee II or Aladdin bicolor. On the other hand, if you garden below 32 degrees latitude, grow midseason or late cultivars. Earlies won't mature properly in your area.

To prevent disease, don't sprinkle corn plants overhead, but irrigate or use a drip system. Supersweets need twice the water of other corn for germination. In dry areas, plant in trenches, 5 or 6 inches deep, or do as the Hopi do—grow several corn plants in a basin. The rainwater collects there.

A living mulch of pumpkins in the patch, planted on 5-foot centers in place of corn that would be set in that spot, is ideal for keeping the soil moist. If you don't want pumpkins, mulch with straw. When the stalks reach 8 inches tall, spray with fish emulsion. Repeat again when the plants are knee high.

Some say that weeds must be kept out of the corn patch. But many Native

Americans traditionally don't weed their cornfields, instead allowing lamb's-quarters, sunflowers, milkweed, wild lettuce, and purslane to grow among the stalks. These plants anchor the soil and contribute to the corn in other ways—companion planting. So if you have any of these so-called weeds in your corn patch, once the corn is knee high, you might want to leave them there (but not wild lettuce if you want to save seeds of your cultivated lettuce). Space the plants as far apart as you've spaced the corn. This doubles the load on the soil, but the benefits of the synergism (one plus one equals three or maybe 3 ½) will outweigh the extra load. If you cultivate, stop when the stalks are knee high, because surface roots must not be disturbed.

Suckers (side shoots) that develop around the base of the stalk give the plant strength and should not be removed. If wind threatens to loosen the stalks, when the plants are a few feet high, hill up earth around the bottoms of the plants to steady the bases. Should a stalk break, just prop it up, even splinting it with a stake.

If plants develop ears at the base (called *tiller ears*), you'll know you've sown that cultivar too close.

If you have space and time enough, when the first planting is knee high, sow a second crop—and a third. Just be sure to take the vagaries of cross-pollination into account. Time the last crop to be ready for harvest a week or two before the first expected hard frost or as long as days and nights stay warm.

Unfortunately, we're not the only ones who find corn tempting. But the only pests I've had so far on my corn were ants, and I just hosed them off—early in the morning: corn can be susceptible to fungal diseases. If you live in a part of the country not so fortunate, choose resistant cultivars.

To baffle raccoons and birds, first try a paper bag over each ear, then a circle of blood meal. An impenetrable baffle: use a length of about 24 inches of ¾-inch strapping tape, the kind with fiberglass in it. Start at the ear an inch above where it's attached to the stalk. Wrap around the ear once, then around the stalk, then an inch and a half or so below the tip, wrap around the ear again. For more deterrents, see The Gardener's Notebook.

There's something else you might be confronted with, and that's a delicate "silvery-grey skinned black" fungus. The description is Diana Kennedy's, the brilliant conservator of Mexican cuisine. Aka corn smut, this is an "excrescence of enlarged and deformed kernels that form under the sheath of green husks around the ears, often forcing them open." With a name derived from the Aztec, the fungus is appreciated in Mexico the way the rest of the world prizes wild mushrooms. Diana Kennedy speaks of *cuitlacoche*'s (or sometimes *huitlacoche*'s) "inky-black extravagance of flavor." Considered most delicious when grown in warm summer rain, the fungus is spread by windborne spores, and if it's in the neighborhood it can turn up in your patch.

If you're dying to taste *cuitlacoche,* grow gourdseed corn (see Dent Corn) and savor an intriguing and historied corn and an unusual fungus at the same time. Gourdseed corn is susceptible to the fungus. But if this sort of thing doesn't appeal, choose fungus-resistant cultivars. Should some spores slip through and you see swellings on ears and tassels that are pale and shiny at first, then gradually darken, carefully pull up the plant, carrying it so the spores don't scatter, then burn it.

To harvest corn at the milk stage, a general rule is to pick three weeks after the first silk appears. When the silk is brown and dry, pull back the husk and pierce a kernel with your thumbnail. If the juice runs clear, the corn's not ready. If thin milk spurts out, it's ready. If the milk is thick, the corn is past its prime—let it dry thoroughly and save it to feed the birds in winter. To harvest, twist or snap the ear off the stalk.

To shuck, winnow, and store field-dried corn. Allow the ears to ripen on the stalk until their husks are crackling dry. Then pick the ears, at once pull back the husks and silk, tie several husks together, and hang without touching in a dry, well-ventilated place—out of reach of any mice—until the kernels are thoroughly dry. To shuck, if the kernels have pointed tips or if your skin blisters easily, wear gloves. Holding an end in each hand deep inside a large bag, try twisting the ear—kernels will fly all over the place. If that doesn't work, hold an ear in each hand and scrub them together, starting at one end—this will loosen the kernels. To save seeds, keep only completely formed kernels and remember to get a good mix of all sorts of ears except incomplete and diseased ones for good genetic diversity.

To winnow the kernels, place them about ¼ inch deep in a shallow pan, take the pan outside on a windy day, and stir the kernels with your hands, letting the wind float away the debris. Or use a hair dryer on its coolest setting in 10-second spurts, then cool the seeds.

Store kernels in an airtight bag in an airtight jar in a cool, dark, dry place.

After harvest, chop up all healthy cornstalks and either add them to the compost pile or, if it's the end of summer, dig them into the patch. Unhealthy material should be burned or tightly tied in a bag and set out with the garbage.

As with many vegetables, there's some confusion in corns. In the Seed Savers Exchange yearbook, for example, multicolored Mandan Bride—I love the name and the corn—is listed by members offering seeds both in the flint corn section and in the flour corn section. The answer? When you get something you like, don't worry what its name is.

Dent, flint, flour, and popcorn are termed *field corns*—the most rugged of the species. Remember that most corn kernels don't take on color until they dry. At the milk stage, they're almost all pale cream or yellow. So when I describe a red or blue or black corn, it's dried.

DENT CORN   *Z. mays* var. *indentata*

Aka field corn, gourdseed corn, grain corn, dent maize. Dents are best for the Southeast and Midwest. Husks of many are very tight and insect resistant.

The distinction among corns lies in the type and amount of starch their kernels contain. In dent corn kernels the centers are soft starch, but the exteriors are as hard as flint. One of nature's naughty tricks—since the inside and outside dry at different rates, a dent sinks into the kernel's crown. Picked at the milk stage and roasted, dent corn has many aficionados. Dried, the kernels are good for hominy, grits, cornmeal, and flour. The great 19th-century Virginia cultivar Bloody Butcher—blood-red kernels with drops of darker red—is one of the most famous dents.

Dent ears are comparatively short, thick, and heavy for their size, and the stalks are uncommonly tall and vigorous, growing to 12 feet, as tall as many fruit trees. I can't see 10- or 12-foot cornstalks easing into a mixed border, but of course you may have just the spot for a patch. Very tall cornstalks can be prone to lodging—cornese for toppling over—which cornstalks are wont to do if they're in soggy or light soil and/or there's wind. So if you have these conditions, look for cultivars that resist lodging and hill them up.

With almost 300 years behind them that we know of, ears of gourdseed corn do indeed look a piece with the sturdy but relatively primitive trappings of American colonial life. The kernels, as thin as squash seeds, have spaces between them that make the creamy white kernels look like gappy teeth. When you see them, you realize how much corn has been bred for appearance.

The plants of Texas Gourdseed corn are very drought and disease tolerant (except for their susceptibility to smut) and they do well in clay soil. In south Texas this fascinating cultivar is considered *el primero* for grinding into flour for tortillas.

Recommended: For exciting color, Bloody Butcher. For large blue kernels grown in droughty clay soils, McCormack's Blue Giant. For white hominy and roasting, Tucker's Favorite and Hickory King. For fungus resistance (particularly smut), Blue Clarage, a heritage semident corn with purple and white kernels that resists lodging and tolerates crowding. For legendary adaptability and dependability in southern heat and soils, Reid's Yellow Dent. For roasting early and then feeding the squirrels,

Pencil Cob—pencil-thin cobs with sweet kernels. For supporting bean vines, Hickory King.

FLINT CORN   *Z. mays* var. *indurata*

Aka ornamental corn, Indian corn, calico corn, Yankee corn, flint maize. Flint corn seeds tolerate cool soil better than most, which makes flint early maturing, welcome in short seasons.

Flint corns, together with popcorn, are considered the oldest of our cultivated corns. Whether you hang them on the door post for harvest joy or grind their kernels into meal, flints have a mysterious nobility about them. They're probably called flint because of the hardness and smoothness of their dried kernels—there's scarcely any soft starch inside. In garden seed catalogs most flints offered are for ornament—kernels come in apricot, orange, red, maroon, pink, yellow, pearly white, red, blue, and some in speckles and stripes. Where grown for food, flint corns are mostly turned into hominy and used for grinding. Like dent, though, they make good roastin' ears when harvested at the milk stage.

Many flints thrive at high elevations. Jicarilla Apache White, for example, has small ears of pearly kernels on 3- to 5-foot stalks that even in the cool high mountains can be harvested in the dried stage in less than three months. Stalks grow 4 to 7 or 8 feet tall, with a tendency to produce two long cylindrical ears. Flint's dried kernels generally store better than those of other corn.

Recommended: To get past "great for Indian corn decorations," look into the Tarahumara flints in Native Seeds/SEARCH's collection gathered in remote corners.

FLOUR CORN

Flour corn is not a separate subspecies but a type of corn whose kernels are nearly completely composed of soft starch. You won't understand until you've ground flour corn kernels in the blender to the fluffiest, silkiest flour imaginable—and then ground flint or dent corn kernels; they'll grind only to a coarse meal.

Recommended: The easiest is Hopi Blue, which I loved. But for color, Mandan Bride. Often kernels on the same cob will be garnet, mauve, lavender, purple, navy, cranberry, persimmon, chocolate, peach, butter, cream, and swirls of all these from a Santa Fe sunset. The Anasazi flour corn is much the same. They grind to gray, however. For drought tolerance, Hopi Pink has an exceptionally long taproot, in addition to making shell-pink flour.

FLOUR/FLINT/DENT CORNS

Over the centuries, communities of Native Americans have come to specialize in their own particular strains of corn—corns that grew best for them, corns that produced the sorts of dishes they enjoyed. Some communities have even bred corns whose ears were mixtures of flour and flint and sometimes dent kernels sprinkled in. There are also plants that produce one cob of flour and one cob of flint on the same stalk. This was wily insurance—if one sort failed, the other sort would make it. If I could, I'd grow them all.

POPCORN   *Z. mays* var. *praecox*

*Aka pop maize. Because the stalks are generally weaker than those of
other corns, sow the kernels or set popcorn plants deeper than usual.
When the plants are about a foot high, hill them up.*

A small packet of rare Cochiti Pueblo popcorn was sent to me from a fellow Seed Saver. On the envelope was written "Very rare!! Hand-pollinate or isolate and pass on!!" I'd never grown popcorn—I thought it was silly. But these seeds I was morally bound to grow. From a 6- by 7-foot patch I harvested 38 small ears. The ears varied from ruby red studded with garnet to all tan to bright and pale yellow with dots of navy blue to yellow studded with black and/or cream. From those ears I gleaned nearly 2 ½ pounds of seeds—and it's not considered a productive cultivar. We popped a handful. I had imagined a bowlful of puffed ruby-garnet-tan-yellow-blue-black-and-white corn. But like all popcorn, the seeds popped white—except for the throats of some kernels, which bore subtle remnants of color, splotches of scarlet or deep yellow or dark blue. The kernels were sweetly crunchy in the center, not at all like the papery stuff you get from the market.

Because you don't harvest popcorn until the seeds are dry on the cob, most cultivars require at least 100 days from seed to harvest. If your season is short, sprout seeds indoors (see The Gardener's Notebook).

Unless you plan to save seeds, it's fun to grow two or three colors of popcorn and let their pollen mingle. You'll have lovely surprises in every ear.

Once Native Americans grew hundreds of popcorn cultivars. Once home gardeners were given a choice of a few dozen. As a result of the back-to-the-land spirit of gardening, more and more cultivars are available. In general, white kernels are nutty and crunchy; yellow ones are particularly tender. Some seedsmen combine ornamental corn and popcorn. Arranged in a centerpiece or beribboned on the door knocker, the luminous, almost heart-shaped small cobs of strawberry corn are charming. But their popped kernels aren't a match for their unpopped looks. Still, for considerations of space, you won't be unhappy if you choose to grow a cultivar with dazzling colors that is crunchy eating. When two cultivars seem of equal value, the one with larger ears will naturally give you more kernels to pop.

Harvest ears when the plant is completely crackly brown and hang as other field-dried corn. Should just the husks be brown and frost or rain threaten before the stalks have dried, harvest the ears and hang them unhusked in a cool, dark, dry place, pulling back the husks immediately. Kernels are properly dry for curing when a thumbnail doesn't leave a dent.

Kernels will be ready for popping when they come fairly easily off the cob. If the air is cool and you plan to eat your crop over winter, probably you can get by with just leaving kernels on the cob and the leaves prettily in place.

The expansion ratios listed in the catalogs are explosion ratios; 40 to 1 means 40 cups of popped corn from 1 cup of kernels, an excellent dividend.

Recommended: They're all easy and delightful. For flavor, Pennsylvania Butter-Flavored is a two-ears-per-stalk heirloom from before 1885. For color, Strawberry, multicolored Calico, Baby Blue, Pink Bo Peep, and Chocolate Pop. For small gardens, Tom Thumb.

SWEET CORN   *Z. mays* var. *rugosa*

Aka sugar corn, sweet maize, sugar maize.

Until the second half of the 19th century most Americans regarded corn as food for livestock, and most of the French still do. Then a few cultivars of sweet corn were introduced, nearly all of them white. When Golden Bantam came along, corn took its place on the table.

But the real hope was to develop corn less ephemeral than a summer breeze. The reason for growing corn at home has always been that the only corn worth eating comes straight from the patch—sugar in standard corn begins converting to starch 30 seconds after the ear leaves the stalk. So the pot was to be boiling before you left the kitchen, and you were to return with your harvest at a trot.

Since the 1950s, breeders have been manipulating the sugar genes in corn. Today's seed catalogs list the fruits of their labors, several sorts of corn that can wait patiently on the stalk or in the fridge past harvest time and still be sweet, sweet, sweet. In fact, as a group, the new strains are called *ultra-sweets*. Are they more desirable than old-fashioned sweet corn? Let's see.

Briefly, so you can make sense of the catalogs. Details follow.

EH: Everlasting Heritage . . . su and se hybrid cross . . . no need to isolate

SE: sugary enhanced . . . su and South American su cross . . . sometimes called homozygous sugary enhanced . . . no need to isolate

SE+: sugary enhanced plus . . . se and se cross . . . no need to isolate

SG: sweet gene . . . sometimes called heterozygous sugary enhanced gene . . . no isolation from normal sweet corn needed, but should be isolated from sh_2 corn

SH$_2$: supersweet . . . from shrunken kernels of su field corn . . . must be isolated from every other type

SU: normal sugary—standard and hybrid sweet corn . . . white, gold, and bicolor corn must be isolated from other normal sugary corns of different colors

Normal Sugary (su and su+ and su++). These are the un-fiddled-with open-pollinated or hybrid cultivars of sweet corn. Traditional sweet corn is not as sweet as more refined cultivars, but there are native American and Mexican corns here that make me shiver with pleasure for their beauty. Black Aztec is my favorite (and dried, it grinds to blue meal). If you've been used to devouring farmers' market or supermarket corn, then you'll find many normal sugary heirloom ears less uniform and perhaps less sweet than those modern hybrids. But one thing these cultivars can offer is matchless old-fashioned true corn flavor and creamy texture.

Too, the genes in these kernels—with generations of experience in doing so—make it possible for them to be sown in cold soil. So don't be too quick to take up with the fiddly new corns. (White and bicolor su must be isolated.)

Supersweet Corn (sh₂). The first ultrasweet, this one has much more sugar than standard kernels; some find it cloyingly sweet. Ironically, the flavor is not a true corn flavor, and kernels are less tender and creamy than those of standard sweet corn.

And there are difficulties in growing it. The seed will not germinate well in cool or dry soil. Seeds are vulnerable to disease and, being smaller, must be planted more shallowly and spaced more carefully. Supersweet cultivars *must* be isolated from all other corn. Should they cross-pollinate, *both* sorts end up tough, starchy, and bland. Newer supersweet cultivars are resolving some of these problems. But supersweets don't convert their sugar into starch the instant they leave the mother plant the way standard corn does. So picked and refrigerated, the ears will keep sweet for up to six days—some contend a couple of weeks. Supersweets rarely grow more than 5 feet tall, and that can be helpful in designing a small garden.

Some of the iridescent bicolors—kernels randomly gold and white on the cob—have one supersweet parent.

Sweetie Series. These are also sh, but with a different genetic combination. Sweetest of all so far: 2 ½ times sweeter than standard sweet corn, but with 30 percent fewer calories. Did we need it?

Sugary Enhanced (se). A cross of normal sweet corn with an unusual corn from South America has surprising sweetness (but not too much), unrivaled flavor, tender kernels, no problems with germination, and doesn't need to be isolated from other corn to hold its quality. Picked and refrigerated, these sugary enhanced ears (aka sugar extended and extra sweet) hold their sweetness for up to three days. In the opinion of many who earn their living growing corn, sugary enhanced is the nonpareil of all hybrids and has the finest flavor of all sweet corn, period. But se cultivars are not as suited to the stresses of northeastern summers as normal su corn.

EH. Everlasting Heritage corn is half standard sweet corn and half sugar-enhanced corn, with some of the virtues of both.

Sugary Enhanced Plus (se+). More fiddling with the genes. Here are two sugary enhanced cultivars crossed for ultra-tender and ultra-sweet kernels.

Sweet Gene (sg). Twenty-five to 30 percent of the kernels on each ear are sugary enhanced, so sugars are higher at harvest time than normal corn—but conversion of sugar to starch can be the same or slightly slower—zip-zip. Few cultivars of this type offered thus far.

If you're just interested in eating great-tasting corn, standard open-pollinateds and hybrids and extra-sweets—but not supersweets—can cross-pollinate all they like and it won't matter much to you. In my first two-cultivars-of-corn-at-once venture, I took literally the catalog's note that Earliglo EH didn't need to be isolated. I blithely grew Hopi Blue corn upwind of the extra-sweet, and at harvest time there were dark blue kernels stippled through Earliglo's cream. To keep colors the way they were meant to be, however, grow yellow corn (which is dominant) *downwind* of white (recessive). Supersweet corn must not only be isolated but also grown *upwind* of all other corn.

To grow miniature corn for pickling or tossing in butter, sow two seeds of a white cultivar (sweetest) 6 inches apart in 2 ½-foot-square blocks to bands 4 ½ feet wide, so you can easily reach in and harvest. Harvest when the ear is about 3 inches long, not long after the silks emerge. Because the plant hasn't brought ears to maturity, often it will send out a second crop, so unless you need the space, leave the stalks in place after the first harvest.

And if you're too busy to deal with them when they reach the infant stage, just let the ears keep on going until you're ready to harvest. So they won't be little-finger size, but even at twice or three times that, they'll be tender and delicate. In fact you get more pickle for your plot if you do let them grow a little bigger. Too, in the beginning you'll have only a few ears ready to harvest—ears don't all grow at the same rate—so you'll have to wait for more to come along. By then the small ones are larger, so you have a motley bunch.

Recommended: These names are simply a place to begin.

Standard or Normal sugary (su): For a first crop, try gold hybrid Early Sunglow—it's cold-resistant, short-stalked, fruitful, and delicious. For OP—Gold: Golden Bantam. Gold for the North and cool coasts: Golden Jubilee. White: Stowell's Evergreen. White shoepeg: Country Gentleman. Purple: Hooker's Sweet Indian. Some people feel that bicolor corn is the best-flavored. Now there's Double Standard, the first open-pollinated bicolor corn. Midseason golden hybrid: Jubilee (wilt resistant). Hybrid white, disease resistant: Silver Queen. Hybrid bicolor: Honey and Cream. White kernels for roasting in the milk stage, delicious indigo-black kernels for grinding when dry: Black Aztec.

Everlasting Heritage (EH): Gold: Kandy Korn, one of the originals.

Sugary Enhanced (se): Gold: highly disease resistant and flavorful Miracle. White: Sugar Snow. Bicolor midseason: Burgundy Delight—purply husks (some call this cultivar an su).

Sugary Enhanced Plus (se+): Gold early: Sugar Buns. Gold midseason: Tuxedo. White early: Pristine. Bicolor: Kiss 'N Tell.

Sweet Gene (sg): Gold: Very sweet Honeycomb and high yielding, disease resistant Sugar Loaf.

Supersweet (sh$_2$): Gold: Early Xtra-Sweet (AAS winner); for southern climates: Hawaiian SuperSweet. White: How Sweet It Is (AAS winner). Bicolor: Honey 'N Pearl.

For resistance to Stewart's wilt, rust, and smut and tolerance of dry soil, gold Tuxedo and bicolor Lancelot, both se.

CORN SALAD. *See Salad Greens.*

COWPEAS.	*See Beans.*

COWPEA RELATIVES.	*See Beans for Drying.*

CRESSES.	*See Salad Greens.*

CUCUMBERS *Cucumis sativus*

Tender annual in the Gourd family, native to southern Asia . . . grows in 5-gallon containers with support. Grow cukes fast and furiously, which is their wont—give the plants soil with lots of aged manure, good circulation of air, full sun (in ferocious climates a little shade is welcome), more water than most, and pick faithfully when ripe.

In a cave near the border between Burma and Thailand, seeds have been found that are the remains of cucumbers grown 11,000 years ago. Likely the fruit was warty, spiny, and ugly, but it surely did travel. Likely an ancient Sumerian, accustomed to cucumbers with his lettuce and cress, would not believe that the long smooth-skinned beauties we slice into our salads are cucumbers. He *might* recognize the stumpy types in a bin at the market that nobody's buying labeled "pickling cukes." Even though sadly dozens of sorts of cucumbers have vanished from the earth, enthusiastic breeding has produced modern cucumbers with many admirable traits.

Perhaps first among the virtues of modern cukes is resistance to disease. If you live in the Atlantic or Gulf states, you can grow cucumbers resistant to downy mildew. In the North there's resistance to cucumber mosaic, powdery mildew, and scab. In the Southeast, anthracnose-resistant cultivars are available and essential.

Attached to these fine fruits are some 50-cent words. To end up growing exactly the cukes you'd like, you need to be sure what slicer, burpless, non-bitter bitterfree, mid-Eastern/Beit Alpha, lemon, pickler, black spine, white spine, gherkins, and bush cukes are—as well as monoecious, gynoecious, and parthenocarpic.

Slicers are the long, sleek cukes we eat fresh. Once this type grew only in the rarefied atmosphere of English and European greenhouses, but new American cultivars will flourish in anybody's backyard. Their strong point is not flavor but that they're productive, they keep well, and they're resistant to disease. For superb flavor and extraordinary crispness, continue to mid-Eastern/Beit Alpha . . .

Burpless: The part of the cucumber that gives people trouble lies in and close to the skin. With traditional slicing cucumbers you have to peel the cuke to make it agreeable. From the Orient come cucumbers with thin, easy-to-digest skins that can be eaten hook, line, and sinker. They are long—up to 2 feet—and to be kept straight must be trained up.

Non-bitter/bitterfree: Many of the burpless cukes are also classed this way. Some are especially sweet, available in both slicers and picklers. Non-bitter varieties are also more resistant to damage from disease-transmitting cucumber beetles.

Mid-Eastern/Beit Alpha cucumbers are the finest flavored of all slicing cucumbers. They have smooth, thin, non-bitter, shiny medium-green skins, extra crisp and juicy flesh, and the ability to set seeds very slowly. In my garden this summer, when the cukes hadn't quite enough sun to satisfy them and five other cultivars played dumb, my hybrid Sweet Alphees knocked my socks off with their flavor and incredible crispness even in the heat of a beastly day. I can't say they're prolific, but they have the virtues of being self-pollinating and resistant to several diseases. I pick them when they're about 4 inches long. My garden will never be without one of these mild Beit Alphas.

More superb cukes are the *lemon cucumbers*—the English have Crystal Apples, similar—pale yellow at maturity—but not as good. Lemon cukes are sweeter than others, delightfully round, open pollinated, prolific, crisp, non-bitter, refreshing, and make splendid pickles, both sour and sweet. These have no disease tolerance, but they've stayed in business for more than 100 years, so they must be doing something right.

Picklers, for the most part, are warty, short, and spiny. These qualities seem related to flesh that best absorbs a pickling solution. Our connection with cucumbers past.

Black spine and *white spine* refer to the tiny prickers that grow from the warts of very young cukes. Just as the sweet corn we pick is at the green stage, so cucumbers are immature fruits of their vines. Black-spined cultivars turn yellow when mature. White-spined fruits are darker green as gherkins and creamy green when ripe. The spines are so soft they can be rubbed off with a cloth.

Gherkin is English for the French *cornichon,* a minuscule cucumber bred to be crisp yet tender when 2 inches long. Gherkins are actually baby slicers, picked just after the blossom drops off. Some (Vert de Massy) can be let go to 4 inches and used for slicing.

Bush cucumber plants were developed after disease resistance and burplessness.

They're a boon to commercial growers since they facilitate mechanical harvesting. But since we can send a self-pollinating vine skyward on a stake and it will take only 1 square foot of space, there hasn't been much advantage to growing bush types that need 3 to 4 square feet.

Then came Little Leaf—a breakthrough pickler comparable to the dwarf-intermediate tomato plant. Two-inch leaves (two-thirds the conventional size) cover a compact vigorous vine that will climb almost of its own accord, set 20 to 30 fruits in hot, cool, humid, drought, and salty conditions, has resistance to all main diseases, sets fruits without benefit of bees, is open pollinated, and produces blocky medium-small cukes that are both good slicers and good picklers. Little Leaf can also tie its own shoes. The AAS winner Fanfare is another semibush slicer with excellent disease resistance and quality.

Monoecious means the vine can produce cucumbers by itself because it contains both female and male blossoms. You can tell the sexes in the clear yellow flowers—the male grows at the end of a bare stalk, and the female is perched sensuously at the tip of a fruit. Vines make many more males than females, and they make them first, so you must wait a bit for fruit to come along. Monoecious is the ancient cucumber form.

Gynoecious means the vine holds almost exclusively female flowers. Fascinating that these vines remain gynoecious only as long as everything goes well. Under stress they'll throw out a male blossom to ensure pollination. Seed companies always include monoecious seeds (easily identifiable) that will produce male blooms at the same time as the ladies bloom so pollination is assured. Males from one monoecious vine can service five to six female vines. Don't forget that some of the cukes you'll be harvesting will be from a pollinator vine you didn't select. You may want to ask its name when ordering. Unlike monoecious vines, the first blossoms out of these boxes set fruit. Generally hybrid gynoecious vines mature earliest and have higher yields than OPs. However, like determinate hybrid tomatoes, gynoecious hybrids mature all at once. You can't be on vacation when they're due, or you might walk through the garden gate into a jungle of oversized fruits and no blossoms setting for the future.

There are other parthenocarpic plants in the garden—fruits that are self-fertilizing and have few or no seeds. That means you can grow these vines under the protection of floating row covers from start to finish and be assured of no insects and reduced disease. Since making seed is what drives the plant kingdom (and the animal, for that matter), and since these plants don't have seed making on their minds, they're free to throw their energy into fruit. But even though the point is no seeds, should a bee stray by and pollinate the blossoms, nothing disastrous will happen.

County Fair $^8/_{87}$ pickler takes this form, and so does Little Leaf. Still, at this point in their breeding, as far as flavor is concerned, these are the Musak of cucumbers.

How to grow the best possible crop? Even if you have a short season, wait until the soil is warm before sowing cucumbers—or start them indoors. Cukes are very tender and grow very fast, so in nearly all climates you'll get a crop before frost. Sow them or set them out under cover at the same time as squash. You're supposed to sow the seeds standing on their thin edge, but lots of gardeners haven't known about this, and their cukes came up just fine.

If you live in the North, warm the soil with black paper or black plastic mulch. When you set out the seedlings, protect them from beetles with floating row covers until the plants have half a dozen leaves—or don't if the cukes are the seedless sort. Leave the mulch in place or mulch with straw—anything to keep weeds to a minimum and moisture in the soil at a maximum. Mulch with straw to keep the soil cool, particularly if you live in a very hot part of the country.

Cucumbers on vines trained up—whether on cross-barred posts, stakes, twine, trellises, fences, or snow fencing—are considerably more attractive and easier to find and pick than fruit lolling on the ground. Many cultivars that will curve or curl into a semicorkscrew on the ground hang nearly straight when growing vertically. But if you haven't the time, place, or strength to set up a support, give the plants a deep, lightly stacked mulch of straw to keep the fruit clean and provide circulation of air. Then when vines start marching on their neighbors, do what professional growers do: vine tuck. Just turn the troops around and head them back where they came from.

Harvest every day to keep the fruits coming—or the new-cuke factory will shut down to ripen fruit in place. Cut with a knife or snips to prevent a tug of war with the vine. Pick long burpless cukes several inches before the maximum size noted on the seed packet. American slicers should be picked at 7 to 8 inches, mid-Eastern/Beit Alphas at about 5 inches, and gherkins at 1 ½ to 3 inches. Lemon cukes will be past their prime if you pick them yellow—pick them pale, no bigger than a large plum.

Recommended: For an easy introduction to cukes, grow lemon cukes, any you find. For flavor, non-bitterness, and crisp texture in slicers, Beit Alpha Sweet Alphee. For flavor in a burpless, Suyo Long Burpless from China is delicious, prolific, and drought tolerant. Orient Express hybrid is delicious, vigorous, and disease resistant. For picklers, high-yielding Dutch-bred hybrid Saladin (an AAS winner) has its fans, ditto Cross Country. But where disease is not a problem, grow Early Russian, an excellent open-pollinated 19th-century pickler. For gherkins, Vert de Massy, Fin de Meaux, De Bourbonne, and Small Green Paris are all excellent, although the vines aren't resistant to much. Amazing and compact, Little Leaf now has an advanced degree—H-19 Arkansas Little Leaf. Salad Bush Hybrid was a 1988 AAS winner. And for interest, Bianco Lungo di Parigi—Long White Paris— creamy white cukes from Chiltern Seeds in England.

For disease resistance:

> ALS = angular leaf spot
> ANTH = anthracnose
> CB = cucumber beetles
> CMV = cucumber mosaic virus
> DM and PM = downy and powdery mildews
> CS = cucumber scab
> SM = spider mites
> TLS = target leaf spot

Slicing cukes: Open pollinated: Poinsett 76—the best OP main crop for the Southeast and Mid-Atlantic coast—has resistance to ALS, ANTH, DM, PM, SM. Marketmore 80—for a cool-season OP main crop in the North and for fall planting in the South—has resistance to CB, CMV, DM, PM, CS. Hybrid: Stokes Early Hybrid and main-crop Turboto have resistance to ALS, ANTH, CMV, DM, PM, CS.

Burpless cukes: Hybrid main-crop Sweet Slice is resistant to all the troubles mentioned with the exception of cucumber beetles and spider mites.

Pickling cukes: Open-pollinated, blocky, drought-tolerant Sumter is resistant to ALS, ANTH, CMV, DM, PM, CS. Hybrid Napoleon is widely adapted and resistant to ALS, ANTH, CMV, DM, PM, CS.

Early bush cukes: Open-pollinated H-19 Arkansas Little Leaf has, the Stokes Seeds catalog says, "amazing yields . . . over a wide range of weather conditions"— resistant to ALS, ANTH, CMV, DM, TLS. Hybrid 1994 AAS winner Fanfare has the same resistance as Sweet Slice burpless.

WEST INDIAN GHERKIN   *C. Anguria*

> *Tender annual in the Gourd family, probably of cultivated origin derived from an African species . . . aka bur gherkin, gooseberry gourd, goareberry . . . grows in 5-gallon containers with support.*

Listed as the Prickly-Fruited Gherkin in an 1865 list of vegetables grown in this country, the fruits should be picked when they're the size and shape of colossal olives. Their rind is light green and astonishingly crunchy. Every time I turn around there's a basketful ripe (once they start turning yellow, onto the compost heap they go). The mass of prickles covering them is fuzzy and nonthreatening. The flesh tastes cucumbery, but it's softer than today's basic cukes—which makes it absorb an extra amount of pickling solution. And the long vines are pretty, resembling watermelon's rather than cuke's vines.

CURLED MALLOW.   *See Salad Greens.*

CURLED MUSTARDS.   *See Mustard Greens.*

DANDELION.   *See Salad Greens.*

EGGPLANT   *Solanum melongena*

Tender perennial in the Nightshade family, native to Africa and Asia . . . aka Jew's apple, mad apple, melongene, aubergine . . . European eggplant grows in 5-gallon containers, Asian in 3-gallon containers. To grow marvelous eggplant, all you need is rich, well-drained soil, water, and suffocating heat.

References in Sanskrit indicate eggplant has been cultivated in India for thousands of years. In contemporary times, if this fleshy berry didn't have remarkable texture and flavor, it wouldn't be a favorite of cuisines so dissimilar as Italian, Greek, Spanish, Japanese, and Thai.

Eggplant may be low in calories, but it's not very nutritious, although its sensual texture and intriguing flavor can make a low-fat meal satisfying. On the other hand, eggplant is strong in antioxidants. It wants lots of heat to grow well—in northern gardens that can mean backing it up against a wall or growing it in a tub in the hottest spot you've got.

Colors! If you're considering tallish purply warm-weather flowers for the border this season—dahlias, salvia, verbena, or prairie gentians—why not use eggplant instead? Leaves on this stately plant are large and velvety and of almost iridescent gray-green-lilac. The bell-shaped blossoms are blue-lavender with yellow stamens. And the fruit! Eggplants can be purple black, gleaming purple with white streaks, pale to vivid violet, red with red streaks, magenta, pumpkin, mandarin orange, orange with green streaks, apple green streaked with purple, green with dark green or white streaks, white, white streaked with purple or purple-and-pink, or yellow. Treat yourself to delectable Listada de Gandia, cream brushed with shocking pink, mauve, and raspberry. Grow it as the centerpiece in a garden bouquet of pastel zinnias with scarlet and sulfur cosmos.

I'll always try something in a ravishing color, but I no longer grow basic black European eggplants—they're at the market. Besides, the long, skinny Asian eggplants are sweeter and nuttier than the large round Europeans—certainly the Asians are quicker to mature and are usually more prolific. The early flavorful hybrid Ichiban (Japanese for "number one") was my first successful eggplant and I still depend on it. From hybrid Tycoon—described as "ferociously productive"—I once counted 90 fruits on the plant. Eggplant shapes can be round, oval, teardrop, and clusters, sleek or deeply ruffled. The fingerlength of Little Fingers, being so small, may not be meaty but they're enchanting.

If you do want to grow traditional European-style eggplants, early open-pollinated Morden Midget did splendidly for us when half a dozen others disappointed. Some say white eggplant is most flavorful, but I haven't found it so. I wish I could report on the crunchy seedy Hmong, brilliant orange and sweet green plum-size Thai eggplants, but so far I've had no luck.

No matter where you live, you'll want to germinate the seeds indoors—they need 80–90°F. Set small stakes at planting time if the cultivar is long- or heavy fruiting. Harvest when the fruits are half the size the catalog describes, before the seeds darken, and while the skins are still brilliantly glossy. Cut—don't pull—off the fruit, taking a bit of stem. Not only are eggplants picked small of the highest quality, but keeping fruit picked stimulates the plant's production.

Recommended: Easiest, the Asian hybrid Ichiban. For inky-purple European-style eggplant, open-pollinated Morden Midget won't fail you. Nor will small early hybrids Dusky and Agoura, purply black and slow to make seeds, which allows for a longer harvest. For creamy white flesh that cooks to a silky texture, Rosa Bianca. For heavenly lavender, Violetta di Firenze, Listada de Gandia, or Bride. For a short season, a friend who grows Early Bird in the North says it produces blossoms the moment it goes into the garden and fruits until frost. For baby eggplants, hybrid Baby Bell/Bambino. For a thrill, investigate the Turkish Italian Orange. Or join Seed Savers and help sustain the gene pool by growing some of a dizzying Asian eggplant assortment of colors and shapes. For resistance to tobacco mosaic virus (always a threat to the nightshades), early pear-shaped Dusky, long cylindrical Vittoria, and oval Blacknite, all hybrids.

ELEPHANT GARLIC.	*See Onions.*

ENDIVES AND ESCAROLES.	*See Salad Greens.*

FAVA BEANS.	*See Beans and Legumes.*

FENNEL, COMMON AND BRONZE   *Foeniculum vulgare*

FLORENCE FENNEL   *F. vulgare* var. *azoricum*

*Half-hardy perennial often grown as an annual in the Parsley family,
native to southern Europe . . . aka finocchio and sweet anise . . . grows
in 5-gallon containers. Fennel wants humusy, fertile, well-drained soil,
a steady supply of water, and shade in the heat of the day where it's hot.
Any check in growth and fennel bolts, so be watchful.*

The fennel of poets is called *Florence fennel*. It has a plump celerylike head with sweet anise-flavored stalks that, raw or cooked, are strange and refreshing. Common fennel is fine for letting the pretty yellow flowers go to seed and for gathering their seeds to sprinkle in breads and through sauces and on bruschetta. Florence fennel is exciting in the border. It can grow waist high, all blue-green ostrich feathers. Well grown, both of these fennels will dominate their corner.

There is a bronze fennel that I found curious in the garden—its color, that of the afternoon light, disappeared. But a friend says that when backed with something contrasting, delphinium or lilies, the bronze makes a striking accent.

The stalks of common and bronze fennels aren't good for eating, but the foliage is. Somehow seedsmen get their fennels mixed up. For three years I couldn't figure out what I was doing wrong because the tough skimpy stalks of my fennel weren't what was described in cookbooks, nor was it the fennel I saw at the market. Order from seedsmen who include the botanical name or who can assure you it's Florence fennel.

Fennel is perennial, but it's usually grown as an annual. The object is the bulbous part, and when you slice it off, stalks grow back, but they're tough and good only for seasoning. In no-frost climates, sow seeds in fall to harvest in spring. Where it's cold in winter and hot in summer, sow in spring. In most parts of the country it's best to sow in early July. My best plants have grown with summer lettuces, under high shade with little straight sun. Harvest the whole plant when the bulb is no more than 3 inches across. And of course the foliage is gorgeous in bouquets.

Recommended: Italian heirloom Romy and Zefa Fino, a bolt-resistant Swiss cultivar.

FLOWERING BRASSICAS. *See Asian Greens.*

FLOWERS, EDIBLE. *See Herbs, Flowers, and Flavorings.*

GARLAND CHRYSANTHEMUM. *See Asian Greens.*

GARLIC. *See Onions.*

GOOD-KING-HENRY. *See Potherbs.*

GOURDS. *See Squashes and Pumpkins.*

GREEN-IN-THE-SNOW MUSTARD. *See Mustard Greens.*

Herbs, Flowers, and Flavorings

Most herbs are primitive plants that grow easily and lushly, asking for little more than their place in the sun. Lavish them with fertilizer, for example, and with the manure you'll spread confusion. While most of the aromatic herbs—which are of Mediterranean origin—will tolerate poor soil, plants will give you their most fragrant and flavorful bits when you give them light, well-draining soil.

As with other edible leaves, once an herb plant is occupied with making flowers and seeds, the leaves usually toughen. But herb flowers are invariably beautiful and edible, and it's pleasing to have them in the garden. The trick is to grow enough of a favorite herb that you can keep pinching the buds off some plants to forestall flowering, while letting others of their ilk bloom their heads off.

Before picking, observe the whole plant and use the harvest as an occasion to do some pruning. Unless otherwise specified, pick a sprig or stalk as long as it can be and at a point where the stalk branches. This way another stem can grow in its place. Pinch off the central tips frequently to keep the plant bushy and pinch off flowers so vigor won't go into making seeds. Harvesting this way promotes bushiness and well-being in the plant.

When dried, very few herb leaves retain their innermost selves. With a patch of herbs growing in the garden and, in winter, a few pots of herbs in a sunny corner indoors, you'll always have juicy flavorful leaves.

In making the following selection, I've chosen those herbs most commonly used in cuisines around the world, and I've added a few whose flavor is unique and, to me, irresistible.

If you live where winters are freezing, you can either grow tender perennial herbs in containers and winter them indoors or grow perennials as annuals, starting with a new plant from the nursery each spring. Most herbs are vigorous growers.

ANISE HYSSOP   *Agastache Foeniculum*

Half-hardy perennial in the Mint family, native to North America and central and eastern Asia . . . grows in 3- to 4-gallon containers . . . start from seed. Plants do well in full sun or with a little afternoon shade and moderately rich soil on the dry side. Self-sows moderately.

Easiest Container Vegetables

baby beets, small cabbages, baby carrots, chard, cresses, cucumbers, dandelions, garlic, kale, kohlrabi, leaf lettuces, Malabar and New Zealand spinaches, mustard greens, small onions (scallions, shallots), peppers, spring radishes, sorrel, spinach beets, bush summer squashes, bush tomatoes, turnips

Easiest Container Herbs

small basils, chervil, Chinese chives, chives, coriander, dill, ginger, lavender, marjoram, mints, oregano, parsleys, rosemary, sages, summer savory, tarragon, thymes

Easiest Container Edible Flowers

calendulas, Johnny-jump-ups, marigolds, nasturtiums, pansies, scented geraniums, sweet violets, violas

To my taste, there's no licorice-flavored herb to compare with the warmth of anise hyssop. This definitely is a mint—the leaves look like large mint leaves, and the spires of blue-purple look like many of the mints. The plant is very pleasing. Starting from scratch each spring, the upright branches are a foot and a half tall by late summer, crowned with flowers the bees adore.

BASIL   *Ocimum* spp.

Most are tender annuals in the Mint family, native to the tropical Old World . . . annuals grow in 1- to 2-gallon containers . . . start most from seed. Basil isn't especially easy to grow from seed, but it's not especially difficult either. Basils want fertile, well-drained soil on the moist side in full sun—this is not an herb of dry stony soil.

For a robust spicy sweet basil, grow the very Italian *genova profumatissima*. It's terrific both as leaves and minced in pesto, and the plant is a vigorous delight.

The choice basil in most of France is a smaller plant with finer leaves and a more refined flavor, *fin vert* aka *fino verde* / fine-leaf. This basil will grow where summers are cool and overcast.

For the most delicate flavor and leaf, choose the delicious melon-size ball of leaves—like a topiary—spicy globe basil. Tiny white flowers stud the plant in midsummer. Make one a focal point up front in the border or use a number more formally as an edging.

For colorful basils, grow Rubin with bronzy-purple leaves. Purple Ruffles was an AAS winner, with deeply cut all-purple leaves. Some strains are thinning, however, and a fair portion of Purple Ruffles' leaves have reverted to green. Opal, probably the first of the purply leaves, is reverting to green even more.

The colored basil I favor is called African Blue. Unlike other basils, this is a perennial, which means you can grow it inside and have sweet basil all winter. In addition to leaves with musky sweet basil pungence, the undersides have a purply blue cast. This basil is most available from herb nurseries as a plant rather than seeds. It grows moderately tall and is very showy with lavender-pink flowers, so set it somewhere you can admire it.

Thai basil is also prettily colored, red stems of blue-green leaves with an anise/basil flavor—and a hint of coriander woven through. Especially good with Asian food, as you can imagine from its name.

Of the many leaves graced with the taste of lemon, few are more richly lemony than lemon basil. Leaves are small and pointed. Mrs. Burns' Lemon Basil is a larger plant with larger leaves and a fine sweet lemon flavor.

As annual basil ages, flavor in the leaves grows slightly smaller and a little bitter but not at all disagreeable. For pristine quality, sow every few weeks through the season and pick just young leaves. Plan to harvest your last leaves before frost, because they'll blacken.

There are about two dozen basils to choose from—large leaves, small leaves, spicy leaves, camphory leaves—each with its special flavor. Basils are charming paired with bright-colored dahlias of complementary size in the border.

BORAGE   *Borago officinalis*

Half-hardy annual in the Borage family, native to the Mediterranean region . . . grows in 1-gallon containers . . . start from seed. Borage likes soil fairly rich on the dry side, but it will take lean moist soil. It likes sun, but it will also grow in the shade. This is one of the easiest herbs of all. Sow seeds once, and borage will return again and again to your garden.

Borage is not a flavoring herb but a plant with exquisite flowers of piercing French blue. Blossoms are five- or six-pointed stars an inch across with a point of black in the center. Blooming several at once on the plant, the flower clusters nod their heads slightly, lending a pensive air to so optimistic a plant. Older blooms fade to pink, so often there is a mix of blue and pink on the plant. Since borage blooms from spring to after frost, you're supposed to clip the plants often to keep them from becoming floppy, but I don't.

The large leaves are fuzzy and heavily veined in all directions, which gives them a rumpled look. Picked young and crisp, they have a mild cucumber taste.

Do try to grow borage where you can see it close up—the blossoms are so lovely. Start by mingling them with chervil for a delicate effect.

BURNET, SALAD   *Poterium Sanguisorba*

Hardy perennial native to Europe and western Asia . . . grows in 2- to 3-gallon containers . . . start from seed. As long as it has sun, decent soil, and average water, very little will keep this plant from turning up all over your garden.

ou can set salad burnet anywhere toward the front of the border with any plant, and it will be enchanting. From a distance you might think burnet a rustic version of maidenhair fern, with its delicate fountain of small round pinked leaves. The flowers, which are sent up in late spring, are faceted ruby buttons, and the flavor of leaves and blossoms is cucumbery. Pick lightly the first year, and then take only the youngest leaves. Older ones get tough and bitter.

CARAWAY   *Carum carvi*

Hardy biennial in the Parsley family, native to Europe . . . grows in 2-gallon containers . . . start from seed. Growing caraway from seed is a cinch. It wants only average soil on the dry side and full sun. Don't try to transplant seedlings, because they send down a long taproot.

araway is the perfect lesson in bienniality for the curious gardener. The first year, the plant grows a foot or so tall, all ferny leaves like a miniature carrot's. The flavor is more like parsley. Of course you can use the leaves as an herb, but don't weaken the plant by taking too many, because the idea is to have it winter over. The second year, the plant can get 2 feet high as it blooms in small creamy doilies like the others in the family, an aspect of Queen Anne's Lace.

The pleasurable thing about caraway seeds from the garden rather than the grocer's shelf is that you can catch them at what I think of as the shelly stage. They're not still green and they're not quite dry, but at a plump stage in between. That comes in June in our garden—caraway flowers in spring. A week or two later, when the seeds turn brown, just before they're thoroughly dry, spread a light-colored cloth under the plant to catch the seeds—otherwise they may burst all over the place. But let a few seeds scatter, and if you don't disturb the soil, you may have caraway plants the following year.

CHERVIL   *Anthriscus Cerefolium*

Hardy annual in the Parsley family, native to southeastern Europe and western Asia . . . grows in 1- to 2-gallon containers . . . start from seed. Chervil is a cool-weather herb, best in spring and fall. If you can give it a breezy spot in bright shade, it might make it through a hot summer. It will take dry or moist soil, although it prefers fluffy moist soil. Chervil will likely self-sow for you, and the lacy, light green leaves can be harvested in a sheltered spot through all but the harshest winters.

*T*hese leaves look as though they're small lacy Italian parsley. Minuscule flowers are a stippling of white. Chervil is delicious planted among the lettuces.

Curled chervil—*Crispum*—has the same uses as the flatter leaf. Some find it even more appealing.

Chervil's flavor is a delicate parslied anise.

CHINESE CHIVES   *Allium tuberosum*

Hardy perennial in the Lily family, native to Southeast Asia . . . aka garlic chives, Chinese leek, flowering leek, Oriental garlic, jiu cai, gau tsoi . . . grows in 1- to 2-gallon containers . . . start from seed. These leaves are as grassy as common chives but thin and flat, not tubular. Their flowers are even more decorative and tasty, sprays of white in mid- to late summer. A clump of many plants, Chinese chives are very adaptable, preferring fine moist soil in the sun but tolerating light shade, less-than-ideal soil, little attention, and extremes of heat and cold.

*C*hinese chives marry the flavors of garlic and chives—a great idea. It's a valuable herb that can live for 30 years and needs to be coddled in the beginning. The first year, don't harvest leaves and don't water unless very dry—this forces the roots deep. Mulch well if the ground will freeze. The following spring, as soon as there are signs of life, gently rake over the clump to pull out debris and to rouse the roots. With the rake, mound an inch or so of soil up around the base—the bulbs have a tendency to push up out of the ground. When the leaves are at least 6 to 8 inches tall, you can harvest a few leaves or all of them. For maximum growth, follow a big cutting with a mild fish or kelp solution, then see how the plant fares. Theoretically, you can take three full cuts each season, but that many may exhaust the plants. Better to have more clumps and take fewer from each, I think. The leaves are most tender in spring.

Daffodil yellow, blanched Chinese chives are among the most beautiful leaves in the garden. See The Gardener's Notebook under Blanching.

Their slender pointed flower buds are used as a separate flavoring entirely—they're more assertive than chive flowers, having the admixture of garlic. You can develop a plant for flower producing or blanching, but not both, since either is a drain on the plant. For flowers, the first season, snip off emerging flower stalks at once. The second season and thereafter, pick the creamy buds when the stems are about 12 inches long but before the buds start to open. Cook them at once in a stir-fry or use as garnish.

Unlike common chives, I've never seen this plant when it didn't look all together—although I've done nothing to groom it. There is burnet around some of our Chinese chives, giving us fountains of froth and spray.

CHIVES
A. schoenoprasum

Hardy perennial in the Lily family, native to Europe and Asia . . . grows in 1- to 2-gallon containers . . . start from seed. A member of the onion clan. Once you have a clump of chives in business, they'll be yours for years. They grow easily from seeds sown in clusters in the garden—a clump of chives is not one plant but many plants close together. Chives will do well in average soil as long as it's well drained. They love water. They'll be cheerful in partial shade but also love their sunshine. Set them where they'll be undisturbed.

Chives are one plant whose leaves don't lose quality when it blooms. Mauve-pink puffs of chive blossoms come in early summer and may be used as the leaves. Chives are a giddy accent plant, the leaves falling every which way. If you set your clump against a small gleaming boulder, the disarray is somehow softened.

To harvest, snip whole outer leaves just above the root rather than take a handful of leaves halfway down. This is not only more aesthetic but also better for the life processes of the plant.

Both leaves and blossoms have a sprightly flavor of onion without being bitter or sharp.

CORIANDER
Coriandrum sativum

Hardy annual in the Parsley family, native to southern Europe . . . aka Chinese parsley, cilantro . . . grows in 1-gallon containers . . . start from seed. Although it loves full sun, here's another leaf that doesn't mind a bit of shade. Well-drained ordinary soil on the dry side is just fine. The plants grow as readily from seeds as any herb, and sometimes new plants volunteer in the fall. Coriander has an uncommonly fast time clock—it blooms and makes seeds lickety-split. Frequent sowings in place (it hates being moved) are the answer. Remarkably free of pests. Coriander is especially vigorous in cool weather.

The flat-leaf-parsley-like plants come and go quickly, but they're so attractive I use them to fill gaps between plants. By the time the coriander has begun to flower and thus be finished, the plants have nicely crowded in. You can eat the flowers or let them form seeds, which you can also harvest and dry. This part of the plant is a spice.

The small round lace-tipped leaves and creamy flowers are pungent, warm, and spicy. The taste of fresh coriander seems to be one people love or hate. Coriander seeds have a different warmth and pungence of their own.

In Thailand, the long thin roots of coriander are an important culinary flavoring—combined with garlic and black pepper, particularly. You may want to grow extra plants and harvest the roots for playing with Thai recipes. Chop and freeze the leaves; no need to waste them.

DILL   *Anethum graveolens*

Half-hardy annual in the Parsley family, native to Southwest Asia . . . grows in 1- to 2-gallon containers . . . start from seed. In full sun, dill grows with alacrity, and if your soil is on the moist side, it may give you baby dill all over the place. Dill gets rank quickly. Best to sow it a couple of times over summer so there will always be sweet young leaves.

Feathery, tall, and fragrant, fresh dill leaves are one of the most engaging of herbs. You can harvest the leaves, flowers, and seeds. The celery-colored flowerheads are small lacy umbrellas. When they turn into seeds, the seeds are small and flattish. Dill can get tall quite fast, so set it toward the back of the border. Its lacy habit is pleasing mixed with the bold strokes of onions.

The taste of dill leaves is grassy, spicy, and clean—as though they'd been dipped in gin.

GINGER   *Zingiber officinalis*

Tender perennial in the Ginger family, native to Southeast Asia . . . grows in 5-gallon containers . . . start from a rhizome. Ginger thrives in rich moist soil and humid warmth. But even if you live in a cold climate, you can grow it indoors in a pot in a sunny window.

lthough ginger's fleshy rhizomes (what we call the root in cooking) give us the richest flavor, the young leaves also taste spicy. If you kept a few pots going, you'd be able to harvest baby ginger, which bears the same relationship to the ginger we find at the market as garden baby carrots to carrots we buy.

At the market, look for plump succulent ginger with a few knobby growth-buds on them. Spring is the best time to do this, or send for a starter plant from a nursery. For each plant, fill a container with equal parts potting mix, peat moss, sharp sand, and compost or well-aged manure. Just beneath the surface, horizontally lay one piece of root the size of an egg. Water thoroughly, then keep the soil mix moist but not wet. Give the plant warmth and bright shade outdoors, or thin light from an east or west window indoors.

It will take a month or so for the first green shoot to come up. After that, never harvest more than one fourth of the young leaves. You can take all or part of the rhizome at any time, but it's best to wait five to six months, until the leaves are flourishing. Once it has sprouted, you can transplant the rhizome into moist rich soil in the garden. But unless your climate is ideal, you'll have better control growing ginger in a pot. Bring the plant indoors before frost.

The baby root—harvested after only a few months—will surprise you with its translucence and delicacy.

Flowers of culinary ginger are not dramatic, but they're tasty. The leaves are strong narrow tropical accents in the border.

HYSSOP   *Hyssopus officinalis*

Hardy perennial in the Mint family, native to Europe and Asia . . . grows in 1- to 2-gallon containers . . . start from seed. Hyssop wants only average but well-drained soil in full sun. It will do with very little water but is resplendent with a modicum.

lthough the taste of hyssop's long slender leaves is bitter and the stems eventually turn woody, this is probably not the hyssop of the Bible— most scholars think that was marjoram.

Hyssop's stems are taller and stiffer and the leaves smaller, but the plant puts me in mind of a skinny tarragon. It's far more beautiful than tarragon, because tarragon doesn't flower. All summer long, airy tufts of blazing blue-violet are among the most exciting blossoms in the garden. Hyssop is generous another way—and perplexing. My blue-blossomed plant, which came from a nursery, presented me with a companion last year, a sibling with pale pink flowers. I can't figure where it came from (a mutant seed of my plant, a running root?), but I'm delighted.

Hyssop has a unique place in seasoning: it's at once bitter and seductive.

LAVENDER
Lavandula spp.

Hardy or half-hardy perennial in the Mint family, native from the Atlantic Islands to the Mediterranean region to Somalia and India . . . grows in 5-gallon containers . . . start with a plant. The best lavender is grown in full sun—important—in light, well-draining, lean soil on the dry and sandy side.

A happy English lavender that began life in your garden transplanted from a 2- to 3-inch pot can be a breathtaking 3- to 4-foot ball in as many years—the centerpiece of its bed. No herb in the garden gives us more pleasure, yet all it wants from us is scant water, no food, and one good clipping at the end of the season to remove the spent flowers.

English lavender *(L. angustifolia)* is the hardiest species and one of the most aromatic. Dwarf English lavender is the hardiest of the hardy—Munstead and Hidcote, for example. I find names are confused among nurseries, at least according to descriptions in catalogs. So don't order by name but by description. By all means, look into the tender French, Spanish, Dutch, and other lavenders that are fragrant and gorgeous—some are even fringed. If you live where there's frost, grow them in pots and winter them in a sunny spot indoors. Then in spring, carry them out to the garden in a scented procession as we do.

Lavender is not an easy herb to use as flavoring—I find its taste more bitter than its fragrance.

LEMON VERBENA
Aloysia triphylla

Half-hardy perennial in the Verbena family, native to Argentina and Chile . . . grows in 5- to 10-gallon containers . . . start with a plant. Lemon verbena likes full sun, although a little bright shade won't be detrimental. Soil can be rich, dry, or average, but should be kept slightly moist.

emon verbena is an airy, woody shrub. In balmy climates it can be pruned to a small umbrella of a tree that will reach 5 feet high. The plant usually goes dormant in winter. Where winters are cold, it must be kept in a container and brought indoors to winter over. A slow but vigorous grower.

Leaves of lemon verbena are so lemony they make your head spin. The leaves have the long slender shape of bay's, but these are very green and, although they don't look it, rough on top. Inconspicuous sprays of tiny white flowers bloom in late summer and autumn.

LOVAGE   *Levisticum officinale*

Hardy perennial in the Parsley family, native to southern Europe . . . grows in 3-gallon containers . . . start from a plant. Give lovage a spot in full sun (or, in very hot climates, part shade) in moist rich to average soil with good drainage.

ovage looks and tastes like a wild celery—the aftertaste has a spicy bite. The plant springs up in the garden about the time the sorrel leafs out, and the pair make a marvelous spring soup. Lovage's stalks are thin and many branched, and the plant can grow 6 feet tall—although ours is in dry sandy soil, and is never more than 2 feet. Flowers are pale gold and tasty, and the seeds that follow are used as celery seeds. The light green and delicacy of the leaves are perfect foils for bolder leaves—I rotate as many of the potherbs and salad plants past lovage as I can.

Wherever you'd use the water-sweet flavor of celery as flavoring, consider using the richer leaves of lovage instead.

MARJORAM, SWEET   *Origanum Majorana*

Half-hardy perennial in the Mint family, native to North Africa and Southwest Asia . . . grows in 2-gallon containers . . . start with a plant. Give marjoram full sun and well-drained soil. Where there's frost, pot up your marjoram and winter it indoors in a bright cool place. This is not a wildly vigorous herb, so never harvest more than a quarter of the plant at a time.

*I*f you like the taste of oregano but have occasionally wished it less strong, kissing cousin marjoram is for you. Marjoram's tiny white flowers are pretty and delicious sprinkled through salad. In the border, the rounded leaves of marjoram next to the tiny leaves of thyme are splendid.

MINT   *Mentha* spp.

Hardy and tender perennials in the Mint family, native to temperate regions of the Old World . . . grows in 2- to 3-gallon containers . . . root a cutting in water or start with a plant. True mints grow only from cuttings, and many fascinating sorts are available from herb nurseries. Mint grows anywhere under any conditions—nothing stops a headstrong mint except solid rock or metal. Lacking rock, grow mint in a container set on an impenetrable material with no cracks.

*I*f you can keep them from escaping, mints cascading down a bank or spilling over rocks or bouncing along the edges of a path are delightful. Don't bother combining them with anything, because they'll soon swallow it whole.

Mints cross with one another with joie de vivre and, like scented geraniums, love to masquerade. There are, at this writing, chocolate, orange, ginger, lime, and grapefruit mints. There will be more.

I suggest collecting the true mints first, parents of all these revelers: crystalline spearmint, appley apple and cream-and-green-variegated pineapple mints, fleshy curled leaves of *crispa* water mint, menthol-scented field and Japanese mints, silvery-leaved horsemint, crème-de-menthe-flavored Corsican mint small as tears, and the quintessential leaf, peppermint.

OREGANO, GREEK   *Origanum heracleoticum*

Very hardy perennial in the Mint family, native to southeastern Europe . . . aka pot marjoram . . . grows in 3-gallon containers . . . start with a plant. To make it think it's still back in the mountains of Greece, give your plant full sun, fairly fertile soil, and water to keep the earth just this side of dry. If it's sheltered, you can pick Greek oregano through the winter up to −20° F.

There are many oreganos, but unless you want to be a collector, don't plant oregano unless it has *Greek* written on the tag. This vigorous plant is wonderfully handsome framed in gleaming white stones.

Mexican oregano, while richly oregano-flavored, is another species, and a tender perennial.

PARSLEY
Petroselinum crispum

Half-hardy (to 20°F) biennial or perennial in the Parsley family, native to Europe and western Asia . . . grows in 1- to 2-gallon containers . . . start from seed. Parsley grows beautifully in moist humusy soil with afternoon shade.

Usually you can buy only one or two sorts of parsley at the nursery, so sending for seeds of smooth Green Carpet or heat-tolerant Decora makes sense. However, starting parsley from seeds takes patience—it's two months to bring it to transplanting stage. You don't have to do anything about the seedlings, though, but give them water and light.

Although curled parsley has the fresh look of a mossy creek, flat-leaf parsley has the pristine taste of the water itself. A good clump of flat-leaf Italian parsley can last several years in a sunny sheltered place in temperate climates. If you have critters, it must be caged or it will be leveled every time it grows an inch.

Parsley at the feet of roses is enchanting.

PERILLA
Perilla frutescens

Half-hardy annual in the Mint family, native from the Himalayas to eastern Asia . . . aka shiso, beefsteak plant . . . grows in 1- to 2-gallon containers . . . start from spanking fresh seed. Once the plants are growing, you'll have them in your garden always, since they self-sow. Give perillas full sun or part shade and good moist soil.

These have the feeling of small leaves of hydrangeas—pinked, seamed, and puckered. Perillas come in two colors, burgundy and green, the green being more flavorful, the burgundy more decorative. Both are absolute musts for the herb fancier.

Perilla's flavor is bright and spicy, a blend of coriander, mint, and flat-leaf parsley with a dash of cinnamon.

ROSEMARY   *Rosmarinus officinalis*

Half-hardy perennial in the Mint family, native to the Mediterranean region, Portugal, and Northwest Spain . . . grows in 3- to 5-gallon containers . . . start with a plant. Ros marinus means "dew of the sea," so let your plant imagine it overlooks the Mediterranean—superb drainage, the sun on its blossoms, the wind in its arms, the mist round its skirts.

I can vouch for blue-blossomed Arp to come through winters of 10°F—it's said to be hardier. Bring it indoors if your winters are colder.

Rosemary's leaves are like short, fleshy pine needles—as pungent and almost as piney. Some cultivars are stiff and upright—Tuscan Blue; others drip down walls like dark green rivulets, sky-blue flowers awash in bees—Santa Barbara. Rosemaries are magnificent in the garden as well as on the table. Silver thyme nestled at the base of gray-green rosemary is superb.

SAGE   *Salvia* spp.

Hardy and half-hardy perennial in the Mint family, native to Asia Minor and from northern and central Spain to the western Balkan Peninsula . . . grows in 2- to 3-gallon containers . . . start with seeds or a plant. Sage couldn't be easier. It appreciates full sun and light, well-drained soil on the dry side.

In late spring, the finely pebbled long oval leaves of garden sages frame purple to azure blossoms—all but those of golden sage, who rightly feels she has no need of flowers to be gorgeous. Blossoms or no, here are more leaves whose culinary quality is unaffected by the plant's flowering.

To be safe, the gorgeous variegated sages—golden and tricolor—should winter in pots indoors if it's colder than 10°F. In the border I scatter seeds of calendulas and zinnias around the sages. The flowers' bright colors underscore the depth of the sages' blues, grays, golds, creams, and greens.

The scent of garden sage is like mountain woodsmoke. It fills the nostrils with sharp sweetness that is almost acrid, and it heats the mouth when you swallow it.

After your garden sages are in place, look into the rest of this extraordinary family. Pineapple and other fruited sages are tender plants, but their spicy, fruity leaves and brilliant flowers are sublime.

SAVORY, SUMMER   *Satureja hortensis*

Half-hardy annual in the Mint family, native to the Mediterranean region . . . grows in 1-gallon containers . . . start from seed. Summer savory has a more refined flavor and more pleasing habit of growth than perennial winter savory, another subspecies. Very easy to grow—just give sun and well-drained soil on the dry side.

Just as I may head for more delicate marjoram when the recipe calls for oregano, I may reach for the summer savory when a recipe calls for thyme. And just as the leaves seem a shorter, greener version of tarragon's, the flavor seems to be bouncy mint mixed with suave thyme.

TARRAGON, FRENCH   *Artemisia Dracunculus* var. *sativa*

Hardy perennial in the Sunflower family, native to southern Europe, Asia, and the United States west of the Mississippi . . . grows in 2- to 3-gallon containers . . . start with a plant. While tarragon isn't tricky to grow, it doesn't often grow with alacrity either. To have plenty to use, it's a good idea to grow two or three plants together in full sun—they won't suffer being close; just keep them watered. If your garden isn't cold in winter so the tarragon can go dormant, you'll have to replace it annually. When ordering or buying from a nursery, know that true tarragon grows from divisions, not from seeds, and Russian tarragon—which does grow from seeds—is a tasteless impostor.

A most graceful plant, with slender shiny leaves, that can reach to 3 feet. Lovely mingled with the twining stalks of a climbing rose. The flavor of French tarragon is rather a minty anise with a trace of lemon and thyme, a bit like chervil but less delicate.

THYME
Thymus spp.

Hardy perennials in the Mint family, native to the western Mediterranean region to southeastern Italy . . . grows in 3- to 5-gallon containers . . . start with a plant. Except where it's hot and humid—where fungus can destroy the plant—thymes are pure pleasure to grow. Give them full sun and good drainage and keep their not-too-rich soil fairly dry.

Whether a creeping mat of tiny green or gray-green or gold-green leaves or a gauzy shrub with purply-pink blooms, there's no thyme I don't find irresistible.

Thyme comes in a nosegay of flavors—caraway, nutmeg, orange, and lemon, as well as the sun-and-smoke taste of French and English garden thymes. The French prefer wild thyme, subtler than any of these. If you were to have just one plant, it should be either wild or French thyme for its purity.

Some Edible Flowers

When you want a mix of colors, order colors you like individually and mix them yourself. Or order a mix and in addition one or two colors you want to emphasize and stir them in. Otherwise, you can get a preponderance of a color that's convenient for the seedsman but that may not be a tint you can use.

All edible flowers can be grown in pots.

Important: Water flowers in the morning so the leaves can dry before nightfall, and at their feet so the blooms don't get waterlogged.

CALENDULAS
Calendula officinalis

Hardy annual in the Sunflower family, native to southern Europe . . . aka pot marigold . . . blooms spring to frost . . . start with seed. Calendulas do well in full sun and average soil and water. They self-sow prolifically. Although a cool-weather plant, calendulas bloom their heads off through

summer in my hot dry garden. But where it's humid, the flowers stop once the heat hits. Sow 'em and grow 'em—that's about it.

E ven though you'll have volunteers, for the lushest blooms, start a new batch each year to revitalize the store. Be good about picking off spent blossoms to keep new ones coming, then in autumn let some go to seed so there will be volunteers in spring. Petals have no flavor, but an incomparable glow.

Rarely, inexplicably, one plant will become a feeding station for aphids—best pull it up. Watch for slugs.

Pacific Beauty, Bon Bon, and Fiesta Gitana are equally delightful—some have chocolate centers. Kablounas are mildew resistant with double centers.

HOLLYHOCKS   *Alcea/Althaea rosea*

Hardy perennial in the Mallow family, native to temperate regions of the Old World . . . blooms from midsummer to early fall . . . start from seed or a plant. Some recommend growing hollyhocks as annuals, but it makes no difference what name you apply to them—hollyhocks self-sow so generously, you can't tell whether it's an old or new plant that's blooming for you. These graceful spires love full sun and good soil on the moist side. Many cultivars will bloom the first summer from seed if you start them indoors early enough.

B eetles are mad about hollyhock leaves. If there are holes in your leaves, look for beetles, pick them off, and drop them into soapy water. If they get out of hand, spray with a pyrethrum solution according to the label.

If you have critters running around in spring, you'll probably need to cage young hollyhock leaves until they're too tall for the squirrels and chipmunks to reach. The flavor of the petals is lettucelike, crisp, and sweet—they're a mallow, like our tasty curled mallow.

MARIGOLDS   *Tagetes* spp.

Half-hardy annuals in the Sunflower family, native from Argentina to northern Mexico . . . bloom early summer to midautumn. Start from seed. Easy heat-resistant marigolds need sunshine and an inch of water each week. Past that, they'll bloom all summer long with whatever else you give them. Marigolds are trouble free if you have no snails.

*D*iminutive yellow Lemon Gem and orange Tangerine Gem marigolds are single petaled, and both flowers and dainty lacy leaves have a light citrus taste and scent. Add color to salads and vegetable dishes with their petals and set nosegays of whole sprigs as garnish.

The hot hues of Paprika, Tiger Eyes, and Scarlet Sophia are even more decorative. Their taste and scent are more pungent, but they're French marigolds, not as piercing as the African strains.

NASTURTIUM   *Tropaeolum majus*

Tender annual in the Nasturtium family . . . blooms midsummer to midautumn or frost, whichever comes first . . . start from seed. Full sun, lean soil, and moderate water will give you the brightest flowers. Nasturtiums volunteer in temperate climates. You can move these plants when they're very small. Nasturtiums couldn't be easier.

*N*asturtium's lily-pad-like leaves, succulent stems, fat buds, gay trumpets, and green knobby seedpods all taste wonderfully peppery. Great mixed in salads, and every part makes a garnish that looks as though drawn from Art Nouveau stained glass. Alaska is particularly recommended for its cream and green marbled leaves, while the gold, mahogany, orange, scarlet, tangerine, cherry, and peach flowers of Whirlybirds perch high on the undulating vines.

These jewels of flowers do attract aphids, so when you bring them into the kitchen, rinse them gently but well.

PANSIES, VIOLAS, JOHNNY-JUMP-UPS, SWEET VIOLETS
Viola spp.

Hardy perennials in the Violet family . . . start from seed.

Pansies: *V. × Wittrockiana*

In a temperate climate, there are cultivars of pansies that can make year-round blooms possible.

Violas: *V. cornuta*

Aka horned violet . . . blooms late spring through midsummer or later.

Johnny-Jump-Ups: *V. tricolor*

Aka heartsease . . . blooms in spring and sometimes through a cool summer.

Sweet Violets: *V. odorata* spp.

Blooms in late winter through midspring and sometimes again in autumn. All will do well in good moisture-retentive soil in sun or sun with bright shade. A light mulch helps keep the soil moist and flowers coming. Pick off spent blooms as much as possible.

These are all great beauties, favorites of the Victorians. Among them are some of the clearest, truest colors in the garden. Sweet violets are the smallest flowers, of intensely pure single color—royal purple, blue, sulfur yellow, white, and almost black. Their dark green leaves can be surprisingly large and glossy and heart shaped. Violets taste the way they smell, only paler. Deep violet The Czar is among the most fragrant.

Monkey-faced Johnny-jump-ups are usually less than an inch across. Johnnies' faces—with a dot in the chin where the fairy touched them—are splashed with purple, red, yellow, orange, light blue, dark blue, pink, primrose, and white. Their leaves are tiny, and they have no taste. The dainty look of Johnny-jump-ups belies their spirit—they are adventurers. Their seed capsules explode, and you can find Johnnies catapulted halfway across the garden from their parents. If you grow just one of this family, let it be these for their rambunctious charm.

Viola's flowers are quarter-size blooms of a single color, fabulous colors of everything that pansies are, and tend to be even purer. If you see a pansy drenched in apricot and you catch your breath, it's a viola. Plants are more compact than pansies, and for some reason they're fussier to grow.

Pansies are a onetime venture, and a pain to start from seed. Padparadja is glowing orange; T&M's Black Pansy has a yellow eye etched in red and purple; Flame Princess's is stunning yellow with scarlet.

SCENTED GERANIUMS   *Pelargonium* spp.

Half-hardy perennials in the Geranium family, native to South Africa . . . bloom from spring to early or midsummer . . . start with a plant. Give full sun and well-drained loamy soil kept on the dry side.

Pinch off spent blooms. Flowers may perish in the heat and humidity of the South—if that's your climate, give them a microclimate that's as cool and dry as possible.

Although closely related, scented geraniums are not among the brilliant flowers we set in pots on windowsills. These flowers and leaves are smaller. The blossoms can be enchanting—they're in pink, white, yellow, red, apricot, and lilac. But it's their leaves that make the plants special. Like those of mints, leaves of scented geraniums have the ability to mimic the scent and flavor of other flowers, fruits, and spices. There are scented geraniums flavored with rose, lemon, apple, lime, chocolate, peppermint, nutmeg, and filbert—all with a basic geranium taste. These are herbs in the sense that you use them for flavoring leaf by leaf.

Some leaves are so fragrant that just brushing against them charges the air with their scent. The rose geraniums are among these; from the catalog descriptions, trying to decide which to grow can break your head. I grow Attar of Roses and Gray Lady Plymouth.

If you live in a cold climate, you can grow scented geraniums in the garden all summer, then lift them, pot them up, and keep them in a cool bright corner for winter. Then, come spring, out they go again.

Because of frost, I must grow mine in a pot, but a friend planted apple geranium—small perky white flowers and felty bright/dark green apple-scented leaves—in her seaside garden. I was astonished at the airy mound it made.

SUNFLOWERS   *Helianthus annuus*

Hardy annual in the Sunflower family, native to North America from southern Canada to northern Mexico . . . blooms midsummer to early autumn . . . start from seed. Sunflowers are easy to grow. They are drought tolerant, but with plenty of water they'll almost double in size. Surprisingly, sunflowers will also tolerate part shade. You'll need to give the extra-tall cultivars the support of stakes or tie them all together with a length of soft cotton.

Here is cheerfulness incarnate. Three can grow in a 5-gallon tub for a welcome at the front door. Pole beans can be sent up tall sunflowers—the stalks can be 10 feet tall!—to the delight of children. There are child-size sunflowers and giant-size sunflowers and sunflowers in between. Colors are golds, oranges, creams, and bronzes—straight from a Van Gogh painting.

If you'd like to taste a sunflower whole, eat it as a bud. You'll find something of artichokes in the flavor, with a little bitterness. I prefer to eat the petals. I snip rags of Mammoth Russian petals into ribbons and toss them with a pasta salad. They're also lovely woven through cherry tomatoes on the border of a plate as a garnish.

Be aware that some people are allergic to sunflower pollen.

Sunflower seeds contain a wealth of nutrients. They are a better-than-average source of minerals and vitamins. Let the seeds dry on the stalk—wrap the flower heads in insect-weight floating row cover as the seeds start to mature, or the birds will get every one. Sprinkle the seeds over your morning cereal before you take some outside to share with the birds.

JERUSALEM ARTICHOKES   *Helianthus tuberosus*

Hardy (to 10°F) perennial in the Sunflower family, native to North America from Nova Scotia to Manitoba and south to Florida, Louisiana, and Texas . . . aka sunroot, sun choke, girasole . . . grows in 5-gallon containers. Find a sunny out-of-the-way spot where the tubers won't become a pest. Plant in loose fertile soil and water regularly.

These tubers are indigenous to North America—a rarity among vegetables (corn, beans, squashes, peppers, and tomatoes belong to tropical America). Native Americans ate them for hundreds of years before the 17th-century explorer Samuel Champlain took a few home to France, where countryfolk loved them. Jerusalem is thought to be a corruption of the Italian *girasole,* which means "turns toward the sun," which these sisters of sunflowers do. And to some the cooked root tastes of globe artichoke. Raw or cooked, I find it tastes like nutty, sweet water.

All cultivars are as easy to grow as anything in the garden.

Traditional roots are roundish, 2 to 3 inches wide, with teeny knobs all over them. Although prolific, old-fashioned knobby roots are a nuisance to scrub and to peel.

New cultivars have smoother roots that are easy to rinse and thin skin that doesn't need peeling. The roots of Fuseau, with buff-brown skin, have roughly the shape and can reach the size of tiny sweet potatoes. Fuseau is also early. Actually, early harvest is not an advantage since the roots are another of those plants sweetened by frost. Red Fuseau roots are dull red, but the plants aren't as productive or as early as Fuseau—they're harvestable after frost. Smooth Garnet also has red skin, and Magenta Purple is very close to that. Carrot-shaped Golden Nugget has yellowish flesh.

The sunflowerlike stalks of Jerusalem artichokes can tower 6 to 7 feet in the air, with masses of golden daisy blooms the size of a child's hand and heart-shaped leaves as big as a child's head. Some blossoms are faintly scented chocolate. The plants are usually too undisciplined even for the back of the border unless you make a scrim in front of them with plants that conform. They make a fine windscreen.

Not all Jerusalem artichokes flower, and not all leaves are enormous. My Red Fuseau doesn't bloom, and the plants come to my shoulder. They'll be there forever because a wee knoblet broken off in harvesting the tubers starts a new plant. The tubers multiply in geometric progression, each producing at least a handful of tubers by the end of the season. That may be a cheerful prospect if you need a corner of the garden in tall green and if you're crazy about Jerusalem artichokes.

For exemplary plants, set in a furrow about 4 inches deep. Cover with a couple of inches of soil, then an inch of manure. Dig up carefully after the first frosts of autumn. Or store the tubers in the ground.

Recommended: Decide whether you want plenty of them that are hard to prepare—that would be Stampede—or fewer that are handsomer and simpler to prepare—Red Fuseau.

KALE   *Brassica oleracea,* Acephala Group

Hardy perennial in the Mustard family, native to coastal western and southern Europe . . . aka borecole, cabbage kale, kitchen kale, marrow-stem kale, Scotch kale, tall kale, tree kale . . . grows in 3- to 5-gallon containers. Kale wants firm soil (in the manner of brussels sprouts) but otherwise will accommodate almost any soil as long as there's good

drainage. For the finest leaves, grow as you would any of the Mustard family, bearing in mind that, being perennial, if kale is happy it can be in that spot for quite a while.

K ale is a nonheading cabbage that most closely resembles the wild plants that evolved into cabbage, cauliflower, broccoli, brussels sprouts, and kohlrabi. The delicious leaves taste like mild cabbage, but with more character.

Kale and collards are fraternal twins. Over the years collards have gravitated south because they're better in the heat and on dry soil. Kale has found a home mainly in the North because it's not crazy about heat but *is* the hardiest of brassicas—in fact no other vegetable can match it. Our Red Russians are the first to start wilting in the summer sun—I use them as gauges for watering. Both kale and collards are improved in flavor by the sweetening effect of frost. What I do with summer's harvest of either is stand the stalks in a jar of water in the refrigerator for a day or two, and that helps duplicate the chill of autumn.

Looking somewhat like elongated blue and mauve oak leaves with ragged indentations, a fountain of Red Russian blue-green leaves, veined and stemmed in lavender, is magnificent.

Another beautiful kale in the garden is the Italian heirloom Lacinato. Its leaves look a bit like large crinkled blue-gray spinach, and the plant grows upright like spinach. Three Lacinatos set close together among green blades of iris and beside the gray leaves and flat sulfur flowers of yarrow make a wonderful study in texture. Both Red Russian and Lacinato have tender, delicious leaves.

These are smooth-leaved kales. Most gardeners are more familiar with the curly-leaved sorts—squinch your eyes, and they're a patch of curly parsley. The Dutch Westland series, thick, frilly, and curled, are among the most flavorful of this type. I've had indifferent luck with the curly types but never failed with the Red Russians.

If you're intrigued by the unusual, grow Pentland Brig. This very hardy kale grows 2 feet tall, and each leaf looks like a cockaded hat. Harvest the top leaves through winter and early spring, the tender leafy side shoots in spring, and *then* the immature flower heads that resemble broccoli in late spring. Available from Bountiful Gardens.

The only problems I've ever had with generous kales are slugs (see The Gardener's Notebook) and aphids, which I hose off with a strong stream of water. They can be debilitating, however, and sometimes I must swathe the plant in insect-weight floating row cover.

In the warmth of early spring, kale will send up flowers, which means eating quality diminishes for a while. Let the plant bloom, harvest most of the very young blossoms for salads and stir-fries, and in time fresh leaves will appear. Young leaves are very good raw. The seeds that you leave to ripen will give you fresh kale for the next year, unless it's a hybrid or unless the plant has crossed with other brassicas. If you want to save kale seeds, you may have to cage your plant (see The Gardener's Notebook).

Cutting stalks at the bottom, harvest kale leaves individually while young, leaving enough for continued growth. Pick the leaves halfway from the center of the plant outward. The center leaves are the kale's future, the outer leaves its past. Today lies between them.

Recommended: For ease, Red Russian. For flavor, the Westland series. For color, Red Russian and blue Lacinato. For versatility and hardiness, Pentland Brig.

ORNAMENTAL CABBAGE AND KALE   *B. oleracea*, Acephala Group

Half-hardy biennials in the Mustard family, aka decorative kale, flowering kale, flowering cabbage, ornamental-leaved kale . . . grows in 3- to 5-gallon containers. Culture is the same as for kale. Doses of kelp emulsion through autumn seem to bolster hardiness. In the Deep South, alas, there's not enough cool weather for good color.

These are the begonias, peonies, and sea hollies of the cabbage kingdom. When nights turn chill, the reds, pinks, purples, lavenders, butters, creams, whites, and blue-greens intensify, and with each frost they become more dazzling. Flowers are mostly edged in green with ombréd or variegated centers. Leaves can be ruffled, curled, frizzed, feathered, or smooth. In the Peacock series, leaves are narrow and fringed, opening from a pink or cream center like a huge three-dimensional snowflake. The Feather kales look like red-and-green or white-and-green three-dimensional tatted doilies. The Japanese have been working with ornamental kales since the end of the 18th century. All are kales, but the names *ornamental* or *flowering cabbage* and *kale* have come to indicate the finish on the leaf—*cabbage* means smooth, and *kale* fancy.

These exquisite creatures lend themselves to the formality of bordering a path or as one captivating moment by a doorway or as companions to other kales and greens in a wintry bed. Plants average 12 inches all ways.

Ornamental kales are slower growing than culinary kales but will grow anywhere. The Peacocks seem the most successful in wet climates—rain falls through the lace of their leaves. When temperatures stay between 25°F and 55°F, the beauties last until a warm spell urges them to start the seed-making process. Then, as with other brassicas, small (and edible) yellow blossoms hovering above them are charming for several weeks. However, a period of mild weather followed by a sudden hard freeze can kill the plants. Should a hard freeze threaten, cover them with a couple of layers of floating row cover or a cloche.

Of course you can eat these as well as look at them. In cool weather young center leaves are tender (outer leaves are tough). Thin-leaved cultivars make the best eating, and the Nagoya and Chidori series are considered superior. The Peacocks are easy and gorgeous. As with other brassicas, they're sweetest—and the colors brightest—after frost.

Recommended: For ease, the Peacock series. Nagoya is also recommended for good eating. The ultra-ruffled hybrid Kamomes have a mild flavor. Otherwise, any beauty that captures your fancy.

KIDNEY BEANS.   *See Beans for Drying.*

KOHLRABI   *Brassica oleracea,* Gongylodes Group

Hardy biennial in the Mustard family, native to coastal western and southern Europe . . . aka stem turnip, turnip cabbage . . . grows in 8-inch-deep containers. Kohlrabi's earth—humusy and in at least half-day sun—must never dry out. Cage it from small nibbling critters.

Kohlrabi looks like a scientist's experiment gone haywire. It's a smallish pale green or purply turniplike swollen stem that perches atop the ground, long shoots with blue leaves stuck all over it darting helter-skelter. Not for the front of the border—unless you're a true gardening nut, and then purple kohlrabi will be beautiful.

The first written description of kohlrabi appeared from a European botanist in 1554. By the end of that century kohlrabi was cultivated in England, Italy, and Spain. These days it's popular only in Israel, Germany, Holland, and Austria. *Kohlrabi* is

German for cabbage turnip. Some say it's a cross between the two; it isn't. Although descended from wild cabbage, its lightly nutted, vaguely cabbagey sweetness is its own crisp self. You'll love kohlrabi.

Pick traditional kohlrabis plum size—larger, and they'll be woody and bitter. However, open-pollinated Giganté and Waldemar and Kolpak hybrids are supposed to stay sweet though large. As for White Vienna and Purple Vienna, the flavor is the same—the purple is only skin deep.

Kohlrabi has a reputation for being easy to grow, but it took me three tries before I pulled one delicious tuber from the ground. I finally discovered I wasn't giving them enough water.

Recommended: The hybrid Waldemar and the basic Asian Purple are best to start with. Kolpak hybrid and Purple Danube come highly recommended. For disease tolerance, open-pollinated Grand Duke tolerates black rot, and hybrid Triumph (a White Vienna type) tolerates yellows, a fungus disease.

KOMATSUNA. *See Asian Greens.*

LAMB'S-QUARTERS. *See Salad Greens.*

LEEKS. *See Onions.*

LENTILS. *See Beans for Drying.*

LETTUCE. *See Salad Greens.*

LIMA BEANS. *See Beans and Legumes.*

MANGEL. *See Salad Greens.*

Melons

Cucumis melo

Tender annuals in the Cucumber family, probably native to western Africa . . . grow in 7 ½-gallon containers.

Melons have been refreshing man since very ancient times, but it wasn't until the Middle Ages that they arrived in Europe. Abroad, for the most part, dessert melons traditionally have been served as part of an appetizer or as dessert. It's the Americans who taught the world to enjoy a fragrant wedge of melon at breakfast.

Netted: C. *melo*, Reticulatus Group

Smooth: C. *melo*, Inodorus Group

Cantaloupe: C. *melo* spp. Cantaloupensis Group

Mediterranean/Tropical: C. *melo* spp.

Culture of these melons is easy if you can give them immensely fertile fluffy deeply dug well-drained sandy loam (one-third to one-half well-rotted manure mixed into the planting hole), full sun, and warmth long enough to ripen the fruit.

Melons can ripen even in short seasons. Start seedlings indoors in good time. In the hottest, sunniest part of your garden (next to the eggplant), create a microclimate that will be a minimum of 65°F night and day. Choose the appropriate early cultivar. Grow it over IRT plastic mulch applied to moist soil one week before setting out the transplants. Shelter the seedlings after transplanting for a month or so with floating row covers—use insect weight as the weather warms up. Be sure to remove the covers when flowering begins.

If you have at least 120 frost-free growing days, you can start melons in the ground when it has warmed.

The quality of the melons you grow will be infinitely finer than most you can buy. These delectable melons fall into three groups distinguished by their rind and a fourth group that's artificial.

The netted (aka muskmelon) type has medium to large fruit, the rind more or less netted, and flesh that's usually orange and musky. Here are the muskmelon, nutmeg, and Persian melons. This is the group for short-season areas. Among these sugary melons are many that don't ship well, so you can treat yourself to an uncommon and fresh-from-the-garden taste.

The smooth (aka winter) type of melon generally has large mildly scented fruit with white or green flesh; the soft rind is smooth or wrinkled. These are the honeydew, crenshaw, casaba, canary, Christmas, and Cavaillon melons. These fruits grow best in warm climates because they need the longest time to ripen.

True (or European) cantaloupes have a hard unnetted rind with green, orange, or pink flesh. They're little raised commercially in this country, and what we call cantaloupe is in the netted group. The perfumed, distinctly flavored orange-fleshed Charentais from France is in this group. True cantaloupes are not as easy to grow as other dessert melons—they don't cope well with too much heat or too much water, and they can go from perfection of ripeness to over-the-hill in a trice.

From the Mediterranean comes a fabulous and evolving group of melons. Sometimes they're described as tropical melons not only because the plants want a long hot growing season to mature (many have smooth/winter melon background), but because of their exotic flavors. These melons have an intensely fruity taste, with aspects of banana, strawberry, pineapple, citrus, pear, and mango thus far. Tropical is a misleading name, however, since they're not native to the tropics, they're man-made.

A considerable amount of mystery surrounds these melons—you'll note that descriptions in seed catalogs are vague. There's so much commerce at stake, nobody's telling what's in a melon's background.

Green- and ultra-sweet-fleshed Galia was an early creation of this group. Melons like it since have been introduced as "Galia-types." Galicum is a superb version. One of the true F_1 hybrids of this group is a netted melon with creamy flesh, Casablanca, developed in Morocco.

Others are termed Spanish melons—*ananas,* meaning pineapples, is one sort. And some are unique, such as the elongated rough green warty melon from North Africa, called *Pinonet Biel de Sapo*—translated, Skin of the Toad. All very exciting.

Geabel, from Chiltern Seeds, is a netted parthenocarpic hybrid, so you have a better chance of getting fruit (see Cucumbers). Its parentage is from all three subspecies.

For the finer points of growing, refer to Cucumbers—melons are in the same family with the same general needs. Because of this relationship, if a bee visits a cuke blossom and then a melon blossom, the resulting melon may be bitter. Try to have a tall barrier between the crops.

If melons are bothered by disease in your neighborhood, it's essential that you grow a cultivar resistant to the problem. There are cultivars resistant to most diseases that will grow in most parts of the country. In the Northeast there's powdery and downy mildew and fusarium wilt. In the South and West it's mostly the mildews. Ask your local agricultural adviser. Where mildew can be a problem as cool fall advances, the trick is to have started the melons soon enough and grown them fast enough so you'll get fruit before wilt or mildew strikes. Beetles can be controlled with hand picking and pyrethrum.

Bugs can spread diseases, but so can you. Always water before 2:00 P.M. and never walk among any of the cucurbits when their leaves are wet—best not to wet them, but water their roots at ground level. In droughty climates you can wait to water until the leaves *begin* to wilt. Although sometimes they'll look desperate in the middle of the day even when their soil is soaked, don't be taken in by this charade.

One 6-foot vine may yield only three fruits, so if space is tight, grow the vine up. But the leaves on the smooth types are large and decorative, so if you have the space, set a fine specimen in your border with companions of geraniums and petunias.

If they're growing on the ground, when melons are the size of your fist, lay a thick bed of straw beneath them, or set them on large stones to keep them clean, dry, and bug free. If you have hungry rodents or raccoons nosing about, you must cage the melons from them at the earliest, or you'll be sorry. Read about the raccoon barrier in The Gardener's Notebook.

Flavor develops in melons two weeks before ripening. As melons get close (count the days on the seed packet to know where you are), gradually withhold water, either stopping completely or watering just enough to keep the vines healthy—depending on your climate. It's the same trick as with tomatoes.

Netted melons don't sweeten once they've left the vine, so it's essential to pick them at their peak. It's easiest to know when a netted melon is fully ripe because it "slips"—separates readily from the vine with a little pressure from your thumb. Smooth melons ripen a bit after they're picked but don't slip, so you must judge by their scent—there should be a lovely melony fragrance at the blossom end. True cantaloupes are ripe when the first leaf above the fruit stem turns pale—sometimes there will be a small crack on the melon close to the stem. They won't ripen further off the vine. Describing signs of ripeness in Mediterranean melons is impossible because each is different. Since many if not most have some heritage from smooth melons, apply the sniffer test—get close to the vine and breathe deeply at the blossom end. If that doesn't work, perhaps the melon has true cantaloupe in its genes so apply the first-leaf test. When you've got a ripe one, write down the signs for next time.

Eat a ripe melon as soon as possible and rejoice.

Recommended for disease resistance:

> FW = fusarium wilt
> PM and DM = powdery and downy mildews
> ALS = alternaria leaf spot

Netted melons: For cool- and short-season areas, open-pollinated Sweet Granite, Iroquois (some FW), and hybrids Earligold (PM), Earlisweet (very sweet) (FW), and Alaska. Earliqueen and Primo hybrids have superior flavor in this category. For flavor in melon country, open-pollinated Old Time Tennessee and Burpee Hybrid. For dependability in melon country, Ambrosia and Gold Star hybrids, also excellent flavor (PM). For disease resistance in hot, humid areas, open-pollinated Edisto 47 (PM, DM, ALS). For resistance to sap beetles, Kansas. For containers, Minnesota Midget.

Smooth melons: Early-ripening honeydew, Earlidew. Early canary, Sweet Thing Hybrid. For melon country, supersweet open-pollinated Marygold, Sharlyn, and Sunrise honeydew types. Disease-resistant honeydew, Crete (PM, DM, FW). Burpee Early Hybrid Crenshaw is earlier than most crenshaws but not early enough for short seasons.

True cantaloupe: For short seasons, wonderfully flavored hybrids Early Chaca, Alienor (FW), Charmel (FW, PM), and Savor (FW, PM). For pleasure, Charentais.

Mediterranean/Tropical types: Galia is good for hot, dry climates and Gallicum for cool climates. For short seasons, Galia offspring Passport, one of the earliest maturing, best-performing. For flavor as well, Casablanca hybrid (PM) and spicy Ha-Ogen.

GOLDEN CRISPY HYBRID MELON

These delightful melons are supposed to grow to 12 ounces, but this summer I skimped on water, growing one plant in a 5-gallon container. To my astonishment the little vine gave me four ripe crispy melons the size and shape of lemons. The skin wasn't any tougher than most cucumbers', the immature seeds were just like a cucumber's, plentiful but silky, and the flesh was cucumbery but sweet. Fascinating and impressive. If it will do that on little water, imagine what it'll do with lots.

WATERMELON   *Citrullus lanatus*

*Tender annual in the Cucumber family, native to tropical and South
Africa . . . grows in 5-gallon containers. Culture is as for Melons,*

except it's even less tolerant of cool weather than netted melons. Remember a straw mulch to shelter the base from the heat.

The flesh of watermelon can be white to garnet-red, with pale yellow and deep orange in between. There are parts of the world where one of these melons will provide the only available pure water. And there are parts of the world where the seeds are the prized part of the fruit—they're roasted in China, and the Hopi use the crushed seeds to oil the stone on which piki, traditional Indian bread, is baked. Hopi watermelons are small (3 to 4 pounds), with sweet crisp flesh the color of lemon ice—and they take less water than modern hybrids. A great treat. The Arikara wild watermelon fits in the palm of one's hand.

There are watermelons that are especially gorgeous—I'm fondest of those with yellow flesh. Yellow Doll hybrid, called *icebox size,* ripens early enough to be harvested in the Northwest—and it's delectable and wonderfully reliable.

Of open-pollinated melons, Moon and Stars is considered one of the most exciting: enormous heirloom melons with yellow or rose-red flesh whose green shell is spattered with yellow crescent moons and stars. Tendersweet Orange Flesh is 35 pounds of heaven. In the South, plain green Charleston Gray No. 133 is an outstanding watermelon for flavor, disease resistance, and yield. However, unstriped melons are susceptible to blotch in southern regions, so see if that problem exists in your neighborhood.

There are delicious seedless watermelons, too, termed *hybrid triploid.* They can be grown wherever watermelons are grown. They are tricky, but the good people at Lockhart Seeds not only offer the cultivars—both yellow and red fleshed—but detailed growing instructions in their catalog. Cultivation of these melons takes lots of attention.

Crisp, sweet, cool, elegant, and soothing watermelon has other virtues too: vitamin A and fiber.

Recommended: Sweet Meat hybrid is a good cultivar for seeds. The rest have already been mentioned.

CITRON MELON   *C.l.* var. *citroides*

Tender annual.

These are small melons with no edible flesh to speak of but with thick rind that can be turned into divine translucent watermelon pickles for the Thanksgiving table. Highly recommended. If you're growing open-pollinated watermelons, however, stagger the sowing times with the citron melons. They can be cross-pollinated and ruin the watermelon crop.

MINER'S LETTUCE.   *See Salad Greens.*

MIZUNA.   *See Asian Greens.*

Mustard Greens

Brassica spp.

In the Mustard family . . . grows in 3-gallon containers. These are the leaves with snap. Sweet-flavored leaves are gathered in Asian greens. These mustards grow fastest in warm weather and don't mind lots of rain. Give them full sun and light soil that's about one-fourth well-aged manure amended with a sprinkling of blood meal, bonemeal, and kelp meal or wood ashes. Keep the soil moist, and in the growing season give weekly treats of thin manure tea or biweekly fish emulsion. You can pick outside leaves in a cut-and-come-again fashion from their youth until they're nearly mature—or as long as you can tolerate their heat.

These are plants with leaves that can be *hot*—tuck one into your cheese sandwich and you'll have the crispness of lettuce and the zing of Dijon mustard all in one. All mustards grow lustily, most are handsome in form, and many are colorful. Some are peculiar to the Orient, some to America's Deep South. Botanical distinctions are blurred. Seeds coming thick and fast from Asian sources may or may not be marked in a way Yankee seedsmen can decipher. So consider ordering mustards another adventure in the garden and keep records of what you like.

These mustard plants are sensitive to the length of the day—like onions. As daylight lengthens and the air warms in spring, they are moved to make seeds, and their leaves become unbearably hot. But then the buds and succulent stalks become the harvest. So give them what they need to grow—and they will grow quickly, on average 45 days from seed to table in warm weather, although some mustards can take three to four months. Most mustards can winter over—if not under a canopy of sky, then under floating row covers, a cloche, cold frame, or blanket of snow. Where there's rain, protect the leaves of fragile seedlings.

As always, to ensure against soil-borne diseases, if they'll be in the ground more than a couple of months, don't grow mustards where other brassicas have grown within four years—but if you're going to whisk them in and out of the spot, you can make it two or three years between plantings.

Plants whose seeds are grown for grinding into prepared mustard are another species, Nigra. These leafy mustards evolved around the seventh century in moist temperate areas in China. Every part of these mustards is useful in the kitchen, from root to leaf to flower bud to stalk—each with its own degree of pungency. Waste nothing.

BROAD-LEAF MUSTARDS · *B. juncea* var. *foliosa*

Half-hardy annual, native to Europe and Asia.

These are fun. The leaves grow slowly in cold weather, then zoom as the weather warms. Sow them in mild climates in late summer or fall, let them winter over, and they'll mind their manners for a few months. Then one day in early spring you'll turn to see a monster over your shoulder. Miike Giant blends sweet with pungent and is beautiful in its enormous way—the leaves can grow 2 feet long. Osaka Purple has slightly more refined purply-red leaves. Small spring-sown leaves of Red Giant fill bare spaces in the border with a coppery glow and catch the light in a salad—Red Giant is also resistant to a number of insect pests.

Bau Sin is another broad-leaf type called *wrapped heart*—large leaves curl inward to form conical or rounded hearts. The plants are slow to bolt, relatively compact, with big heads and broad, thick stems that are tender and tasty while young, much prized for pickling. Chao Chow/Chaozhou or Swatow Large Headed is similar but pungent and strong. It resembles head lettuce, but instead of leaves, the curved layers are stalks.

Leaves in a smaller scale of fellow brassica arugula are charming woven through these mustards.

Recommended: Easy to sow in spring, Red Giant. For unusual shape and good flavor, a Bau Sin type.

BROCCOLI RAAB/RABE   *B. Rapa,* Ruvo Group

Half-hardy annual, native to Europe . . . aka rapini, rapa, rappone,
turnip broccoli, Italian turnip, Italian kale.

RAPINI/TURNIP GREENS   *B. Rapa,* Rapifera Group

Hardy biennial, probably native to Europe. Grow both plants as turnips,
covering them with insect-weight floating row covers—flea beetles and
other bugs can be a problem. Harvest leaves as for any mustard.

There's a real problem with names here. Seedsmen whom I regard treat these two as one—I couldn't find one source offering true rapini, but lots of broccoli raabs aka rapini are offered. As you can see, they're the same species, different group, and the confusion lies in the fact that they're both grown for their leaves and buttons of tight little buds that look like sprouts of broccoli.

To unravel them, the flavor of broccoli raab's leaves and buds is mustardy sweet, its leaves are softly glossy. The leaves of rapini are softly prickly, and the flavor has a mustardy bite. In fact true rapini are turnips developed for their greens and given a fancy name. They generally come in two shapes: cut leaf and strap leaf. The cut leaves are deeply indented like oak leaves, and the strap leaves are relatively smooth around the edges.

You still can't be sure which rapini you're getting from the seedsman, but there are clues. If it's recommended for spring sowing, it's probably broccoli raab—especially if there's a word like *Italian* or *European* in the description. If it's recommended for fall sowing/overwintering and there's a phrase like *strap leaved* in the description, it's probably rapini aka turnip greens. Rapini will give you florets early in spring.

Sweet Rocket, a country flower with small edible pink flowers (also a brassica), likes the same conditions and adds a light touch to these greens of broccoli raab. Rosy-hued sweet alyssum is charming among rapini.

For either plant, individually pick leaves and shoots—leaving the main stem—when the buds are no bigger than the tip of your thumb. If the days are cool enough, you can harvest another crop—perhaps a third. But once the buds open, as with all brassicas, everything turns HOT.

Recommended: They'll be different, but Shepherd's Garden Seeds' Broccoli

Raab, Stokes Seeds' Rapine (Spring Raab), Johnny's Selected Seeds' Spring Raab, and Comstock, Ferre & Company's Early Pugliese are all quality greens of the broccoli raab type. Stokes's Salade (Fall Raab) and Orol Ledden's Raab for Fall Planting (Rapa or Italian Turnip) can be trusted to be tasty rapini.

COMMON OR LEAF MUSTARDS   *B. juncea*

Half-hardy annuals native to Europe and Asia . . . aka Chinese mustard, Chinese leaf mustard, Chinese mustard green, India mustard, gai choy, karashina, bamboo mustard. These fast-growing leaves bolt quickly.

When you read the word *mild* about a mustard, likely it's one of these. When you see *frilled*, it's one of the next. Curiously, common mustards are as scarce as hen's teeth in catalogs. (Look for mustards under "Greens" when "Mustards" aren't listed.)

Plants vary from 6 to 12 inches tall, leaves may be deep or bright green, rounded, shiny, and pinked around the edges or long and deeply indented. Young leaves have a rather lettuce-crossed-with-spinach-crossed-with-mustard taste—but a mature leaf will give the broad-leaved mustard's zing. Sometimes, if a plant has overwintered and bolted, the flowering shoots grow thick enough to peel and use as pickles.

Recommended: Easiest, Savanna Hybrid is a good example of this type—early, productive, delicious, and slower to bolt than nonhybrids.

CURLED MUSTARDS   *B. juncea* var. *crispifolia*

Half-hardy annual native to Europe and Asia . . . aka mustard greens, southern curled mustards, ostrich plume.

Leaves are very curly, often stiff and crisp. The Asian cultivar Green Wave and the American Southern Giant Curled are opposite sides of a coin. Their deeply frilled leaves could be plumes for a hat, but they're rugged.

The plants have a regal bearing but a naughty way of tweaking the nose when you eat their leaves raw.

Recommended: All are easy. For salad, beautifully ruffled Old Fashioned Ragged Edge, superb quality for warm climates. Spicy slow-to-bolt Green Wave (an AAS winner in 1957) does best in the North.

GREEN-IN-THE-SNOW MUSTARD   *B. juncea* var. *multiceps*

Hardy annual, native to Europe and Asia.

I first picked these seeds to grow for winter because I loved the name. The plant grows upright, but the dark green leaves, although deeply serrated, have no particular charm. However, I find great charm in picking them in the snow, bringing them into the kitchen, and tearing them into a simmering pot of minestrone. Their flavor is spicy-mustardy. Where it's bitter cold, grow them in a cold frame. Companions of parsley add panache.

Recommended: Another name that appeals to me is Snow Cabbage/Shia-Li-Hon, the strain from Evergreen Y. H. Enterprises.

NETTLES.   *See Potherbs.*

NEW ZEALAND SPINACH   *Tetragonia tetragonioides*

Tender perennial in the New Zealand Spinach family, native to Japan, the Pacific Islands, Australia, Tasmania, New Zealand, South America . . . grows in 3-gallon containers. Provide sandy soil, after-

noon shade where it's ghastly hot, and enough water to keep plants from wilting.

I've found New Zealand spinach temperamental. I'd sown seeds profusely for several springs and only last year did a few deign to come up. The small spade-shaped dark green leaves *are* attractive and can cover 2 to 3 feet in the North—in the South they may climb trellises. Sow seeds among red petunias. New Zealand spinach, which tastes like spinach without the edge, is famous for enduring the sort of heat that makes spinach collapse. In fact it doesn't really get started until the days are in the 80s.

OKRA *Abelmoschus esculentus*

Tender annual in the Mallow family, native to tropical Asia . . . aka gumbo, gogo, gombo, lady's-finger . . . grows in 3- to 5-gallon contain-ers. If you have a long enough warm season for cowpeas, you can grow okra. Then you won't need more than full sun and good garden soil with an inch or so of compost or other humus worked in.

Okra flowers, creamy yellow with red throats, look like a cross between hol-lyhock and hibiscus, okra's cousins. I placed three plants of Red Wonder, which grows 5 feet tall, in the center of the main bed, then bordered them with cream, yellow, cherry, and pink Lilliput zinnias. When the setting sun backlit the okras, the orbs of their pale yellow flowers became moons, and the red in their stalks, pods, and maplelike leaves was suffused with an otherworldly glow.

So many people say they hate okra, but virtually none of them has tasted okra fresh from the garden.

There are fine early okras that are the ones to use in cool weather. Annie Oakley II hybrid, perhaps the highest yielding in cool climates, is the one that's done best for me. But there's also Blondy, Evertender, Dwarf Long Green Pod (all open pol-linated). Plants range from the dwarf cultivars, which are 2 to 3 feet tall, to stan-dards, from 4 feet up. Older cultivars have prickers, but spines are being bred out of okra fast. Most pods have ridges, but Emerald Velvet was developed with round smooth pods.

With the exception of the strongly flavored Little Egypt and Star of David, taste in okra is similar in all cultivars. So in warm climates you can choose with an eye to height, yield, and color.

In the North, warm the soil with black paper or plastic mulch and leave it in place for the season to capture as much heat as possible. Be careful not to disturb the roots when transplanting and keep warm with floating row covers until pollination time, when you must lift them away. In the South you can of course sow directly in warm (65°F plus) ground.

Too much nitrogen and you'll get leaves in place of pods, so don't fertilize while growing. As with any fruiting plant you must keep pods picked so more will come along. Cut off with a knife when pods are 2 to 3 inches long.

Recommended: Quick-growing open-pollinated Clemson Spineless is best for flavor—and best for the Cotton Belt. Hybrid Annie Oakley II is probably the surest cultivar to start with everywhere else. For color, Burgundy and Red Wonder.

The Onion Clan

Allium spp.

The Amaryllis family . . . grow in 2-gallon containers. For the finest onions, give them full sun, deeply dug loose soil, and good drainage— raised beds are ideal. From planting to harvest, pull up every weed you see and keep the soil moist but never wet (dry soil encourages bulbs to split). And finally, if you're sowing seeds, they must be no more than two years old.

One winter I read a gardener's description of growing the great English white onion, Ailsa Craig. I sent for seeds. That summer, my swath of Ailsa Craig onions with their blue-green stalks 4 feet in the air delighted me more than anything else I grew. From that success I avidly expanded my repertory to other alliums—shallots, potato onions, multipliers, topsets, Welsh and Japanese bunching onions, leeks, elephant garlic, garlic, rocambole, chives, and Chinese chives. From the garden they taste infinitely richer and livelier than ever they did from the market.

Some of the clan grow from seeds, but more are what is called *multicentric:* without benefit of bee or hours of darkness or pull of the moon, one bulb sunders itself into several bulbs, mirror images of one another. Few vegetables are less bothersome to grow.

Onions are accommodating. I've grown fine onions with five hours of sun and the rest bright shade, but I notice that those in full sun do best. If your soil isn't sandy loam, dig in sand to make it friable—or mix compost or other organic matter to lighten clay soils. Before planting, spread an inch or more of your best well-rotted compost or manure—preferably rabbit or poultry—and a veil of wood ash over each square foot where the bulbs will be. Be moderate with fertilizers. Too much and the bulbs can grow so lush they turn mushy. Dig amendments in to the depth of a foot, pulling out weeds and rocks.

Have your own seedlings well hardened (see The Gardener's Notebook). If sets have arrived in the mail and they look dry, set the roots in an inch of water for an hour or so before planting. When planting, dig down about 3 inches with a trowel where each onion will be and sprinkle in from ½ to 1 tablespoonful of bonemeal—as you do when planting daffodils. Return the soil and plant with the root ends just deep enough in the soil to keep the bulb from rolling away. Always water with a weak solution of liquid fish or kelp or B-1 when you transplant.

N.B. If onion seedlings accidentally get frozen, spray them with cold water and then shade them from the sun. They will thaw slowly and can survive.

When the soil warms up, mulch. Use pebbles or stones to hold warmth and keep down weeds—use 1 or 2 inches of grass clippings or leaves if you need to keep the roots cool. Leave a diameter of a few inches free around each plant so the necks won't rot. Should the soil start crusting despite the mulch, scratch the soil loose around the bulbs with your fingers so the bulbs can pop to the surface—onions like to grow at least half out of the ground.

Then, something like 40 to 60 days after planting, sprinkle blood meal and wood ashes around the plants.

Remember that fall and winter alliums must be well mulched to preserve nutrients and moisture.

You can set almost any of the onion family up front in the border. Their leaves have strong thin vertical lines, and should you ignore them until they flower, the round puffs of flowers are handsome, too. I have a patch of garlic growing now mixed with drifts of white sweet alyssum and sapphire-blue lobelia at its feet, and it's enchanting.

BUNCHING ONIONS: JAPANESE AND WELSH   *Allium fistulosum*

Half-hardy to very hardy perennials, of cultivated origins . . . aka Japanese or Chinese or Oriental bunching onion, Spanish onion, ciboule, two-bladed onion. Bunching onions will grow and produce in ordinary soil, but you'll have finer plants longer if the soil is rich. Therefore, culture is as for basic onions. Bunching onions generally are trouble free.

Bunching Versus Common Green Onions—aka Scallions

All onions go through the stage when their bulbs are soft and their leaves are long, supple, and green. Some are immature common onions that might otherwise go on to be cured—the way a green summer squash can be the immature stage of a cured pumpkin. Some onions are finest at this stage and are not traditionally cured—a separate species called bunching onions are the best example of this type.

What distinguishes bunching from common onions is that, although bunching onions can be grown from seed, many divide into a clump at the base in the manner of multipliers. One seed can turn into 20 onions at once, and each of these onions, planted singly, can do the same. Onions are usually harvested individually from the cluster, but never more than half at once. New onions will fill the spaces in a month or so.

Green onion is the correct term for onions at this stage, but since most people call them scallions, I will too.

Bunching onions invest no energy in growing large bulbs because they form no bulb at all. As they grow, their tubular dark green stalks and usually white stems just grow taller and taller, a foot and a half or more in the air. These add incomparable snips of onionness to stir-fries, soups, omelets, Chinese pancakes, salads, and are great for dipping into coarse salt and breathing deeply as you chomp your spicy way up. Bunching onions tend to be more pungent than scallions, with greater depth of flavor.

Bunching onions have been prized for cooking in China for centuries. They were first mentioned in Chinese writings around 100 B.C. It's thought they crossed the East China Sea to Japan 1,000 years later. Today bunching onions are as ubiquitous in Asian kitchens as bulbing onions are in ours. And in this hemisphere bunching onions have landed in two camps. Those that came to

Europe from Asia are called *Welsh onions*. These are good onions, but they're much the plain souls they were in the Middle Ages.

Aristocratic Japanese/Oriental onions, on the other hand, have been refined by Japanese breeders for years. Thus cultivars under the Japanese banner are considered lustier than the Welsh, both in the garden and in the mouth.

Both Welsh and Japanese onions can be slipcovered in red. Although the flesh is white, if you harvest the onions while the skin is tender, you can grill them unpeeled and the red will stick. Timed to mature in autumn so the cold will deepen the color, Japanese cultivars Red Beard and Santa Clause (how'd that *E* get on there?) are a gorgeous crimson. These are the most appealing of all onions on the relish tray.

In addition to pure bunching onions, there are crosses between the common onion and bunchers. One of these is Beltsville Bunching. Beltsvilles are mildly flavored with crisp fine flesh, and their bottoms are slightly rounded. They top the list of bunching onions to grow in hot dry weather. These onion crosses also overwinter well, and scallions may be harvested very early the following spring from an autumn sowing or in two months from a sowing in spring. But you can snip stalks in the manner of chives and topset onions almost year-round. The old-fashioned bunching onions should not be left in the ground if it freezes. The leaves will be all right, but the bulbs will get mushy. Shelter them in a cold frame (you can move them easily). Replant in spring when the ground is workable.

Nebukas. One of the things that's happened with Japanese onions is that strains forming a single stalk have been developed into an art form. Their pure, straight shafts grow 20 inches long and over an inch wide. In this country these cultivars are offered in seed catalogs with suggestions for growing them in the usual scallion way. Since the stems on these onions coarsen relatively quickly, for tender leaves, these onions must be harvested 9 to 10 weeks after sowing—that's why 60 to 75 days is usually listed as the harvesting date.

But in Asia, the raison d'être of single-stem bunching onions is to become nebukas, stalks painstakingly blanched beneath a shroud of soil that emerge moon-white and exquisitely tender—the same process and principle as for white asparagus. Like leeks, this luxury onion takes long months to produce, and some are harvested a year and more after sowing. And like leeks, these onions will produce two crops—just cut off the bulb an inch above the ground.

Nebukas are fascinating to work with. I followed Joy Larkcom's instructions in *Oriental Vegetables* for growing them classically—transplanting them twice and giving them a year. The bulbs we harvested were a magnificent foot long and as thick as my thumb. Poached, they had to be cut with a knife, but they were sweet and tender. Although much longer, the nebukas weren't whiter than the leeks I'd planted at the same time and didn't fuss over. To grow nebukas often, I suggest you blanch them like leeks. To grow nebukas once, have the adventure of growing them traditionally. A bank of their thick leaves is majestic in the border, but you may want to soften the stiffness with Bright Lights cosmos.

Bolting in bunching onions usually begins in spring of the second season. To keep the patch going, in spring before the plants have a chance to start making flowers, pull up the cluster of onions and tease the roots apart (a sturdy chopstick is a good tool) while keeping the roots moist. Immediately replant the young ones from the outside of the clump, each on its own. In turn these will multiply. Take the center onions to the kitchen or the compost.

Recommended: For onions that divide: Of the Japanese strains, Evergreen White Bunching, with silvery skin and a habit of dividing continuously, is an exemplary cultivar and a good place to start. It may be sown in spring or fall. For milder onions, grow the generic and very hardy Welsh Onion (sometimes called White Welsh or Early White). For overwintering nebuka, Kincho and Hardy White Bunching.

COMMON ONIONS

Allium Cepa, Cepa Group

Half-hardy biennials, native to western Asia.

COOKING AND SLICING ONIONS

Mature common onions have an ancient and colorful history. In Father Abraham's Chaldean city of Ur, prepared onions were sold by street vendors to accompany fried fish and grilled meats. Herodotus notes an inscription on the Great Pyramid citing the expenditure for onions, radishes, and garlic needed to sustain the laborers building it—1,600 talents must have been an impressive sum, else why carve it on a pharaoh's monument? Not only are onions' flavor appealing but also their shape. In the 15th century, Mohammedan Persian architects drew on the sensual shapes of the bulb when creating the great mosque of Tamerlane in Samarkand—floating onion domes against the sky. After this came the onion domes of the Taj Mahal in India and of St. Basil's Cathedral in Moscow.

These brilliant domes were inspired by four shapes: globe (fundamentally round), flattened globe (an O on its side), tops (like most beets and turnips), and torpedoes (also called *spindle* or *bottle shaped*). They can be large. Or they can be tiny.

The pearl onion in your martini is called a *pickler*. The onions your grandmother creamed for Thanksgiving are called *boilers*. In some instances the only difference between cultivars of picklers and boilers is their size at harvest.

I love the process of growing onions, I love the variety of cultivars I can produce for the kitchen, and I love how they look in the border. Their long, finger-thick stalks are strong vertical strokes, but enough stalks droop and dangle to keep the plants from being formal. Because most onion bulbs grow from half to almost completely out of the ground, their skins of gold, flax, cream, red, and crimson catch the light—especially the way I grow them, in clusters of half a dozen. Around and between them, I set mounds of Summer Sun petunias. It's extraordinary how their buttery yellow brings out the warmth of each onion's color.

Pleasure in growing cooking and slicing onions begins with their seeds. In fact what distinguishes common onions botanically is that they reproduce from seed and not from division, as shallots, potato, and topset onions do. Their seed is a speck, half a sphere, as shiny and black as coal. When the seedling emerges, a loop of bright green thread, peaky at the top, backs out of the soil, tail over teakettle. Soon one leg frees itself from the seed, rising awkwardly at first, stretching, nodding, then moving airily in a tangled dance.

From seed is one of three ways to grow these onions. Seeds will always provide the greatest selection. However, you must be able to trust the seedsman to send you fresh seeds—they are 100 percent viable for just one year and 50 percent viable for two years. Of course, you have to fuss with seeds longer than you would transplants, which is the second way of growing onions.

At the nursery and through mail-order sources you can buy seedlings that have been started the same season. Selections of transplants are limited, but clearly you'll save time and trouble over seeds. These plants are pricey and perishable. Much less expensive are sets, which is the third way of getting onions into your garden.

Sets are miniature onions, babies started the previous year, then pulled and dried. Many cultivars take this break in their growing cycle in stride and will go dormant until popped back into the soil. You'll commonly see sets in baskets at the nursery, hardware store, or garden section of megamarts—yellow and red ones and maybe whites. No cultivar names are attached, no promises. Since you don't know their name, you can't know how their internal clocks are set—and you can't be sure they're suited to your day length. Sets are valuable when your season is very short and you didn't sow seeds the previous summer for overwintering or your soil is too wet for bulbs to be in the soil for months and months—or if you're plagued by pests, since many insects find the skins of sets too tough to penetrate. But unless heat treated, onions grown from sets can go to seed prematurely. If they've been heated to a certain degree, the dormant flower in the bulb is zapped and the bulbs don't bolt (you won't know whether this has been done, either). Size also affects bolting. Sets bigger than ½ inch bolt readily. Stuttgarter is more bolting insurance—it's slower than Ebenezer types. Some say sets are the surest way to grow onions. I'd say, try everything else first. To grow your own sets from seeds, see the box on pages 134–35.

Once you've decided on the form you'll start with, can you grow any onion you want? What's this in catalogs about degrees of latitude and onions north and south and how long a day is?

Common onions grow in two stages. First, leaves and roots sprout and grow—these will nourish the bulb to come. Then, at a preordained moment, a mysterious and magical moment, all energy is withdrawn from the leaves and roots and poured into forming layers of a bulb. Although the bulb in an onion looks dramatically different, botanically it's simply more leaves, their bases in embryo, wound around and around. This change of focus in the plant's growth occurs when the hours of darkness in a day correspond to the hours of darkness woven into the plant's genes. This happens no matter whether the roots are thick and strong and the leaves lush and lusty or the seed has scarcely germinated.

So the common onion is one of Mother Nature's sensitive progeny. But they're not uncooperative: They're photoperiodic—*photo* meaning "light" and *periodic* meaning "recurring at regular intervals." Onion bulb growth is regulated by the hours of darkness around the plant in each 24-hour period. These hours are in relation to proximity to the equator. In summer, during the onion's season of growth, days are shortest close to the equator, the days lengthening north and south of it. Then to know which cultivars will grow best in your garden, you must know its latitude!

According to how many hours of darkness the plant needs to form a bulb, common onions have been divided into three categories. Perversely, somebody named them not in terms of the regulating darkness but of the sunlight in which they grow. The term is *day length*. The box on pages 134–135 explains.

Briefly, when you grow short-day onions in the North, the bulb-forming mechanism kicks in when there are 12 hours of light each day—in March or April—and before you know it, you have to harvest the onions at a small size to save them from flowering and going to seed. However, a sweet southern onion will still taste sweet. That is, it *should*.

In the South, because there are never going to be 14 or more hours of light, the bulb-forming mechanism of long-day onions will never be activated—you'll have lots of leaves and no bulbs to speak of, i.e., scallions.

Can Somebody Tell Me Where We Are on This Map? I Want to Order My Onions . . .

Short-day onions are keyed to 12 to 13 hours of daylight, which occur between 24° and 33.5° latitude.

If you live on or south of a line drawn across this country from San Juan Capistrano, California, through Lubbock, Texas, to about 3 miles north of Pawleys Island, South Carolina, short-day onions will grow big and sweet for you. In fact, short-day onions are characterized by their mildness and sweetness. Bermuda onions are the aristocracy of this type. There are white, yellow, and red Bermudas, all wonderfully mild. A Bermuda onion is one of the parents of the enormous apple-sweet onions of Vidalia, Georgia, and Maui, Hawaii—a flattened globe called Granex 33.

The many microclimates across the South can make growing largish onions difficult. Your growing season may be hotter, cooler, drier, or more tropical than the onion's genes can handle. Not only day length but also weather affects the common onion's growth. Plants are happiest producing leaves and roots in cool weather, but they need pleasant weather—at least 60°F—to form bulbs. In a perfect world, when the hours of dark coincide with those programmed into the onion, that day would turn warm as well—not hot, just warm. Over 104°F, the reverse

Some cultivars are considered day-length neutral. A group of such onions, pleasing to slice, are handsome torpedo-shaped reds. In the far North these grow a slender 1½ to 2 inches wide and perhaps two to three times as long, but in the warmth of the middling states they can get twice that size. None are good keepers, but their soft rosy flesh is lightly pungent, and they're sensual in still lifes and centerpieces.

Sweet Onions: The chemistry of the soil has much to do with the sweetness of the onion it nurtures. Sulfur in the soil—essential to plant growth—is pulled into the bulb. The more sulfur in the soil, the more sulfur in the onion. Lots of sulfur is why a bite of a raw storage onion can make you gasp—the more sulfur, the longer the happens; bulbing is inhibited. If unfriendly weather strikes, try again with another cultivar. Perhaps if short-day onions haven't done well for you, you can try intermediate-day (or medium-day) cultivars.

Intermediate-day onions form bulbs where there are 13 ½ to 14 hours of daylight—between 32° and 40° latitude.

Draw a line a generous 100 miles south of the northernmost edge of short-day onion territory, then draw another along the top of California's Mendocino County through the top of Kansas to Normandy Beach, New Jersey. The most successful areas for these onions are usually the central valley in California and the middle and south Atlantic states.

Where winters are mild in this territory, onioners can conceivably have it all ways: grow long-day onions from spring through summer, short-day cultivars from midsummer through fall, and something like the amazingly adaptable Buffalo over winter.

In long-day onions the switch from forming leaves to bulbs is flicked on when there are 14 ½ to 15 hours of daylight—some require 16 hours or more. These onions are hardy and grow above the 33.5° latitude—the northern defining line of short-day onions.

Probably the best-known northern onions are the flattish globes of Walla Walla (aka Walla Walla Sweet). Seeds were brought to Washington State in the last century by a Frenchman from Corsica. Walla Walla's creamy-white flesh is best eaten raw. For cooking onions in the North, look to the golden Spanish. They are generally globe shaped and milder than most intermediate- to long-day types.

onion keeps. It's the sulfur that's released from the onion's cells when we slice into them that makes us cry. We don't cry when we bite into a true Walla Walla or Vidalia. The soils of the Pacific Northwest and a strip of land in eastern Georgia have one thing in common—they're low in sulfur. The Vidalia and Walla Walla onions have in common their sweetness—and the fact that they don't keep. All sweet onions can be eaten raw.

There's no way to lower the sulfur from the soil à la Vidalia and Walla Walla. What you *can* do if you're wild to raise sweet onions is grow them in a container. Experiment with very light, sandy, low-sulfur soil mixes.

Past day length, soil, and weather, there's the consideration of length of growing season for onions. Big bulbs take their own sweet time to mature. Should you have a very short growing season and wish to grow cooking and slicing onions from seed, you can do it two ways. Sow an early cultivar indoors 10 weeks before your last expected frost date in spring and grow it over summer to mature in August or sow in August for a lazy crop to winter over and mature the following June. You can do both, using a dual-purpose cultivar such as Buffalo.

Flavor is different between spring-sown and summer-sown crops, even with the same cultivar. When cultivars such as Buffalo and Walla Walla are started in early spring, by late summer they will be a nice size and pleasingly mild when compared to most onions. But sow them in late summer, let them sleep through winter, and by the following summer they'll be large if not enormous and supersweet, their potential utterly fulfilled.

North or south, if your soil is well drained so that it doesn't stay cold and wet, or if you can protect young onions from bitter cold, overwintering is the way to realize the full sweetness of the sweetest onions.

However, if water is in short supply in your part of the world, and rain or melting snow is skimpy in winter, best reflect on how reasonable it is to have something in the ground that must be kept moist for 10 months or more.

For onions through winter, in the North sow seeds of Walla Walla the second or third week in August (not earlier, not later) outdoors in flats or in a seedbed, three to four seeds per inch. Don't fertilize at any point—succulent growth freezes easily and is susceptible to disease. If you expect temperatures to be in the minuses in winter, the onions must go into a cold frame. Whether they end up in a frame or outside in a sunny sheltered place, prepare a couple of inches of good friable soil (nothing like the spectacular soil of summer). Two months after germinating, or when the stalks are the thickness of a pencil, either thin them lightly where they are (leave a few extra as a hedge against losses) or transplant them into place, two to three seedlings per inch.

If you expect the air will be colder than, say, 20°F, protect the onions with a floating row cover before the freeze hits—one or two layers, depending. You may want to add an insulating layer of leaves on top of the row covers. Whatever works without crushing or smothering the plants.

For onions in a frame, open the frame and let the babies breathe as often as there's sunshine, never letting their soil dry out. In spring, when the crocus blooms or as soon as the garden soil is dry enough to prepare, transplant the onions into their permanent places as though you'd just raised them in a sunny corner of the house.

In the South it's a little trickier to overwinter onions due to the vagaries of temperature. Lots of winter days in the 30s and 40s can cause short-day onions to bolt come spring. Still it's worth a try. Proceed as for northern overwintered onions, only you probably won't need the cold frame.

After you've chosen your seeds, the best way to raise seedlings is in soil blocks. This is a wonderful system and particularly suited to onions. Six seeds are dropped into the dimple in a child-size block. That many in so small an area? Yes! The method has been proven in the field to produce an especially high yield of medium-large bulbs. And, as I've said, bunched this way, they make delightful fountains of green in the border.

But why not sow onion seeds where they'll grow rather than sow them in blocks and transplant them? For one thing, it would be giving weeks to soil that might otherwise be productive. Onions can take a couple of weeks to germinate in the soil but only 2 days in a bubbling water bath.

It can be another 2 to 3 months before they've got themselves in gear and can be set in the ground for growing. For another, onion seedlings are more vulnerable to having the life choked out of them by weeds than most plants simply because they're so fragile. In fact weeds among onions cut the *final yield* by 4 percent each day. A few weeks of weeds, and you've got a patch of weeds instead of onions. And it's miserable trying to pluck weeds from a tangle of onion threads. You almost need tweezers, because you mustn't disturb the onion's roots—an onion's roots are shallowly spread within a 6-inch radius of the plant. For another, as happens with mustards, transplanting strengthens the plant. Many trim the tops back to 4 inches when they transplant, hoping the energy will go into the bulb and root system. Some cut Spanish onions back 2 or 3 times, while still in flats. Others argue that the cut can be such a shock to the little plant's system that it may never fully recover and productivity can decline. I don't trim.

Success with onions comes when the plant is well served in both its phases of growth. The bulbs will be only as good as their leaves and roots.

As the onions mature, watch for stalks with little domes at the tip. These are flower buds. Snip them off at the base the moment they appear so strength will continue to go into the bulb, not the flowers-then-seeds. Eat them.

If you're growing onions to store, remember that the drier they are when sent to storage, the longer they'll keep. The drying process should begin when the first leaves start to yellow. When that happens, withhold water. That's why it's a good idea to place onions out of range of a drip system or other in-place watering device that will water the area no matter what. Twisting the tops prevents rain from gliding down the leaves to the heart of the onion and causing it to rot. It's not fatal if storage onions are watered to the end, but it makes it more difficult to be sure they'll be bone dry.

When to harvest? When it's "tops down," the circuslike expression used in the trade—when about three-fourths of the leaves have fallen over and the bulb comes easily from the ground. If there's any resistance when you pull, it means the roots are still alive—it's best to wait until they've stopped growing. Drying onions left in the soil invite earthworms to feast on the roots and fungal diseases to invade. If frost is in the air but your onions are still as happy as clams, you must speed the harvest along. The traditional method of rolling over the onions or bashing them with a rake to break the stalks sounds like farmer's fun, but this can damage tissue at the neck, inviting spoilage. Break the leafy stalks gently with your hands. Then lift the bulbs up a bit with a digging fork, disengaging the roots. Be as careful as you can not to pierce the bulbs. Keep them dry—if rain threatens, cover with something waterproof, but remove it the moment it stops raining so you won't steam the onions. Within a week you should be able to pull the bulbs. Once it's tops down, don't put off the harvest.

To harvest, gently wrest the onions from the soil—never yank—and shake off the earth from the roots. Do not brush or wash them, for any bruise or dampness might be an occasion for spoilage.

You can eat the onions any time now, but for storage, they must be cured. Arrange the bulbs in a single layer with space around them on something above the ground that provides circulation of air, such as lath or 2-inch chicken wire. Pull the leaves through the holes so the bulbs can be held in place, root side up, not touching. Place out of direct sunlight in a dry airy corner of the garden. Should rain threaten, or the days be overcast, gather them up and dry in an airy place indoors. A fan to circulate the air helps. I can't emphasize enough that the onions must be *dry* to keep in storage. When the neck of the bulb is brittle, the onion is ready to store— it can take one to three weeks. Use onions with thick or double necks first: they won't keep as well as the others.

Braid the tops of a few of the handsomest onions and hang them in a cool, dry, airy place—not picturesquely beside the stove. Onions without leaves generally last longest, since air can get to the necks and finish the drying process. Snip off the leaves ½ inch above the bulb. Turn the onions a couple of layers thick into a mesh bag or an airy basket or holey bin. In our cellar, where there are mice, I've stored onions successfully all winter in big covered plastic garbage bins that I made lacework of with an ice pick—a million holes. Store off the floor in a dark dry place with a constant temperature about 32°F—or as close as you can get to it. If there's no place in your house below 40°F, best refrigerate them. Relative humidity must be below 70 percent. Keep them away from apples, which emit a gas that will have your onions sprouting prematurely, and from potatoes, since the gas onions and potatoes produce will shorten the storage lives of one another. Check every week or so and send any bulbs that are spoiling to the compost or sprouting to the kitchen.

Storage onions. These are the ones at the supermarket. If you want your own cured onions to keep for a long time, there are points to look for when you choose a cultivar. If it's mentioned, the thickness of an onion's neck is important. You want necks to be as slender as a swan's. Thin necks dry fastest and thus become a sealed entrance to vulnerable flesh. Conversely, thick necks—a result of the onion's heritage or too much nitrogen or too little phosphorus in the soil—inhibit the bulbs' keeping qualities. A veteran onioner has noted that you can tell whether an onion is going to be a good keeper if it has a small tight neck and the root end is quite flat. Roots sprout most easily when the root end is ridged or elongated, and a sprouting onion is on its way to perishing.

In addition to neck and tail configuration, potential for storage is linked almost invariably to pungence. Pungence comes from the onion's sulfur, which is a preservative—just as dried fruits are treated with sulfur to keep their color and flavor bright. Onions that keep sound and true for months and months—growing sounder and truer by the minute as the sulfur content increases—can fell an onion lover with one raw bite. That's why the unusual hybrid Sweet Sandwich is so appealing. When harvested, the bronze globes with white flesh are as pungent as can be. But after a couple of months in storage these slicing onions are amazingly mellow in a wintry salad or sandwich. The longer they keep, the sweeter they become—the opposite of traditional keepers. Breeders are working on producing more onions for storage that take less of a hero to eat.

I've never had a lick of trouble with my onions, and likely you won't either. However, a couple of insects equally enthusiastic about your onions might be lurking. Mostly in the North, there are onion maggots, and mostly in the South, thrips. To discourage onion maggots, sprinkle the soil with diatomaceous earth and wood ash when you plant the onions. Spray thrips with insecticidal soap every 3 days for 14 days. Consult your agricultural extension agent if the problem worsens.

If you find onions you admire and want more of but you can't locate them in any form again—as once happened with my small, flat, golden Italian button onions, Borettana—you can try to reproduce them from seed. Set them in a cool dark place until they sprout—or at least some do. Plant them in spring or fall as you would a set and let them flower and make seeds. Pray they're not a hybrid, because if they are, you can't know what you'll get. Onion seeds cross easily, so if these aren't the

Maybe This Year I'll Grow My Own Sets from Seed . . .

Choose a long-storing cultivar suitable to your day length—Red Creole (Creole C-5) is a rare short-day cultivar that qualifies. A superior long-day cultivar for sets is open-pollinated Golden Mosque, a cross of nonsprouting Stuttgarter and early Ebenezer. The sets are ovals, but the mature onions are round.

To keep the finished bulbs small, sow seeds in place very thickly on only moderately good soil: commercial growers of sets sow 60 pounds of seed per acre as compared to 2 to 4 pounds for cooking onions. Weed faithfully, but don't water as copiously as usual and don't fertilize. They should be stressed not enough to crack but enough to keep them small. Bend over the leaves if they haven't started to yellow when the bulbs are no more than ½ inch in diameter. Larger, and they're prone to bolting when you plant them next spring. Pull, cure, and remove the tops at the neck. Store as usual, but with special care. If you have lots, you can try to suppress the forming of flowering stalks by storing the bulbs at 70°F. Some of the bulbs will dry and perhaps be a loss. If you've none to spare, store loosely in net bags in the refrigerator at 32°F. In spring any that have gotten away from you and are wider than ½ inch should be grown for scallions.

only onions growing within one square mile, you'll need to cage them (see The Gardener's Notebook).

Many excellent open-pollinated cultivars—some heirlooms, some newly developed by breeders—are well suited to kitchen gardens. The same caution about open-pollinated seeds as always applies particularly to onions. Strains will wax and wane, so purchase OP seeds only from seedsmen with a sterling reputation, such as those I have listed in the back of the book.

Don't buy onions in any form unless the day length of the cultivar is mentioned or you know it from another source. Without that information you're growing onions in the dark.

Some very mild and sweet onions are white inside and out—for example, many strains of White Sweet Spanish, Early Supreme, White Bermuda. But white-skinned onions can also be pungent as the dickens. You can be sure your white onions will be sweet only when you grow a sweet cultivar yourself.

But what about a red onion that's *red*—not white—inside? I think red onions are as aesthetic an accent, raw or cooked, as my larder affords. I'm always disappointed when I peel away brilliant red skin and find milky flesh beneath. If red inside and out matters to you, read catalog descriptions carefully.

Past that, you could go crazy with the multiples of things you want in an onion and where it can be grown and all the cultivars all the catalogs say are marvelous.

Recommended: If you're trying onions for the first time, I'd suggest the high-yielding adaptable yellow hybrid Buffalo, whose relative insensitivity to day length makes it growable from New Mexico to British Columbia, from Georgia to Maine. Buffalo is one of the earliest onions from seed—and they'll keep until Christmas. You can also sow Buffalo in August for wintering over. Best sown in spring from 35° to 50° and in summer from 30° to 55° latitude if winter lows don't exceed −10°F.

Reliable: short—Early Supreme, Texas Grano types; intermediate—hybrid Buffalo and OP Sweet Spanish types; long—Ailsa Craig and hybrids Norstar, Canada Maple.

Red (or at least pink) inside and out: short—Red Granex hybrid, Red Creole; intermediate—Italian Red Torpedo; long—Mercury, Red Man, Benny's Red, and early hybrid Lucifer.

Sweet: short—hybrid Granex 33 (fall or spring sowing) and OP Texas Grano 502 (fall sowing); intermediate—Candy; long—Walla Walla Sweet (late summer sown).

For storage: short—OP Texas Grano 1015Y, OP Red Creole; intermediate—Spano (but only medium-long storage); long—Copra, Sweet Sandwich, all hybrids (Capable, Duration).

PR: (Pink Root—resistant to a disease of the soil) short—Texas Grano 502 PRR, Early Supreme; intermediate—Early Red Burger and Stockton Early Red; long—Vaquero (also resistant to fusarium).

For sets: In the North from your own seeds, yellow Golden Mosque. Storebought, flat nonsprouting Stuttgarter, a northern European cultivar that does better the farther north it grows. Red sets could well be Red Creole or the adaptable open-pollinated Red Wethersfield, large, flat globes with red-rimmed white rings. And one classic white for sets for short and intermediate days is flat, fine-grained White Ebenezer, brought to this country from Japan in the 19th century.

Torpedo shapes are day-length neutral. These are variously known as Red

Florence, Rouge de Florence, Red Lucca, Italian Red Torpedo, Red Torpedo, Torpedo, Italian Blood Red Bottle, and Florence Long. Lucca and Florence are close to 44° latitude. And so, roughly, is the South of France, where Red Simiane—sweet and pure white in the center—is prized. Jan Blüm of Seeds Blüm says her Simiane, with red skin and sweet red flesh, "does well from Florida to Quebec."

Finally, for climates where the weather is not conducive to onions: In areas as diverse as eastern Oregon and across a swath through Idaho, Colorado, and the high plains of Texas, an onion that does well is the long-day hybrid Vega. It's a large tan globe, mildly pungent, and a relatively good keeper.

GREEN ONIONS/SCALLIONS

Aka spring onions, salad onions. Culture is the same as though you were growing these onions full size.

In an early stage of their growth, common onions are pencil-slim with small tender bulbs, so many gardeners just toss out their Walla Walla or Ailsa Craig seeds and pull them young. Anything wrong with that? Only that it's underemploying those gifted cultivars. A little like calling in Marilyn Horne to sing the alphabet song.

But because everyone can't be a star, there are common onions suited to being harvested at this tender stage—when they have no skin to cloak the tenderness of their tips. For some reason seedsmen and breeders have conditioned us to expect scallions with sparkling white tips, although one or two are purply-red. Anywhere in the country, you can sow these onions as soon as the soil can be worked in late winter. Although they're best when spring sown, you can sprinkle White Lisbon seeds in a sheltered spot in autumn, let them winter over, and there will be scallions in spring. Harvest when the onions are the thickness of your little finger or as you like.

I'm partial to onions, and I'm partial to golden and orange and tangerine calendulas, and I almost always mix them together.

Recommended: White Lisbon makes a graceful scallion, very like a teardrop. It has all the virtues—sweet snowy bulb, juicy greens, crisp through and through, vigorous, tolerant of both heat and cold, and it's among the earliest. Southport White Globe, which can go on to form a fine, large white bulb (a particularly good keeper), is popular especially in the South for fall planting as an overwintering scallion.

Burgundy is a red onion not wasted when pulled young—about a month behind White Lisbon. You might mix the seeds and sow them together for a long and pretty harvest.

All these cultivars are open pollinated. To save their seeds, you'd best cage them (see The Gardener's Notebook).

PEARLS, PICKLERS, AND BOILERS

Aka summer onions. Culture is as for the big guys.

Here are more onions that are also cookers-and-slicers-in-the-bud but have been bred to be delectable when their bulbs are as big as a dowager's faux pearls or bigger. You rarely see these onions at the market, and when you do, they're packed in small baskets, absurdly priced. You can buy them frozen, with or without cream sauce, but they can't compare with the texture and flavor of fresh onions. Although many are their best at latitudes of 40° and above (the upper limit of intermediate-day onions), they'll grow anywhere—a little smaller in the South, a little larger in the North.

Sow them thickly, don't thin, and harvest singly or in bunches when the bulbs are the size you want. Just about foolproof.

Recommended: Purplette is an amusing and versatile mini-onion, with purply-red skin that turns the white flesh pink when cooked or pickled. With its delicate flavor and festive color, Purplette may be harvested from scallion to walnut size. Actually, all these onions are tasty from pearl to boiler size, although some have been bred for specific sizes. Tear-drop White Portugal (aka Silverskin) is either day neutral or a short-day onion, depending on the catalog. It's one of the classic pickling onions.

Of pearl onions, luminous Quicksilver Pearl is perfectly round and ultra-thin-necked. To pickle for martinis, there are flattish mild Pompeii Perla Prima. A little larger is Barletta, an elegant, pure white, slightly flattened, round European onion. And don't forget the sweet Bermuda onion, Crystal Wax Pickling.

But my favorite of all the small onions is the button shape of what the Italians call *cipollini*. They're traditionally pickled, but I love to use them every which way. They're long-day onions, and they keep for several months. I am grateful to Renee Shepherd for making Borettana Italian heirlooms—cipollini—available.

ELEPHANT GARLIC   *A. Ampeloprasum*, Ampeloprasum Group

Hardy biennial, native to Europe, North Africa, and Asia . . . aka great-headed garlic, Levant garlic. Culture is the same as for garlic, but it can take two years for a clove to form more cloves.

*E*ach clove of elephant garlic—not garlic but a form of leek—can be as large as an entire garlic bulb, and bulbs can weigh a pound. For all its size, the flavor is mild. You can cut the flesh of peeled raw cloves into matchsticks and toss them in a salad. Where it's extremely cold, plant in the spring. You might find the resulting bulb is one solid clove rather than a cluster. Replant in fall or spring and hope you'll have big separate cloves to harvest. Always remove any flowering stalks (the seeds are sterile). Bulbils, miniature bulbs, can form around the roots of this plant.

GARLIC   *A. sativum*

Hardy perennial, perhaps from a wild Asiatic species. For a fine crop of garlic, choose a spot of loose, well-drained, moderately fertile soil—too rich, and you'll get lush leaves and skimpy bulbs. You'll have markedly superior results in raised beds or even mounds. Garlic loves sun and just enough water to keep the bulbs not too wet and not too dry.

*G*arlic is as rich in its history as in its contribution to the table. All the ancients grew garlic. The Egyptians held it in such esteem that for 15 pounds of the bulbs a healthy male slave could be purchased. The Talmud sanctioned garlic as an aphrodisiac. Hippocrates treated all manner of infections and disorders with garlic, and Roman soldiers carried garlic with them as a source of stamina and courage. Ancient Chinese scholars wrote treatises on garlic.

Green garlic, pulled young and sweet from the ground, is, mysteriously, a secret kept from most of the world. It's like a garlic-flavored scallion, the white part small and slim or round as a walnut, depending on its age when you pull it.

I find growing garlic—especially when harvested green—easier than growing any other onion, except perhaps shallots. Like shallots, garlic is propagated from its cloves (seeds, when formed, are generally infertile). For green garlic you can plant sound cloves from bulbs you buy at the market, which is what I do. This practice is frowned on by garlic specialists, who say you get out of the ground garlic only as good as you put into it, and they tend to think that what's at the market isn't as good as what they offer. But eaten at the immature stage, there's not much difference in flavor between cultivars. Inspect every clove scrupulously before planting so you don't unwittingly plant disease.

To plant garlic, I poke a hole with my finger in sunny loose soil, press in a clove pointy tip up, cover the hole, and pat it firm. When I'm done, I water the buried cloves thoroughly. Garlic is very hardy, so I plant a few dozen cloves every few months and let some winter over in the cold frame. This way we almost always have green garlic. Usually I can harvest after a long month, before bulblets form.

Sometimes, if I'm distracted awhile, what I find when I pull the plant is a fat round bulb that looks like a boiling onion. I'm always fascinated by how it got so round from a crescent. If I really lose track of the cloves I've planted, the round bulb will separate into cloves. This takes from five to eight months.

Garlic for drying. For garlic that you will dry and cure, the larger and plumper the bulbs from which the cloves come, the larger the resulting bulbs will be. The size of individual cloves in the bulb seems not to matter, since all have the same genes. If your source is garlic from the market, be certain you taste one clove from each bulb before you commit to it. A pure-white-skinned cultivar from the market is probably California Late. It can be mild and lovely. But a beautiful mauve-skinned garlic—perhaps Silverskin—can be sharp and as hot as can be.

Market garlic is better than none, but there is a realm of unusually beautiful and delicious garlics available from specialists. Most likely the seedsmen will ship in autumn. Long cool or chilly winters give the plants a chance to establish themselves and time to develop strong roots and leaves before they start their bulb-making business in spring. For cured garlic, autumn planting is recommended for all but the coldest climates—there, a February or March plant is recommended, and some seedsmen will ship bulbs then. A garlic clove's sprouting mechanism is triggered by cold, so if your earth is warmer than 50°F, break the bulb into cloves, mix with damp sand, cover tightly, and refrigerate until the cloves sprout, anything from a few days to a few weeks.

To keep bulbs for drying and curing, withhold water as the leaves begin to yellow and let the bulbs cure in the ground for two to three more weeks, until approximately one third of the stalks are brown and dry (yellowing moves from the ground up). Tie the leaves in a Japanese-style knot, if you mind that they look ungainly. Then lift the bulbs carefully with a small gardening fork so the cloves don't scatter or the bulbs bruise—as with onions, bruised bulbs will be the first to rot. Snip off the roots to ¼ inch and brush off any earth, but leave the stalks intact if you expect to braid them. Dry on racks in a warm, airy spot out of direct sun until the bulb wrappings are papery but the stalks are still flexible, a week or two.

If you've a big crop of cured bulbs, why not braid them?

To make a thick braid for hanging dried garlic, lay two bulbs crossed on a work surface before you (it may be your lap). Have the bulbs at the top, close together, their stalks down. Lay a third bulb (the bulb again at the top) running straight up and down between the first two. Begin the braid by wrapping this center stalk around the crossed stalks of the others. Add the next bulb (if its bulbs are small, you can add two at once), setting it slightly below those already braided and best side out. Braid as usual, pulling the stalks snugly, since they'll shrink and loosen as they dry. Each time you bring an outer stalk to the center, add another bulb. When the braid reaches the length you like, usually a foot to a foot and a half, wrap and tie the stalks with raffia (florists and crafts stores have it) or cotton string.

Hang your beautiful garlands not in the kitchen over the stove (too hot) but in a cool, dry, dark place between 50°F and 60°F. Well-cured bulbs of many cultivars can keep for a year. Be sure to save some for replanting.

Recommended: For your first try at drying garlic, grow something dependable and prolific such as Chet's. The flavor is mild, the cloves are large, and they keep exceptionally well. If you have cold winters, try the purply-brown, richly flavored Spanish Roja, brought to Portland in the late 19th century by Greeks—thus it's also called Oregon Blue and Greek Blue. The blue is for its thick blue-green stalks and leaves. And when you see purple artichoke garlic offered, send for some and grow it. The bulb is formed of cloves overlaid on one another—like the petals and hues of a Violetto artichoke.

Once you've grown such fine, rare garlic, you'll never cook with supermarket stuff again.

ROCAMBOLE GARLIC   *A. sativum* var. *Ophioscorodon*

Very hardy perennials, native to southern Europe . . . aka serpent garlic, topsetting garlic, purple skin garlic, ophio garlic. Culture is the same as for garlic.

A country name for rocambole garlic is *clown's treacle*. One of nature's tasty pranks, the plant looks like a loop-the-loop for the little people, with tips shaped like chocolate kisses on long, thin stalks that whiz up and away and swoop and circle dizzily. Rocambole is garlic's answer to topset onions. Like some topset onions, this garlic can taste hot as Hades. It forms cloves underground and miniature bulbs *(bulbils)* on the tips of main stalks in place of flowers. Mauvy-crimson bulbils that look like kernels of strawberry popcorn are caught in a bundle the size of a coat button.

Rocambole will usually produce more cloves underground than culinary garlic if you remove the seed stalk—do this as the cluster of bulbils begins to form. If you want to increase your supply by planting bulbils, let the cluster mature. A single bulbil may be planted as in topset onions, but it will be a couple of years before bulbs are produced. Harvest green leaves as for green garlic.

Rocambole is traditionally planted in fall, although it may also be planted in spring. However, a spring-planted clove will give you an immature single round at the end of the season—like my garlic described earlier. Replant it in fall and you'll be rewarded with big fat cloves the following spring. Harvest when leaves begin to yellow but while there are still half a dozen green leaves on the plant. Well-cured cloves keep for three to six months.

Some feel this is the finest-flavored garlic of all.

LEEKS

A. Ampeloprasum, Porrum Group

Half-hardy to very hardy biennial, known only in cultivation. Culture is the same as for almost everybody else in the clan. In hot summer areas, half-day sun and high shade are best.

Leeks are majestic and stalwart. Their leaves, drenched in blue-green, are broad and flat, with the hand of strong linen. The leaves grow straight and tall above the stem, beautifully plaited in the round. The non-bulbing tips are uncommonly sweet.

Leeks are as ancient as onions and garlic, cultivated in Mesopotamian fields thousands of years ago. Khufu, the pharaoh who built the pyramid at Giza and who fed his laborers onions at great expense, rewarded his court magician with 1,000 pears, 100 pitchers of beer, 100 bunches of leeks, and an ox. Leeks have been on European tables since the emperor Nero ate quantities of them, believing they would enhance his voice. Today leeks are most celebrated by the Welsh. In the 6th century, an abbot-bishop named David advised his countrymen going to fight the Saxons to wear leeks so as to recognize one another in the heat of battle. Now David is the patron saint of Wales, and on St. Davey's Day, Welshmen sport a leek in remembrance.

For the most efficient use of the soil, and because transplanted leeks are usually more vigorous, start seeds indoors. Seedlings germinated in soil blocks should be transplanted into a larger container as for onions, then separated and planted individually. The larger the seedling when it goes into the ground, the finer the leek will be. Transplanting size—time for blanching—is two to three months old and 6 to 8 inches tall.

Blanching is traditional leek care. It makes the stem as sweet and tender as possible. It's my experience that growing the plants in a trench is the most efficient way of blanching leeks. The process isn't troublesome, because it's done over a period of months. Besides, it's a process that's mysterious and primeval.

The trench doesn't have to run in a tidy line. And it doesn't have to be contiguous—a curve of a few feet here, a crescent of a few feet there. And of course the trenches can be in the border. Knee-high leek stalks have an insouciant ease. Placed toward the back of the bed, some of leeks' loveliest companions are small stars of annual tall-growing phlox.

Were your leeks going to be in competition for quality and size, you'd dig your trench 2 feet deep and a foot wide, then fill it with fine compost 8 inches from the top. But for fine eating quality, after preparing your soil as usual for an onion, dig a trench 6 inches deep and as wide, placing the soil along the side of the trench. Pull out all rocks. Trenches can be a foot apart.

Keep the roots of the seedlings moist while they're waiting to go in. Lay the seedlings from 2 to 6 inches apart in the trench—closer if you plan to pull them young and slender, farther if you plan to let them get big. The root end should be centered, and the rest of the little leeks should lie against a side wall. You may or may not have a bit of leaf sticking above ground. Water gently with vitamin B-1 solution.

But circumstances might make it preferable to dibble individual holes 6 inches deep 6 to 12 inches apart in the same good soil. Planting and blanching are as for trenches. Three weeks after transplanting, start blanching (see The Gardener's Notebook).

Although they are prey to the same demons as common onions, leeks seem to grow with less bother. Floating row covers will handle most problems, as will a no-nonsense spraying with the hose in the morning.

In theory, if early, midseason, and late leeks are sown together, you can pull sweet tender leeks for most of 10 months. However, which leeks are early, midseason, and late seems to change from catalog to catalog. Although the form of the leek—slender or broad—is in its genes, how fast it grows and to what degree are largely up to you and your weather.

Scallion-size leeks of some cultivars (Varna, for example) can be harvested in two months from sowing. They will be milder and more delicate than any green or bunching onions. Standard early leeks should be ready for their first harvest in late summer. True midseason leeks start in December, and very hardy late leeks are the rare vegetable you can pull from the ground from late January into April.

Your beauties can stay in the ground the year-round—until they start to bolt. Where summers are hot and humid, think leeks. They are more tolerant of such weather than most of the onion family.

Leeks fall into two categories: overwintering and nonoverwintering. But the temperature of the *soil* is how you choose, not the air. Hardy leeks can be tougher and stronger flavored than nonhardy leeks, so if you need them, read catalog descriptions carefully—and order from a seedsman in the North.

Leeks beneath the snow . . . If you'll be wintering leeks over and the air will get colder than 20°F, as the hard freezes approach, cover the plants with a foot-deep mulch of straw or a sackful of leaves or sawdust or a cloche for insulation—just be sure they can breathe. Now you can dig leeks easily. If your weather is so cold the ground would freeze even with this insulation, lift the leeks as late in autumn as you can, keeping their roots intact. Plant them on a 45° angle close together in a sheltered cold frame. Or plunge them into a bucket of moist sand and keep them in a dark place at 32°F and very high (90 percent) humidity. You should have leeks through most of the winter, and you can replant them, if you wish, to continue growing in spring. Just don't let the roots dry out.

Leeks are one allium that grows well on heavier soils. For example, in the maritime Northwest, leeks do beautifully on silty clay (generously amended, of course, with organic matter).

Although leeks can occupy a patch of ground for 10 months or a year, they are a worthy crop and considered good value for the space. If each person in your house ate 12 leeks a season, that would take only 3 square feet of your garden, the equivalent of about one staked tomato plant. Leeks do need constant moisture, though, and if water is at a premium where you live, you'd best reflect on how many you can manage.

Harvest a leek as soon as it's a size you want to eat. Lift it out gingerly with a very long weeding tool, since the fragile stems can snap.

After wintering over, around the middle of spring (or anytime after four to six weeks of cold weather) your leeks will likely send up a flower stalk. If you nip out the stalk and feed the plant, you'll gain time in which to harvest—except there will be a hard core in the leek you harvest, the stem of the flower. But if, after removing the plant's seed-making machine, you should leave the leek in place much longer, the leek may make an end run and produce small bulbs with cloves in them at the base of the plant. These are called, appropriately enough, *leek pearls.* When you finally do pull the leek (sometime in late spring), separate and plant these bulblets immediately, at the same level they were next to the leek—they'll be ready for the fall harvest. Once the leek starts procreating like this, it's no longer palatable.

Do let one or two of your leeks flower and go to seed. Most cultivars are open pollinated, so seeds will faithfully reproduce their parent. Not only are leek flowers beautiful as all allium flowers—plum-size poufs of various shades of rose composed of myriad tiny clusters of even tinier flowers—if you'll run your hand over them after the seeds have dried, in time you'll find tiny seedlings around the plants. You might want to collect the rest of the seeds on the stalk. As for the seedlings in the ground, cover them with leaves or straw to the depth of a few inches or a foot, depending on your winters. I've read that such seedlings have survived −24°F. In early spring, after the seedlings have begun to grow, move them to where you want them with the rest of your new leeks.

Sometimes after seeds have formed on the flower, conditions are such that among the seed clusters tiny bulblets—*bulbils*—sprout. Set them an inch or so apart on a shallow container of moist potting mix. Sprinkle with mix to barely cover the bulbs. Spritz with water. Grow as common onion seedlings. They should be ready to plant in the garden in a month or so.

For the thrifty among us, Mother Nature has provided a way of propagating two leeks from one. You can plant an inch of the bottom with its roots—the cut just above soil level—and have a new leek a couple of months later. You can do this with market leeks.

Recommended: All leeks are delectable. Generally speaking, the earlier the cultivar, the less hardy. Extra-early: Varna and French Summer (aka Kilima). Early: for flavor and quality, Otina. But for your first leeks, begin as I did, with King Richard. It is vigorous, tolerant, and delectable. And versatile; it can produce stems 12 inches long, and it's also excellent pulled at baby size. Midseason: Giant Musselburgh or Musselburgh Improved is a grand old hardy cultivar that can be harvested mid-season on, proving fat leeks are just as tasty as skinny ones. Autumn Mammoth/Argenta the same. Late/overwintering (particularly hardy): Scotland, an heirloom, overwinters wonderfully. The Danish cultivar Durabel is milder and tenderer than most and is also late to bolt. Alaska has dark blue-green leaves and long, thick, sweet stems. The leaves of ultra-hardy Blue Solaise turn a lovely violet in the cold. (It's said the hardier the leek, the bluer its leaves.) Broad London/Large American Flag is short and broad. Lyon Prizetaker has especially fine flavor—an English favorite. For disease resistance, Arcona.

POTATO AND MULTIPLIER ONIONS   *A. Cepa*, Aggregatum Group

Usually hardy perennials, probably native to Asia, but not known in the wild . . . aka ever-ready onions, nest onions. N.B. Once they are finished, never follow multipliers with radishes. There will be too much

*nitrogen in the soil from the onions, and the radishes will bolt. Culture
is the same as common onions.*

Once, potato onions were so prized in this country they were given as wedding presents. These large-spirited onions have declined because onions from seeds are faster and cheaper to produce and because seed onions grow bigger. Like rocambole garlic, these bulbs rarely produce seed. Instead they are increased by division, the plant creating several bulbs joined at their bases. In the border, you won't see gleaming bulbs, however, just a spray of tall green stalks. They grow and multiply underground, like potatoes. I combine potato onions with red romaine lettuces in the border. Thin blades of onions and ruffly rosy leaves, very pleasing.

Multiplier onions and potato onions are essentially the same. Pearl and boiling onion sizes—up to an inch across—have come to be called *multipliers* and larger onions *potatoes*. Multipliers are used principally as scallions, although when they reach pearl onion size they can be pickled. Where winters are mild, these onions keep sweet, turning pungent as the days get hot. Sometimes the snowy skins of white multipliers are tinged with rosy purple—from a distance, a cluster looks like a nosegay of baby roses. Some think white multipliers are the most delicious of all onions. I don't quite agree, but they are lovely. Yellow multipliers are so like shallots they're sometimes sold that way. Although multipliers will keep increasing their cluster, potato onions are far more valuable in terms of their return for the amount of space.

Potato onions are like the good child in the corner that everyone forgets is there because she makes no fuss. The flavor of potato onions is mild and sweet. Potato onions store better than most culinary onions grown from seed. They are bothered by fewer pests. Some are drought tolerant. Potato onions can handle temperatures below freezing in the ground when they are planted and mulched properly.

With a flattened globe shape, there are still heirloom yellow, red (pale pink flesh), and white potato onions available. I'd probably begin with yellow ones, because they're adapted to everywhere in the country except southern Texas and Florida (too hot). The red have finer flavor, however. And the white, though smaller, are finer still (Southern Exposure Seed Exchange's White Potato Onion especially). Occasionally one or another will form a cluster of tiny bulbs on the tips of stalks instead of flowers—use them for cooking.

These have fewer diseases than common onions, but because of either the onions' juiciness or their good flavor, voles can be a nuisance; see The Gardener's Notebook.

Once you have potato onions in hand, you never need buy them again. Prolific, they'll increase their weight at least threefold every year—as many as eight times. It's been said that, with the exception of staked tomatoes, potato onions produce the most abundant yield per square foot of any vegetable in the garden. One bulb set in the soil in the fall (the time for planting) will produce a cluster of scallions for cooking and slicing. A bulb the size of a small plum usually produces one or two bulbs the size of an orange. An orange-size bulb forms something like a dozen bulbs ranging from small to large plum size. Most potato onioners plant an assortment of sizes so they'll have a variety for eating, storing, and planting. By and large, these onions are as worthy as any but the fanciest common onion.

You can also grow potato onions in pots indoors in a sunny spot for onion greens in winter in the manner of shallots. Follow shallot directions.

To harvest multipliers as scallions, either cut leaves from the outside (up to ⅓ of the foliage) or pull the whole bunch. If you try to pry apart bulbs from a cluster, you'll make a tear, opening the rest to disease. Even though they are joined at the base, each of the cluster is wrapped in its own skin, and each has its own roots. Their country name *nesting onions* is apt, evoking the image of eggs heaped in a nest. Sometime in summer the greens die and turn brown, as we've seen with common onions, and they're ready to harvest, dry, and cure. In its turn, each of these onions has the buds of leafy shoots within it.

Although they're usually planted in autumn, 19th-century farmers with many mouths to feed planted them when setting out seedlings and sets of common onions. Spring-planted onions have less tendency to go to seed. But autumn-planted onions seem to outproduce spring-planted ones considerably. The only difference between curing these and common onions is that you dry and cure a cluster as a whole, then separate it for storing.

To plant bulblets and bulbils, harvest, separate, dry, and cure potato/multiplier onions exactly as you would cooking and slicing onions. You can leave the mother bulblets in the earth for several years, and then it's wise to divide them. From the end of July through October in cold climates, and from mid-October through December in mild climates, place them on top of the ground, as for sets. These are probably the hardiest of all onions, and their fresh greens are particularly welcome in bitter winter when few other onions are harvestable. In well-drained soil in a sheltered spot they can take hard freezes. Then in late winter or early spring, you'll have sweet onion greens to harvest.

Recommended: For heirloom multiplier and potato onions, those from Southern Exposure Seed Exchange and Kalmia Farm.

SHALLOTS

A. Cepa, Aggregatum Group

Usually hardy perennials, probably native to Asia, but not known in the wild. Culture is the same as for common onions.

Small—best between the size of a hazelnut and small walnut—shallots are the aristocrats of onions. They are usually mild and sweet, but sometimes they can be assertive, and sometimes they're touched with the warmth of garlic. What's more, shallots are beautiful. Skins are gold, brown, and rouge-red. The flesh can be rosy, pale yellow, or pure white.

Shallots, multiplier, and potato onions are essentially the same onion. The difference among them rests in a fine botanical point. In potato onions the whole group of leaves emerges from the throat of the bulb, sheathed as one. In shallots, each leaf is sheathed by itself. But unlike potato onions, shallots sometimes—rarely—flower.

Shallots are a cinch to grow. Day length is rarely a consideration, and they require no care past common onions, despite their great price at the market.

Gray shallots, called the *true shallot*, are reputed to be the standard culinary shallot, but they can become unpleasantly pungent. They must be planted in the fall, partly since they're likely to dry if stored through winter and partly because hot weather makes them taste fierce. This way bulbs can mature in cool weather. In the South, try growing Drittler White Nest Onion shallot—it will grow in Florida and southern Texas where cousins potato onions won't. And you can use shallots in place of potato onions, although they're much smaller.

In temperate climates you can plant any sort of shallot in autumn and soon have green shallots. Like green garlic, green shallots have extraordinary delicacy and warmth.

Shallot greens. In some cuisines shallots are valued principally for their green leaves, which are much more delicately flavored than scallion greens. Come autumn in the North, set half a dozen shallots upright in deep pots of light soil mix—allow about 6 inches between them and leave one fourth of the shallot perched above the soil. Water enough to keep the mix moist but not wet and set in a sunny spot indoors. All winter you can cut delectable greens that will come again.

Recommended: Prince de Bretagne, the cultivar from Brittany with lavender flesh and pure sweet shallot flavor, is the most elegant of all. Begin there.

ORACH. *See Potherbs.*

ORNAMENTAL CABBAGE AND KALE. *See Kale.*

PAK CHOI. *See Asian Greens.*

PARSNIPS *Pastinaca sativa*

Half-hardy biennial in the Parsley family, native to Eurasia . . . grows in deep 3-gallon containers. For fine sweet-spicy parsnips, sow fresh seeds in sunny, smooth, light, loose soil; give them constant moisture and patience. Manure added to the soil must be aged. For smooth, long roots, don't overfertilize. Because the roots can run deep, you must prepare the soil deeply. If yours is stony, use a crowbar to carve out holes about 18 inches deep and 3 to 4 inches wide. Fill these holes with nonrocky soil and sow the seeds on top. Seeds must be spanking fresh.

In this house we esteem the underappreciated parsnip. But in this garden we have tried to grow the long sweet creamy roots without success. In the process, I've discovered parsnips need lots of sunshine. I've come as far as having some leaves sent up. The delicate leaflets along the stalk are lovely, like a rabbit's foot sort of fern. If you can, place them next to violets.

In cold-winter climates, parsnips are sown in early spring, and they're most flavorful if allowed to grow and slumber under deep mulch until the following spring—that's one year! Where winters are mild, sow the seeds in summer and harvest through winter until spring. As with many other vegetables, cold turns them sweeter. But they must be harvested (just like carrots) before sprouting flowers; otherwise they'll be woody.

Recommended: Harris's Model, a model open-pollinated parsnip.

Peanuts   *Arachis hypogaea*

Tender annual in the Pea family, native to southern Brazil . . . aka goober, groundnut, grass nut, earth nut, monkey nut, pindar . . . grows in 5-gallon containers. Because they can tolerate light spring and fall frosts, you can grow peanuts as far north as Canada. Give them full sun. Warm light soil on the sandy side enriched with compost is ideal—not manure; it has too much nitrogen, and you'll get more leaves than peanuts. If you have clay soil, loosen it to friable with organic matter. Peanuts also like humid weather, so spritz the air with a fine spray from the hose now and then if yours is dry. Keep the patch weeded. Peanuts need at least 110 warm days to mature.

Spanish peanuts have the sprightliest taste, the plants are most compact, and they do best in cool climates. Children like larger, longer Virginias because they're mildest. The pods hold just two to three nuts but are easily shelled, and the plants are productive—50 to 60 pods per seed. Even larger and longer Valencias contain up to five nuts per shell with rich peanut flavor.

When the soil is warm and dry and you're ready to sow, shell the pods carefully, because you need to plant the whole peanut with its skin intact. Inoculate the seeds as described in The Gardener's Notebook. Shelled seeds germinate faster, but if you're all thumbs on planting day, just tuck the unshelled pod in the ground and don't worry.

When the plants are a foot or so tall, draw up the soil around them as you do for potatoes. This keeps them cozy.

After the yellow butterflies of flowers have been fertilized, they turn their faces toward the earth. They drop their petals and touch the tip of their flower stalk—called a *peg*, in peanutland—to the earth. Gravity pulls it voluptuously into the soil. In the dark beneath the earth a baby peanut—or two or three or four—soon appears. Above the ground the cloverlike leaves make a delicate bush, often a foot and a half high and even wider. Indeed you can place these plants around the front of the border. Mingle with a carpet of brightly colored rust-resistant Royal Carpet Mixed snapdragons.

Mulch the plants from the time they emerge to flowering time. Then, of course, you must pull back the mulch so the pegs can plant themselves. When that is done, gently return the mulch around the pegs. It will be about six more weeks before you can harvest your goobers.

If water is scarce, peanuts are fairly drought tolerant, and you can skimp until flower buds are forming. They'll need water then and just after the pegs have rooted. Water with a drip system or soaker hose so the soil won't crust. If it does, sprinkle a veil of grass clippings, sawdust, or spent straw over the ground to soften it.

Aphids are about all that bothers peanuts. Spray them off with the hose, but gently.

When the leaves turn yellow, wriggle your hand down carefully into the soil and find a peanut to see if it's mature—if it looks like a good old familiar peanut. If frost threatens and the pods aren't ready, protect the plants with a couple of layers of floating row covers, because usually there's a warm spell after the first frost, as you know.

To harvest, gingerly loosen the soil all around the plants with a digging fork, then pry up the whole plant—pods won't be more than 6 inches below the surface. Shake off the soil and lay plants bottoms-up so the pods will air-dry. Pods should cure for a couple of weeks on the plant, then for another week or so off the plant on a sheet. This may be done outdoors unless rain or humidity threatens.

If your season is short, warm the soil of the peanut patch with black plastic film as soon as you think of it in spring. A southern exposure is best. You can sow seeds in paper pots indoors a month before planning to set them outdoors—and that's not until the soil measures 60°F a couple of inches below the surface. Once the seeds or seedlings are in, keep everything sheltered with floating row covers until days are truly warm—the covers can stay in place the whole season if it's coolish, since peanuts are self-fertile.

Recommended: For Spanish, Pronto or Early Spanish. For Virginia, Jumbo. For Valencia, Tennessee Red is the one I grew and loved. Peanuts are easy.

$\mathcal{P}$eas

Pisum spp.

Dwarf peas grow in 5-gallon containers, tall peas in 20-gallon containers or a half-barrel with support. Just choose a sunny site with loose, humusy, well-drained soil (important) that you won't need for about three months. When supporting vines, the more sun and air around the plants, the better. And don't forget the inoculant (see The Gardener's Notebook). Always try to water your peas at soil level or, if with a hose, before noon on a sunny day. Water on cool leaves begs for mildew.

      I expect raccoons and their ilk have been feasting on peas as long as man, which has been since Neolithic times. Peas found in a cave near the Burmese-Thai border, peas of a size and sort that suggest they may have been cultivated, have been carbon-dated at nearly 10,000 B.C. The peas are what we consider "field" peas, small and coarse. Field peas would be the peas man ate for the next 11,600 years.

GARDEN PEAS   *Pisum sativum* var. *sativum*

Half-hardy annual, native to Eurasia . . . aka English pea, green pea, common pea.

In the 16th and 17th centuries gardeners and horticulturalists in both the New and the Old Worlds began to eat green peas fresh. Fresh peas are actually the immature seeds of the plant—properly called *berries.*

Pea flowers are self-pollinating—that is, they don't need wind or insects to carry pollen from one plant to another—so the work by those 16th-century breeders was done by selection, then hand-cross-fertilization. Because their climate is generally perfection for peas, the English took up the cause and have developed superb cultivars of garden peas.

With the appropriate cultivar, soil, weather, and defense against critters, growing peas is easy. But that's not the whole of it.

As productive as some cultivars are, it takes an awful lot of plants to provide more than a few meals' worth. How many? About 25 plants yield about 1 ¼ cups shelled peas—what I consider *one* fresh-peas-from-the-garden serving. Under optimum conditions, planted closely as possible in a band 4 inches wide beneath a trellis 6 feet tall, there could be 1,458 thriving pea vines. They would give about 58 generous servings. That's merely two weeks of peas each night for a family of four, and no seconds. By contrast 6 feet of staked tomato plants would have you scrambling for the canning jars.

As with corn, the sugar in peas begins converting to starch the moment they're plucked from the plant. That's why even peas at a farmers' market can't compare to the ones you've just brought in from the garden. So peas are a must, no matter what.

Selecting the best peas to grow for a foolproof crop is crucial and a bit more complicated than just picking those with the finest flavor. Since peas have a relatively low yield for space, one element is how many pods on the vine (some have double pods) and how many peas in the pod. This is not unlike corn: how many ears to a stalk and how many rows of kernels to an ear. Another factor to be considered is how easy the pods are to shell. As much as we adore petits pois, for instance, there's nobody within shouting distance of this garden with the time or patience to shell more than one meal of the teenies.

Sorting out pea seeds. Wrinkle-seeded: With few exceptions, deeply wrinkled seeds produce the sweetest and meatiest peas on the most prolific vines. Their abundance of sugar causes these peas to shrivel as they dry.

Round seeded: Either green or creamy white, when dried, these seeds (peas) stay smooth and round. They are the hardiest peas and fastest to mature. They are also the most tolerant of poor growing conditions. Round seeds are best for sowing when weather—too cold, too hot—is a factor. Containing less sugar, their flavor is inferior to wrinkled seeded peas. In catalogs, round seeded peas get comments like "a useful crop." That's like saying they're nice.

Early peas—52 to 62 days from sowing: Usually shorter vines that ripen peas in eight to nine weeks from sowing. The English classify peas as first early and second early, but the two groups come to fruition within a matter of days.

Main crop—after 62 days: The division between earlies and main crop seems arbitrary, but generally these peas are on taller vines and fruit at least a week or so later than earlies.

Bush (dwarf): The vines grow from 1 ¼ to 2 feet tall (sometimes a little more) and generally bear small pods that tend to mature more rapidly than larger ones. Often recommended for small gardens, in fact these waste pea-producing space, and unless you read that the pods are produced on top of the plant (a trait being developed increasingly), it's stoop labor to pick their peas. The fruit of most bush cultivars tends to mature all at once, which is good for commercial growers and for processing for the freezer, but not good for a long spell of lazy harvesting and eating.

Midsize (half-dwarf): The vines are from 22 inches to about 3 ½ feet tall. An ideal size for growing and picking if you don't have room for tall vines or interest in picking from a ladder. Actually, few seedsmen make this distinction—the shorter vines are included with dwarf peas, and the taller ones with tall peas.

Tall (trellis): Vines that grow 3 ½ to 6 or more feet tall. Of course they need more than pea sticks for support—a fence, a trellis, nylon netting, or rows of twine or wire stretched between posts. As with beans, there's always a moment at the end of the season when I realize that, before I can put away the netting, I have to pull out all the tiddly tendril bits. Supports of brown untreated twine (it comes in a giant roll and is very useful in the garden) can simply be rolled up with all the vines and added to the compost. Tall cultivars tend to take proportionately longer to mature and to bear over a longer period of time.

Semileafless (afila): There are only a few small leaves on these plants. Instead the vines are wreathed in tendrils. Growing 6 to 10 inches apart, the tendrils wrap around one another, and everybody holds everybody up while they grow 2 feet tall. With pea sticks or brush available, this attribute, one might think, is in the realm of a botanical gimmick and of no advantage. But it *is* an advantage where the climate is damp and peas easily mildew. The strong tendrils hold the plants off the ground, and circulation of air and light is superior. These plants also withstand strong winds, they're easy to cover against frost, and pods tend to grow at the top of the plant, so picking's comfortable. You can grow these semileafless plants as an intriguing low hedge, too. Disadvantages are that the pods tend to be smaller in this form, overall yield is not quite as abundant as from the standard vine, and they seem to have less resistance to stress. They're better for cool than hot climates. But how are they to eat? Young tendrils are delightful in a stir-fry, and although the flavor of our Novella peas was average, catalogs describe Novella II as tasting from very good to sweet. Remembering that strains of seeds vary from one source to another, it's possible. It took breeders 20 years to produce this form, and the hope now is to do the same for sugar snap peas.

Double podded: Usually the plants open the season with a crop of single pods; then, as the season advances, crops of double pods grow increasingly heavier. Double pods don't double the harvest—because of the strain on the plant—but they probably do increase it about one third. The trend in breeding these days is definitely in double pods. If you choose to grow one of these types, be prepared to give them all the water, sun, and nourishment they need to ensure they fulfill their potential.

Triple podded: Once there were Triplet petit pois and Trio garden peas with lots of triple pods, but the stress of producing so much fruit takes its toll, and the plants seem to fold prematurely. Gone.

Petit pois: Bred for tiny peas, these can have as many as 10 peas per pod. Generally they are delicate and sweet.

As for when to sow your seeds, the line in catalogs generally is "plant in early spring as soon as the soil can be worked." I never know what that means because there's the January thaw when suddenly the air is balmy and there's no trace of snow or frost. I've always yearned to sow peas then, but I know that February with the possibility of 10°F is coming. So "as soon as the soil can be worked" is misleading. Peas will germinate in soil as cold as 40°F, and pea seedlings are frost tolerant but not frostproof. The optimum temperature is 50°F. Should you plant on raised beds where the soil is warmer on top, that's a help. The thing not to do is plant peas in soil that's both cold and wet, because then they'll rot.

Six weeks before the last expected frost—or before you expect the weather to settle—is the wisest time to sow. But don't forget you can use floating row covers (one or two layers) to shelter young plants if you find you've rushed the season. One layer will shelter peas down to about 25°F. In the hot South and West, best sow peas in autumn.

To prepare for planting, if your soil is clay, either work in some sand or hoe up the soil to make a raised bed. Peas want phosphorus and potassium (potash), not so much nitrogen that they'll produce lush vines and no fruit, and a not-very-acid soil (don't grow peas near conifers or oaks, which will probably have a buildup of acidic soil around them). Over the soil, sprinkle veils of wood ashes (potash), bonemeal (phosphorus), and oystershell lime (if your soil has a pH of more than 6.5—see The Gardener's Notebook). Then spread an inch of lovely rich manure and/or compost on top and use a spade to dig and mix everything in. At planting time, moisten the seeds in a bowl of cool water, lift into another bowl, dust with fresh inoculant, and stir to blend so each seed is lightly coated. Sow very thickly.

Pea sticks. Unless they're the very short semileafless types, everybody in this family needs help standing straight. Even if the catalog says "needs no support," your peas will be happier if they have something to cling to. Pea vines sprawling on the ground are like everything else sprawling on the ground—a feast for slugs, snails, grasshoppers, and other hungry types and susceptible to disease due to little circulation of air. Pea sticks, each lurching in its own direction, give a delightfully loony air to the patch. Use any brush—slender shrub and tree trimmings—and set them close enough so every vine will find support.

Once peas are planted, it's very important not to compact the soil around the plants or to sog them with too much water. The roots need air, and without it your harvest can be reduced by half. That's why you mulch pea vines only when they're about half-grown and only if the soil doesn't stay moist. The vines produce best if the soil is on the dry side at the time of blossoming, so until they flower, give them just ½ inch of water a week. After that, just keep the soil moist.

If there are rabbits around, a sprinkling of agricultural lime on peas' leaves may repel them. To be certain, erect a buried fence. For quail or other nibbling ground birds, cover the seedlings from the instant they emerge with floating row covers sealed to the ground with boards *and* use a yellow balloon bird scare (see The Gardener's Notebook under Birds). If there are field mice, squirrels, and chipmunks, you *must* cage the peas with ½-inch chicken wire. Read about raccoons and deer in The Gardener's Notebook.

In temperate climates using the appropriate cultivars, you can harvest peas from some part of May through some part of September or even October. In warm climates you can have peas from fall to very early spring. The thing to do, if there's space, is to sow several cultivars with early to late maturing dates all at the same time, as you would corn.

The gardening establishment considers autumn peas inferior to those planted in spring. Since you can't taste them side by side and since they're garden-fresh peas after all, I smile and plant autumn peas, a rambunctious cultivar like Maestro. Soak the seeds overnight (not essential in spring because the soil is moist) and keep the earth cool with an airy mulch of straw or shredded newspaper or shade the bed with shadecloth from the nursery or an old umbrella thrust in the ground. See that the soil never dries out until the peas have sprouted. Should the air be hot, wave the hose at your vines in early morning or before noon at the latest for a refreshing shower.

Time and the caprices of climate . . . You'll probably do a double-take as I did at the Territorial Seed Company numbers for garden peas. Alderman is given as being ready to pick in 120 days—that's 78 days later than in Harris's catalog and 50 days later than Stokes's. In Oregon, Maestro is ready to pick in 110 days, and in Burpeeland, 61. Soil heat units (they are high for sand, low for clay) and your micro-climate determine days to maturity. So do *your* numbers accordingly.

As with other fruiting vines, your pea factories will shut down if you don't keep picking their fruit. Because the peas can grow past the *moment suprême* in a day or two—particularly with petits pois—if garden pea pods are bright green and shiny and if you can feel the peas bursting plump inside, pick them! Garden peas should spurt juice when you press them. Begin harvesting at the bottom of the plant and work up. Harvest petits pois just when the pods begin to swell. To prevent pulling up the whole vine with one pod (I've done it), hold the stem of the pod with one hand as you gently tug off the pod—or better yet, snip off the pod—with the other. Check the vines *daily*. If some pods get by you and turn leathery, just simmer them into pea soup, whiz them in the blender, pass them through a food mill, and they'll be lovely.

By all means, mix bush peas—blue-to-gray-green foliage, small white butter-flies of blossoms, translucent green dangles—into the border. With their pea sticks at rakish angles, their vine tips askew, such insouciance is a match for the scarlet-copper-gold of nasturtiums.

Most every garden pea of quality is a—by now—old-fashioned open-polli-nated cultivar. It's nice to know that if you're careful you can save some of your peas and grow them next year. And so on.

Garden peas, whether seeds are wrinkled or smooth, will not cross with any other members of the Pea family. Pea flowers are self-pollinating, but there's always our dear friend, the wind. For the purest strains, separate cultivars by 50 feet or cage or bag them; see The Gardener's Notebook.

Recommended: Except as noted, all cultivars listed here are wrinkle-seeded, and all have proven their worth for years. When you're browsing the catalogs, remember that ready-to-pick dates vary widely, depending on the source's climate.

Earlies: Maestro are sweet, disease resistant (nearly immune), long yielding, many berried, productive, half dwarf, and widely adapted. You might prefer to start with the remarkable Green Arrow/Green Shaft—flavorful, disease resistant, double podded, easy to pick, many berried, and a half dwarf. Knight is much like Green Arrow. Others with their admirers are Burpeeana Early and Daybreak. *Main crop peas:* Half-dwarf Lincoln is fabled for being flavorful, disease resistant, and long yielding. Multistar has multivirtues: good flavor, double pods, disease resistance, and productivity.

For *coastal areas:* Choose early peas and/or those resistant to downy mildew. *Double podded:* Olympia, Oregon Pioneer, Patriot. *Dry climates:* choose early peas and/or those resistant to powdery mildew. *Easy to shell:* Alderman/Tall Telephone, Thomas Laxton. *Flavor:* Oregon Pioneer, all the petit pois. *For freezing:* Stokes says commercial freezers prefer dark green peas such as Daybreak, Olympia, Oregon Trail Pea, the Novella type, and Triplet. Johnny's recommends Bounty and Daybreak; Harris recommends Frosty. *Heat tolerant:* Wando. *Petit pois:* Argona, Giroy, Petit Provencal, Precovelle, and Waverex. *Productive:* dwarf Progress No. 9/Laxton's. *Round seeded:* Douce Provence doesn't have the highest yield of all such cultivars, but it may have the sweetest flavor. For heavy crops, try old reliable Feltham First. *Semileafless (afila):* The Novella series and Curly, an improved Novella. *For successive sowings:* Kelvedon Wonder is an English favorite all-around pea for sowing first thing and then straight through the season.

Perhaps because they grow in misty weather—or, as a second crop, in the stress of hot weather—peas are more susceptible to coming down with something than their cousins the beans, which grow in the warmth of the sun. If this will be your first time with peas, or if you've had bad luck with them, ask your county agricultural or extension adviser if you have disease in your neighborhood and, if so, which. Then plant the appropriate disease-resistant peas. *Bean yellow mosaic virus:* Knight, Maestro. *Common wilt:* Alderman, Argona (petit pois), Knight, Maestro, Progress No. 9, *Downy mildew:* Green Arrow, Lincoln. *Fusarium wilt:* Green Arrow, Lincoln, Petit Pois Giroy. *Leaf curl virus:* Green Arrow. *Pea enation virus:* Knight, Maestro, Oregon Pioneer. *Pea and bean mosaics:* Olympia. *Powdery mildew:* Knight, Maestro, Olympia. *Top yellows:* Petit Pois Giroy.

SNAP PEAS/SUGAR SNAPS
P. sativum var. *macrocarpon*

Half-hardy annuals.

Of course it's rare in a gardener's lifetime that a new vegetable is created. Sugar snap peas, the plushy eat-'em-all-up peas in the pod—born in 1979 of a plant of rogue peas—are not true inventions but rather a ravishing refinement of snow peas. The difference between snow peas and sugar snaps is that the peas in snow pods are nubbins and the pods themselves are thin (technically they lack parchment), while sugar snap peas in the pod are fully developed and the pods are thick and succulent. Sugar snaps, besides being delectable, are twice the vegetable, twice the harvest, of garden peas.

Although sugar snaps can yield well in both hot and cold weather—we had lovely pods in withering July—all is not pig heaven with these peas. Vines grow at least 6 feet tall, which makes picking a stretch, and they lack resistance to disease. And, as sweet as they are, the pods have snow peas' inedible strings.

Sugar snap peas grow sweetest, surprisingly, with a little heat. You're told to pick the pods when they are fully round—taken too soon, and their sugars won't have developed completely. But if you pick them three-quarters filled, they'll be less starchy. Rush them to the salad bowl or pot.

Now that the dust has settled, some pea aficionados have given up growing sugar snap peas and returned to their garden pea favorites. The time may come, but so far the sugar snaps, as delicious as they are, haven't the intense sweet pea flavor of the old-fashioned Lincolns. I give my pea patch over to garden peas because I think them incomparable for flavor. On the other hand, sugar snaps don't need shelling.

Recommended: Double-podded Super Sugar Mel is presently the first choice for ease and flavor; it also has some heat and disease resistance. Where hot weather comes all too swiftly, Sugar Ann, an AAS winner, matures two weeks earlier than sugar snap, and it's almost as sweet. If you hate stringing peas, try Sugar Daddy. It has no strings, but its flavor is not up to the others, and the soil must be warm before it is sowed. Both Sugar Ann and Sugar Daddy grow on dwarf vines.

SNOW PEAS
P. sativum var. *macrocarpon*

Half-hardy annuals . . . aka edible-podded peas, sugar peas, Chinese peas, mangetout.

Legumes and the Soil

When you grow peas, you're doing more than your soul and belly good. Your soil will profit. All legumes gather nitrogen from the air and fix it in nodules on their roots, which release it into the soil. When the last pea or peanut or bean has been popped into your mouth, chop up the vines with a hoe and turn them into the soil for fine green manure before you plant a summer or autumn crop. Then in fall, toss some unfinished compost into next year's pea bed.

These vines are not cultivated for their peas but for their edible pods. Snow pea pods are harvested while the peas are tiny. Should you be distracted and that stage get by you, the pods will be tough—you can shell the peas, but they won't be very sweet. These are a mainstay of Asian cuisine, so I buy these seeds from an Asian seedsman.

Recommended: Little Sweetie is the rare snow pea that's stringless. It's early, dwarf, and tolerant of July heat and most pea diseases. Oregon Giant is early and disease resistant, and its pods are thicker, its peas larger and noticeably sugared. There are other tasty and productive snow peas, but these two offer a clear choice between stringlessness and sweetness.

SNOW PEA SHOOTS   *P. sativum* var. *macrocarpon*

Aka pea tendrils.

In China, there are cultivars of peas grown specifically for their leafy shoots, never mind the peas. If you grow your own, they'll be even more delicious than the ones in Asian markets because you can pick them much smaller, 3 to 5 inches long. The pods, vines, tendrils, leaves, and any flowers attached are all edible and have a sweet crunchy pea flavor. But try not to permit flowers—they'll toughen the vines. Where you've picked, two shoots will grow.

You can sow a pea shoot cultivar or simply pick the tender tips of any young pea vines—particularly those of the semileafless sorts or a dwarf edible podded pea such as Little Sweetie. They'll continue to grow, and you can take a second crop or even a third if they're vigorous and it's not too hot. Finally, they'll be tough.

The very young shoots wilt rapidly. The bigger guys at the market are three times the size of the pea shoots you'll harvest, and that's why they hold up. Pick yours just before eating.

SOUP PEAS/PEAS FOR DRYING
P. sativum var. *sativum*

Sow as early as you can so there will be time for the seeds to dry in the pods.

Until you've held the iridescent, smoky cocoa-mauve pods of Raisin Capucijners in your hand, you haven't fulfilled your pea-growing potential. I can't remember where I first heard of them, but I've grown them a couple of times, and they're heaven. Just the color of the pods dangling amid their green leaves is pleasure enough, but the dried brownish peas are large and delicious. The 2-foot vines are short enough so they can find places to duck their heads inside a wire-covered cold frame—what I've had to do to get peas past the critters this year.

There is also Blue Pod Capucijners—smoky blue pods with gray peas. And Round Green, for green pea soup.

These are round peas, remember, very tolerant to early plantings. And not sweet; they're for soup. Let the pods stay on the vines until they're crackly dry, but catch them before they twist open.

Peppers

Capsicum spp.

Tender perennials in the Nightshade family, native to tropical America . . . grows in 3- to 5-gallon containers. Peppers are demanding. They want a sheltered spot of nourishing soil drenched with light, days in the 70s and 80s, nights in the mid-60s and low 70s, and ample water to create well-developed root systems. If traditional cultivars don't get

*this, they'll drop their blossoms and won't form new ones until the tem-
peratures again are perfect. But new cultivars have been bred to handle
un-pepper weather. Once you've chosen peppers that will thrive under
your circumstances, all you have to do is grow the strongest, leafiest
plants you can.*

SWEET AND CHILI   *Capsicum annuum* var. *annuum*

Bell, cherry, squash, bull horn, banana, globe, top, snub nose, pendant, blocky, lobed . . . ivory, lemon, butter, gold, lime, dark green, chocolate, orange, tangerine, brick-red, crimson, lavender, purple-black . . . thin walled, thick walled, waxy, smooth . . . sweet, bitter, nonbitter, mild, hot, very hot, fiery . . .

One of his companions described eight combinations of white, violet, and yellow in the skins and flesh of peppers Columbus carried from the New World back to the Old—"pepper more pungent than that from Caucasus." They were peppers grown for generations by Olmecs, Toltecs, and Aztecs.

In the garden, peppers are one of the first plants you can think about putting up in the front of the border. Whether 12 or 48 inches tall, the plants stand erect, the white stars of blossoms (up to an inch across) against pert, glossy green leaves are lovely, and the fruits are as ornamental as anything on a Christmas tree. Basils of all sorts are engaging companions.

Which peppers should you grow? The question is which peppers *will* grow in your neck of the woods.

Where it's too cool all summer, try Gypsy hybrid. Where peppers might not grow, try Gypsy hybrid. It was my first successful pepper, grown in seaside Malibu. Green-gold Gypsy combines earliness with fine flavor and fruitfulness. If there's time, it will ripen to orange-red. Gypsy is a thin-walled tapered sweet pepper. For smallish glossy green-to-red sweet peppers, the best early cool-weather-tolerant cultivar is Ace Hybrid.

If you live in a marginal climate, give peppers the sunniest spot in your garden—next to the eggplants—and warm the soil with black paper or plastic mulch. Shelter seedlings through iffy weather with floating row covers or cloches. Remove the mulch when the days warm up and replace it in a couple of weeks with organic mulch such as grass clippings or straw.

Where it's very hot, you can grow most any cultivar, but pick those whose leaves protect fruits from the scalding sun. Lacking the filtered light of trees, inter-crop peppers with tall tomatoes. Or drape 30 to 40 percent shadecloth over the plants once fruit starts to develop, then remove it toward the end of the season as the sun's rays ease. Sprinkling the plants with cold water in the heat of the day also helps prevent the plant from peevishly dropping its blossoms.

Peppers are grouped according to shape: cherry (to 1 inch, yellow or purplish, ornamental, not the spicy cherry peppers), cone (conical—to 2 inches long, also ornamental), cluster (to 3 inches long and very pungent), bell (our dear sweet friends), capsicum (mostly elongated, to 12 inches—the condiment peppers, from cayenne to New Mexico).

In both cool and hot climates, small peppers and chili peppers are easier to grow than those that are large and sweet. That's because in general smaller-fruited peppers tend to be earlier, more vigorous, and better yielding than large types. In my short-season mountain garden, the only sweet pepper I can get to ripen is Gypsy, but I've had sensational luck with brilliant shows of small Auroras, Sweet Pickles, and incandescent tiny Thai chili peppers. My hot Auroras and Sweet Pickles turned from yellow to purple to orange to red—in no time there were all these colors on the bush at once because each pepper was at a different stage.

Part of what makes small-fruited cultivars easiest is their greater heat tolerance. In fact chilies need more heat to crop well than sweets—the more heat goes into them, the more comes out. That means your jalapeños in Seattle won't have the fire-power of jalapeños in Taos. My hot peppers have been plenty hot. Still, in the North, grow Early Jalapeño for maximum flavor. And bear in mind that with so many seeds out there passing through so many hands, one strain of Serrano can be wimpy while another numbs your head.

In humid climates it's wise to separate chili from sweet pepper plants. Wild chilies are more susceptible to disease than cultivated plants, and some of your most interesting chili seeds may have been collected in the wild.

If I lived in chili country—six to seven smothering hot months—I'd grow chilies from all over the world I can't buy: San Juan Tsilé, long, hot, flavorful chilies propagated by elders of a New Mexican pueblo . . . Ají Rojo, said to be an Incan favorite, long, narrow, and very hot . . . Aci Sivri from Turkey, another long narrow pepper that can be mild or fiery hot. Each summer in my patch I'd grow more of the earthy chilies that make Native American, southwestern, Mexican, Italian, Spanish, Caribbean, African, and Asian dishes hum. If you live in chili country, the seedsmen listed under Chili Peppers in Sources offer you this world.

Then from among peppers that you know will grow in your garden you can select the best tasting. On the whole, when ripe, smaller cultivars are considered more intensely flavored, sweeter, and juicier than large ones, but there are very sweet, very large juicy peppers such as Vidi, a Lamuyo type. (Lamuyo is a European type of sweet pepper, large, and almost twice as long as it is wide.) Sweetness enters the pepper only after it has matured—without exception the best-tasting peppers are ripe ones. Europeans are bewildered by Americans' settling for sharp and bitter green peppers when we could be enjoying rich, ripe, red or gold sweet ones. Stokes Seeds's John Gale, a man preoccupied with peppers, is fond of saying that eating a pepper green is like eating an unripe apple. Final ripe colors of sweet peppers are gold, orange, red, and chocolate brown. The deeper the color, the richer the flavor and store of vitamins A and C.

Speaking of colors, no vegetable offers such a glorious palette. But the days-to-maturity listed in catalogs are days from setting the plants out to picking the peppers *green*—mature they are not. Add four to six weeks more for ripening before there might be color.

Then which color would you like? Red? Since most of the world's peppers finish red, all you need do is look for an appealing cultivar. Lipstick is early and luscious. Ace is considered the most reliable for rouging up. Orange? Ariane, a sweet, blocky bell developed in Holland to honor the royal House of Orange, is a royal treat. Gold? Quadrato Asti Giallo is a huge, blocky Italian bell with a touch of spice in its sweetness. (Since golden peppers tend to be softer when ripe, harvest them just as they turn their final color.) Purple or lavender? These peppers are on their way to ripening red, so the purple/lavender phase lasts only a few days, and the flavor is unripe green. Lorelei is a stocky bell the color of eggplant—its green flesh beneath the skin makes it dark. But in the newer lavender peppers, flesh is cream or pale yellow, so the dark skin glows from beneath, making it lavender. Islander begins violet, then turns yellow, then is streaked with orange, then becomes rich dark red. To harvest at the purple/lavender stages, wait until these peppers start to deepen in color; otherwise they can be bitter. Chocolate peppers? They can be exceedingly sweet. The bell Sweet Chocolate is the favorite—it ripens from dark green to deep mahogany. Eat these raw or cook them very quickly (e.g., stir-fry) to keep the skins rich brown; otherwise they'll turn green. Black? Blackbird, a purple and brown cross, changes from green to brown to purply-black to deep red. It, too, tastes green. Ivory? As with orange, white/cream/ivory is a rare color in peppers, but unlike orange, it's transitional. The cultivars Dove and Ivory Charm practically start waxy white, changing very little until they end pale yellow-gold. Decorative, but they still taste like a mild *green* pepper.

And what will you do with your peppers? For stuffing, slicing raw into salads, chopping into sauces and soups, and preserving in oil, the thick walls and crunchy

Ristras

From New Mexico comes the custom of stringing up long red chilies to dry in the sun. Actually, you can do this with any peppers that have thin walls—those with thicker flesh can spoil before they dry.

Thread a stout needle with cotton string and pass it through the stems or through the top of the peppers. If your air is anything but bone dry, leave an inch between the peppers for good circulation. If it's easier, you can instead tie each stem along the string. Hang in the sun to dry. If your air is at all moist, best hang them indoors. Once rattle-dry, the chilies will keep their quality longest in a dry, dark, airy place.

flesh of bells are best. Then there are long, tapered, thin-walled Italian frying peppers, sometimes mild, sometimes hot. They're comparatively flat so they fit comfortably into a skillet, and their thin walls soften quickly in oil. Long, fire-engine-red New Mexico chilies are traditional for drying and threading on stout string in bunches or festoons called *ristras* in Santa Fe.

At the other end of the scale, under-an-inch cherry peppers are delightful in a basket with drinks or as pop-in-the-mouth pickles—cherries come both mild and hot.

If you find a pepper you like, set a few of them in a window until they dry to brittle red, store their seeds in the freezer, and sow them as usual in spring. Never hesitate to try growing seeds from peppers you've liked. Even though they may be hybrids and their seeds won't grow true, they'll be interesting.

In choosing a cultivar, look for words like "provides good fruit coverage. . . ." That means lots of leaves. The fuller the canopy of leaves, the finer the fruits.

Germinate the seeds indoors no matter where you live—they need a steady 80°F. Set in 2- to 3-inch pots. For maximum harvest, give seedlings warm days and nights. Do *not* harden them off, but wait till the night air is consistently 65°F; the air temperature is more critical than the soil temperature.

If you harvest all the first fruits from your plants in August, you'll considerably increase future yields.

To harvest, cut peppers with a bit of stem attached, rather than twisting or pulling them from the plant.

Having succeeded with your first season of peppers, venture forth. Next year, grow your own paprika peppers and grind your own spice come autumn. Dry them as *ristras,* then grind with the skin, adding about 10 percent of its volume in seeds. And grow pimiento peppers for marinating and having in the refrigerator all winter.

As perennials, peppers are relatively long lived. If your winters are cold but you have a sheltering place with bright light and good circulation of air that won't get colder than, say, 30°F, carefully dig up your favorite pepper plants, set each in a suitably sized container, and bring them in. When the soil is toasty in spring, transplant them back in the garden, to a new place. Or let them stay in a container, repotting as roots fill the pot.

Recommended: For sweet peppers, start with hybrid Gypsy in warm gardens or Super Sweet Banana in cool ones. For chilies: the adaptable and unusual manzano or the incomparable habanero. For resistance to tobacco mosaic virus: Gypsy hybrid. For sweet bells: early hybrids Bell Star and Lady Bell, quick-to-redden hybrid La Bamba, open-pollinated Purple Beauty, Golden Summer hybrid, lavender hybrid Islander, open-pollinated orange Corona, Chocolate Belle hybrid. For preserving: open-pollinated Pimiento L. For chili peppers: Fresno Chili Grande, Santa Fe Grande, and Tam Jalapeño No. 1. Italian frying type Espana hybrid and deep bell-shaped Redwing have resistance to potato virus Y, tobacco etch virus, and the tobacco mosaic virus.

Heat-Tolerant Plants and Cultivars

Many fruiting plants won't set fruits in great heat, so what to grow if you live where daytime temperatures in summer are routinely in the 80s and 90s? There are many possibilities—here are a few for starters. In addition, many are drought tolerant (D).

AMARANTH, LEAFY
BEANS, DRY: Aztec Dwarf White (D)
BEANS, LIMA: Florida Butter, Sieva, Willow-leaf White (D)
BEANS, SNAP: Romano, Genuine Cornfield, McCaslan (all D)
BEANS, SOUTHERN PEA: Mississippi Silver (D)
CORN: Breeder's Choice, Hopi Blue (both D)
CUCUMBERS: Poinsett, Salad Bush, Marketmore 86 (D)
EGGPLANT: Thai Long Green
LETTUCE: Little Gem (D), Kagran Summer
MELONS: Ambrosia, Planter's Jumbo
NEW ZEALAND SPINACH (D)
OKRA: Lee, Annie Oakley II, Cowhorn, Green Velvet, Emerald
ONIONS: Papago
PARSLEY: Decora
PEAS, FOR DRYING: Mexican Soup Peas
PEAS FRESH: Wando
PEPPERS, SWEET: Cubanelle, Gypsy, Gator Belle, Sweet Banana
PEPPERS CHILI: Thai (all D)
RADISH: White Icicle
SPINACH: Bloomsdale Long Standing
SQUASH, WINTER: Upper Ground Sweet Potato, Arikara, Waltham Butternut, Santo Domingo (all D)
SWEET POTATO: Beauregard, Sumor, Vardaman
TOMATO: Better Boy, Heatwave, Kootenai (D), Solar Set

POTATOES
Solanum tuberosum

Half-hardy annual tubers in the Nightshade family, probably native to the Andes . . . aka white potato, Irish potato . . . grows in half-barrels or big planting bags. Potatoes do best in the North. In the South, where they're called Irish *potatoes, the heat, drought, disease, and insects that come with an intensely hot summer make growing potatoes impossible. That's why sweet potatoes are a favorite—they gobble up the heat. Instead, Irish potatoes are planted from the middle of January to March for a late spring harvest, and then again they're tucked in the ground in August to harvest in late fall. Potatoes need sun and water.*

High in the Andes, the corn that sustained life closer to sea level didn't grow because the air was too thin. But hundreds of sorts of potatoes of all different colors and shapes had grown wild in that air for millennia. Potatoes were venerated. The Incan unit of time was as long as it took to cook a potato. And until *conquistadores* carried potatoes back with them to Spain, the tubers were a secret from the world. Myths surrounding the tubers gathered until in the 18th century Europeans imagined eating potatoes would "increase seed and provoke lust, causing fruitfulness in both sexes."

Lust aside, potato plants give pleasure to the eye. Knee high, the branches with their dark leaves have a graceful arching habit, and blossoms are quarter-size yellow-centered stars. For the most part, if the potatoes are violet, the flowers are violet and the leaves have a violet cast. If the flesh is blue, the flowers and leaves are bluish, too, which is helpful in identifying potatoes in a mixed patch. For all but the last couple of weeks of their lives (the time when the potatoes are ready to be harvested), the plants are lush and decorative. I tuck nasturtiums in front of them, and the vines mingle marvelously.

Most books tell you potatoes are not a crop for small plots, adding patronizingly that you can get perfectly good potatoes in the store. But four plants in less than 4 square feet will produce an abundance of small potatoes harvested "new"—the skin so thin it can be rubbed off with a fingertip. Simply because you *can't* get a variety of fine-flavored potatoes at the market do I feel that, second only to tomatoes, potatoes are an obligatory kitchen garden crop.

Most books also tell you not to plant potatoes from the market. But should you find an appealing variety there, take it home. I once bought tiny rose-gold potatoes in New York in October, stored them in a brown bag in the butter keeper of our refrigerator till May, then planted them. Every one grew. What's the worst that can happen? One year I lost the use of 6 square feet of garden for a few weeks because walnut-size red potatoes from the market *didn't* sprout. But I would be remiss if I didn't tell you that a market potato might also carry scab or another disease. You have to decide whether it's worth the risk.

In choosing potatoes to plant, think about how you'll cook them. Often catalogs will describe the flesh, often they won't. Waxy potatoes (relatively high in moisture and low in starch) are best when a potato must hold its shape, as in salads, gratins, sautés, and chips. Fluffy potatoes (low in moisture and high in starch) are best when you want a dry light potato for mashing, baking, soup, and deep frying. If the potato in your hand is unknown, cut off a piece, fit it back in place, then turn it upside down and lift. If the pieces stick, the potato is starchy, but if a piece falls, it's not. New potatoes have less starch than those that have been stored, and you can count on a russet to be starchy.

What about color? All Blue, besides being a medium-size potato that's thoroughly blue and delicious, is a vigorous cultivar, one of the best I've grown. For fingerlings, try Purple Peruvian; although it's rather mealy, it's drenched in purple and keeps and keeps. Round Blue Andean has dark blue skin, creamy yellow flesh with a purply ring around the edge. Other blues and purples are splashed with stars and stripes.

Blossom has red skin, red flesh. All Red has bright red skin and rose-pink flesh. Viking Purple has purple skin splotched with bright pink. Alaska Sweetheart is red on the outside and pink on the inside and tasty. Red Gold has light red skin and butter yellow flesh.

When choosing potatoes, always remember their origins, the high cool Andes. If you live in an area of intense summer heat, choose early (quick-to-mature) cultivars and grow them in the freshness of spring. Summer heat or no, early potatoes grown in spring and early summer are less bothered by disease and produce higher yields than late cultivars grown under the stress of warm weather. If well mulched and protected with a floating row cover, young potato sprouts can survive light frost—and even if they're shot down, more will appear. If late potatoes are a must, choose the most disease-resistant strains available, give optimum care, and don't be disappointed if yields are puny. In cloudy climates, clear plastic is beneficial for pre-warming the soil. Remove the plastic when the potatoes go in.

If there's room and time and fair weather ahead, why not grow early, midseason, and late potatoes all at once?

With potatoes, the tuber itself is usually the seed (although true seeds born of the bush's applelike fruits—don't eat these, they're toxic—are more and more used in propagation). The healthiest potato, then, has the potential for making the best vine. Certified disease-free seed potatoes from a reputable nursery are the safest to plant. Although choices are skimpy compared to the hundreds available from the Seed Savers Exchange, it's risky planting potatoes from an unknown bed, because they might bear disease.

When the potatoes arrive, write its name on each in indelible ink. You'd be surprised how easy it is to confuse them between arrival and planting time. Then sprout the potatoes—that is, you want to produce the translucent shoots that are so annoying when they appear on potatoes in the larder.

Sprouting potatoes. You can set unpeeled potatoes just as they look on your plate into the earth, and they'll grow. But to become a plant, they must first make sprouts. If you help them to do this indoors, a process called *chitting,* you'll be way ahead in having a crop. And this way you can see which potatoes are viable and which may not be, so you won't waste space.

Often potatoes in storage will sprout without any help, especially when you don't want them to. Those eager beavers are the guys to plant.

Along about the turn of the year, place the tubers in something airy like a basket, the ends with the most eyes (tiny dents that are dormant buds) facing up. Keep them in a light place at 40–60°F for about six weeks. Sprouts should be sturdy and at least an inch or so long. Discard unsprouted tubers and any that are soft.

Tubers the size of eggs or smaller should be planted whole. Whole potatoes produce the most generous crops. You want no more than three sprouts per potato, so snap extras off. If you have larger potatoes but not many of them, you can use a clean sharp knife to cut them into pieces, each containing two or three eyes, with plenty of flesh around the eyes and no blemishes. A one-eyed potato will make a plant, but it will take considerably longer. Each piece should weigh at least 2 ounces. Let the cuts dry for at least a day (some dust the cuts with sulfur to inhibit disease, but I don't), then plant.

I should assure you right now that, unless you live in an area plagued by insects, rain, or alkaline soil or where potato diseases are endemic (your county agricultural adviser will tell you), potatoes are an easy crop to raise well. If you really can't grow potatoes, try white sweet potatoes instead. To grow great potatoes, I've found there are just a few essentials.

Plant potatoes where no member of the Nightshade family has grown for three or four years. That's how you'll avoid soil-borne disease. If, in the past, other nightshades have had problems in your garden, grow them as far from your potatoes as you can. Raspberries, too. The only time that any of my potatoes have ever taken sick was the year they were next to the raspberries. It may have been coincidence, but some think there's an element in the thorny plants that lowers potatoes' resistance to blight.

As for the soil, Lynn Ronniger of Ronniger's Seed Potatoes surprised me when she said potatoes, being light feeders, grow well in average soil—my books say it must be rich. The best soil, she says, is old pasture, where sod has been dug in and decomposed. The Ronnigers grow cover crops to get the same effect. Lynn also surprised me on the subject of adding manure to the soil where potatoes will be grown. Apparently no matter how well aged, manure can cause scab on the potatoes. Scab is a disfiguring fungus that can linger in the soil for years. Happily, it affects only the outside—the potato's flesh is safe to eat. Lynn said they've had reports from many customers who have had the same experience. I wonder whether this might be a concomitant of particular soils. I've always added manure to my potato soil, and I've never had scab.

Make sure the soil fits the potato's need for acid—acidity in the soil helps prevent scab. The pH should be between 5 and 6.8.

To plant, with a small spade or hoe, dig a trench 3 inches wide and 5 inches deep if you're going to use comfrey leaves, 3 inches if not. In heavier soils, dig an inch or so shallower. If you have some, line the furrow with comfrey leaves. Comfrey plants will be in full leaf at potato-planting time. The leaves help potatoes resist disease. With the hoe, loosen the soil on the bottom of the trench, chopping in the leaves if you've added them. Add an inch of soil, so the potatoes don't come in contact with the leaves. (When I asked Lynn Ronniger whether they'd ever used comfrey leaves with their potatoes, she said no but added that the leaves should really be composted. Lynn said that anything that's decomposing next to the tubers while they're forming can cause scab. Since it wouldn't be practical to compost the leaves separately, I cover them with soil so the potatoes won't come in contact with the fresh decomposing matter.)

Set in the potatoes, sprouts up, cut sides down, directly on the soil. Cover with a few inches of half earth and half compost. Now lightly pile on 10 to 12 inches of straw or straw mixed with old leaves. The covering must be airy but complete, since potatoes turn green in the presence of light, and that makes them mildly toxic.

As the sprouts emerge and turn into vines, keep piling on more of this mulch around (not on top of) the vines to maintain this 10 to 12 inches. Called *hilling up*, this mulch conserves water and enriches the soil when it's dug in after harvest.

Now provide the required water. Last summer, a drought year, our potatoes were given every one of the other necessities except water. There were shockingly few tubers, and those there were didn't grow beyond cherry tomato size. A hard lesson. When you do water, try not to water potato plants overhead. If humidity is high, the leaves can mildew.

Pull all weeds or smother them with mulch. But that's true of growing most every plant in the garden.

Most every year one of the gardening magazines has an article about raising potatoes in a wire tower or tire or barrel or pure straw. I tried straw. Theoretical advantages are that you don't have to dig a trench (you can either lay the potatoes directly on the ground and the straw deeply over them or lay a deep bed of straw over cement, for that matter, and the potatoes on the straw with more over them), weeds can't grow through the straw, water is conserved, when the crop is ready you just pull back the straw and pick from a nest of potatoes, and at season's end the straw adds humus to the soil (given soil beneath). The only part that worked was the conserving water part, and the only folks happy with the potatoes were the field mice. The experiment convinced me more than ever that you can't beat beautiful dirt.

Anytime after the plant blossoms, you can dig walnut-size potatoes. However, not all potatoes produce flowers. If, by the end of August, there are none, you can work your hand down to see what you've got below ground.

When the vines do sag and the leaves turn brown, their potatoes have matured. If you can, leave the tubers in the ground two to six weeks longer and do not water. The skins will toughen, and the tubers will last longer in storage. This long underground storage period is why I either distract the eye from the drying vines with flowers or set only plants whose potatoes I want to eat tiny in a prominent position in the garden—I can whisk the plants away before they brown.

There is food for the senses in digging potatoes. I use my hands to bring up the tubers, because when I dig with a fork I invariably spear some (I cut those up and cook them right away). Best time to harvest potatoes is in the morning, when the tubers are cool. You kneel or sit in the earth and slip your hand into the soil beneath the bush. Push your hand along, pressing, pulling, fondling, feeling, cajoling the earth, the tangle of roots, to reward you with its round or fingerling or crescent or oval fruits. When you find one potato, there will be more, of varying sizes. Then you ease the fruit from the threads tying it to the plant and pull the potato up out of the ground. It smells wonderful. I close my eyes when I'm digging potatoes.

At summer's end, to avoid anything you don't want overwintering in the soil, harvest all the potatoes. To keep them, lay the freshly dug potatoes—the earth brushed off them—in a single layer in a dark place at around 70°F for a week to heal any tears in the skin, then store in a cool, dark place with good circulation of air. Meanwhile, turn as much of the mulch into the soil as you can.

While you're at it, you can dig one wheelbarrowful of any sort of old or new manure into every 25 square feet of next year's potato bed. And chop in comfrey leaves. Then sow it to winter rye. In spring, a month or so before planting, turn over the green manure, and boy, will you have potatoes!

Recommended: For flavor and texture, the buttery richness and silkiness of yellow-fleshed potatoes. Some of the favorites you can't buy but can grow are Mrs. Moehrle's Yellow Fleshed (small to medium, my favorite), Lady Finger (yellow skinned and almost as thin as a finger), Bintje (yellowish skin, a widely grown yellow potato), Kroop Nebber (Swedish, small crescent shaped), Desirée (rosy skin, said to be Europe's favorite red potato), and last summer's discovery, Cherries Jubilee (bright pink skin and pink creamy flesh). In France, Ratte fingerlings are considered finest of all. Ronniger's sells them as La Rote or Larota.

For disease resistance, white early baker Norgold Russet, mealy midseason Bake King, late russet Butte, late yellow-fleshed Carola.

For the South, needing heat tolerance, stick to the early and midseason potatoes such as early white-fleshed Anoka, midseason Red LaSoda, a good keeper, and midseason all-purpose Kennebec.

For dry soils and heat, early baking Norgold M.

For good keeping, early Bison ("simply the best all-around white-fleshed red potato ever developed" says Ronniger's), midseason Yellow Finn, and late Blue Victor (white flesh).

Any potato you've grown yourself will be delicious beyond description.

POTATO AND MULTIPLIER ONIONS.   *See Onions.*

Potherbs

Grows in 2- to 3-gallon containers.

My old *Larousse Gastronomique* tells me that for potherbs—*herbes potagères*—greens used in the preparation of broths and soups, the French regard only these six as classic: chard, lettuce, orach, purslane, sorrel, and spinach. My new

Larousse adds that these greens are also served as vegetables on their own, mixed into salads, and arranged as garnish.

But what, precisely, is a potherb? Dictionaries advise that it is an herb that's boiled in a pot and eaten. And what is an herb? The botanical definition is a plant grown from seed without permanent woody stems. That does make lettuce an herb. And lettuce simmered and buttered a potherb. But not in this country. Or, really, in much of present-day France.

As reckoned by gardeners and cooks, what makes a green a potherb is a we-know-quite-well-what-we-mean subtlety not yet in *Webster's*. Potherbs are greens with the breath of the wild still in them. They grow easily to the point of rankness. Their flavors are, on the whole, an aspect of *green*. Few have named cultivars—neither nature nor plant hybridizers have taken these Cinderellas and turned them into princesses as they have lettuce and spinach and chard. In our gardens potherbs are for quickly filling the greens gaps and allowing us to admire the resourcefulness of nature. They're best in early spring, harvested by the leaf, in a cut-and-come-again way.

AMARANTH/TAMPALA   *Amaranthus* spp.

FOUNTAIN PLANT   *A. tricolor* var. *salicifolius*

Tender annuals in the Amaranth family, native to the tropics . . . tallest grow in 5- or 6-gallon containers . . . aka Chinese spinach, Joseph's-Coat. Amaranths are one of the most heat and drought tolerant of potherbs yet thrive in humidity. The less fertile the soil, the more brilliant the colors, but for the finest plants the soil should have an inch of aged manure worked in before sowing.

I love thinking about the ancientness of these leaves. In Greece amaranth was sacred to Ephesian Artemis. Invested with properties of healing, it became a symbol of immortality and was used to decorate both tombs of the dead and statues of living gods. On this continent southwestern Native Americans have used amaranth leaves as potherbs and ground their seeds for grain for centuries.

Amaranth is a plant of immense variety and virtue. It comes in many forms, most easily divided into leafy, grain, decorative, and weedy amaranths. The leaves and tender stalks of all amaranths are edible, and the flavor of young plants is like a zippy spinach faintly touched with artichoke. Amaranth leaves are richly colored, some extravagantly. Most of those offered in catalogs are of the tampala type, with leaves 2½ to 4 inches wide. Merah's largish leaves are dark green splashed with magenta, Hijau's are splotched with lime, Pinang's with green-gold, and Joseph's-Coat with all three colors. Flaming Fountain and Red-Leaved Tampala are pure scarlet. Red Stripe Leaf and Lal Sag are ready for the table in a month. Most of these cultivars grow the same size as spinach, fetching in the front of the border around gaillardia, but some, such as tampala, can reach 4 or 5 or even 8 feet tall, striking in back with sunflowers.

Harvest while the leaves are small, tender, and sweet and before the plants flower, picking from the outside first. Rich in calcium, iron, protein, vitamins A and C, leaf amaranths nourish in so many ways.

In the North, one spring sowing will give greens all summer. In the South, sow every couple of weeks to keep greens coming.

All amaranths are host plants for tomato spotted wilt virus, so it's best to keep them from tomatoes and vulnerable peppers, potatoes, lettuce, celery, and spinach.

Recommended: Hijau is one of the most widely adapted.

GOOD-KING-HENRY   *Chenopodium Bonus-Henricus*

Hardy perennial in the Goosefoot family, native to Europe . . . aka mercury, allgood, goosefoot, wild spinach. Full sun, lovely soil, and water.

It is thought the Romans introduced Good-King-Henry to England. The only perennial among the Goosefoot potherbs, it's up in February or early March, a pleasing sight. The rich green mild-flavored leaves are arrow shaped, slightly wavy, on long slim stalks—the plant grows in clumps like spinach, but the leaves are smaller. This is not a front-and-center vegetable because it's not particularly interesting and the flowers—small beige-green balls on stalks—are dull. But new shoots can be cooked like asparagus. For color, plant some red mustards beside it.

For the best start, don't harvest until the second year. The leaves wilt rapidly once plucked, so this is a cut-and-cook-it-now sort of vegetable.

NETTLES, STINGING   *Urtica dioica*

Hardy perennial in the Nettle family, native to Europe and Asia. If you have a moist, out-of-the-way corner with decent soil and full sun or high shade, consider planting nettles.

Nettles are hosts to nearly a dozen insects-on-our-side, insects that are fond of insects that are fond of beans, for example. And a number of butterflies prefer nettle food for their caterpillars. Nettles are said to stimulate the growth of plants, to increase the potency of aromatic oils in herbs, and to aid the formation of humus—thus they're valued in compost. Nettles are high in nitrogen—nettle tea can be as much a tonic for the garden as nettle broth is tonic for the gardener. Nettle leaves hold the highest source of vitamin E in the plant kingdom, and they are also rich in iron, sulfur, potassium, and calcium. Their flavor is basic potherb green, lighter than spinach, and refreshing in early spring.

In a list drawn up in 1672 of "such Plants as have sprung up since the English planted and kept cattle in New England," nettles were "the first Plant taken notice of." Being that tenacious, you'd expect nettles would be easy to grow, but I've found the tiny seeds infuriatingly difficult. Finally, I sprouted some in a saucer.

There are two species of nettles, Roman, an annual which grows to 3 feet, and Stinging, this perennial that can stand 6 feet high in moist woods, but under cultivation they're usually half that tall. In summer nettles produce insignificant greenish catkins. Bee Balm is a fetching companion with its red or pink poufs. Nettles increase by spreading roots, so set them in a utility patch and keep an eye out. Their stalks, stems, and undersides of the toothed heart-shaped leaves are covered with fine bristles that sting like crazy—the pain lasts about 10 minutes, although the juice of dock leaves instantly stops the sting. In Danish folklore the sting of nettles is protection against sorcery, and a clump of nettles marks the dwelling place of elves.

Harvest young tender leaves and rinse them with gloves on. In the kitchen, rub leaves with salt and the stingers will vanish—cooking them has the same effect.

ORACH   *Atriplex hortensis*

Red Orach   *A. hortensis* var. *atrosanguinea* c.v. *rubra*

Hardy annuals in the Goosefoot family, native to Asia . . . aka mountain spinach, garden orach, butter leaves. Well watered and grown in humusy soil, the plants can grow at least 6 feet tall, although 2 to 3 feet is more common. Soil too salty or alkaline to support spinach or chard will grow dandy orach.

Even if you can grow spinach and chard, orach is slower than either to bolt in hot weather. The flavor of orach is mild and spinachy and it can serve in all of spinach's ways. The smallish arrow-shaped leaves come in three colors: green, yellowish (often called *white*), and red. I suggest red—I'd rather color than not, and in autumn it sends up sunset-pink sprays of seeds. Dark red and gold coreopsis make a delicious companion to red orach.

Start with fresh seed each year. Pick the leaves young, before they become too strong. And don't be abashed if your leaves don't look like those in photographs. So close to the wild, there are probably dozens of strains being handed around.

Ancient Romans boiled orach, it has been in English gardens since the 16th century, and all three were in American gardens by 1805.

SORREL, GARDEN

Rumex Acetosa

Hardy perennial in the Buckwheat family, native to Europe and Asia . . . aka sour dock. Growing terrific sorrel is a snap. My clumps cling to the side of a sandy slope. I water them when I must, I don't feed them, but every day as I pass by I tell them how beautiful they are, and I snap off all but a few seed stalks in spring.

If I had to choose one potherb for my garden, sorrel it would be. Sorrel is the first green to perk up in spring and the last to fold in winter. The plant grows in lush foot-high clumps that look as though they're all leaves. The large leaves, crinkled and arrow shaped, are rich bright green, and their flavor is like lemon in spinach without spinach's aftertaste of iron. The wind whisks seeds from those stalks through the garden, and in no time there are a few sassy new plants. You can never have too much sorrel, because the leaves melt to nothing when cooked. You're supposed to renew the plants after three years (euphemism for pulling them out and starting over). Some of ours are nine years old, but they don't know that—they're still in splendid form.

Our sorrel isn't bothered by slugs, and so far we haven't any snails in this garden. But sorrel is a favorite hiding place for these horrible creatures, which makes it easy to gather them up by dawn's early light.

Nip stalks of outer leaves at the base of the plant, leaving center leaves to increase the clump. Actually, there's always something to pick year-round, even when it's 10°F.

Recommended: Blonde de Lyon and Large de Belleville.

French Sorrel
R. scutatus

I'd read about French sorrel over the years, then came across it in the Richters catalog, which said the "smaller leaves are more concentrated in flavor and a little will therefore go a long way. . . ." I thought I should try it. But Richters has a minimum order of six plants, no small expense. I had to dream up five other plants I could use.

Richters has an ingenious shipping system of cells within cardboard within boxes—the stock arrives as fresh as May. When I finally got down to the little plant I was curious about, I was dumbstruck. That morning I had spent a long hour pulling up small spade-shaped green leaves that grew in rosettes all over the bloody garden. And there, after a 2,000-mile journey from Canada, was a bright and shiny new little plant of the same. So, some might consider French sorrel a weed. If you have it, toss strands of it into a salad or a soup and be glad.

Spinach Beets
Beta vulgaris, Cicla Group

Hardy biennials in the Goosefoot family, native to the Canary and Madeira Islands, the Atlantic coast of Europe, the Mediterranean region to southern Russia, Syria, Iraq . . . aka leaf beet, perpetual beet, perpetual spinach. Grow and harvest as chard.

Little known in this country, this form of chard is grown enthusiastically by the English. Although the beetlike root is insignificant (not part of what you eat), the leaves are smooth, succulent, and dark green—larger than spinach and smaller ribbed than traditional chard. The flavor is a mild chard. The plants are useful in summer when spinach bolts, and, well mulched, will winter over and greet you in spring. They grew generously for me on fairly dry inhospitable soil, with candytuft drifting in and out.

Pumpkins.
See Squashes and Pumpkins.

Purple-flowered Choy Sum.
See Asian Greens.

Purslane.
See Salad Greens.

RADISHES   *Raphanus sativus*

*In the Mustard family, native from Europe to eastern Asia . . . grows in
2-gallon containers. To grow crisp, succulent, tasty, elegant roots—
whether fast and crisp or slow and plushy or flyaway rattails—you must
provide rich, loose, light, stone-free soil that holds moisture and has good
drainage, and water, water, water. Give full sun for cool season radishes
and shade in the heat of the day for summer cultivars. It's important to thin
seedlings according to the packet so no radish will be squeezed for space.*

As ancient a crop as beer is a brew, radishes were munched many thousands of years ago by the pharaohs, who washed them down with beer. The Greeks fashioned turnips of lead and beets of silver as gifts for Apollo—but they made radishes of gold.

Those early radishes were probably large and coarse and wildly hot. As radishes came under cultivation, they grew smaller, sleeker, milder.

The ancients knew that color is crucial to appetite. If a dish is vibrant, it will be appealing—and will somehow taste the better. The bright and subtle colors of radishes, their nippy flavor, and their crunchy texture can subtly add to the success of a dish—a meal.

Some hues in radishes have come and gone—wannabe goldens that were in fact muddy yellow and an oblong named Martian, green top and white tip, inside and out.

They're not difficult, but radishes need what they need. Large radishes require lots of leaves to nourish them and consequently lots of space. When there are half a dozen leaves, feed with manure tea.

Most radishes are sensitive to the length of the day (as are onions). As the days lengthen, so will the radishes—and they'll get hotter in taste. For the best flavor as summer advances, sow the mild, long, French Breakfast types. Short round radishes are suited to the short round days of spring and autumn.

If your soil dries out quickly, dig in organic matter. If your soil keeps wet—it looks dark and the particles seem packed so close they can't breathe—mix in clean sand to lighten it. If your soil is hopelessly mucky, spring radishes suited to the situation are Cherry Belle and Red Boy. If diseases threaten, sow resistant cultivars. Soil that's well drained is your first line of defense against disease. And if your soil is decent only a few inches down, grow short radishes.

Long and indented radish leaves form rosettes of dark green. They're so attractive that you can place them anywhere in the landscape where low (3 to 12 inches) greens would be useful for a month or two (unless you're plagued by flea beetles, in which case it's easiest to grow radishes under cover off in a corner, I'm afraid). As for radishes in crop rotation, they are brassicas, prey to brassicas' troubles. If I grew a preponderance of large radishes, the kind that are in the ground for two months or more, and if I lived in an area vulnerable to soil-borne pests and diseases, I'd rotate radishes with brassicas. But since their cultural needs are more those of root crops than of leafy brassicas, I place them with roots.

Breeders are shortening leafy tops so radishes can be grown closer together, thus increasing yield (there's less competition for light). But spring's flea beetles can decimate short tops, so protect these cultivars with insect-weight floating row covers immediately after sowing. If row covers aren't feasible (you're counting on the pretty leaves to show in the landscape) and if your neighborhood isn't susceptible to other radish problems, grow cultivars with lots of leaves and interplant with members of the onion family to minimize flea beetle damage. To protect against maggots, use row covers.

Unless you're really stuck for space, given two cultivars of equal value, one with short tops and one with lots of leaves, I'd go for the leaves, because you can pick young ones here and there for tasty, nutritious, prickly additions to wild salads and also cook them as greens. I was surprised to find a new offering of radishes specifically grown for the greens—like certain cultivars of turnips. I remember trying to find recipes for radish greens years ago, and nobody had ever heard of eating a radish leaf. Evergreen Y. H. Enterprises now offers hybrid Radish Leaf, Four Seasons. Leaves are smooth rather than prickly and delicious for pickling.

Catalog descriptions get excited about everything else in radishes but flavor: crispness, lack of pithiness, how long the radishes hold in the field, tolerance for heat, length of tops (important commercially for bunching), fineness of taproot, durability of color, uniformity of shape. Generally speaking, the flavor of radishes tends to be hottest when grown in heavy soil and hot weather and just before they go to seed. If some radishes go to seed, you'll find their four-petaled flowers in shades of purple, pale yellow, or white charming and good in salad. When the flowers turn to seed pods, you have a whole 'nother vegetable to harvest. The little green pods have been likened to sugar snap peas in their crispness. So don't get upset if you forget to pull radishes and forget to cut their flowers.

PODDING / RAT-TAIL RADISHES   *R. sativus* cv. *Caudatus*

Hardy biennial, developed in southern Asia . . . aka aerial radish.

These are terrific. No roots to speak of, but after the plants have gone to seed, there are plushy, tender, radishy, long, slender, tapered, purply-brown pods. People love them until you tell them the name—which they too closely resemble—and then your friends turn pale, clutch their throats, and won't go near them. The trick is not to say the name—but who can resist? I grew only a few, so I mostly ate them myself, with great pleasure, chomping on them as a reward for weeding.

Harvest while they're peppery and crisp for a wonderful addition to stir-fries and salads. These are not for any but the utility part of the garden, since the tails whip out and about with glee.

The purple are the prettiest.

SPRING RADISHES — *R. sativus*

Half-hardy annuals.

These days there are radishes suited to harvesting in spring, summer, and autumn/winter. Spring radishes are among the most quickly realized crops in nature—there's something to pop into your mouth and crunch on in about three weeks. Twenty-eight sorts of radishes were cultivated in America in 1865. Today catalogs offer something like 150 open-pollinated cultivars alone—although the grays and browns seem to have disappeared, as have most of the purples. Long Scarlet, Wood's Frame, and Early Scarlet Turnip White Tip are surviving spring radishes from the 19th century.

Spring radishes *must* be sown to mature in cool weather; otherwise they'll be hot and pithy. Sow them as soon as the ground can be worked, under floating row covers or cloches if need be. Round red Ribella, a refined Cherry Belle, is particularly good for early sowing. If you love radishes, continue sowing every week or two until a long month before your days will be in the 80s.

The reason you can't sow just once and pull spring radishes over a period of time is that few cultivars can hang on to their pristine crispness and mildness in the ground more than a few days once mature. It's wise to mark your calendar so you can catch the little rascals at their best. The idea of sowing a seedsman's mix that matures at different times is tempting, but then the only way you'd know whether your radish is ready would be to pull it up.

Most spring radishes will keep for a couple of weeks in airtight containers in the refrigerator (store with their leaves on and don't rinse until serving). Where it's cool all summer, you can just keep sowing spring radishes. Where it's hot, sow them again from late summer to early fall, to mature in the cool of autumn—they're hardy enough to take first frosts.

Spring radishes come in three basic shapes and five colors. Rounds—traditionally called *turnip rooted*—and ovals, like olives or beets, are the fastest growing and most forgiving. Round/oval radishes can be red, dark red, purple, pink, yellow, white, or red dipped in white. French Breakfast types are like a child's little finger. Brilliantly red and often snowy tipped—most appealing—they're firm rather than crunchy and must be pulled at 1 ½ to 2 inches because they turn hot and hollow in a trice. Carrot-shaped icicles, when pulled 4 to 5 inches long, are crispy-crunchy. Icicles can be red or white, tapered or cylindrical. Unfortunately, French Breakfast and icicle radishes are more susceptible to disease than rounds and ovals. And white radishes have more problems than red.

Color in spring radishes can be as bright as red patent leather—Cherry Belle, Poker, and Fancy Red II are crimson knockouts. Or hues can be soft and luminous, like the rose of Pink Beauty and the whites of Snow Belle and Icicle Short Top. But sometimes the color's washed out. I find this true of some of the radishes in the Easter Egg collections I've grown—yet a friend's in New Mexico were gorgeous. An enchanting notion, the radishes are round or oval and white and various shades of red, described as pink, lavender or lilac, and purple. The vivacity of the colors and whether or not they're hybrids depend on the seedsman. Easter Egg radishes are not one cultivar that scatters color randomly into its seeds the way some corns do but are the likes of Snow Belle, Plum Purple, and Ruby mixed in a packet. Purple in radishes resembles blue in petunias—wishing don't make it so. So far, the color is a dark blue-red, but perhaps true purple is just around the corner. The flesh of all these radishes is white.

For flavor in a round radish, the exemplary Cherry Belle, an AAS winner, is fine and mild. So is Pink Beauty when eaten young. Pontvil is my favorite French Breakfast type—it grows quickly, and doesn't rapidly grow hot and pithy, a flaw in most of this form. And Icicle Short Top is tender and mild—the folks at Harris Seeds say it's the best white radish they've grown.

But pull a walnut-size white turnip called Tokyo Cross from the soil (a hybrid, it's ready in about 35 days), wipe off the earth on your jeans, and bite. All the crispy snap of a great radish, but sweeter. Tokyo Cross is almost my favorite radish.

It's traditional to mix seeds of these fast-growing roots with those of lazy parsnips and carrots. Radishes not only mark the places where the slow-growing roots are going to be but also lustily break ground for them. I used to do this, but I don't anymore. I'd rather let carrots and parsnips march to their own drummer instead of being hustled along by radishes.

Recommended: Start with reliable Cherry Belle, or Red Pak if disease is a problem. And do try Tokyo Cross turnips. More disease-resistant radishes are Red King, Fancy Red II, Fuego, and Red Prince.

SUMMER AND AUTUMN/ WINTER RADISHES

R. sativus Cv *Longipinnatus*

Hardy biennials . . . aka Japanese radish, daikon, mooli, Chinese radish.

Here are the radish heavyweights and keepers. If you find radishes the size of baseballs appealing, grow German Giant—scarlet skin, pungent crisp white flesh that, thinly sliced, tastes great with beer. Jumbo is actually sweet. These are also spring sown and seem not to get woody despite their girth.

Although India's mooli radishes—long tasty white ones known in this country as *daikon*—are also fundamentally cool-season crops, tapered hybrid Summer Cross No. 3 may be sown from late spring until autumn, to harvest from midsummer on. These medium-hot radishes crisply fill the summer radish gap. Even though they may have more tolerance for heat, it's wise to give summer radishes airy shade. Planting them in the asparagus bed is a tradition. By then the asparagus is past harvesting, whiling away the hours until next spring, so their roots are delighted at the occasional manure tea brought by their guests.

For crisp radishes to pickle or store in the manner of carrots and beets, in mid- to late summer, sow pungent pure white Miyashige. For unusual radishes in autumn, try Green Flesh, which can grow over 12 inches—much of which sits saucily on top of the soil—but should be pulled smaller. Chinese green-fleshed radishes are juicy and lightly hot. By contrast, Black Spanish Round, rough and ready, has translucent white flesh that can be startlingly brisk but pleasing. These are also great keepers, lasting five months or more in the refrigerator or moist sand. Where there's no frost, sow mild stump-rooted Okura in autumn to harvest in late winter. To sow radishes anytime of the year except when days are freezing, mild daikon-type All Season (Tokinashi) will be ready in about two months.

The fantasy autumn radishes, Chinese Beauty Hearts, are native to the land around Beijing. They are large (a pound or more) and crisp and sweet. Ovals or rounds, Beauty Hearts have dull green shoulders and white bottoms. But slice into them and, with luck, find flesh with sun rays of rose, from shell to watermelon pink—luck because the seeds are unpredictable. The fabled radish is treasured as fruit in northern China. Sow Green Skin and Red Flesh the end of summer—perhaps you'll have some for sculpting into water lilies and roses for your Thanksgiving table.

Recommended: Hybrid Summer Cross No. 3 is the easiest long radish I've grown.

RHUBARB   *Rheum Rhabarbarum*

Hardy perennial in the Buckwheat family, native to Manchuria . . . aka garden rhubarb, pie plant, wine plant . . . grows in 7 ½-gallon containers. Remember that the green leaves are poisonous. *For a long-lived plant, dig a generous hole in well-drained soil, mix in about one-fourth aged manure and compost if the soil isn't moisture retentive but is well draining. In cool climates, cover with black paper mulch until the earth warms. Set the top of the crown level with the surface. Once established, heap well-aged manure around the plant before leaves emerge in spring and repeat in autumn. When the weather warms, mulch up to its chin with straw or newspaper to keep the roots moist. Water deeply, keeping the soil moist.*

You must grow rhubarb if only to see the voluptuous way it emerges from the ground. My three-year-old Valentine, which I thought was dead last autumn (drought, drought), is unfolding now in early April. The leaves, like dark green China silk, are bunched, crushed, gathered, folded, ruffled, crimped, and crenellated as they dreamily push their way up through the heap of winter-sheltering straw. With each day the heart-shaped leaves grow more enormous, the stalks more crimson, the fountain of green more dazzling. Yes, you must grow rhubarb.

When I first grew rhubarb, I fell for the story that it will take whatever soil it can get and be happy on its little scrap heap. It won't, it wasn't. My next piece of bad advice was that rhubarb didn't mind half-sun. It did. (Where summers are very hot, however, rhubarb is grateful for a little afternoon shade.) Now the dear thing is in full sun, and it's a blithering success. If I had a garden on a large scale, my rhubarb would be splendid toward the back of the border set off by a passel of white and yellow daisies.

You can pick up healthy rhubarb divisions at the local nursery in spring, but more unusual cultivars are available through the mail. Seeds add a year to the first harvest, and seed-grown plants are never as vigorous as those begun from root divisions.

The first season, it's important to let the roots grow strong, so pick no stalks. Once stalks are 6 inches high, give them a collar a yard wide of compost, leaf mold, or strawy manure. When the stalks are a year old, harvest sparingly for four weeks. The year after, harvest until the stalks begin to come up skinny, usually mid-July.

To harvest, snap off outermost stalks by holding near the base and pulling with a slight twist (don't cut with a knife; you may slip and cut the crown, and stubs left from cutting will decay). Don't take more than one fourth of the stalks at one time and stop harvesting when you've taken half the stalks. After harvest, feed with fish emulsion. Always snip off any flowering stalk at the base, then stick it in water—it will blossom and be lovely for a very long time.

If you live where it's too warm for the plant to go dormant in winter, try growing rhubarb as an annual. Sow seeds in January and harvest in May until hot weather stops the production, then harvest again when shoots start growing in autumn.

Recommended: Valentine and Canada Red or Chipman are two with cheery red stalks that keep a blushing color when cooked. McDonald (aka Sutton) is also red but turns muddy in the heat. The old cultivar Victoria has green stalks and is no longer recommended.

RUTABAGAS

Brassica napus, Napobrassica Group

Hardy biennial in the Mustard family, origin unknown . . . aka Swede, Swedish turnip . . . grows in 5-gallon containers. As closely related to turnips as broccoli, rutabagas are a breeze to grow. Just give them a sunny patch of rich, well-drained soil. The only problem is they can be in the ground for six months. But the yield is high, about 3 pounds of delicious roots per square foot. Like turnips, rutabagas don't do well in heat, so timing is important.

Rutabagas sound funny. Mashed rutabagas sound terrible. I made James Beard's mashed potatoes with rutabagas on blind faith one Thanksgiving, and everybody fell into their plates. In France they call such things as rutabagas *la belle laide,* the beautiful ugly one. You must try half a dozen for mashing their nutty, sweet, slightly turnipy golden flesh with butter and cream. Forget the potatoes.

To work around the heat they don't like, if the air is hot, soak the seeds overnight before sowing and be careful not to let the ground dry out until the seeds germinate.

At sowing time, dig in an inch each of compost and/or rotted manure and a veil of wood ash and bonemeal. Water the plants consistently and treat with manure tea when there are a dozen leaves per seedling. Although the cultivar Marion has resistance to clubroot, it's the better part of valor to protect the crop from airborne diseases with floating row covers from the moment of sowing. If mice become a problem—it hasn't happened to me, but it will—you'll have to cage the plants with hardware cloth.

If there's no threat of pests or disease in your garden, the smooth leaves are handsome enough to add their blue-green to the border. The prettiest mix I ever made with rutabaga was mingling it with Giant White Hyacinth Flowered candytuft.

You can harvest rutabagas once they're the size of a small orange. Don't let them get enormous—nothing should get enormous. Where it doesn't freeze, you can leave the roots in the ground until early spring, picking their leaves a few at a time for winter greens or salads. Rutabaga tops can tolerate frost, but their flesh will rot if their ground freezes and then thaws. If your ground does that, pull the plants in good time, cut off the leaves an inch from the crown, and dip the root in a warm pan of half water and half melted paraffin. Kept in a cold place (with other overwintering roots), the wax will preserve the roots for months.

Recommended: The strain of Laurentians is tasty and dependable for starters. The English know their Swedes, though, and Garden Purple Top Acme is recommended by Chiltern Seeds.

Salad Greens

Grow in 2- to 3-gallon containers.

A friend said, "I remember the first time I ate at your house—I'll never forget the salad. I didn't recognize a single thing—it was fantastic!" That's why I've gathered all the salad plants together in one entry: it would be a shame if you missed one scrap of leaf.

My distinction between salad greens and potherbs is that I mostly use the greens raw and mostly cook potherbs, but all go raw into salads.

When you're looking in catalogs for an esoteric green, you need to be resourceful. If it's not listed as miner's lettuce, for example, see if there's a collection called "Salad Greens," "Greens," "Exotic Vegetables," or "Herbs." And *then* you may have to look under its "also known as," and sure enough, there it will be, claytonia.

Harvest these greens as potherbs—when very tender, stalk by stalk, leaf by leaf, unless you're ready to cut a whole head off.

AMBROSIA   *Chenopodium Botrys*

Half-hardy annual in the Goosefoot family, native to Europe, Asia, and Africa . . . aka feather geranium, Jerusalem oak, sticky goosefoot. Past water, ambrosia neither wants nor needs special attention.

I'm very fond of ambrosia for wild salads because it resembles no other leaf. The medium-size dark green leaves grow in a deeply lobed shape like an oak leaf. They are prettily veined and slightly succulent. In a European book the leaf's scent is described as "unpleasantly aromatic," so obviously soil and climate make a big difference with flavor. In this garden I enjoy ambrosia's clean spiciness. In time there are clusters of fuzzy nothing-colored flowers (characteristic of the Goosefeet). Because it's lank, I set it in a potpourri of wild greens in a utility bed. When it's happy, it self-sows, which is pleasing. An easy plant for beginners.

ARUGULA   *Eruca vesicaria sativa*

Half-hardy annual in the Mustard family, native to the

Mesclun, Misticanza, and Wild Sorts of Salads

These are mixes of plants that were somebody's bright idea long ago—mesclun in southern France and misticanza in northern Italy (saladini is English gardener and salad connoisseur Joy Larkcom's version). The notion is to mix seeds of a variety of plants that grow compatibly, that are companionable in the salad bowl, and that provide a lively play of color, texture, and flavor. Classic Provençal mesclun is simply baby leaves of lettuce, endive, arugula, and chervil. In Italy's Piedmont district, where chicories especially grow to perfection, the tradition is said to be five chicories and four lettuces.

Then everybody got into the act. And why not? It's great fun. The basics are spiked with dandelion, corn salad, purslane, sorrel, orach, and every delicate leaf from flat-leaf parsley to bronze fennel.

This is an amusing way to get acquainted with a range of salad possibilities. But the patch can look unkempt after the first young flush unless the collection has been put together with great care.

In my garden I take enormous pleasure each time I go out at dusk with my basket to pluck a few leaves here, a few sprigs there, composing the salad on the fly, so to speak. It's never the same because leaves and flowers come and go. But it's always exquisite and richly flavored.

Mediterranean . . . aka rugula, rocket, roquette. To grow passels of arugula, just throw out the seeds on sunny soil and keep watering.

Rocket was cultivated in medieval European gardens, and before that, ancient Romans grew it. A handful of the smallish dandelion-shaped green leaves gives salad such style and verve.

There is a newer cultivar with cut leaves like a maple's and yellow flowers. It's called Rustic and it *can* be in the front of the border. Ours is with alyssum. Once they're up, I don't thin seedlings officially—I just occasionally pull up a plant by mistake when I'm harvesting for salad. August-sown arugula can slumber under blankets of snow for ages, then spring into life after the snow melts. It will bolt— send up white stars of flowers—and although the leaves will be markedly hotter, the whole flowering stalk will be good to eat.

As lush as arugula can be, it's best kept with other devil-may-care mustards in a spot where it won't have to conform. Perhaps it's called *rocket*—its English name— because it grows from seed to maturity in a flash.

Sow a pinch of seeds often, since young sprigs are mildest and finest. It's also its best in cooler weather. A kitchen garden essential and a pleasure to grow.

Recommended: Both the classic and the Rustic from Shepherd's.

BUCK'S-HORN PLANTAIN   *Plantago coronopus*

Hardy annual in the Plantain family, native to Europe . . . aka hartshorn, star of the earth. The plants are happy in light or sandy soil (they're especially fond of sea air), but give ample water to keep the leaves supple.

This is a wild little thing with a Raggedy Ann charm and a lettucey taste. The bright green leaves are long, very thin, and deeply lobed at the tips—like a buck's or hart's horn. And they grow in a ground-hugging spray—like a star of the earth. In the 19th century they could be found in French and American country gardens. Set three or four with their spidery green leaves at the edge of a patch of pinks with their spidery blue leaves. Pick the leaves while very young— mature, they toughen.

A caution: Somewhere in the supplying pipeline are seeds named Buck's-horn plantain but sublabeled Minutina and/or Herba Stella. The plant has nothing to do with the one I've described—instead, the leaves are radishlike and hot.

CHICORY, COMMON   *Cichorium Intybus*

Hardy perennial in the Sunflower family, native to Europe . . . aka radicchio, blue-sailors, succory. Chicories grown for their leaves require the same nurturing conditions as lettuces, with particular care that they not be crowded and wilting leaves be kept picked to avoid rot. Plants wintered over need excellent drainage and protection from rain.

Chicories grown for their roots want soil that is friable, rich, lightly moist, and well drained, but they are more tolerant of imperfect conditions than chicories grown for their leaves.

The lineage of chicories is ancient. There isn't one that isn't beautiful. Many are unpredictable to grow, matters of climate and season. But every year new cultivars that deal with difficulties are offered. In habit of growth, chicories resemble lettuces and dandelions. So play with them, half a dozen types at a time, just as you play with lettuces and milder leaves. Just follow the recommendations on the packet—every chicory has its quirks.

A distinguishing feature of chicory is that the leaves are bitter. Smaller and inner leaves are sweeter than larger and outer ones. Leaves are sweeter after cold weather. But don't think you have to make salads entirely of chicory and then grin and bear it. Ribbons of bitterness can be threaded through mild greens to great effect. To minimize the bitterness of all the leaves of a plant, blanch it (see The Gardener's Notebook). Otherwise, the centers of heads and bunches are naturally blanched as leaves grow around and around them, so you might harvest only the centers and feed outer leaves to the critters.

Since chicories are perennials (albeit short-lived), you'll have their flowers the second year. They are sparkling blue (blue-sailors) and shaped like daisies. If you never ate a leaf, you'd be glad you grew chicory just for its abundant flowers over summer. They open at dawn and fold their tents at noon. Most chicories grow low, and the tallest can be kept to a couple of feet. If you have enough plants so that harvesting doesn't leave anyone threadbare, place these beauties in the border where they can show off. In summer they are particularly charming among Peter Pan zinnias.

Because they have elevated chicory growing to an art, certain towns and regions of northern Italy have come to be associated with the shapes of chicory.

Verona, in the Veneto region, and, on the Gulf of Venice, Chioggia indicate chicories with firm round heads. In garnets and rubies marbled with white or cream, these are the chicories that have come to be called *radicchio*. The leaves of these exquisite heads are as crisp as baby cabbage and at once sweet and bitter. Chioggia also comes variegated.

Although Giulio may be sown in spring because it's slow to bolt, most radicchio chicories should be sown from late June to early July and where they will grow (transplanting only stresses their native instability). Don't be alarmed when these red balls of fire commence as ruffly bunches of green. They will metamorphose, or most of them will. All will be tasty chicories, but not all will form heads or turn red.

When you read in catalogs that a chicory produces a head "without cutting back," that's because, in the cool of autumn, traditional chicories must be cut to within an inch of their leafy lives so they'll send up a head that turns red with cold weather. Newer cultivars don't need cutting back. Giulio is one of the most widely planted of these, and it has grown beautifully for me. Harvest these chicories when firm and the size of large oranges.

Castelfranco, also in the Veneto, gives us chicories that grow as the Veronas and Chioggias, only their hearts are softer and their leaves are richly variegated. Colors are marbled from bloodred and burgundy to roses, bronzes, creams, and greens. Castelfrancos don't need cutting back to produce round heads. Castelfranco is more tolerant of heat and milder in flavor than most chicories. Sow in early summer for late-autumn harvest and protect the colors from blazing sun.

Grumolo chicories have rounded green leaves that grow upright in summer, then furl themselves into soft rosettes in cool weather. These decidedly bitter chicories are from the Lombardy in northern Italy. Grumolos may be sown from spring to fall, but midsummer sowings will give you chicory from autumn to spring, although some plants may die down in winter. These are extremely hardy, and if you leave an inch of stem when you harvest heads in autumn, very early spring will bring small green rosettes. After you harvest these, more sprouts will come.

Spadona is a green smooth- and narrow-leaved chicory as hardy as Grumolo. It is nonheading, which means you pick individual leaves, sown spring to fall.

Sugar Loaf is just-green-leaves with an enticing name and long elegant romainelike heads with broad outside leaves. The leaves are densely packed and crisp and may be picked at every stage. Usually sown in June and July, to get through a frozen winter, Sugar Loafs need the shelter of a cloche or cold frame. Inner leaves are sweet, outer leaves more bitter. Another way with Sugar Loaf chicories is to broadcast lots of seeds in spring or fall and harvest them as seedlings. Snowflake is of this type, but who can resist growing a chicory called Crystal Hat?

Treviso, of all the red leaves named after Italian towns, may be the handsomest of chicories. Just north of Venice, Treviso has given us crunchy wine-red heads that are small, pointed, and elegant—its shape is something between a heart of romaine and Belgian endive. Sow in mid-July and don't be concerned if the plant grows green—those leaves are just the protective wrappers. Trevisos may be difficult, but you can do it. Early Treviso will probably need cutting back to get a head, and hybrid Nerone de Treviso won't.

Catalogna (or Catalonia) is one of the dandelionlike chicories—deeply cut rich green leaves and slender white ribs. Catalonia is the cliffy province along the Costa Brava in Spain, and this chicory looks wild enough to have danced with gypsies. Although the dandelionlike bunches can grow 18 inches tall, mine, under the high shade of a black oak, grew a tender 10 inches, plenty for me. Sown in late summer and sheltered through winter, leaves may be harvested cut-and-come-again straight through. They can be splendidly bitter. Catalognas are also called *asparagus chicories* because tender shoots pop up from the roots in early spring—Puntarella is the cultivar. Blanch the shoots by covering with a box or flowerpot, and when they reach 4 to 6 inches, harvest them by cutting flush with the earth. In winter in southern Italy, its tender bitey leaves are boiled like potherbs and dressed with oil and lemon juice.

Capuchin's Beard (*barbe de Capucin*, Capuchins being monks) is a venerable wild chicory that resembles Catalogna—long leaves, deeply cut—but it's more bitter. Sow from late spring to early summer. For greater sweetness, blanch these bunches also.

Magdeburgh and Soncino are two of the best types grown for their roots—ground dark-roasted chicory roots blended with ground dark-roasted coffee produce a New Orleans brew that's piercingly French. While the roots develop over summer, their young dandelionlike leaves can be plucked for salads or cooked as a potherb, although the warmer the weather, the more bitter the leaves. Seeds for root-harvested chicories are best sown in spring and the roots lifted after the first autumn frost.

N. B. Even if it looks as though you've lost a chicory plant to rot, don't pull out the root. Just cut back the leaves and care for the plant as though it were dormant. You may have a Sleeping Beauty awaken come spring.

Belgian endive. We've talked about chicory leaves for their own sake, noting that when you cut back leaves and leave the root in place, sprouts come forth again weeks or months later. Those that sprout in the garden are called *nonforcing chicories.* Those that sprout well indoors are called *forcing chicories*—Belgian endive is one of these. Witloof (it means "white leaf" in Flemish) is the traditional forcing chicory, sending up plump, firm, gilded white sprouts called *chicons.* Directions for growing your own Belgian endive are in The Gardener's Notebook.

Recommended: For leaves, start with easy Sugar Loaf, or perhaps Catalogna Special. Fuss with Magdeburgh chicons once you've got your chicory bearings. And why not do your own Belgian endive!

CORN SALAD, COMMON   *Valerianella Locusta*

Hardy (to about 5°F) annual in the Valerian family, native to North Africa and Europe, western Asia . . . aka lamb's lettuce, mâche, feld-salat. Corn salad asks only for full sun, ordinary soil, and water when there's no rain.

Perky as jaybirds, lamb's lettuce, *mâche, doucette, bourcette* are all diminutive names for the thicket of dark green, slender, spoon-shaped leaves Americans call *corn salad*. The slightly plushy leaves are tender and sweet.

Corn salad grows easily, but it grows very slowly, and you think it will never get there. But then it does, and you can pick leaves to your heart's content. Thickly sow small-seeded types in late summer and again in very early spring—or midwinter if it's balmy. If it's chill and there's no shelter of snow, protect the plants with floating row covers. Sow large-seeded heat-resistant types for your main crop over summer.

One winter I grew corn salad bordering cream, red, and green kales, and the effect was charming. Always leave at least half the plant when you pick. When it goes to seed, let some plants flower, because the little blue blossoms are delightful—and it means a new crop. We always have corn salad from volunteers in early spring. Another splendid crop for beginners.

Recommended: Every cultivar has its virtues, but I'm partial to the cupped leaves of Coquille. The classic Verte de Cambrai has larger leaves and is delightful. Gayla is supposed to be an improved Verte de Cambrai, but I'm not sure what's wrong with the old one. Where it's constantly damp, Elan and Vit are mildew resistant. For heat resistance, the larger-leaved, large-seeded Piedmont.

CRESSES

To grow sprightly cress, provide humusy, moisture-retentive soil, at least half-day sun, and lots of water.

Seedling crops—masses of tiny hot leaves cut halfway down—are ready to pick in from 10 to 14 days. Cresses get crotchety in hot weather. A mouthful of cress seems to me as close as I want to get to spring tonic.

GARDEN CRESS   *Lepidium sativum*

*Hardy annual in the Mustard family, native to Egypt and western
Asia . . . aka broadleaf cress, peppergrass, curled cress.*

Confusion reigns here. Garden cress isn't what's offered. Broadleaf cress,
curled cress, and peppergrass are, and no one seems to be sure of what they are. This
is my experience with the seeds I've grown:

The leaves of broadleaf cress have the flavor and color of watercress, but they're
pointier. They also need less water, and they self-sow. Ours were sprinkled through
the cutting celery—an excellent place, because the two enjoyed the same circumstances, and you can snip for salads in one kneel.

Curled cress seedlings are curled—as they mature, they quickly turn into lacy
leaves resembling cutleaf Italian parsley. They are peppery hot, but if you harvest
center leaves from old plants and outside leaves from young plants, you'll have the
mildest. Xenophon claims the Persians ate this cress even before they knew how to
bake bread. The leaves grow very quickly, and there can be four or five cut-and-
come-again crops from one sowing.

Actually, seedsmen don't always know which cress they're offering because the
supplier doesn't know (or care, frankly, since cress isn't exactly a major item). So it's
silly to try to untangle the names; just read the description in a catalog you trust, and
order what appeals.

Recommended: Reform broadleaf cress grows with the greatest of ease, as does
fine curled cress.

PINK CRESS   *Amaranthus tricolor*

Perennial in the Amaranth family.

This pretty little cress, low with delicate lance-shaped leaves brushed with pink,
is drought tolerant, and its leaves are a delightful decoration. It's not a mustard,
you'll notice, so the flavor is comparatively mild. I've sown these among garden
pinks (peppermint pink dianthus) to delicious effect. Not always available.

UPLAND CRESS   *Barbarea verna*

*Hardy biennial in the Mustard family, native to Europe . . . aka land
cress, early wintercress, Belle Isle cress, American cress, scurvy grass.
Give these bouquets dappled light, moist soil, and shelter.*

These low-growing rosettes of deeply toothed, shiny green leaves lend warmth to salads through winter—with your eyes closed, they're watercress. Pick leaves from the center until hot weather comes, when their snap will make you gasp. I've set a few plants to one side of dwarf goldenrod—charming.

WATERCRESS   *Nasturtium officinale*

Hardy (to −10°F) aquatic perennial in the Mustard family, native to Europe . . . grows in 3-gallon containers. Set in fertile soil in bright shade and keep constantly moist or grow in a pot with a big saucer that keeps the pot's feet wet.

The Romans thought the sharp bite of watercress cured madness. Because I have no watery spot, I grow a succulent large-leaved watercress in a container in a cool bright place and fill the saucer with water daily. There aren't masses, but I can pick crisp stalks for sandwiches and salads. When the fast-growing roots choke growth, I simply float a few stalks in a jar of water, and when they root I plant them in the pot in fresh soil.

DANDELION, COMMON   *Taraxacum officinale*

Hardy perennial in the Sunflower family, native to Europe and Asia. All you have to do for dandelions is provide fertile soil, some sunshine, and keep the soil moist but never marshy or mucky.

Dandelions have only recently been cultivated—wild types were pleasing enough. Now leaves are broad or narrow, fleshy or thin, fringed or smooth, hairy or bare, and the plants vary considerably in height and manner of growth. All have a bitterness akin to escarole's. You can also cook dandelion leaves as a potherb—sprinkle on the basil—make a delectable wine with the flowers, and roast the root as you would chicory.

Dandelions among the purple and green perillas are delightful, or mix with Chinese celery for marvelous leaf textures. Keep the flowers picked! My books mention blanching to make the leaves milder—what some people will do to keep busy! But if you're curious about white dandelions, see The Gardener's Notebook.

Some of my books also instruct me not to pick the leaves the first year but to give them their due as perennials and wait until the second year. I've never managed to do this.

Seedsmen offer French and Italian cultivars of dandelions, but remember that "Italian dandelion" is a chicory. Dandelions and beginning gardeners are made for each other.

Recommended: The French cultivars Ameliore and Montmagny.

ENDIVE AND ESCAROLE   *Cichorium Endivia*

Hardy annuals or biennials in the Sunflower family, probably native to India . . . broad-leaved endives aka Batavian endive, scarole, or chicorée scarole. Endives and escaroles respond to the same tender loving care as chicories grown for their leaves, except these need richer soil. Give lots of sun for crops sown in summer and fall, some shade for spring-sown crops. These heads are as susceptible to rot as chicories and lettuces, so superb drainage is essential.

*E*ndive is thought to have been created by a cross of wild chicories. Botanically, endive is distinct from chicory in that endive's flowers are self-pollinating. Culinarily, endives and escaroles are less bitter than chicories—*piquant* best describes their flavor. And they are easily blanched, which makes them all the milder (see The Gardener's Notebook). But blanching is by no means essential.

Endives are the easiest to identify of all greens in the chicory family. They're the large floppy open bunches with succulent ivory stalks and finely cut, curly, frizzy green leaves—*chicorée frisée* is their French name. Some grow nearly flat to the ground in a breathtaking starburst. Some grow in a giddy tangled mound.

You might begin with exquisite petite cultivars such as Très Fine and Galia and then add to your collection. Curly endives are fairly tolerant of heat, so you can sow them from early spring to midsummer. In very warm weather, blanching the heads makes leaves tenderer. Green Curled Ruffec is more than 100 years old, deeply cut, and relatively hardy. I've overwintered it at 10°F under just two layers of floating row cover. Salad King, called the giant of curled endives, is another that's cold tolerant.

Somehow *escarole* has become the name for broad-leaved endives (it has no botanical standing). These leaves also grow in loose open bunches and are green only (never red or variegated). The tender crisp leaves are either ruffled or curiously twirled—like loops in ribbon bows twisted to catch the light. Edges of leaves can be smooth or faintly toothed. Some escaroles in their early stages can be indistinguishable from smooth-leaved chicories in their early stages. There is unquestionably a difference in shape and performance, but there's scant difference in flavor among escaroles. Their broad leaves turn more bitter in warm weather, but they're hardier than curly endive—they will sweeten with a few degrees of frost. You can blanch escaroles or not. Some are self-blanching; the heads grow thickly enough to shade the inner leaves.

Recommended: Green Curled Ruffec endive and Nuvol escarole. Any escarole with Cornet (horn) or Fullheart in the name will be a beautiful plant. For extra hardiness, Perfect escarole is hardy to −7°F.

LETTUCE, GARDEN   *Lactuca sativa*

Half-hardy biennial in the Sunflower family, not known in the wild. For superb lettuces, keep them moving rapidly—make every minute a growing minute. That means rich, well-drained, humusy soil—lettuces go crazy with a couple of inches of a mixture of aged chicken manure, compost, straw, and sawdust hoed into the top few inches of soil—abundant moisture (the ground kept moist but not sodden) or spraying the leaves with a liquid from the sea once a month, and no crowding—eat those thinnings!

Lettuces were cultivated 3,000 years ago by the Babylonians and even earlier, it is said, by the Chinese. Lettuce seeds were sealed in Egyptian tombs, and lettuces were served to Roman emperors. In the Middle Ages lettuce was on European tables, mostly eaten hot. By 1865 seedsmen offered 113 varieties to America's gardeners. Today we can choose from 300. And the USDA collection in California numbers roughly 800 cultivars from all over the world. New lettuces are being offered thick and fast, which can work against us. In 1988 I clipped a rave about the flavor of Red Rapids—a fancier found it the "best of the red" loose-leaf lettuces. The review sank to the bottom of my study, and when I came across it four years later and decided to order Red Rapids, Royal Red had taken its place in the catalog. When you find a cultivar you like that's at all unusual, let one plant make seeds and save them.

It's easy to save lettuce seeds because lettuce is self-pollinating and rarely are there crosses, even when cultivars are grown beside one another. It's safe to say that most if not all the lettuces offered in catalogs are open pollinated. All the yellow florets on a lettuce flower open at the same time, stay open from 30 minutes to a few hours, then close forever.

But if you have wild lettuce growing outside your garden, and should you be saving seed, it's imperative you go on a grim mission and pull all the prickly devils up, or you'll have to cage the cultivated lettuces you're growing for seed.

Mosaic virus (the plants turn yellowish and are stunted) can be transmitted through infected seed. Aphids spread the disease. If you have the problem, destroy affected plants and seeds and use resistant cultivars.

Garden lettuces are divided into classes based on habit of growth. Each has its advantages and its beauty so it's good to know which is which—except authorities don't agree on where the distinctions are drawn. Most gardeners would say there are five forms. From easiest to most challenging to grow well, they are *looseleaf, butterhead, romaine, crisphead, and Batavian.*

Looseleaf. This fetching lettuce grows in an open habit like a floppy bouquet. These are termed *nonhearting* lettuces—there is no curled heart—but the bouquet can gather around a central rosette. Looseleaf (aka bunching) lettuce leaves are smooth, curled, ruffled, frilly, finely cut, pointed, or lobed. Colors can be all manner of greens or reds with bronze tips, rose blushes, or splashes of cream or burgundy. Looseleafs are the most decorative, least demanding, and among the most heat-tolerant lettuces you can grow. And they're the fastest: leaf lettuces can complete their life cycle in just 40 days. Sow looseleafs regularly through the growing season and just keep picking.

You'll love the fascinating heirloom Deertongue (aka Matchless) with its sensuous leaves. Black Seeded Simpson, with flavorful, curly, lime green leaves (inexplicably, slugs glide past it in my garden), and Oakleaf, shaped like oak leaves, delicate, sweet, vigorous, and long producing, are three of the best-loved, most dependable looseleaf forms. The savoyed-leaved Ruby is perhaps the darkest red, but Red Sails is easier to grow and widely adapted, although I find its flavor thin when compared with the great lettuces of this world. Red Fire is a superior red, slow to bolt. I love Lollo Rossa, green leaves tightly furled and tipped with rosy scarlet. These lettuces respond to day length. Long summer days turn a red leaf magenta; short days turn it bright red.

Butterhead. These lettuces look like great big cabbage roses. Their leaves are succulent and fragile and tear if you blink at them, which makes them devilish to ship and pricey at the market. But you can feast on a whole head of homegrown buttery butterhead every night and twice on Sunday if you like. Butterheads are the royalty of lettuce—they have an air of laissez-faire refinement about them. Butterheads form a head but with indifference to conformity—leaves ruffle here, nestle there, swirl around and about as they please. Perhaps the best-known butterhead is Bibb lettuce, which first grew in amateur horticulturist John J. Bibb's garden in Frankfort, Kentucky, around 1850. Often Bibb, Boston, and butter lettuce are used interchangeably. But even though all Bibbs are butter lettuces, not all butter lettuces are Bibbs. Bibb can also be called *limestone lettuce*. Generally, butterheads are slower to bolt than looseleafs.

Romaine or Cos. If the lettuce has long, narrow upright leaves that are smooth or crinkled with fleshy center ribs, it's a romaine or cos. These leaves are tightly folded at the base and the head grows up, usually on the straight and narrow. It's possible this form was discovered on the isle of Kos, off the Turkish coast, thus the name. The lettuce was introduced to France at the papal court, then seated at Avignon, so it was called Roman lettuce, *laitue romaine*. Curiously, although drawings of lettuces found in Egyptian tombs show romaine's shape, there are far fewer romaine cultivars these centuries later than other sorts. Of the USDA collection of around 800 lettuces, less than 10 percent are romaines. It's rare to find more than two or three cultivars offered in any catalog. Romaine leaves come in basic green, in reds from rose to cranberry—it depends on day length—and with hearts from ivory to pink. These lettuces are slower to grow than most looseleafs and butterheads, but in terms of value for space, they have other lettuces beat. A well-grown head of Valmaine, for example, can provide 2 pounds of lettuce in 1 square foot. Sow romaines about 8 inches apart; six weeks later, cut the leaves down to an inch or two, then turn to other salad plants while the stalk sprouts another crop, for picking six weeks after that. Romaines' succulent leaves are the most tolerant of heat, cold, and drought, and generally they contain more vitamins A and C than other lettuces. In exchange for all this, romaines need at least partial shade in hot dry summers and more generous supplies of nitrogen than basic lettuce. The romaine lettuces of commerce, so often past their prime, are leathery—instead grow juicy Little Gem or Diamond Gem, perhaps the best-flavored lettuces of all. The most widely grown romaines are Parris Island types, and if you get a cultivar with 318 after it (the numbers will increase with new issues), it will mature earlier, be heavier, and grow taller than the standard. Romulus is an exceptionally sweet romaine, Rosalita is deep purply-red with a yellow heart, and Rubens is a smaller romaine with painterly scarlet leaves and chartreuse heart.

Crisphead. These supermarket favorites, aka head or cabbage lettuces, are familiarly called *Iceberg*—which, in fact, is the name of the best-known crisphead lettuce cultivar. Homegrown, you can't imagine how gorgeous this lettuce is—both in terms of flavor and beauty. Colors here are water-green to ruby-red, with hearts from celery-white to rose, and the leaves may be glossy or matte. While the crisphead plant is young, leaves may be picked individually as with the other lettuces. You'll probably be surprised to find your crisphead lettuce has lovely curled or frilly outer leaves. As the plant matures, leaves in the center begin to curl around and around inward, densely layering themselves into a smooth ball. If you are mad about red and the crunchiness of head lettuce, try Cerise, Rosy, or Pablo. These lettuces are the best choice when the soil is dry and poor. In general, crisphead lettuces, while slowest to mature and most challenging to grow, are the most resistant to bolting. However, where nights are hot, these lettuces will bolt immediately, so don't even bother trying.

Batavians. Batavians appear to be a cross between crisphead and looseleaf lettuces, with the head forming in a rather frilly, elongated way. They have especially crispy, crunchy leaves, which you can pick individually, and full but tender tasty hearts. In catalogs, lines can be wobbly between American Icebergs and European Batavians—Iceberg began life as a Batavian—and it's not particularly useful to straighten them out. Webb's Wonderful has been called both. So has Ice Queen (Reine des Glaces), one of the most beautiful of all lettuces, a swirl of deeply cut, rich, delicious, pointed green leaves. Rosy-leaved Verano is clearly Batavian and one of the tastiest. These lettuces are particularly tolerant of heat and cold.

Nothing disastrous happens if you sow any lettuce any old time—there's always a harvest, even though it may be cut prematurely short. But if a cultivar's sowing guide is not observed, the genes of those seeds aren't given a chance to shine. Lettuce is a cool-season vegetable. All cultivars grow well when daytime temperatures are below 75°F and nights are above 40°F. That's a pretty narrow range. Because lettuce is such an important vegetable to so many cultures, an impressive amount of selective breeding has been done to expand the season. Today we have strains that handle conditions that by rights should be fatal to the fragile leaves.

In catalogese, *spring* lettuce means the cultivar grows true to form—it will bolt when the weather gets hot. Seeds of spring lettuces should be sown indoors three to four weeks before they're moved into the garden, where you'll cover them when the air is 28°F or colder. With the protection of a cold frame or floating row cover, lettuce is hardy to 20°F. Spring lettuces thrive when the air is light and the sun is thin. When heat hits, they flower and die. Butterheads and crisphead lettuces are the preponderance of cultivars sown for spring, and they can be grown in any part of the country.

Around the time you set tomatoes in the garden is the time to put away the packets of spring lettuce and switch to *summer* cultivars. Romaines, crispheads, and Batavians are generally best in the heat. In all but the most torrid climates, summer lettuces may be sowed through summer until a couple of weeks before the first expected frost. They'll carry through that first frost, being hardy, and give you leaves through the Indian summer that usually follows first frost.

It's wise to sow summer lettuces directly, since transplanted lettuces seem to have a tendency to bolt more than those sown in place. It's fun to crouch in front of a bed and simply sprinkle lettuce seeds over it, sparingly, then ruffle the patch with your hand as you would a child's hair, thereby lightly covering the seeds with earth. (Black-seeded lettuces want full light, so don't cover them with soil at all.) You could sow the seeds in soil blocks or paper pots, since the roots won't know they're being transplanted and you'd have more control over expensive seeds.

Where summer days are consistently 80°F or more, to keep ahead of bolting you must sow lettuces often and pick while the plants are young. The easiest way to time sowings is to sow when seedlings from the previous sowing emerge. Sow or set lettuces in high shade—such as beneath a tall tree whose branches begin well over your head. Or plant lettuces among pole beans, tomatoes, or corn (make sure it's a crop that likes its feet wet). There the plants can rejoice in light but not be blasted with sun. A gentle misting with the hose in the heat of the day can mean the difference between lettuces bolting and not.

When lettuces bolt, their leaves get bitter. Not that it does much good, except that you'll know to harvest and eat faster, but you can predict bolting. In leaf lettuces the new leaves in the center quickly get smaller, darker, and thicker, and in head lettuces, when you squeeze them, bolting is imminent when the heads become rockhard. Bolting usually begins around Labor Day.

Below the 50th parallel, around Labor Day it's time to sow the lettuces that will winter over. Several strains have developed the ability to shine through the short, cold, wet days of a temperate winter. With shelter from battering winds and rains, a bred-to-it cultivar can be perky when the air is 20°F. The bronzed butterhead Brune d'Hiver, well over a century old, is amazing. I just pull back the floating row cover and pick lettuce leaves all winter. If you have no warming, sheltering snow, set your winter lettuces in a cold frame. Winter Marvel and Rouge d'Hiver are two more extra-hardy, delicious, overwintering cultivars.

As soon as you've put away the New Year's horns and rattles, you can sow short-day-tolerant forcing cultivars of lettuce for harvesting a couple of months later. There aren't many of these offered, and the seedsmen keep changing their minds about a given cultivar's virtues, but I have sown Akcel, a deep green French butterhead, in the chill of February, and it was exciting harvesting lettuce in April.

If yours is a temperate climate, you can sow fast and slow cultivars at the same time—a traditional method with corn and tomatoes. Sow them as a bouquet in one place or plant each separately if you'll be replacing early lettuces with transplants of other crops. Don't be surprised if, given deep mulch, lots of water, and shade, heat-tolerant spring-sown lettuces last most of summer.

You can harvest leaves of all lettuces individually, always from the outside. With crisphead lettuces, you may pick down to the finely curled head, and then you can't pluck any more. But if you've spaced hearting lettuces closely, take up every other one when they're half-hearted, leaving room for those in the ground to fulfill their potential. Pick either in the cool of the morning while the leaves are still crisp with dew or just before you prepare them in the evening. Once the sun has softened their leaves, it's hard to get the crispness back. Leave about 2 inches at the base, and most plants will sprout anew. Or, when they're the size of your fist, cut a whole head for a luxe individual salad. For the most vibrant red in red looseleaf lettuces, harvest the leaves while young, since the color fades to green as the plant ages.

Most heading lettuces can double their weight in the 14 days approaching maturity. So don't slack on the water.

Do remember that each source has its own strain of a named cultivar. One man's Bibb is not another's.

Recommended: Utterly dependable are Black Seeded Simpson and Oakleaf looseleafs, Tom Thumb and Sierra butterheads, Diamond Gem and Winter Density romaines, Reine des Glaces and Webb's Wonderful crispheads/Batavians. For crispheads in the East, grow Ithaca and Salinas. In the West, Simpson Elite is a new slow bolter.

Malabar Spinach   *Basella alba*

Tender perennial in the Basella family, probably native to Africa and Southeast Asia . . . aka Indian spinach . . . grows in 5- to 10-gallon containers. Happiest in warm, rainy climates with a bit of shade in the heat of the day. In temperate climates, give full sun. Soil need be only moderately fertile. In places such as Florida, seeds sown in August make rapid growth through autumn.

This is one of the few greens that thrive in heat. Young leaves and slender stalks are fine in salad. I've never cooked them, but a mess of the leaves seasoned with hot chilies and mustard oil is popular in the lands where the plants are native. When cooked, the flavor is strong and the texture gluey.

From a distance, leaves of Malabar spinach—somewhat heart shaped, slightly ruffled, with veins etched in fleshy dark green—look like large tropical leaves of violets. The cultivar to grow is Rubra. It has red stems, which contrast wonderfully with the rich green leaves (smaller than those of vigorous all-green vines). Red-stemmed vines trailing up a pole or down from a hanging basket are handsome—they can reach 6 feet where it's hot, less than half that where it's cool.

Harvest tender leaves, pruning as you pick, with an eye to keeping the plant in pretty proportion.

If you had a place where you could mingle Malabar spinach with Grandpa Ott's purple morning glory, that would be a peaceable part of the garden.

A Beginner's Garden

Make it a delectable salad garden. Leafy greens from seeds might be: *arugula, dandelions, Black Seeded Simpson lettuce, red oak leaf lettuce, purslane.*

Vegetables from seeds might be: *Kentucky Wonder snap beans, lemon cucumbers, any scallions, Lady Godiva pumpkins, Parat Red radishes, Sweet 100 tomatoes; cocozelle zucchini.*

Add some sweet and chili pepper plants from the nursery.

Herbs and flowers from seeds might be: *Pacific Beauty calendulas, chives; flat-leaf parsley, Scarlet Gleam nasturtiums, Russian Mammoth sunflowers.*

From an herb nursery: *African blue basil, rosemary, lemon thyme, spearmint.*

And from the market, set cloves of garlic in the ground for green garlic.

MALLOW, CURLED
Malva verticillata var. *crispa*

Hardy annual in the Mallow family, native to Eurasia. Grow this decorative, undemanding addition to salads and garnishes in full sun, average soil.

Small purple or purply-white flowers with petals like geraniums cluster up and down the centers of tall stalks. Leaves are lobed and crisped and curled along the edges. This old-fashioned back-of-the-border plant was once cultivated for salad, and its time is coming again. Leaves and flowers are delicately flavored with a slight lettuce taste. The plants can get rank, so I mix them among stately things such as tall okra. Mallows are easy.

MINER'S LETTUCE
Montia perfoliata

Half-hardy annual in the Purslane family, native of British Columbia . . . aka claytonia. Give these delectable plants light, fertile soil and at least a half-day of sunshine.

Skidding into a meadowy home plate or swinging through a vacant lot with Rover, you've seen miner's lettuce but never known it was meant for salad. Miner's lettuce is the curious rounded triangle of a leaf that dips like a bowl in the center, from whence springs a tiny white flower—a bit like a miniature water lily pad. In our mountaintop garden, leaves are at most an inch across, and the whole plant is about 6 inches wide and 8 inches tall. A California native has fleshy leaves up to 5 inches wide and grows in a 12-inch mound—that must be what sustained miners in the Gold Country.

Pick the leaves (they taste like mild, fleshy spinach), leaving an inch of stem, and more will come. Seeds sown in summer and sheltered in autumn will provide greens through winter and spring, then they'll self-sow. If seedlings turn up out of place, they are easily moved.

PURSLANE
Portulaca oleracea

Tender annual in the Purslane family, probably native to India . . . aka pusley, verdolaga. Given fresh seed, purslane's easy to start in good soil, and once the tiny golden flowers bloom and go to seed, you can stop worrying about purslane ever after.

Europeans have cultivated purslane for centuries as a salad plant. It's crunchy and lemony. The native purslane in our garden is a low creeper, with thin red fleshy stalks and tiny fleshy green leaves that grow in nickel-size clusters. Over summer our purslane drapes itself charmingly over the rocks outlining the bed. This purslane makes a fine living mulch, preserving water and cooling roots of larger plants in hot weather. It's particularly good with tall plants such as corn and beans. I sprinkle the tiny seeds over the bed after I plant the bigger ones and think no more about it.

The leaves of the variety *sativa* (called *kitchen-garden* in Europe) are dime size and especially succulent—plants can grow knee-deep. The leaves of gold cultivars are paler, fleshier, and the plant more sprawling. The leaves of green cultivars are thinner, the tang is more pronounced, and the plant is more vigorous. I'm partial to the gold. I mix them with the golden feverfew toward the middle of the garden, as these purslanes have a floppy habit. For salads from either green or gold cultivar, pick whole stalks, leaving a couple of leaves at the base for growth.

Purslane is as generous with nutrients as it is with its seeds: the plant is the foremost land source of omega-3 fatty acids, and it's packed with vitamins and minerals. Some otherwise perfectly reasonable gardeners consider purslane a scourge. True, it's a plant that can take hold and crowd out less spirited souls—but I wouldn't be without it.

SAMPHIRE
Crithmum maritimum

Hardy perennial in the Parsley family, native to the seashores of Europe . . . aka rock samphire. Set samphire in a sunny place up close where you can admire its primeval charm—and give it a smooth white rock to set off its tracery.

Samphire—the word comes from "Saint Peter's herb"—is "of a spicie taste with a certaine saltnesse." Squinch your eyes and the foot-high plant might be a branch of delicate green coral washed up on a beach, and in fact samphire grows wild on English Channel cliffs and dunes. I smile when I pass mine growing out of a pocket of earth between small boulders at the top of the garden stairs. Had I known of its ties to the sea when I sent for seeds, I might not have tried growing samphire in the mountains. Because of samphire, I'll try anything.

You'll need only one plant because samphire is a perennial and you're not going to eat that much of it. I pick its tender leaves and then caraway-like sprays of blossoms from early summer until hard frost—they are cucumber-crunchy, with a light lemony/anisey/celery taste. One of my favorite salad surprises.

SHEPHERD'S PURSE   *Capsella bursa-pastoris*

Hardy annual in the Mustard family, native to temperate regions . . . aka mother's heart. Given rudimentary attention and a little shade, the plant will reward you with leaves most of the year.

These saw-toothed leaves in a graceful rosette offer nearly twice the vitamin C of oranges and ample vitamin A as well. Their flavor is mustard/dandeliony, a delicious fresh bitterness. You surely have shepherd's purse in your garden now. In the chill of autumn, some of the veins and leaves may be brushed with red. Do start with seeds from one of the sources listed, because cultivated leaves of shepherd's purse are larger and tastier than wild.

Pick leaves young, then let a few flowers go to seed for the future—but first strew some in a salad. The plant can grow over a foot tall, but leaves are tastier when they're smaller. Mix a few among butter lettuces for jagged against smooth.

SALSIFY   *Tragopogon porrifolius*

Hardy biennial in the Sunflower family, native to southern Europe . . . aka vegetable oyster, oyster plant; flowers: John go to bed at noon. Use fresh seeds. To grow plump salsify roots without hairiness or forking, prepare the soil as for parsnips, only expect the roots to grow 10 inches long. Mulch plants with peat or straw and keep the soil moist and free of weeds all season.

The root of salsify looks like a big beige carrot. The dark green leaves are long, slender, flat, and pointed, rather like a lily's. In spring of the second year the plant sends up mauve daisylike flowers. The blooms close late in the morning, thus their country name, John go to bed at noon. In English gardens salsify was grown as an ornamental long before its root was brought to the table. I grow half a dozen plants among lettuces—the reedy leaves of salsify and ruffles of lettuces delight me through summer.

Salsify is a forgotten vegetable in this country—if ever it was remembered—curious for one that is so versatile. The cooked creamy white flesh of well-grown roots is surprisingly succulent, almost waxy, with a silvery hint of oysters. Don't let the oyster part put you off. The flavor is subtle and delectable. Salsify in the garden can be enjoyed five ways.

From spring-sown seeds, roots can be pulled late autumn through winter. After they've been sweetened by frost, harvest a few roots in November—soak the soil before digging. That's one. Then mulch the rest with straw to winter over. Pull some when the ground softens between freezes. Then in early spring, those few left will send up tender shoots—the English call them *chards*—tender greens with the exquisite taste of spring. When they're about 5 inches long, into salads they go. That's two.

Feed the roots with fish emulsion after this harvest, and in a few weeks you can harvest shoots again. Sometimes even a third crop is fine and tender. These you might cook as a potherb. But by now the root is exhausted and not fit to eat.

Salsify and chicory are cousins, and long ago some resourceful gardener applied the same blanching notion that creates Belgian endives from sprouting chicory roots to these shoots. It worked. They are great fun; see The Gardener's Notebook. Because they'll be sporting pots in the flush of spring, I grow these plants in a utility place, throwing out pinches of ferny-leaved chervil to share the moist bed over summer. That's three.

Salsify plants that I want to flower the following year I rotate through the border next to perennial alliums—potato onions, Chinese chives, chives, and bunching onions. In early spring, up come salsify flower buds on tender stems. Some buds will be cut before they open and the bunch tossed in butter until tender-crisp, a tasty and charming garnish. That's four. Let the remaining flowers bloom, since they're so lovely, and bring them into the house for an arrangement. That's five. Once the plants have bloomed, however, the roots are too fibrous to harvest, so they must be pulled up and a new patch begun.

Salsify has no problems to speak of, unless you're plagued by aphids. A good spritz of the hose will knock them off. Harvest the root when you can feel down into the soil that the top of the root is about 1 ½ inches wide. To prevent breakage, soak the soil well and use a spade from the side to dig up gently. Salsify has an alter ego, scorzonera.

Recommended: Giant and Mammoth Sandwich Island are the standard cultivars, both excellent.

SAMPHIRE.   *See Salad Greens.*

SCORZONERA   *Scorzonera hispanica*

*Hardy perennial in the Sunflower family, native to Europe . . . aka
black salsify, Spanish salsify, viper's grass, black oyster plant. Culture
and harvest are the same as for salsify.*

Salsify and scorzonera both have cream-colored flesh, but salsify's skin is
beige and scorzonera's black. Although different genera, the two are often
spoken of in the same breath because they both have a subtle taste of oysters—in scorzonera this flavor lies in the skin.

Scorzonera's leaves are dark green, long, broad, and flat—very attractive in the
border and a fine addition to salads. A clump can stand 2 feet tall. They are handsome planted among brightly colored chili peppers. In the second spring there are
double-daisylike flowers of sunshine-yellow, also fine in salads. Unlike salsify, the
roots will still be edible after it has sent up flowers.

Recommended: Gigantia.

SHALLOTS.   *See Onions.*

SHEPHERD'S PURSE.   *See Salad Greens.*

SNAP BEANS.   *See Beans, fresh.*

SORREL.   *See Potherbs.*

SOYBEANS.   *See Beans, fresh.*

SPINACH

Round-Seeded: Spinacia oleracea var. *inermis*

Prickly-Seeded: S. oleracea var. *oleracea*

Hardy (20°F) annual in the Goosefoot family, native to southwest Asia . . . grows in 2-gallon containers. You'd think spinach wouldn't be fussy, but it is. For first-rate leaves, give it compost-rich soil with the right pH (see The Gardener's Notebook) and keep it moist at all times. And no crowding—this is one plant that must be thinned and meticulously weeded.

The seeds of the plant take two forms, prickly and smooth. Although there are exceptions to the rule, if leaves are dark and crinkled—called *savoyed*—the seeds are smooth—best sown for hot weather. If the leaves are lighter green and smooth, the seeds are prickly—best sown for harvesting through cold weather. Where winters are temperate, you can sow any spinach you like as often as you like from autumn till spring.

Spinach marks a summer's day. When it finds itself basking in 15 hours of light, or when the days warm to 80°F (particularly if it began life in cool weather), the plant thinks "Time to make seeds!" and up shoots a flowering stalk. The End. To work around this problem, sow an extra-early cultivar like Crystal Savoy as early as you can work the soil in spring. Floating row covers will shelter the seedlings against snow, if need be. Because these plants will flower once warm weather comes, mid-April sow the lightly crinkled Indian Summer, which is excellent eating and essentially ignores summer heat.

For a constant supply of spinach, you're supposed to sow every two weeks. When I'm pressed for time, I don't bother with the very early crop, I just sow a goodly number of seeds of a mix of cultivars once in late spring and pick leaves in a cut-and-come-again fashion until they all bolt. If I put them in a spot with little direct sun but bright light, sometimes they won't go to seed until the end of July. Where summers are hot, best forget spinach until late summer or fall. Instead sow Malabar or New Zealand spinach or perpetual beet if you're crazy about spinach's flavor.

Deep green bursts of ruffly spinach leaves are charming setting off polyanthus primrose, whose crinkly leaves resemble spinach's.

My spinach places are usually under tall oak trees, with about three hours of sun and the rest bright shade. If you have no such place, create one by growing spinach between rows of bush beans, celery, or tall brassicas. Despite what older books tell you, never add fast-acting nitrogen-rich fertilizer to spinach's soil. It will release the oxalate in spinach, the nitrites. Just enough compost or old-fashioned aged manure to loosen the soil is all you want.

Asian spinach. In moderately cold winters I've had sensational luck with Asian spinach. Slightly different from ours, they're extra-hardy, fast, and very tasty. Sheltered in a cold frame with a couple of layers of floating row covers over the plants, these spinaches can handle 15°F or even less outside. Cold makes the leaves very sweet. I sow this winter crop in August, sprouting the seeds between damp toweling in the refrigerator (spinach doesn't germinate well in warmth). One day I'll remember to sow spinach again in September—sheltered with mulch or snow, tender leaves will pop up in very early spring. Overwintered spinach wants a sprinkling of blood meal when growth begins in spring.

There are only a couple of reasons you might have problems with your spinach. If you sow it very late in spring, ill-equipped cultivars can be stressed in summer heat. Or if you water overhead in the afternoon, leaves won't have a chance to dry, and mildew can develop in the cool of the night.

To harvest, gently pinch off stems of side leaves at the base, always leaving about half the plant to keep it going. You can forestall bolting a bit by keeping the largest leaves picked.

Recommended: Probably the easiest well-flavored spinach to begin with is a classic crumpled Bloomsdale—Stokes Seeds' Longstanding Bloomsdale Dark Green, for example. Extra cold hardy is Winter Bloomsdale (aka Cold-Resistant Savoy), with its heavily crinkled leaves, and the Asian sorts, of course. Melody, Estivato, Bloomsdale Savoy, and Tyee have also prospered for me. And Low Acid spinach is good for people who shouldn't eat much oxalic acid. Another heat-tolerant spinach (besides Indian Summer) is Italian Summer hybrid. Asian spinach—take whatever your favorite Asian catalog offers—my favorite cultivar Shoshu has been dropped.

SPINACH BEETS. *See Potherbs.*

Squashes and Pumpkins

Cucurbita spp.

Unless otherwise stated, tender annuals in the Gourd family: C. max-ima (autumn and winter squashes and pumpkins), of cultivated origins, probably South America; C. mixta (cushaw, winter squashes, pump-kins, silver-seed gourds), native to Mexico and Guatemala; C. moschata (winter squashes, pumpkins, Canada pumpkins), of cul-tivated origins in America; C. pepo (summer and autumn squashes and pumpkins, gourds, marrows), of cultivated origins, probably North America . . . grow in 2-foot-deep containers. To live up to their poten-tial—which can be staggering—squash plants need warmth, full sun, well-drained and very rich soil, and lots of water. When a squash plant wilts from lack of water, it will produce smaller fruit as a result. Still, squashes are the most tolerant of cool climates of the Gourd family. And if summers are superhot, vines will be grateful for a little shade in the afternoon. Mulch heavily.

Where seasons are brief but squash appetites are enormous, warm the soil before sowing or planting seedlings with black plastic mulch.

The cultivation of squashes began thousands of years ago in southern Mexico, where today children of the gifted Mayans raise a brilliant array of squashes with loving hands. Over the centuries squashes were carried to every part of the Americas. It was a heritage plant for Native Americans here by the time the Pilgrims arrived.

Squashes are nutritious; they stick to the ribs yet are easily digested. And you can eat squashes at every stage from flower to seed-bearing fruit. More than nour-ishment, it's a rare squash that isn't a beautiful plant to look at. The forms of squashes are myriad and marvelous. Ready or not, they will be a focal point in the border. They're very appealing and most practically placed at the edge of the bor-der—their abundance softens the edges. If you move fast, you can aim them right, and they won't get in anybody's way.

By *aim* I mean that squash plants generally send out one main vine that marches hell-bent in one direction. Pumpkin vines are usually directable, being slender and supple. Summer squash vines, however, can get intimidatingly large, and they're not a bit supple, so after a point you can't direct their march. If it's an informal border, it shouldn't be a problem.

With summer squash you're continuously harvesting, and you end up having squashes only near the tip of the vine, having stripped the vines bare of all the others. With winter squash, of course you'll leave the fruits in place along the vine—an element to consider in landscaping.

Whether your season is long or short, plants will have a better chance against marauding bugs if you start seeds in paper pots indoors two to three weeks before you expect the weather to be warm and settled. As soon after that as the seedlings have three leaves, set them in the garden without disturbing their roots. (Don't start seeds earlier, because squashes grow vigorously, and once potbound, the roots never recover.)

Native Americans grew their squashes in hills, which, in northern latitudes, warmed soil earlier than soil resting deep in the chill. The practice is to leave a couple of plants per hill. I make mounds rather than hills and grow squashes one by one because I like to set them through my beds. But even a little rising helps keep lower branches from getting soggy when watered. If the plants aren't directly over a drip system, I dig a deep channel around each for irrigating.

Where each squash will grow, dig out 2 feet of soil in each direction and fill the hole with a mixture of half or three-fourths (I'm not kidding) well-aged rabbit or steer manure or composted straw and the rest as close as you can come to well-draining loam. A solution of blood meal as a foliar feed is recommended once a month.

Although lots of water makes squash vines that fly through the air, plants can survive without irrigation, enduring even a few weeks without water. They'll stop setting fruit, and they'll wilt alarmingly, but they'll recover—especially heritage cultivars with drought tolerance in their bones. Squashes haven't been a favorite crop of Native Americans for hundreds of years for no reason.

If squash disease and insects are a serious problem in your neighborhood, the moschatas are the most trouble-free winter squashes. Or keep the vines protected with floating row covers from start to finish. There are summer squashes that don't need pollination, and you can hand-pollinate blossoms of the rest. Another technique to try after female flowers appear: lift the covers every three or four days just for two hours, as soon as the bees are up in the morning, so they can work them.

Patrol the garden in the middle of the afternoon, early in the season and in the middle of the season, looking around the base of the plants, on the fruits, and under leaves for beetles and bugs. Squash them. If you get desperate, spray with a mixture of Rotenone and pyrethrum, both natural insecticides, or sabadilla dust, a botanical insecticide that works.

Once a plant shows signs of not recovering from a disease or attack, pull it out and burn it or bag it and send it to the dump. In fact, pull up an ailing plant at the first symptom, lest it infect others.

The squash tribe is complex, and it behooves us to know which is which. Why? Because each of the four species has its virtues and its shortcomings. Whether you're choosing squashes to grow or squashes to take home from the market, it's comforting to be able to make an informed choice. If you come upon a squash and want to know its breeding, the stem—botanically, the *peduncle*—will tell.

Maxima. The maximum in size and, many feel, in flavor. Flavor doesn't reach its peak in maximas until about two months after storage. Most fruits are enormous—some have grown to 600 pounds. Shapes are rounds to oblongs to turbans— buttercups, bananas, Hubbards, marrows, turbans, and the sort of pumpkins the fairy godmother called as a coach for Cinderella. Maximas are fine textured, and most keep reasonably well, with quality not diminishing over time. Shell colors can be orange, yellow, pink, gray-blue, white, and green, and some can be gorgeously rainbowed. Colors of the flesh are rich and deep. Seeds are white, tan, or brown with cream-colored margins. Vines are very long. Velvety maxima leaves are huge, round or heart shaped; stems are round, thick, soft, and corky. The aristocracy of the family, maximas can be more susceptible to wilts and insects than the rest of the clan.

Mixta (termed *argyrosperma* by some). These squashes have a tropical heritage. Most are curved-necked or pear-shaped cushaws, some of which are grown for their seeds. Mixtas are little grown in the North because, like moschatas, they don't thrive where nights are cool. But cushaws are grown in the South and Southwest because they stand up to heat and drought. Flesh is pale yellow to cream, long keeping, but fine texture and sweet flavor are not its long suits. Shells are orange, green, white, or yellow—some have vivid patterns in several of these colors. Seeds are long and white or tannish, with distinct margins, and it's the tasty seeds for which many mixtas are grown. Vines are long. Mixta leaves are large, hairy, and often splashed with yellow or white; stems are thick, angular, corky, sometimes warty, and flare slightly at the fruits. Mixtas are the most drought tolerant of squashes, and they have good resistance to beetles and borers

Moschata. There are squashophiles who believe the moschatas are the sweetest of squashes. Most commonly cultivated are the butternuts. The moschatas also include flat cheese pumpkins—especially fine keepers—and golden cushaws. Seeds are beige with a darker edge. Blossoms can be huge and beautiful. Vines are long; leaves are large and hairy but not prickly. Slender, slightly angular stems are distinctive because they broaden at the fruit in five rounded knobs. Although they don't do well when nights are cooler than 60°F, established moschatas are enormously vigorous and resist insect damage.

Pepo. Here are our well-loved zucchinis, crooknecks, pattypans, vegetable marrows—all the summer squashes—acorns, vegetable spaghettis, Delicatas, Sweet Dumplings, and most of the pumpkins. Pepos are as flavorful as they're going to be right after harvest. Fruits take many shapes, and while most of the mature fruits are orange, some are green, gray, white, yellow, or multicolored. Flesh is cream to orange. Pepos are fastest to mature, but on the whole the shortest keeping—many must be eaten within a month of harvest. Seeds are white with white margins. Most of the squashes that grow as bushes are pepos, but pepos may be long-vining, too. Pepo leaves are 6 to 12 inches long and prickly—they give me a rash when they touch my skin, so I wear long sleeves and pants when working around them. Stems are very prickly, hard, and sharply five-angled—when cut, the end makes a star. Bush cultivars of pepos are vulnerable to borers. Either grow several of these crops a couple of weeks apart and harvest what you can or stick to vine cultivars with built-in resistance.

If raccoons live nearby, pepos are the prickly deterrents you need to keep safe your corn and other raccoon-tempting crops. Pepo squashes have been called nature's barbed wire fence.

Squashes are as ancient and their genetics as tangled as any fruit on earth. Natural crossing can irrevocably change the seed under one's hand in a season. The seed is only as reliable as the seedsman—and reliability isn't the whole issue. Personality and taste come into play. The seed you're offered in a catalog is what appeals to the person who composed the collection. How can you know if you share his/her view of the world?

For example, serious plantsmen I know grow Arikara, a pre-Columbian maxima, and offer seed through Seed Savers Exchange, noting it's an excellent keeper. Another squash specialist I know offers Arikara commercially, noting "poor keeper."

The Difference Between Summer and Winter Squashes

Summer squash, with its tender skin and ghosts of seeds, is eaten at the immature—i.e., green—stage, the way kernels of sweet corn are eaten while young and "green." Clearly it's called *summer* squash because it's ready to eat in summer. Winter squash has a hardened shell and seeds ripe for sowing, and it takes almost until winter for it to reach that maturity.

You can let any summer squash ripen and then cook and eat it in the manner of winter squash. You can also eat the fruit of any so-called winter squash in the green stage in the heat of summer—maybe it will be delicious, maybe it won't. (See Cocozelle.) Acorn squashes are tasty at all stages.

However, after centuries of those who love them breeding squashes, certain cultivars have come to be regarded as being best eaten in certain seasons.

And yes, pumpkins, as glamorous and as much given to fairy tales as they may be, are just another winter squash.

Vining vs. bush cultivars—quality and quantity vs. space. Who knew that leaves on Mother Nature's vegetable plants were more than pretty things that shake and shimmer in a breeze? As with asparagus, peppers, beans, and tomatoes, the more leaves, the better yield and often the better flavor. It's the same for squashes.

Leaves are like solar collectors for a heating system. They pump energy into the plant, which pours the energy into the fruits. In squashes this energy takes the form of dry matter—pleasing texture, and sugars—pleasing taste. No bush cultivar can compare in quality or quantity of squashes with closer-to-the-wild long-vined sorts.

Which brings up an interesting point. With few exceptions the squashes we eat at the immature stage—summer squashes—are bush forms of pepos. They aren't asked to go for the gold. The golden and orange and red and blue squashes of winter spring from the energy of long leafy vines. The great pumpkins we cherish are also pepos, but the long-vined sort.

But there are ways to pare down winter squash vines without sacrificing fruit quality. Pinch off the ends—the growing tips—of vines once they've reached 4 feet or as much as you can accommodate. And if resources such as length of growing season and space and even water are limited, you can thin the fruits, too—four winter squash to a pinched plant will ensure the best possible flavor in those fruits.

If you wish seeds of open-pollinated squashes to come 99 $^{44}/_{100}$ percent true, grow just one cultivar of all species except moschatas—and none of those. Or grow as many of everything as you please and have the fascinating job of hand-pollinating them. Cover your female flower with a paper bag or a plastic screen to keep it pure.

Gourds will also cross with squashes and wreak havoc. Timing, timing.

Not to worry when the first exciting blossoms on your plants dry up and fall off. This is the plant's way of revving up—clearing its throat. Squash plants are one of those that grow both male and female flowers. Usually male flowers are produced first, all by themselves—there are no ladies for the bees to carry their pollen to. In some cultivars there won't be female flowers until the vines are really humming—4 feet long! You can tell male blossoms easily because their stems are slender all the way to the base. The slender stem of a female blossom ends in a rounded bottom beneath the flower—a nascent squash. When you pick squash blossoms for stuffing and sautéing, unless you have so much squash you could scream, leave the female blossoms, potential squashes, and take the males—but of course not all of them.

Later in the season you're liable again to have female blossoms fall barren to the earth—the plant can't support any more children. That self-pruning is done by every plant in your garden.

Saving seeds of your favorite squashes. Another reason to be cognizant of the squashes' species is this magical mystery: the cells that will develop into the skin and flesh of a squash were already formed in the female flower's ovary before the flower ever opened. Therefore, the open-pollinated seed you have in your hand—if it came from a reliable source—will grow into the squash you expect no matter whose pollen fertilizes the ovary. But the cells that will develop into the *seeds* of that squash are formed by the union of the female flower's ovules and the male flower's pollen. Therefore, the open-pollinated seed you will have in your hand next summer will grow into whatever squash is created by the two flowers.

A study has proven that male pollen from moschata can fertilize a female maxima flower. There are plantsmen who believe moschata will also cross with pepo. And some say pepo will cross with mixta. Everyone agrees that when squashes of the same species grow within a quarter of a mile of one another, pandemonium breaks out. Some say within two miles. A lusty group! You won't know about this hanky-panky when you harvest the squashes. It will be evident in the next generation when the seeds have borne fruit. The fruit may or may not bear similarity to its parents.

SQUASH SEEDS

Some cultivars have been developed for their seeds, which you can roast and nibble for their valuable nourishment. Some even have no hulls. Naked Seeded/Lady Godiva/Godiva are pumpkin-shaped pepos with inedible flesh but seeds without hulls. Being pepos, the vines are long and prickly, so train them up a trellis if you're crazy about squash seeds for roasting. Mini-Jack is a pumpkin grown for its hull-less seeds.

Recommended: Veracruz Pepita's seeds are long and narrow—Pepita has grown well in the cool Pacific Northwest—and Silver Edged's seeds are large and white with—yes—a silver edge (both are mixtas).

SUMMER SQUASHES   *C. pepo*

Of cultivated origin, probably North America.

Summer squashes are classed as bush squashes, which means that they won't devour your garden in the process of giving you pounds and pounds of good eating. That's the first thing about summer squashes. All you have to do is pick the squashes faithfully. As with other fruiting plants, when a squash is left on the vine, the plant pours its energy into making that fruit's seeds mature and doesn't make new flowers, so that's the end of your summer squash harvest. A happy and productive summer squash plant can yield hundreds of fruits; its winter squash sibling can give you 30 fruits of acorn squash size.

How many summer squashes should you grow? For the two of us, for variety, I grow one zucchini, one pattypan, and one crookneck. That gives us a different shape of squash every couple of nights, some to dry and some for friends.

Drying is the only means of preserving excess summer squashes I find palatable. You do it in shreds, and come winter, you can't imagine how grateful you'll be to have fresh-tasting zucchini in the minestrone. They'll keep for years.

Summer squash vines are most decorative in the border, especially close to the big lavender—fine, upright, gray-green lavender and sprays behind lush green leaves and golden blossoms.

COCOZELLE SQUASHES *C. Pepo* var. *Melopepo*

You can tell if your long, slender dark green squash is cocozelle rather than zucchini if it has greeny-yellow or light green stripes down the sides. Sometimes they're fluted. Young squashes will be ready for the table about 10 days earlier than zucchini—or most any other summer squash for that matter. At that point in the season those 3-inch squashes are bliss. Cocozelles are fine-textured and tasty.

Zucchina Costa Romanesca is fluted, prized in Italy, where it's picked so young the blossom's still attached. The exquisite pair are quickly sautéed in olive oil. Fiorentino is another fluted squash, traditionally harvested when it's as long as a strand of spaghetti.

When other summer squashes hit their stride, you can let these *ragazzi* keep on growing. They'll be fully matured with yellow flesh in about four months—the first winter squash to enjoy on a chill autumn evening.

Recommended: Choose just plain Cocozelle from a reliable seedsman, as well as the others mentioned.

CROOKNECK SQUASHES *C. Pepo* var. *Melopepo*

Crookneck squashes can take a longer time pulling themselves together than others, but they will make up for it by producing steadily until summer's end. Harvest at 3 to 4 inches.

The bright yellow, slightly warty, thin curved necks and bulbous bottoms of crooknecks seem to have the sunniest flavor of summer squashes.

Despite the fact that all good seedsmen aim to give me the best squash to satisfy my yen for creamy, sweet, gold, warty yellow crooknecks, I know that Johnny's Selected Seeds' Yellow Crookneck is not going to taste the same as Territorial Seed Company's Yellow Crookneck, and both will be different from Lockhart Seeds' Early Yellow Summer Crookneck. Seeds will have been chosen specifically for conditions in the North, the Pacific Northwest, and central California—and seeds will have strayed a long way from the nucleus of yellow crooknecks when only a handful of seedsmen were raising them. My garden has aspects of all these areas in it. So what I do is grow a different strain each year and keep notes.

And that's why I always include an open-pollinated yellow crookneck among summer squashes, so when I find one that really rings my bell I can save its seeds and know I'll have it to enjoy forever.

Flavorful hybrids are coming along, though, and they can be counted on to be consistent, at least for a while. Many are also more resistant to or tolerant of most of the diseases that frustrate squash growers. The skin of hybrid crooknecks has no warts.

There are also straightneck crooknecks. Even though they're zucchinilike in shape, they're paler and fuller figured than zucchini. Early Prolific Straightneck is an open-pollinated cultivar that won an AAS award—in 1938! It's still holding its own in catalogs, with creamy yellow flesh that's tender and succulent. And the exuberant Multipiks and Sunbars are straightneck kin to other yellow squashes with a precocious gene (see the box on page 224).

And, there are yellow semicrooknecks. Dixie, a hybrid from Early Yellow Summer Crookneck, is said to do well under adverse conditions, and it has delicious, creamy yellow, smooth flesh.

Recommended: For flavor, see those already named. If it's important that necks don't break when you harvest your crooknecks, grow early, vigorous, bright yellow Sundance. Crookneck (some say it's a semicrookneck) Supersett is tasty and high yielding and resistant to cucumber mosaic virus and watermelon mosaic virus, race 2. Hybrid Golden Girl is a tasty straightneck.

PATTYPAN/SCALLOP SQUASHES   *C. Pepo* var. *Melopepo*

Aka custards. Harvest the size of small daisies.

I find the old-fashioned flat, scalloped pattypans have a nuttier and spicier taste than most other summer squashes. One of the charmers of the garden is Sunburst, the butter-yellow hybrid pattypan with the dot of green at its base. Sunburst is buttery through and through and really needs none, just a few specks of nutmeg and parsley. Golden Bush Scallop matures a couple of weeks after other pattypans, but its flavor, too, is worth waiting for, and it will keep you in golden pattypans till frost.

For old-fashioned, sweet, pale green pattypan, I've loved both Benning's Green Tint and Early Green Bush Scallop, a Benning's strain—both are delicious. As with crookneck, I'd rather grow an open-pollinated pattypan, but the pale green AAS winner Peter Pan is a hybrid that grows easily everywhere, is tasty, and is of high quality. And for the contrast of dark green skin and pale green flesh, hybrid Scallopini is sweet and productive.

To taste a pattypan said to date from before 1722, grow White Bush Scallop (or its sibling, Early White Bush Scallop). Fruits are flat and pale green with creamy flesh, although they can get tough if not picked small. Wood's Prolific is another heritage white scallop.

Precocious Yellow Summer Squashes

Squash breeders and a joyous gene in gourds have given the world a whole heap of brilliance. The "precocious yellow" gene causes squashes to turn a heartstopping yellow uncommonly early in their growth, to create more female flowers, which increases the crop, to forestall effects of the cucumber mosaic virus (even when the plant is infected), to have a rich hint of the taste and scent of pumpkins, and to be higher than other summer squashes in beta-carotene, the valuable precursor of vitamin A.

These golden jewels are Sunburst scallop, Butterstick zucchini, Supersett crookneck, and Multipik and Sunbar straight summer squashes. More are on the way.

ZUCCHINI SQUASHES   *C. Pepo* var. *Melopepo*

Aka courgettes.

Ah, zucchini. A joy in July and a joke in September.

But can you imagine summer without zucchini? Zucchinis seem to get tastier and tastier, probably because more and more are being offered. At the end of summer I usually like the one I just grew the best. Last year I fell in love with Butterstick, a nutty-tasting golden hybrid. Although the bush didn't give me heaps of fruits, what came was divine and over a long period, and I don't think I'll ever be without it.

There's no sound that melts my heart more than the echo of a bee humming to herself from the bottom of a squash blossom as she stuffs pollen into her baskets. Someone had the brilliant idea to develop a zucchini just for its flowers. Butterblossom did only moderately well for me, but I was fighting critters tooth and nail, and perhaps mice got their share of the flowers. As it turns out, the catalog I bought it from has dropped Butterblossom, so perhaps it wasn't me.

The wealth of zucchini colors and shapes includes dear round squashes. Ronde de Nice has light green skin and smooth flesh tastier than most zucchini. I haven't found it easy to grow, and I've heard that from others. But once you've got it going, you'll be thrilled. Harvest plum size or larger for stuffing. Hybrid Gourmet Globe is darker than Ronde de Nice and striped, but it, too, has exceptional flavor. Hybrid Sundrops are oval, but I found the plant's name more memorable than its fruit.

At the heart of the zucchini matter, of course, are the green ones, and here it's a zoo. Every description of every zucchini in every catalog is superlative. But they're talking about appearance and yields and ease of picking more than taste.

That narrows the field. After Ronde de Nice (which has two points for its peerless flavor and round shape), there's Greyzini. A medium-light green hybrid, I think it's the best of the straight zucchinis I've tasted. The compact vines produce early and abundantly and over a long period, and it's very widely adapted. For an open-pollinated version, its forebear was Grey Zucchini, a most superior squash because its yield is also extended over a long period. Black and Dark Green are other open-pollinated cultivars that get high praise for flavor.

Seeds of Change offers White Egyptian Zucchini. It bears plump 9- to 10-inch creamy green fruits.

Recommended: For flavor, those already mentioned. For self-pollination and good flavor, Type 1406 from Cook's Garden.

WINTER SQUASHES AND PUMPKINS

In catalog descriptions, dry flesh is better on the plate than moist-fleshed squash. For pies and cakes, it's the reverse.

To get the sweetest, meatiest squashes from each plant, thin it to three or four fruits. Winter squashes cannot get overripe. As long as the vine is healthy, the squash will wait patiently to be harvested. It's crucial to harvest before frost. If mature, the heftier thick-shelled maximas will scrape through a light frost. But if their vines are killed, immature squashes must go to the compost pile, or dig them in. Unlike the green tomatoes you can bring indoors to ripen, immature squashes are finished off their vines.

Because you want the viningest, leafiest plants, you must either send winter squash vines up a trellis or fence (and support the fruit with slings) or give them their liberty on the ground. These magnificent plants are thrilling to look at in the border. Even before the fruits turn autumn-gold and orange and red and blue, green squashes of all shapes are appealing. When planning your garden, see if you can find a place for at least one glorious winter squash to mix with herbs and flowers in a main bed.

For what it's worth, one squash breeder believes that in maximas, at any rate, all-green or green-and-orange-mottled fruits are sweeter than fruits that are pure orange.

For well-cured, thick-shelled squash, be prepared to use a hacksaw or an axe to cut it up for cooking. Smaller, softer shells will surrender to a sharp stout knife and a mallet—using four hands, please.

Where it's cool and/or damp in early autumn, vines of squashes can mildew. That's not a problem for summer squashes that are finishing, but it's the end of winter squashes as well. So try not to get water on leaves and stalks from midsummer on and never water after 10:00 A.M.

The Winter Squash Eating Calendar

These delectable, satisfying, sunny, low-calorie (a third to less than half the calories of potato) vegetables not only come in a bunch of shapes, they also vary in size. Since some don't keep and others do, a winter squash-eating plan can carry you worry free through winter, spring, and even summer. As squash keeps, it develops more and more beta-carotene.

Assuming squashes are in storage by the beginning of November . . .

Acorns through October. Baby Bear pumpkins through November. Stripettis through December. Black Forests through January. Sweet Dumplings and Delicatas through February. Sweet Mama buttercups through March. Blue Kuris through April. Cheeses through May. Waltham Butternut through June. Green Hubbard Improved through July. Tahitian Melon (moschata) through August. Arikara through September—but before this, Autumn Gold pumpkins will be ready!

One great thing about having a mammoth winter squash on your hands is that its flesh, steamed and pureed, freezes more palatably than almost any other vegetable or fruit.

Also in shorter seasons, it's wise to bring unfertilized female flowers and infant squashes into the kitchen after the first of September. This way the plant can concentrate on maturing and flavoring the fruits it's got.

As for other maturing fruit-on-the-ground, cushion the squash on straw or newspapers or a large smooth rock to preserve its shape and its shell.

To harvest and cure, leave an inch of stem on the fruit, making a clean cut with clippers or a sharp knife. Either line the wheelbarrow with something cushioning or carry fruits individually to where they'll be cured—no nicks, scratches, or bruises. For circulation of air, cure winter squashes in a single layer on a screen lined with straw propped above the ground—or some such arrangement. Curing dries and hardens the shell and can take one day in cool sunny weather or three days where it's damp. Before storing, wipe fruits with a solution of 1 tablespoon chlorine bleach in every cup of water. Air-dry thoroughly, then store fruits between 50°F to 60°F at 50 to 70 percent humidity. Cool, dry, and dark. Don't stack squashes, but let air circulate around them. Every few weeks, inspect for rusty or black patches—signs of spoilage. Bring the affected squash into the kitchen and trim and cook and eat or freeze it. Particularly watch any fruit with warts. Dips between bumps can hide spoiling organisms.

ACORN SQUASHES   *C. Pepo* var. *Pepo*

Because pepos mature fastest, acorns are among the best choices for short seasons. Acorns are easy to pick and to cook. Their flavor is pleasing.

It's hard to tell when acorns are mature—they color up before they're fully sweet. The test about not being able to dent the shell with your thumbnail doesn't pertain to these small squashes—they can be ready before that time. Check the calendar according to the days to harvest on the seed packet (starting from the day you set seedlings in the garden). When the day comes, bake a squash. If it's ready, you can harvest the rest or leave them on the vines until frost threatens. Harvest well before frost.

Acorn squashes are tasty eaten at the immature stage. Zapallito del Tronco—glossy dark green skin with golden flesh—is offered as a round summer squash that matures into a winter squash. But a newer cultivar, Table Gold, can do the same thing. With golden orange rind, it's sweeter, more tender, and less fibrous than green-skinned acorns. And its pale gold flesh has three times more beta-carotene. Leave two to four squashes on the plant to mature and harvest the rest as summer squash, starting 50 days from sowing. Mature fruits weigh 1 to 1 ½ pounds.

For the rest of your acorn winter squash, consider Ebony Acorn. It's one of the best-flavored acorns, doesn't need sun curing—just grab one of its green-black fruits from the vine, rinse off the earth, and stick the squash in the oven. Ebony Acorn will keep for three to four months after harvest, a long time for pepos. Table Ace is also green-black with delicious orange flesh.

For a taste of the first acorn offered in this country—1913—grow Acorn/Table Queen/Des Moines. The ribbed, dark gray-green fruits with thick orange flesh come from wandering vines. Many consider this still the highest-yielding, finest-quality, nuttiest-tasting acorn squash extant. And it stores well.

Jeff McCormack of Southern Exposure Seed Exchange tells me the pale gold shell and golden flesh of the Missouri heirloom, Thelma Sanders' Sweet Potato, is the best-tasting acorn he's found.

Recommended: The original Acorn in one of its avatars and Thelma Sanders', with Table Gold and Ebony Acorn second. By the way, a fuss has been made about the white hybrid acorn Cream of the Crop, an AAS winner. In a tasting of seven winter squashes at *Sunset* magazine, for its blandness, Cream of the Crop came in last (Sweet Mama buttercup was first).

BANANA SQUASHES · *C. maxima*

Except for Pink Jumbo Banana, a squash that should be harvested before it's more than 75 pounds or 2 ½ feet long, whichever comes first, cultivars of bananas are as scarce as hen's teeth. If your only experience with banana squash is a slab from the market, then visit someone who's growing the squash or grow it yourself to see the beautiful, cylindrical, warm pink.

Since they grow so large—there don't seem to be any small banana squashes—there are no early cultivars for short seasons.

Recommended: Pink Jumbo Banana.

BUTTERCUP SQUASHES · *C. maxima*

At the bottom of buttercups is a raised bellybutton of contrasting color, as though the fairy touched it there. Fruits are shaped like drums or tops or turbans.

For shorter (4-foot) vines, hybrid Sweet Mama has won compact-squash taste tests again and again. Fruits average 2 ½ pounds, are tolerant to fusarium and squash borers, and keep for five months. Sweet Mama is dark green and resembles a kabocha. Forest green Black Forest is a buttercup without the button, like a smaller kabocha. However, many regard Burgess—3 to 5 pounds of gray-flecked, dark green drum with thick, dry, orange, sweet potato-like flesh—as the quintessence of winter squash.

Recommended: Burgess Buttercup because it's open pollinated. Sweet Mama hybrid will have to take care of herself.

BUTTERNUT SQUASHES   *C. moschata*

Butternut is the plain Jane at the dance and not the prom queen, but butternut gets picked for a whirl more than anybody realizes. Looking like a very large tan pear with a long, thick neck, butternut hides a surprise inside—warm orange flesh that keeps and keeps and a comparatively small seed cavity at the base. Butternuts are the most nutritious of the winter squashes, with nearly twice the beta-carotene and vitamin C of Hubbard, the runner-up.

An AAS winner, the Waltham strain of butternut is one of incomparable quality and flavor. The flesh is rich, sweet, and dry, and the preponderance of fruits are uniform—the odd crook in the neck turns up, but it has no effect on flavor. Fruits are 3 to 6 pounds, depending on the seedsman, on vigorous vines.

One semibush hybrid, another AAS winner, has been given raves for flavor and productivity—Early Butternut hybrid. Its vines still go flying, but they're more compact than Waltham.

Ponca Butternut is a newer butternut, earlier and smaller than Waltham, but more prolific. Both are good keepers. Zenith Hybrid's fruit is smaller and heavier, and there's half again as much of it as of Waltham Butternut.

If squash borers are a problem, the solid stems of butternuts will thwart them.

Recommended: For flavor and aroma, wonderful Waltham. Ultra Butternut Hybrid is three times the weight.

CHEESE SQUASHES   *C. moschata*

With thick orange flesh, these squashes are large, flat, and ribbed, resembling fluted wheels of cheese. Magdalena Big Cheese will cover your garden with 50-pound orangey-tan ancestors of one of the oldest squashes in America.

Just plain Cheese, a tall cheese shape, weighs 10 pounds, is an excellent keeper with delicious flesh, and rare.

Rio Mayo Big Cheese is a name that embraces a variety of colors and shapes suited to low, hot desert regions. Seeds can be sown in winter, spring, or during summer rains, then dry-farmed (see page 256).

Recommended: Cheese, by all means.

CUSHAW SQUASHES   *C. mixta*

These are the squashes for long, hot, droughty summers.

I don't have the climate for cushaws, but the pale yellow flesh of Santo Domingo, a dark-and-light-green-striped squash from the Santo Domingo Indians, is said to make an incomparable pie. It can be eaten in the immature stage for summer squash, and its roasted seeds are tasty. Santo Domingo is tolerant of drought and can go two to three weeks between waterings.

Tennessee Sweet Potato is a white, pear-shaped heirloom with pale yellow flesh of fine quality. Green-Striped Cushaw is the most popular cushaw outside the Southwest—its flesh is lightly sweet and rather coarse, suited to pies and squash bread.

Recommended: Green-Striped Cushaw, for starters.

HUBBARD SQUASHES   *C. maxima*

There can be a great deal of Hubbard squash when you grow it. Not only are plants prolific, but squashes are huge. Happily, Hubbards are the best keepers.

Golden Delicious has a very hard shell (it looks like a pumpkin in the shape of a child's top) that makes it a superb keeper. Unsurpassed for freezing.

The classic Warted Hubbard is 8 to 10 pounds of thick, dry, sweet, fine, deep orange unstringy flesh beneath a hard, very bumpy green-black shell. Growing on vigorous vines, it has the true Hubbard shape, which is that of two chocolate kisses stuck together. The flesh freezes beautifully and makes great pies. Green Hubbard is a blue-green-shelled heirloom from the 1790s. Many seedsmen offer Green Warted Hubbard, except it's really Green Hubbard Improved, which is also offered as Hubbard Improved Green.

Blue Hubbards are 10 to 20 pounds of bumpy, ribbed blue-gray squashes with fine-grained, very sweet yellow flesh. They're a New England favorite—beautiful in the garden and fine eating.

Golden Hubbards have an orangeish shell and fine, sweet, dry flesh. They're about 10 pounds and mature earlier than the green and blue Hubbards.

Perhaps the best Hubbard news of all is sweet Blue Ballet, a 4-pound version of Blue Hubbard, and Mini Green Hubbard, a 2½-pound version of Hubbard Improved Green. These are welcome in the North because they'll be mature and tasty within a short growing season.

Recommended: For flavor, Golden Hubbard. For short seasons, definitely the minis—Mini Green Hubbard and Blue Ballet.

KABOCHA AND OTHER JAPANESE SQUASHES   *C. maxima, C. moschata*

These squashes grow most vigorously in warm climates.

You know what happened to names of Asian greens when they crossed the Pacific Ocean. Japanese winter squashes have not escaped the same fate.

Kabocha (Ka BOH sha) is a Japanese term for little pumpkin.

In this country—at this writing—we grow two sorts of winter squashes (some resembling what we think of as pumpkins) developed in Japan: Green Hokkaido and Orange Hokkaido.

Green Hokkaido squashes are basically buttercups—round or squarish drum shapes lightly or markedly ribbed. Small children can carry them for jack-o'-lanterns. In Japan there are several sorts of Green Hokkaidos, and they're slowly being released to our seedsmen. So far we have nonhybrid maxima Green Hokkaido and very warty moschatas Chirimen and Black Futtsu. Hybrid maximas are Delica, Butterball, Home Delight, Sweet Delite, Honey Delight, and Naguri.

In Japan the shells of mature Green Hokkaidos are different colors. The ones we know are matte dark gray-green or blue-green. I find them exquisite—they remind me of Chinese pottery. Flesh is invariably fine, nutty-sweet, thick, dry to the point of being buttery-flaky, and warm orange.

So in this country—here comes the leap—*kabocha* has come to mean the Green Hokkaido type of squashes we know. When you see squash described as kabocha in a catalog, you'll know what to expect. It's my favorite winter squash.

Orange Hokkaidos are shaped like globes and teardrops. They were developed from good old American Hubbards—a gift of ours handsomely returned. *Orange* in the name refers to the flesh, since the shell of Blue Kuri is Blue Hubbard blue. It's flesh is orangeish yellow. Red Kuri is red through and through. To my surprise, not everyone warms to Red Kuri's taste—it's been called "distinctly different." I don't know what that means, but it's a reminder of how individual our palates are.

Uchiki Kuri, should you see it offered, is Japanese for Red Kuri.

Tetsukabuto is a maxima/moschata cross. It has a small scar on its blossom end, which denotes, Pinetree Garden Seeds tells us, "better flavor than the other Japanese squashes with larger blossom end scars." It's dark green and roundish with sweet, nutty, deep yellow flesh. A good keeper.

Recommended: For flavor, any of the kabochas née Green Hokkaido. Honey Delight hybrid is one of the best.

More maxima winter squashes. Sweet Meat—up to 15 pounds of slate-gray skin and thick, dry, fiberless, golden-orange flesh nearly as sweet as the buttercups—is a favorite in the Northwest.

For drought conditions, Arikara is a pre-Columbian squash grown by Arikara Indians of the northern plains. Similar in shape and keeping quality to Hubbards— it keeps for 10 months—smaller (10 pounds) Arikaras grow especially well in the Midwest. Where the leaves join the vines, the plant can set down roots. Arikara just keeps rooting itself, reaching into the soil, drawing sustenance from it. Who needs water? This capability also makes the plant less vulnerable to vine borers. Fruits can mature as early as 72 days, and it makes good pie.

For those who don't like winter squash too sweet, there are Chestnuts. They're deep slate-green the size of buttercups and shaped like turbans without the top knot. Their orange flesh is wonderfully dry and not sweet—in storage, they become moister and lightly sweeter.

More moschata winter squashes. Should you have six months of warm days, Tahitian Melon/Tahitian may be the sweetest of winter squashes. It's very long keeping, and its sweetness increases in storage. Fruits are from 8 to 20 pounds and resemble a graceful, long-necked, golden butternut. Vines are mildew resistant. If your season is marginal, at least try to have this splendid squash by starting seeds indoors and using floating row covers at the beginning and end of the season.

For hot, dry, or droughty places, Upper Ground Sweet Potato—an Appalachian acorn-shaped heirloom—is rampant but reliable. It has orangeish flesh with butternut flavor. Fruits are more variable in this strain than most, which bothers some people and not others.

More pepo winter squashes. The cream-with-green-stripes of small Sweet Dumplings don't appeal to me as much as the vivid coppers and golds of other squashes, but these are dear. Each is an individual serving of orange flesh, and as sweet as can be—and they're open pollinated.

Delicatas/Sweet Potatoes are usually mentioned in the same breath with Sweet Dumplings because they're an elongated version. They're even sweeter than butternuts and very fine grained, with an iron-hard shell. Neither Sweet Dumpling, Delicata, nor Sweet Potato requires curing, and they store for three to four months. Sugar Loaf is a fine strain of Delicata, tan-and-green and blockier, but it won't store as long.

PUMPKINS

Cucurbita spp.

To get the biggest possible pumpkins, in addition to the usual nurturing, when all the pumpkins have set that you expect to mature by the first frost, remove all flowers and baby fruits and cut back each vine to the first pumpkin. Harvest before frost or in time for Halloween, whichever comes first. For jack-o'-lanterns, leave 3 inches of stalk. Sow miniature pumpkins at least one week before other winter squashes to avoid cross-pollination.

In this country any squash that ripens to orange and is the least bit round is called a pumpkin. And of course they're not a separate item botanically. One of the biggest thrills in the garden is growing pumpkins. Partly because they're so vivid, partly because I know there's scrumptious eating just waiting in the patch. Later on, the sight of an orange pumpkin in a corner of the wintry entry hall lifts my spirits.

The basic pumpkins you buy at the market or pumpkin stand are delightful and make fine jack-o'-lanterns. So that frees you up to grow fantasy pumpkins in your patch . . .

Rouge Vif d'Etampes is gleaming copper-red, deeply fluted, big and round and flattish—1 to 1 ½ feet wide and ½ foot tall. Flavor is less the point of this pumpkin than its origins in a French fairy tale. But well grown, vines are productive, and fruits can reach 25 to 30 pounds with sweet flesh. And it's a maxima, so it keeps better than pepo pumpkins.

Considered the finest general-purpose pumpkin, Small Sugar—also known as New England Pie—was introduced before the Civil War. It has the sweet, fine, dry yellow-orange flesh we expect in winter squash and a small seed cavity; it's bright orange and pleasingly flattened and ribbed. Small Sugars weigh a generous but not overwhelming 6 to 8 pounds. An open-pollinated pepo.

A little-known treasure, Sugar Baby/Honey Pumpkin, is the favorite of Jeff McCormack of Southern Exposure Seed Exchange. It's a Minnesota heirloom from the 1880s, the same shape but half the size of Rouge Vif d'Etampes. Dry, sweet orange flesh, another open-pollinated pepo.

Connecticut Field was introduced in this country before 1700, and it's still everybody's favorite for an all-purpose pumpkin—for pies, freezing, jack-o'-lanterns, and the just plain joy of having such a vibrant spirit in our midst. Bright orange Connecticut Field has been called Big Tom and Yankee Cow in its past. Just for that, it never lets you know what shape it'll turn up in. It gets to be 10 to 15 pounds and is slightly ribbed. If unpredictability is not for you, Howden is a predictable open-pollinated Connecticut Field.

An offspring of Small Sugar (the Papa was a seeded sort without hulls), Baby Bear is a pumpkin patch kind of pumpkin, lightly ribbed and bright orange inside and out. Size is between the miniatures and the small pie pumpkins, about 1½ pounds. Baby Bear is warm orange, softly ribbed, and has a sturdy handle. But you're not supposed to carry pumpkins by their handles, because they may break—the stems and then the pumpkins. Because of its parentage, the flavor is lovely and the semihull-less seeds are good toasted. Developed by Johnny's Selected Seeds, it's an AAS winner.

Small pumpkins were developed in China 500 years ago. From 3 to 6 inches in diameter, Mini-Jack isn't the teeniest, nor is its flesh edible, but it's round, bright orange, and its seeds have no hulls—so you can use it for decorating, then toast the seeds. Sweetie Pie and Jack Be Little are the most appealing miniatures. They're 3 inches wide, 2 inches tall, with the flattened, deeply ribbed look of storybook pumpkins—they'll keep for a year and are edible. Munchkins are almost the same. All three are high-yielding, open-pollinated pepos.

There's a waxy, white 10- to 15-pound, rather globe-shaped pumpkin named Lumina. When you carve it, the bright orange flesh makes the ghostly shell glow from within—before the candle's even lit. Be sure not to stress Lumina (no lack of water, no skimpy soil), or it will turn pale blue with fright. Harvest while slightly immature to keep the white from deepening. (Actually, after a couple of months in storage, Lumina is one of the most delicious pumpkins.) And there's a mini-white version of Sweetie Pie called Baby Boo.

If you want to see how big a pumpkin you can grow, Atlantic Giant has been coaxed to the size of nearly one-third ton. These guys want 20 square feet to themselves. Remove all blossoms until the middle of July so strength can go into the vine and thus the leaves. Leave two main vines and only one pumpkin on each. Feed with manure tea every 10 days from late August. You can make 400 pies from one fruit. Big Max gets only to 100 pounds or so, but it can be turned into four-score pies. But the giants are not the best for cooking.

If you have curious raccoons in the neighborhood, I recommend marking the perimeter of your transplants faithfully (see The Gardener's Notebook). Or try a circle of blood meal.

Recommended: For flavor, Small Sugar is superb, with heirloom Sugar Baby also high on the flavor list—and it's particularly resistant to mildew and other disease. For a short season, hybrid Autumn Gold is ready to pick in three months from sowing and will be a lovely deep orange—10 pounds in a globe shape, and makes fine jack-o'-lanterns—a 1987 AAS winner. For space, Spirit is a short-vined type.

VEGETABLE SPAGHETTI SQUASHES   *C. Pepo*

With every other squash, the aim is to get rid of the fibers in the center. Spaghetti squash is where all those banished fibers went.

Rather than grow the same squash you can get at the market, take a flyer on Stripetti, a cross between Delicata and vegetable spaghetti squashes. The harder shell (from Delicata) makes this a good keeper, and the strands (with Delicata flavor) sweeten with storage.

Recommended: These *are* fun to bring into the kitchen. Buttery yellow Pasta is a hybrid improvement on other spaghetti squashes.

GOURDS, EDIBLE

Grow gourds as squashes, with full sun, average to fertile soil, and ample water to make succulent fruit.

Gourds are more than just colorful water dippers, birdhouses, and musical instruments—many of them are delicious. Here are some of the most interesting. All are an adventure.

Angled Luffa (Luffa acutangula). Also called *Chinese okra* because of ten ridges running down the fruit. Pick them 4 to 6 inches long. The fruits have a summer squash flavor. The long vines have butter yellow blossoms. Soak seeds 24 hours before sowing.

Bitter Melon (Momordica Charantia). These look like warty cucumbers; cooked, they taste like crunchy quinine-flavored peppers. All over Asia, the fruit is welcomed as cooling in hot weather. Pick fruits young and as close to cooking as possible. The beautiful dark green leaves and tendrils are edible but *very* bitter— send vines up a trellis. Seeds must be fresh and are best germinated on paper towels. The warmer and more humid the climate, the better for bitter melons.

Chinese Fuzzy Gourd (Benincasa hispida). These are a baby form of some of the enormous, waxy-shelled Chinese winter melons. The long, slender, fuzzy-as-can-be squashes are amusing to grow, and their delicate flavor is a cross between cucumber and zucchini.

Cucuzzi/Hercules Club/Lagenaria/Calabash (Lagenaria siceraria— also, incorrectly, *longissima).* For a dramatic effect grow one of these vines against your house. Heart-shaped leaves are the size of dinner plates, flowers are small creamy trumpets, and all you do is water, then stand back while the long slender gourds keep coming. I find the babies bitter, so I harvest when the fruit is at least 8 inches long. The taste is summer squash. I once turned a mature fruit into the base of a vegetable salad for 24.

STRAWBERRIES   *Fragaria* spp.

Hardy perennials in the Rose family, native to northern temperate regions . . . grow in 5-gallon containers. Strawberries are easy to grow given superb soil. Spread 2 inches of compost or well-rotted manure over where you'll set strawberries and dig it in—add whatever else you may need to make the soil humusy and well draining. Provide frequent and deep soakings, especially when plants are producing fruit. If drainage is poor, grow strawberries in a raised bed.

Wash aphids off with the hose and diligently pick off slugs and snails.

Unfortunately, strawberries do not tolerate salty soil and water. If yours is saline and you're dying to grow berries, grow plants in containers and dilute the water with bottled water.

Strawberries can be grown and harvested in every part of the country. Where winters are cold, you must shelter the plants under straw, leaving the mulch in place until the last frost is past. Strawberries need their nip of frost to go dormant and rest from all that berrying, so where there are two months or less of frost, grow strawberries as annuals for harvesting in winter.

Unlike most fruits, which require a waiting period before plants are of bearing age, you can plant strawberries in spring and have some to eat by fall. And straw-berries are self-fertile, so even just one plant would give you fruit.

Harvest strawberries the moment they're tender and fragrant, nipping off the stem at its base. Pick daily, to keep berries coming along.

Order certified disease-free stock so you don't borrow trouble. Don't grow strawberries where there have been potatoes, peppers, or tomatoes within the last four years—these plants may have hosted verticillium wilt, which would affect the strawberries. Homegrown strawberries are almost always disease free, but should yours develop wilt or rot, pull them out and don't plant strawberries in the same spot for four years.

ALPINE STRAWBERRIES   *F. vesca*

> *Very hardy perennials native to the Alps . . . aka* fraise de bois.
> *Alpines like just morning sun in areas where summers are temperate.*
> *Where summers are hot, give them bright shade (under the high*
> *branches of a tall, airy tree) all day.*

Alpines' official name is *woodland strawberries*, and you'll bring a patch of the forest into your garden with these diminutive plants. The berries are typically slen-der and long, although some are turning up round these days. They're not much bigger than the tip of your little finger, wonderfully fragrant and sweet. Blossoms are white, but the fruit comes in rosy red, golden yellow, and creamy white. Fruit is available usually from midsummer to midautumn. Leaves are thumbnail size and, in the case of white berries, exquisitely marbled cream and green. Birds aren't inter-ested in white strawberries for some reason.

Unlike their larger cousins, alpine plants have no runners. This means you can set them anywhere and they'll neatly stay put, forming a fluffy mound—rather than, like their cousins, hopscotching here and there, starting new plants. Alpines are enchanting mixed with dark blue lobelia along the front of the border.

Something else about these plants: if you don't manage to harvest a berry, it will thoughtfully dry up and topple off its stem—unpicked garden strawberries get mushy and rot.

Alpine strawberries are propagated either by dividing an older plant or by sow-ing seeds. Seeds are infinitely less expensive, and you can grow more unusual cultivars. Because they are so small, plants aren't heavy bearers. To have a bowlful of woodland strawberries once in a while, grow a dozen plants or so per person.

Recommended: For finest flavor, Alexandria (relatively large berries) and Baron Solemacher. Improved Rugens bears heavily later in the season. Alpine Yellow and the white Variegated Strawberry *(F.v. Albo-Marginata)* are enchanting. Temptation is an everbearing alpine that will give fruit from midsummer till fall from a January sowing. Pineapple Crush is also creamy white and has a trace of pineapple in its flavor.

GARDEN STRAWBERRIES   *F. × Ananassa*

These robust plants like full sun and will soak it up even in hot climates. Set plants so the crown is above the soil and the top roots are ¼ inch below the soil. For maximum harvest, plant in rows and let runners fill in until plants are about 7 inches apart, then pinch off runners. A mulch of manure or compost is especially important for everbearing plants, since they do so much work. If, in midsummer, their leaves turn pale green, give them a dose of manure tea.

There are now two classifications of garden strawberries.

The old-fashioned sort, spring- or June-bearing, are generally regarded as the finest-quality berries of all. The plants rely on long winter nights to set flowering in motion. Fruits come in a rush for a few weeks in late spring or early summer.

Everbearing or day-neutral plants flower and fruit through the season, never heavily at any one time. These are especially recommended where the growing season is short, since you won't lose a whole crop to late frosts as you would with spring-bearing berries.

By growing both spring-bearing and everbearing plants, you'll have berries through the season.

A runner in a plant is a tendril that dances out of a mature plant, finds a spot it likes, develops rootlets on the tip, and plants itself in that spot. I've seen garden strawberries plant themselves in everything from a lawn to a gravel path. I've never grown these in a row except to have them bordering a bed—which they do enchantingly. And I let the runners run where they like—sometimes I'm delighted to have a new plant; sometimes I pinch the runner off. Healthy garden strawberry plants in blossom and in fruit are charming and exuberant. When their fruiting time is past, they can begin to look a little sorry. When their leaves turn brown in cold weather, they're not pretty at all. So think about that when you place them.

Where the climate is mild and cool, spring-bearing plants need to be replaced every three or four years. Where it's hot, they'll last longer. Everbearing plants should be replaced every other year in most places.

Of the more unusual cultivars, New York 1593 is called *Black Beauty* because it has deep-purple skin and flesh. Pink Panda has pink flowers—the warm pink of wax begonias. Its fruit is secondary in quality to its flowers, but you can use a plant or two for accent in a mixed hanging basket.

Recommended: The following are spring-bearing. For flavor: Sequoia, Cavendish, Sparkle, Jewel. For northern areas: Cavendish, Sparkle (especially for preserves and freezing), Blomidon. For the Northwest: Shuksan or Benton (especially recommended for the mountains). For the South: Earlibelle. For warm summer areas: Jewel. For warm winter areas: Tioga. For the Southeast and South Central: Cardinal. For disease resistance: Surecrop. For stressful conditions: Midway. For outstanding everbearing plants: Tristar (superb flavor) and Tribute.

SWEET POTATOES   *Ipomoea Batatas*

Tender perennial in the Morning-Glory family, perhaps native to tropical America . . . bush cultivars will grow in a bushel basket . . . aka (incorrectly) yams. Sweets tolerate heat better than any vegetable we grow; optimal temperature is 70–85° F. They will flourish, however, if temperatures don't dip below 65° F or climb above 95° F. I've produced a modest but exciting crop in that range. If you live where there's frost, minimum sweet potato growing requirements are 3½ frost-free months—two weeks to warm the soil after the last frost, then three months for maturing the earliest cultivars. Certainly there are microclimates and heat-gathering tricks that would make it possible to grow sweets almost anywhere. But a notch above the 42nd parallel—Boston, for example—is the dividing line between growing sweets easily and making it a project.

Sweets' ideal soil is a loose, rich, well-draining, slightly acid sandy loam. If yours isn't like that, dig in compost, sand, and oak leaf mold or pine needles to approximate it. For maximum warmth and drainage, raise the bed about 8 inches high, making it 3 to 4 feet wide. In the North, you can warm the soil with black paper or black plastic a week or two before the last expected frost date, then wait until the earth is cozy before setting the slips—usually one to two weeks after the actual last frost.

There are two sorts of sweet potatoes, and it has long been a custom in this country, particularly in the South, to call those with sweet, moist orange flesh *yams,* and those with dry, mealy yellowish flesh *sweets.* True yams are tropical/subtropical plants, a staple in much of Africa, Asia, the West Indies, and Latin America. If you're in a market with clientele from those countries, it's likely the elongated tubers with whitish (or maybe purplish) barklike skin and starchy white (or maybe red) flesh that the sign says are yams really are. Otherwise the tubers in the bin at the supermarket are sweet potatoes no matter what the sign says.

Unless you live in the South, where sweet potato slips are a commonplace at the nursery, you'll have to either start your own or send away for them. In my part of the world, I haven't found a market sweet potato that will sprout—all are treated not to—and I haven't found a nursery within a couple of hundred miles that sells slips.

As a child I used to poke three toothpicks around the bottom half (two-thirds is better) of a sweet potato, stick the tuber in a glass of water covering the bottom inch, and put it in a light, warm place (but not sunlight). In a few weeks the bottom would be a tangle of roots and the top a myriad of shoots. In time each shoot would send up a cluster of leaves. If you buy a sweet whose flavor you like and it sprouts this way and you have a long enough season to chance growing what might be a 150-day cultivar, gently pull or twist off the rooted sprouts. Each is called a *slip,* and it's a new plant. It's possible to get as many as 50 slips from one large potato. Don't plant whole sprouting tubers, though; you'll get wonderful vines and no sweet potatoes.

Covering tubers in moist sand or sawdust or vermiculite in a box and keeping them between 75°F and 80°F is another way of starting slips. I tried this in the oven with just the warmth of the pilot light and inadvertently baked the potatoes. Heating cables at the bottom of the box are better. Up to the point of cooking them, it can't get too hot for these tropical children.

However you do it, start slips about six weeks before you plan to set them in the ground.

Should the slips be ready before the earth is warm enough to receive them, cover the roots in a deep flat of moist potting soil and nurse them along in a sunny window or under lights with other seedlings until it's time to go outdoors.

It's important to set (*set* is sweetpotatoese for plant) the slips in the late afternoon. For potatoes of uniform size, space slips evenly. Should you have more slips than you can grow, use the largest, since these make the healthiest plants. It's traditional to use a stick or broom handle to push the slips down into the earth, 5 to 6 inches up to their leaves. Pat the soil around the roots, then water in thoroughly with a weak solution of fish emulsion. Once the plants are on their feet, see that they have ¾ to 1 inch of water weekly, either from rain or from the hose. Too much water will rot the tubers; not enough will stress the vines. Plants are very drought tolerant, but they shouldn't go thirsty.

Everybody agrees on how to raise spiffy tomatoes, but unaccountably four different sources will give you four different opinions on the finer points of growing sweets. Some tell us the plants are light feeders; some say heavy. Some say the tubers want rich soil; some lean. I go by the folks who grow sweets commercially. They amend the soil, and they fertilize while the tubers are growing.

The situation is this: the vines need nitrogen for vigor—some but not much. As with beans, lots of nitrogen will give you galloping vines and scant fruit. The tubers need phosphate and potash for splendid roots.

I dug enough compost into the soil to make the earth friable. Sprinkled a very light veil of blood meal over the soil (the nitrogen), a very light veil of steamed bone meal (the phosphate), and a slightly heavier veil of kelp meal or wood ashes (the potash). Worked it in with a fork a foot deep. And I covered it with black paper mulch, which I'd never used before.

A month later, two weeks after the last frost, I set five fine slips in a row a foot apart, west of the corn and south of the cukes and fuzzy melon, in my "needs heat" bed. For scent and color through the patch I mingled purple-leaf Thai basil, bangles of brilliant gold and orange nasturtiums, and dangles of royal purple beans that climbed up the chicken wire lattice next to the melons.

Sweet potato vines are as lovely as anything in the garden. Their dark green or blue-green or sometimes reddish heart-shaped leaves and ombré rose-to-violet trumpets of blossoms remind us they are cousins to morning glories. My five plants tumbled over the basil and rolled up and over melons and cucumbers on the other side of the trellis.

Sweets are vulnerable to a number of insects and diseases—particularly in southern climates—and some types of soil fungus are transmitted through the soil on the tubers. Order plants from a seedsman with a reputation for quality and integrity. If you're getting samples from nonprofessionals, ask for slips with no soil attached. If that's not an option, when they arrive, scrub the tubers of all soil. Finally, before importing tubers in packages that will escape the agricultural inspector's eye, check with the county to make sure there's no quarantine from the point of origin.

To minimize problems, rotate sweets through your garden, start with healthy slips of disease-resistant cultivars, and do your best to give them optimum growing conditions. Should the vines suddenly look puny, contact your county agricultural agent for help.

In the North, grow your crop on black paper or black plastic all season and don't mulch further. The hotter the soil, the better.

In the South, where there's no question of the soil being amply warm, after the slips are established—a couple of weeks after planting—mulch around them deeply with spoiled straw or leaves.

An added advantage to mulch with these vines is that it keeps them from touching down on the earth and rooting and making baby tubers in that spot, which would divert strength from the nest back at central.

Dig the potatoes before the soil turns as cold as 55°F—cold is very harmful to the tubers—or before frost, whichever comes first. If the vines are hit by frost, harvest the potatoes at once. Some plants have a habit of growing their tubers some distance away from Mama. Dig at least 2 feet all around the plant to catch the whole family.

Handle very carefully. A scrape or cut in the skin is an invitation to destructive bacteria. The more you handle sweets, the faster they disintegrate.

Sweets must be cured carefully for best quality in long storage. Dry them on dry ground for several hours after digging. Brush off excess earth but do not wash. Then lay them on a sheet in a very warm (85–90°F) place. Add a tub of water for room humidity. After two weeks, move them somewhere at 55°F. Store them without touching in a dark, dry, well-ventilated place, safe from mice.

As with some winter squashes, sweet potatoes become more richly flavored after storing as their starches convert to sugar. Well cured, they can keep for six months. As always, inspect the potatoes from time to time and eat any that show signs of flagging. Then save some of the best sweets in storage to make slips for next year.

White Sweets

Growing conditions in much of the South make Irish potatoes difficult if not impossible to grow in the heat of summer, and Sumor—as well as White Crystal, White Triumph, Old Kentucky, Hayman, White Yams, etc.—fill in for the Irish there. Blindfolded, you can't taste the difference between them and buttery, sweet Irish potatoes. Delightful discovery for us in the North.

Recommended: For flavor and moist orange flesh, Jewell and Porto Rico. If you join Seed Savers, send for a sample of Ginseng Red or Old Orange, a bush cultivar with intensely orange flesh. For golden skin and golden medium-dry flesh, All Gold, except it's no longer available commercially—only through Seed Savers. If that's your taste, keep an eye out. For short seasons, the easiest to find is Georgia Jet—good flavor, high yielding, said to be the best for the North. Like Georgia Jet, sweet white Sumor is ready in about 90 days and has lots of flowers. On the southern shore of the East Coast, white-fleshed, sweet-scented Hayman is legendary. For colors, there's Red Wine Velvet, beet-red skin, purple stems, green leaves, moist yellow-orange flesh—another available only through Seed Savers. Vardaman is a bush cultivar with reddish leaves and orange skin and flesh. And for white, Sumor and Old Kentucky. The whites have less vitamin A, however.

TOMATILLOS

Physalis ixocarpa

Tender annual in the nightshade family, native to Mexico . . . aka Mexican green tomato, Mexican husk tomato, Mexican ground cherry, jamberry . . . grows in 3- to 5-gallon containers. Tomatillos grow with alegría—merriment and joy. Their culture is the same as for their cousins, tomatoes.

Tomatillo vines roll and tumble across the garden, while among the heart-shaped leaves small yellow trumpets dangle and fat green, buff, and purple paper lanterns rustle in the breeze. All over Mexico the fruit swelling inside the lanterns will be ground into *salsa verde,* a piquant sauce for eggs at breakfast, tortillas at lunch, grilled fish or chicken or meat at dinner.

Tomatillo is a yanqui name—the plant is as freighted with names as fruit on its vines. Across the United States we have *tomatillo,* little tomato; in Mexico *tomate verde,* green tomato; *tomatitio verde,* green little tomato; *tomate de cáscara,* husk tomato; *tomate de bolsa,* bag tomato; *tomate de capote,* cloak tomato; *fresadilla,* little strawberry; *tomate manzano,* apple tomato; *miltomate,* corn tomato; and *tomate milpero,* cornapple tomato.

There's an aspect of the plant in each of these names. The glossy, firm, round fruit can be as tiny as wild plums but as large as plums cultivated and cared for. The fruit is light green because it's picked unripe—ripe, it turns gold—but there are purple cultivars that, when picked, are brushed with violet. Each fruit is wrapped in a papery husk—which, according to their names, may seem baggy to one person and to another as capacious as a Spaniard's cloak. There's a stickiness on the fruit, too—

perhaps an experiment toward a natural defense against insects. Ripe, the flavor of the fruit is sharp-sweet like strawberries; underripe, it has the soft tang of apples. *Miltomates* are tiny fruits whose vines have ambled through Mexican cornfields generation after generation.

Tomatillos fruit earlier but for as long as tomatoes, and they're more tolerant of cold. For sauces, pick just after the husk changes color from green to buff. For jam, let the fruit inside the husks ripen. To enjoy raw in salads, harvest anytime. Usually I plant tomatillos near summer squashes since they have the same needs.

Purple De Milpa has good flavor, and it's great fun to husk—with the size, shape, and gloss of a crab apple, the fruit looks as though it's been colored with crayons by a child. There are triangles of purple where the husk has split and the sun struck the skin. The rest is purple scratched over green. Each year a few volunteers spring up.

Recommended: Purple De Milpa for sheer joy.

TOMATOES   *Lycopersicon Lycopersicum*

Tender perennial in the nightshade family, native to Andean South America . . . aka love apple, gold apple . . . grows in 5- to 10-gallon containers. If the cultivars are suited to your climate, and if they have ample sun, rich soil, uninterrupted water, and no weeds, you'll grow great tomatoes. After all, volunteer tomatoes grow like Topsy. Just be sure any compost you use has fully decomposed—tomatoes are particularly vulnerable to disease that might be pulsing inside a half-rotted piece of potato or other nightshade.

Twist a fat ripe tomato warm from your vine. Bite into it, and its juices will spurt, your nostrils will smart, your mouth will pucker, your mind will race, your chin will dribble, and everything you'd hoped for from your garden you'll hold in your hand.

Europeans didn't have the pleasure of biting into a tomato until the 16th century, when Spanish conquistadores brought back seeds for golden tomatoes from this hemisphere. The Spanish, French, and Italians ate tomatoes but not the English. Most people in the world never really ate tomatoes until the middle of the last century. And now, ironically, the tomato is losing its luster as comparatively tasteless, tough-skinned tomatoes are being grown to meet the needs of growers, shippers, and marketers.

What makes a tomato immortal? Flavor, of course. Unlike peppers, eggplants, and peas but like potatoes, beans, and corn, flavors in tomatoes are forcibly distinguishable one from another and can be memorable. People speak possessively about the buttery warmth of their Yellow Finns, the meaty richness of their Royalty Purple Pods, and the ineffable delicacy of their Silver Queens the way they speak about the lush sharp sweetness of their Marmandes. Then there's texture. A great tomato is juicy without being watery. Firm without being mealy. And there's color. The eye triggers the brain, and few sights can set a mouth watering faster than the slicing of a luscious deep, dark, ripe red tomato.

I was shocked to read a woman's tasting notes on half a dozen tomatoes she'd grown—two of my favorites she particularly mentioned as being insipid and dull. Then I remembered my conversation with the owner of an herb nursery who told me she was constantly surprised at the differences in people's perceptions of flavors.

It's sad but true that open-pollinated strains are, taken as a whole across the country, across the world, uneven. For example, no tomato is reputed to have richer flavor than the Amish heirloom Brandywine. I grew it and was disappointed to find the fruits ordinary. Now Brandywine is described in one catalog as "slightly purplish red." In another the flesh is "pink-red." In another, "dark pink-red." In another, "pink." Is this just imprecise language, or are the four Brandywines four slightly different strains, as I think they are?

That's why it's so pleasing when you find an open-pollinated tomato you're mad about. You can tie a ribbon around the finest fruit on the finest vine, save its seeds, and then grow it again next year, certain of how it will taste. That's true, of course, for every vegetable in the garden.

Hundreds of tomatoes are offered in catalogs, and by now I've grown more than my share of them. But only a handful have distinguished themselves in my memory. Still, it's a handful we in this house can't be without. And *any* tomato you pick fresh from your garden will taste better than any from the market. My list, obviously, is hardly definitive. There are so many tomatoes on other gardeners' lists I haven't tasted.

To start your own list, just match up seeds that are best for your climate and season with the flavors and colors you'd like. If you live in an area where tomatoes are susceptible to disease (ask a neighboring gardener or your county extension adviser), choose cultivars with built-in resistance.

What about starting with plants from the nursery? Sure, if you're pressed for time. But those cultivars are hybrid Mr. Everyman's Tomato—no individuality. When I've grabbed tomato seedlings at the nursery because I was late getting in seeds that year, I've only been disappointed in the fruit. Use seeds.

What do *determinate* and *indeterminate* mean in catalogs? Determinate tomato vines are self-limiting. They're short. Fairly early in the season, flower clusters blossom at the tip of the vine, and that is the end of forward motion. Determinate tomato plants usually are well-behaved shrubs, and I often set them in the middle of a flower bed. On determinate plants nearly all the tomatoes ripen at once—helpful in areas with short seasons or if you want to get all your canning done in one fell swoop.

Indeterminate vines have leafy shoots at their tips instead of flower clusters, and those shoots continue to grow, and the plant continues to flower and fruit until frosted or exhausted. The vines are long. An indeterminate plant spreads its crop over a longer season and generally speaking is more productive and more flavorful.

Should you be in the enviable position of having little frost and a long growing season, you can plant early-, mid-, and late-season cultivars all at once the way you can potatoes and corn and just keep eating.

Early in the nineties, breeders presented the world with a marvelous combination tomato plant: dwarf intermediate. Plants have the indeterminate all-season-long habits of flowering and fruiting and the tomatoes have the superior flavor, but the bushes stop at 3 to 5 feet. The plants are especially decorative—their leaves are thick, dark green, and crumpled or quilted.

Any number of genetic characteristics determine sweetness and flavor in tomatoes, but fruits from indeterminate vines have traditionally been considered to have the best taste. The components of flavor are produced in the leaves, then sent to the fruits. Indeterminates have a higher ratio of leaf to fruit; therefore, more leaves result in more intensely flavored fruit, just as with peppers. More leaves also give the fruit better protection from the scalding rays of the sun and other weathery insults. But growing tomatoes is worlds easier than growing peppers.

When you see tobacco-leaf foliage mentioned, the leaves will resemble their potato cousin's, which are especially handsome.

As much as I can, I mix tomato plants in our borders. Their leaves are dark and perky, their blossoms dainty, their fruit shining and, in time, colorful. Determinate tomatoes are jolly with other bushes such as peppers and dahlias. And golden splashes of gaillardia are charming at their feet.

Fresh tomatoes in winter. When you're making out your tomato seed list, remember there's a group of cultivars whose long suit is not terrific flavor or rich color, but the fact that they ripen very slowly and hold their quality for a very long time in the process. You start them a little later than the rest of your tomatoes—usually late spring—and then pick them before frost while they're green. Then wrap and keep them in a cool room as described later in this section, where they can take weeks if not months to turn rosy in the dark.

Attention Smokers

Smokers must wash their hands before touching any nightshade plant—tomatoes, tomatillos, potatoes, eggplants, peppers. The tobacco in cigarettes, cigars, and pipe tobacco may transmit disease to which fellow nightshades are vulnerable.

Probably the most successful is Burpee's Long Keeper; different seedsmen offer different strains of it, and each strain tastes different. One I've tasted is bland, one smartly acid, so ask. When ripe, the skin is pale orange-red and the flesh rosy red.

Sowing and planting. Even if you have warm weather and a long season, it's wisest to germinate the seeds yourself, since tomato seeds germinate best at around 80°F. The moment they've sprouted, turn them into a 3-inch paper pot filled with quick-drying potting mix—i.e., nothing with a lot of peat moss in it. (N.B. Next to the cultivar's name on its stick, also note by *D, I,* or *SD* whether the plant is determinate, indeterminate, or semideterminate. That way you'll know how to support and space the plant when you set it in the garden.) Keep the plants 6 to 12 inches under bright light for 12 to 14 hours each day if you can. The air should be around 60°F. *Water the seedlings sparingly.* Kept on the dry side, the seedlings' roots will develop but the plant will stay short, which gets the plant off to a better start when it goes into the ground.

When the air is at least 50°F, take the plants outdoors for the day, then bring them back in at night. This hardening prepares them for the great world. Around the time the pome fruits bloom, transplant the tomatoes into the garden.

If you haven't prepared the soil the autumn before (usually I haven't), then around the time you sow the seeds or as soon as you can work the soil, prepare the planting holes. Lots of well-aged manure in them—equal parts earth and manure. If it's been a chill winter, lay clear plastic mulch over the bed, then remove it at planting time. Many successful tomato growers leave the plastic mulch in place all season.

Seedlings should be set out before they flower. If yours are so vigorous they've made flowers, pinch off the flowers—difficult to do. On planting day, thoroughly moisten the soil and the roots of the seedlings. Then pinch off the lowest pair of leaves and set the plant in the hole with these nodes well below the surface. They will form roots in place of leaves, a bit of botany that's always fascinated me. If you're going to stake them, set the stakes now.

As they develop on indeterminate vines, you must pinch off the little suckers that appear between the main stalk and the side branches that form. This keeps the vine from sapping its strength with shoots instead of fruits.

Vine support. Indeterminate tomato vines can grow the way they do in the Andes if you provide clean mulch (straw, leaves, pine needles, or newspapers) for them to sprawl on and if slugs aren't a problem. Let loose on the garden, these vines can grow 10 or 15 feet long, and they'll be their most productive due to deeper penetration of sun and better circulation of air. The first year I grew Marmandes, I let them ramble, and they were impressive—actually they're semideterminate. They grew 12 feet long. The fruit is a little smaller and takes longer to ripen than tomatoes grown upright, and yield per square foot of garden is greater when tomatoes climb up.

In the Northwest, where the ground will be wet when tomatoes are ripening, decay takes a toll of fruit on the ground. Determinates don't mind the support of a 3- to 4-foot stake, but unless the crop is heavy, it isn't necessary. Although ingenious systems have been devised for supporting tomato vines, any system should be simple. Everything should be kept simple in the garden.

A trellis is handsome, but I find the easiest and most straightforward support is a stout stake. Stakes should be 1 to 1 ½ inches square, redwood, with 1 foot buried firmly in the ground and at least 5 feet above it (6 feet is necessary with crazies like Sweet 100 cherry tomatoes). Tomatoes are easiest to pick when staked, but finding stout 7-foot redwood stakes, for some reason, is difficult. Every week, just tie the new growth to the stake—use baling twine or, if aesthetics are not an issue, old stockings.

Another style of support is a cage. Store-bought cages are tall funnels of four stout wires with three or four rings holding them together. They're flimsy and frustrating, and I try not to use them—but sometimes when I have a dozen tomato vines flying through the garden, I resort to them. The best cages for growing tall tomatoes—sturdy yet easy to deal with—are cylinders of galvanized wide-mesh (so your hand can slip through and come out with a tomato) wire fencing cut in 5- to 6-foot lengths. The cage should stand at least 5 feet tall or as tall as you can get the wire. Make a slightly overlapping circle of the wire and tie with baling twine (not wire, or you're liable to get scratched). Every foot or so around the bottom, secure the cage to the ground with wire coat hangers snipped in half (the top lopped off). Or drive four stakes into the ground around the cage and tie the cage to them. The harvest may be a little later than from tomatoes grown on stakes, but this method is considered the ultimate way to grow indeterminate tomatoes. In autumn the cages are easily dismantled.

The commercial growers' method of support is a string trellis. For me this was a labor-intensive disaster, frustrating from start to finish. Since you must plant tomatoes in a new bed each year, digging up and then resetting the posts and hanging all that twine again is a bloody nuisance.

Mulch. You must mulch to conserve water and to keep down weeds. Mulch is crucial to healthy tomato plants. A base of newspapers makes the foundation.

Leaving 6 inches open around the stem for air, lay down about ½-inch of black-and-white newspapers. Lay the papers in open sheets, so they'll decompose more easily, not whole sections. On top of the papers, spread 6 to 8 inches of any mulch you like. The newspapers should keep all the weeds underground and the rest will aid in conserving moisture. When the plant is strongly established, you can pull the mulch a few inches closer to the vine. With black plastic, make sure you cut slits in it to let water through.

The most critical element in growing tomatoes is water. Too much water will make the fruit watery. Drying out can disfigure the fruit. Under most circumstances, from the time the first blossoms appear until harvest, keep the soil evenly moist, not wet, with irrigation. To keep tomatoes moist in great heat, plant them between patches of sheltering taller crops such as corn. If you have water-retentive soil, you might be interested in experimenting with growing tomatoes under water stress—see the box on page 255.

The only other problem I've had came one day when I noticed great holes in some of the leaves on a plant. I could find no insects. Time passed, and the leaves got lacier. I looked it up in a book. I sprayed the vine with a stream of water from the hose. He flailed about something fierce, and I was dumbstruck when I saw him—one of the most extraordinarily camouflaged creatures I've ever seen. The tomato hornworm is a gigantic caterpillar *exactly* the color of the leaves with incidental white stripes. I picked him up with a stick and dropped him into my slug jar (soapy water). A lepidopterist friend says the hornworm smells like the tomato plant—"You are what you eat."

There are lots of tomato-growing gizmos out there, but you don't need them. One development that is a blessing is the floating row cover. With the protection of a layer or two, well-hardened seedlings can tough it out through the last frosts of spring—going into the ground a week or 10 days earlier than without the covers—and venerable vines can survive the first frosts of autumn, producing through Indian summer.

Hastening the fruit. Early in August, unless you have lots of warm weather ahead, pinch off the top growing-point shoot of indeterminate vines, leaving two side leaves above the first flowers. From then on, all strength will go into the fruits. At the same time, to get the largest, most flavorful tomatoes from determinate plants, pinch off half the blossoms before they set fruit. Then, around the first of September, remove all flowers and newly set fruit (either fry them or make green tomato piccalilli), leaving the larger fruits on the vine to ripen. If you have no interest in a lot of green tomatoes for frying or piccalilli, about six weeks before the first expected frost, stop watering—or cut down on water considerably. The stress forces fruit to ripen. Surprisingly, if there's no frost, tomatoes will still be ripening on their vines in November without any water at all. They're less fragile than you might imagine.

Ripening and harvesting. Tomatoes generally ripen from the base of the vine up—I wonder whether it has to do with the warmth of Mother Earth. So even though the tomatoes on top of the plant are green, start looking around the bottom for red or yellow fruit when they're of a size that looks promising. Harvest the fruit when it smells like a tomato and its color is uniform—about one week after it first begins to take on color. Pick by gently twisting the fruit on the stem in a sideways motion. Tomatoes picked vine-ripened have far more vitamin C than those ripened off the vine.

If you live where there is frost, you must be decisive about harvesting the remaining green tomatoes at summer's end—otherwise you'll wake up one morning and find them mushy and gray. So get a basket and pluck away, inhaling that sharp peppery scent of succulent tomato leaves and vines being snapped. There are discoveries. Under Romas I've found nests of ovals in Easter egg hues ranging from warm red to rose to gold and apple-green. In the Yellow Currant vines I'll inevitably find thickets of ripe Yellow Currants I missed, and I'll feel obliged to gobble them up as I pick.

If Jack Frost is pressing at the garden gate and you haven't time to harvest, on a dry day cut down the stalks, lay them on several inches of dry straw, and cover the plants with two or three layers of floating row cover—and, if necessary, several more inches of straw. With this protection the tomatoes can keep for several weeks, and you can gather them as you need them. I've also heard of packing tomatoes on vines supported by a stake with a tepee of several inches of straw. Use twine to tie the straw in place against the elements, but keep it airy underneath so nothing molders. You can reach through the packing and pick tomatoes.

Ultimately the vines should be chopped up and added to the compost heap and the last tomatoes either stored indoors or made into piccalilli.

Now is the time to dig in manure or compost. Take the newspapers to the compost pile, then spread the enrichment over the summer's mulch and turn both into the soil. In the bed where you'll be growing tomatoes next year, sow Crimson clover or fava beans. Then a month before planting, chop them up and turn into the soil. And begin the splendid cycle all over again.

Keeping the harvest. The best way to ripen green tomatoes (most delicate fruits, for that matter) is to wrap them individually in paper. It could be newspaper, but that's so utilitarian and besides, who wants to eat ink? Point is to keep the skins from touching, in case a fruit goes bad.

Do not wash the fruit, but gently rub off all dirt. Tomatoes with blemishes must be taken to the kitchen and cooked. Wrap the rest in white tissue. Wherever you have a spare drawer in a cool room, lay in the tomatoes, a single layer. If you're organized, you'll put them in some order of ripeness, eating right to left. Optimum temperature is in the 50s, optimum humidity is high. Circulation of air can be what usually whistles through a chest of drawers. Every week or so, check your hoard. You can tell by spots of dampness or an odor if there's a problem.

I've kept Longkeepers for three months this way. If I'd had more, they would have been around longer. It's grand slicing your own fresh, organic blush-red tomatoes in December.

Recommended: The single best all-around tomato to grow your first time? Because you can't buy one like it (except, perhaps, at a farmers' market) and because it's as luscious fresh as mixed into pasta, the lusty, deeply ribbed Italian heirloom, Costoluto Genovese.

For flavor after Costoluto in my book is golden Taxi. It fruits early and abundantly, and the flavor is as glowing as its brilliant yellow—at once tangy, sugary, intense, light, golden. Your summer garden should never be without a yellow tomato, and mine will never be without Taxi. Golden Mandarin Cross from Japan is a superb hybrid. And funny-looking Marmande, classic French heirloom, is bumpily shaped, but there are lots of tomatoes two months after setting seedlings in the garden, even where summers are cool. To me the combination of its smooth texture and shining flavor can't be beat.

Bonny Best and Brandywine are more great tastes. Stokes Seeds' hybrid Ultra Magnum VFT won a taste test with Yellow Brandywine.

For an early beefsteak, Nepal, the closest I'll get to a beefsteak tomato in my short season. For some reason, every year I'm startled afresh at how good it tastes. Johnny's 361 is a new compact, early beefsteak.

For orange, Valencia, as vibrantly flavored as if it were an heirloom from Spain instead of native Maine. Caro Rich and Double Rich are persimmon-colored tomatoes with more vitamin C than oranges and gorgeous flavor to boot. I grew them for the first time this year, and I can't understand why they're not in every catalog. Orange tomatoes are another kitchen garden imperative. If you're a bagel fancier and you love lox over cream cheese, try a luminous slice of the delectable Golden Mandarin Cross, instead.

More colors: White Wonder is extraordinarily sweet and tasty and translucent. Pink-purple-bronze Purple Calabash—who could resist the catalog's description, "ruffled fruits identical to ones figured in 16th-century herbals"?—are quite as ruffled as Costoluto Genovese, but sampled side by side, the Calabashes are very sharp, whereas the Italians have a richer, rounder flavor. Red-and-yellow Striped German is luminous and delicious. And Big Rainbow is layered green, red, and gold and has sweet fine taste.

For flavor in hybrids: French Dona and Lorissa. New tomatoes they may be, but they're full of sassy old-fashioned charm. So is the intensely yellow delectably flavored Golden Mandarin Cross. Remember never to refrigerate tomatoes.

For sun-drying: The ancient Italian way of preserving tomatoes by drying in the sun is one of the most joyous rituals of summer. When I read that the small salad-size Principe Borghese was a favorite sun-drying tomato in the homeland, I grew a bush and dried an incredible amount of fruits. The pieces dry to bite size, which makes them easy to toss into a dish rather than forcing you to cut up leathery slices. Given half a chance, the gregarious Principe *loves* to turn up where you least expect it the following summer.

For disease resistance: In more than 20 years of growing tomatoes, I have never had any blight or bother—just one tomato hornworm. But there are parts of the country where disease is in the air, and if you garden there, here are the keys to catalog descriptions in choosing resistant cultivars. The most prevalent diseases are symbolized by letters following the cultivar's name. For severe problems, consult the specialized tomato catalogs (see Sources).

A = alternaria blight
ASC = alternaria stem canker
F = fusariam wilt (two "races," F1 and F2)
N = Root-knot nematode
T = tobacco mosaic virus
V = verticillium wilt

Generally, tomato plants grown in the East and Northeast will be most vulnerable to F, T, V; southern and other humid areas to F, N, T, V; as well as assorted droops and wilts; and western areas to F, N, T, V. Hybrid tomatoes that combine disease resistance with good flavor: Big Beef and Dona.

If a plant becomes afflicted, in all cases burn it or bag it and send it to the dump. When you grow tomatoes next year, it's essential to move the crop to a spot where there haven't been nightshades for four years and not to grow another member of the nightshade family in the troubled tomato patch for four years. To make the soil repugnant to nematodes, grow marigolds in the tomato patch.

Where tomatoes are slow to set fruit and ripen in cool weather, choose cultivars that are indeterminate, extra-early (they'll fruit as soon as genetically possible), and early-blight resistant. Kotlas (formerly Sprint) and Early Cascade are two such. Although they won't be as razzamatazz as tomatoes grown in the shimmering heat of Kansas, these "subarctics" can produce tomatoes with lively flavor. My beefy Nepal (said to have originated in chilly Nepal) shone in taste tests when grown in cool weather. Oregon Spring V suits this climate. And look into the provocative selection of Siberian cultivars—Galina's, Olga's Biggest, Gregori's Altai among them. The dwarf intermediate Stupice (from Czechoslovakia) is flavorful, early, and high yielding—even in cool San Francisco. Earlirouge V and Marmande VF also set fruits at low temperatures.

Where blossoms won't set because of heat—or the blossoms set but the fruit is thick skinned and tasteless—one way to have good tomatoes is to concentrate on the small-fruited cultivars. Smaller strains tend to set fruit better, and they'll crack less in the heat—see the cherries, currants, and pears that follow. But breeders have been working on cultivars that set larger fruit in the heat. Heatwave was bred specifically for the South and Southwest. Claims are that it sets fruit between 90°F and 96°F, with good flavor and no cracking. Cal-Ace VF is also good for arid climates. Solar Set is said to produce lots of flavorful 8-ounce fruit at 92°F and high humidity. For the Mid-Atlantic and Florida coast, Homestead 24F is a late-season, open-pollinated cultivar that's meaty, flavorful, and has good leaf coverage. Others for hot, humid climates are Ozark Pink VF and the multidisease-resistant Tropic VFN/T. Crimson Sweet Earlirouge V is fond of extremes—cold *or* hot.

One traditional way to get tomatoes all through hot summers is to plant a vigorous early and a midseason heat- and crack-resistant cultivar at the same time. Start with Oregon Spring. It was developed at Oregon State University to tolerate cold, but the challenge of one stress is as good as another: Oregon Spring has cropped both early *and* late in the hot-as-blazes summer of the San Joaquin Valley.

So your first crop ripens in late June or July, the plant shuts down in the heat of summer for a rest (you can cut it back to about 14 inches), then it starts fruiting again in the fall. Meanwhile, your midseason cultivar, Heatwave, is kicking in. Be sure to dig an extra amount of moisture-retentive compost or other humus into the soil for these brave plants. Lighten their burden by picking fruits continually as they ripen. If blossoms seem reluctant to set fruit, gently give the vine a shake in the middle of the day to free the grains of pollen.

Kootenai is a crack-resistant tomato from Russia that tolerates drought and poor soil and still yields tasty crimson fruits. Flora-Dade VFF does well in limestone soil. For tomatoes that do well in a range of adverse conditions, try Campbell 1327 VF and Traveler.

Every list of tomatoes is temporary. New cultivars come along—heirlooms resurrected, hybrids reformulated—every year.

Cherry Tomatoes   *L. Lycopersicum* var. *cerasiforme*

My Sweet 100 cherry tomato, a hybrid indeterminate, grew so unreasonably tall and ratcheted out so much fruit that it began to make me nervous. Not a few times did I wonder who was in charge. If only the flavor of the fruit had been as extravagant as the plant, but no, to my taste it was all cloying sweetness and no sharpness. There is now a Sweet 100 Plus. Don't those guys know when to quit?

The German-bred, open-pollinated Gardener's Delight (aka Sugar Lump)—a prolific early cherry tomato with honeyed tangy flavor—has challenged the likes of the Sweet 100s (although to many Sweet 100 will always be the best). Sweet Chelsea, a larger, better-behaved indeterminate hybrid, is reputed to have sugariness combined with a rich tomato taste. And century-old Red Cherry, an indeterminate with tangy, sweet old-fashioned flavor, is the pet cherry of many. One cherry tomato that's on my list of won't-be-without is Gold Nugget. The fruit starts early (it sets blossoms particularly well in cool climates) and continues through most of the summer. It's abundant (especially in the beginning, when you're hungry for tomatoes), the plant is compact, and the golden orbs not only have true tomato flavor but, like Oregon Spring, if not pollinated, they're almost completely seedless (the jellylike substance lies between the walls and soft flesh of the tomato, but there are only amorphous seeds in it). Hybrid Sun Gold is a newer yellow cherry with remarkably sweet tomato flavor. Then there's Green Grape, an interesting determinate heirloom. It's grape shaped and over-the-hill-cucumber-green smudged with yellow. I was astonished at its sweetness, juiciness, and bright tomato flavor. It was the favorite in a recent tasting of all sorts of tomatoes, including heirlooms and hybrids. Our Green Grapes are larger than the catalog describes—small plum size, rather than an inch across. The color is odd but luminous. Camp Joy, a vigorous open-pollinated cultivar with full tomato flavor, also has its fans. Cherry tomatoes are even more delightful in the border since there's so much more fruit to catch the light.

Recommended: To start, grow at least one Sugar Lump/Gardener's Delight and one Gold Nugget. They're gorgeous together. Sun Gold, too, is a must. For tomatoes in high heat, Red Cherry and hybrid Mountain Belle VF. For disease resistance, Sweet Million FNT.

Water Stress:
Smaller Sweeter Faster Fruits

Under certain circumstances, when grown on restricted amounts of water, tomato, squash (at both summer and winter stages), sweet pepper, eggplant, melon, and watermelon plants will produce fewer and smaller fruits, but fruits that are intensely sweet and flavorful. Under the same circumstances, chili peppers get markedly hotter.

As with every organism on earth, the thrust of a plant is to reproduce itself. When deprived of water normally needed to make seeds, the plant is termed *water stressed*. According to a professor of plant pathology, "God tells the plant it's going to die, so it thinks it has to produce more seeds faster." Under water stress, water is lost from the tissues, a chemical reaction between starch and water takes place (hydrolysis), and an increased concentration of sugars results. Extra sweetness in the fruit is due in part to this increase in sugars and in part to the fact that the fruit's usual amount of sugars isn't thinned by moisture in the tissues.

Near Santa Cruz, California—the heart of artichoke land—Early Girl tomatoes are being grown in clay soil without irrigation. The area does have morning fogs in summer—droplets of water are absorbed through leaves—so they're not growing completely without moisture, but they are water stressed. The vines produce only a few small tomatoes, but they're uncommonly delicious—they fetch higher prices than standard tomatoes at the market.

Other California farmers are growing a whole range of winter squashes—acorns to kabochas to spaghetti—in heavy clay without irrigation. Early watermelons—Sugar Baby, in particular—are also being raised this way. Native American melons—notably Hopi and Navajo—are grown in sand without irrigation and although small, are juicy and sweet.

(continued)

Growing crops with whatever moisture Mother Nature bestows is called *dry farming*—a practice as old as agriculture itself. On Navajo and Hopi lands, annual rainfall can be as little as 8 inches, equally divided between summer and winter. Melons, corn, beans, winter squashes, and chilies are raised on about 4 inches of moisture altogether. Native field corn has traditionally been sown 10 feet apart in all directions and 12 to 18 inches deep—only a heavy or consistent rain can germinate the seeds. No seed of modern corn could emerge from that depth. Native red cling peaches dry-farmed in catch basins at the bottom of tall cliffs are small but juicy and heavenly sweet.

I've used the technique at the end of the tomato season to ripen fruit the last few weeks before a killing frost. I withdraw water—some or all, depending upon the circumstances. Those babies stare at me reproachfully, but their fruits ripen fast and are delicious. The circumstances to be considered are the soil, the climate, and the cultivar. Super-water-retentive soil like clay or humusy sand or loam will release moisture for a couple of weeks—particularly when deeply mulched. If the sun is pounding relentlessly, I risk things moving along so fast the plants die before the fruits have a chance to ripen—but a gentle autumn sun sustains the vines. Naturally those cultivars with vigor in their genes and those acclimatized to my part of the world do best.

So even if you garden in droughty territory, take heart—and grow delectable nightshades and melons.

CURRANT TOMATOES
L. pimpinellifolium

Native to Andean Peru and Ecuador.

Smaller-than-your-thumbnail golden orbs on sprays bursting from a vigorous knee-high plant, Yellow Currants are golden inside and out, and Red Currants are bright red. Both have shimmering sweet tomato flavor. The vines are even more never-say-die than Red Pears. We've had both currants still fruiting in November, long after frost had knocked over everybody else. And I haven't had to sow them in years, since plants volunteer with joy. Sprays of tiny reds and golds are absolutely enchanting on the plate. Past watering occasionally (they're very drought tolerant), I don't exactly take care of my currants. They've been taking care of themselves beautifully for generations and don't need me.

Against all rules, I've grown Yellow Currants, or rather they've grown themselves, in the same place for years. If I had one sign of disease or weakness in the bushes, I'd stop them in their tracks. But I'd be crazy not to keep such a good thing going.

The Red Currants aren't as generous with their seeds, so I save a few seeds and sow them each year. They're enchanting with their tracery of vines and tiny red fruits skipping through the basils. I don't stake them, but I probably should.

Recommended: Grow both.

PLUM/PEAR TOMATOES   *L. Lycopersicum* var. *pyriforme*

These vines are indeterminate and prolific. The problem is that the name Red Pear probably is a different cultivar with each seedsman. If you're lucky, you'll get a small (cherry tomato size), perfect, red-pink teardrop, one of the most aesthetic shapes in vegetables. And the flavor should be heirloom delicious. Red Pears have been grown in this country since before 1850 and probably by the Indians of Mexico and Central America long before that. The fruit ripens a little after the early tomatoes and continues long past the first frosts. Heirloom Yellow Pears have been taken up by the catalogs, I see. They are the lemon-yellow counterpart of reds, except the Red Pears fruit a little longer into autumn. You could start with either one and have success.

Again, do give your tomatoes the pleasures of mixed company in a border.

Recommended: I've grown Roma, San Marzano, Nova, Ropreco, Bellstar, San Remo, and Viva Italia; and Viva Italia is the best so far. In summer I use them for quick fresh sauces. I put up a couple dozen quart jars of plum tomatoes for quick winter sauces. For disease resistance, Viva Italia and Spectrum 385, both hybrids, both resistant to VF1F2NA. For growing in great heat, Yellow Pear, Roma VF, and Azteca VFN.

TURNIPS   *Brassica Rapa*, Rapifera Group

Hardy biennial in the Mustard family, probably native to Europe . . . grows in 2-gallon containers. Turnips need loose, fertile,

well-drained, stone-free soil with half-day sun. So they'll grow quickly,
fine-fleshed, and sweet, water consistently and feed manure tea when
half a dozen leaves appear on the seedlings. Thin so no roots will be
stressed.

Okay, so you think you hate turnips. Unless you've grown your own turnips, pulled one from the earth not much bigger than a walnut, and stood in the sunshine and savored the tender-crisp, bitey-sweet white flesh, you haven't eaten turnips. Did 7,000 years of farming teach the Sumerians to pull turnips small? And when the naturalist Pliny wrote about the long, flat, and round shapes of Roman turnips, did his cook prepare them young?

Some turnip roots are still as long as carrots (De Croissey) and as flat as a child's top (Just Right hybrid), but most are pleasingly round. A colorful few have ochre flesh (Golden Ball) or red skin that tints the white flesh like beets when cooked or pickled (Ohno Scarlet and Scarlet Ball—perhaps the same Asian turnip). Some have shoulders of violet and bottoms of cream (de Nancy and Purple Top Strap Leaf). And many are snowy white through and through and of exceptional quality (the rounds and globes from Japan).

But these are just the roots. Far and away the most nourishing part of the vegetable is its greens. The deeply cut leaves must also be harvested very young, or it takes steaming the daylights out of them to make them tender. Cultivars are available that are more greens than roots—Shogoin is a prime example.

Culture for turnips is very like that of radishes (they're not closely related, surprisingly). They grow best in cool weather. Turnips sown in early spring, which must get in and out of the ground before days reach 80°F, are more demanding than when sown in late summer with nothing but cool weather ahead. The small delectable whites—Tokyo Cross, White Lady, Presto, and Tokyo Market—are ready in about 30 days. Newer ones are White Lady hybrid and Yorii Spring. The beautiful and flavorful purple-and-creams—de Nancy and the Purple Tops—are ready in 40 to 50 days. The 19th-century heirlooms Golden Ball and Scarlet Ball are ready in around 60 days. All must be pulled as soon as they're mature, or they'll get pithy in the ground—mark your calendar. Sow again about one to two months before the first frost of autumn—a little cold will sweeten their roots.

For what the English call *maincrop turnips*—turnips sown in midsummer to be harvested large in autumn—I suggest the pride of Vermont, Gilfeather. It's creamy white, remarkably sweet, and can grow the size of an orange without getting hot or pithy. Another heirloom, Purple Top White Globe, is good for keeping through winter along with autumn/winter radishes, carrots, and beets in a cold place. Or sow them in early autumn, cover them with a cloche or floating row covers against hard freezes, and you'll have greens in earliest spring.

If flea beetles or maggots are a problem in your area, protect the turnips from start to finish with insect-weight floating row covers. If there are problems with disease in your soil, grow the 30-day cultivars, none that stay in the soil longer. And certainly rotate turnips through the garden faithfully with other roots. If you have some double-red English daisies—and you should—move a handful to the turnip patch.

Recommended: Fast, crisp, and delectable Tokyo Cross.

WINGED PEAS. *See Beans and Legumes.*

A Low-Maintenance
Kitchen Garden

Choose perennials (P) first. Although they may take effort to put in, they'll be comparatively effortless for years. Mulching—done in moments—is required to keep them easily maintained.

Annual (A) vegetables, to be low maintenance, must have the sun and water they need and fertilizing once or twice during the growing season. However, if the soil is nourishing (either in the ground or in a pot), they can get by without fertilizing.

If you are plagued by slugs and snails, you'll have to strike the leafy greens from this list.

Those in *italic* are the ultimate in low maintenance.

[1]Biennial—they'll live for two years. But I find when they're happy and their flowering shoots are picked off, they last longer.

[2]Need lots of moisture, which may or may not require attention in your garden. Otherwise the usual inch of water a week is required.

[3]Self-sows or spreads in most areas if you don't disturb the soil, which gives you a new crop with no effort.

VEGETABLES AND FRUITS

[1]chard
dandelion (P)
eggplant (P; Asian are easiest)
endive, curly (A)
escarole (A)
Good-King-Henry (P)
[3]*Jerusalem artichoke* (P)
kale (P)
[1]lettuce

mustard greens (A)
New Zealand spinach (P)
okra (A)
onion, bunching, potato (P)
rhubarb (P)
[3]*sorrel* (P)
spinach (A)
[3]strawberries (P)
[2]watercress (P)

HERBS

basils (A)
[3]*borage* (A)
[3]*burnet, salad* (P)
[3]*chervil* (A)
Chinese chives (P)
chives (P)
dill (A)
lavender (P)

lovage (P)
[3]*mints*, most (P)
[3]*oregano* (P)
[1]parsley, especially flat-leaf
[3]*perilla* (A)
rosemary, Arp (P)
sage, garden (P)
thyme

EDIBLE FLOWERS

Mulching and watering are needed, as is occasional spritzing with the hose to keep off aphids.
[3]*calendula* (A)
[3]Johnny-jump-ups (P)
marigold (A)
[3]nasturtium (A)

THE
GARDENER'S
NOTEBOOK

AAS—All-America Selection

$\mathcal{E}$ach year, from 75 to 100 new cultivars for the home garden are grown beside the best existing cultivars of the same plant—a new white eggplant beside the best old white eggplant most closely resembling it. This takes place in 26 gardens across the United States and Canada. Judges can identify trial cultivars by number only. Finally only 3 or 4 plants are selected for the annual award. *Merit is based on vigor and a broad adaptation for the home garden.* Flavor, I'm told, is equally important.

If you've not had success growing something you like or if you live in an area that is—for whatever reason—marginal for gardening, choosing a cultivar that has "AAS winner" after a name will give you a running start. It may not be the most interesting or the most flavorful of what's out there, but it will likely grow for you.

Annual

$\mathcal{H}$*ortus Third:* "Of one season's duration, from germination to maturity and death."

Ants

$\mathcal{I}$n the garden I let established trails alone as long as they're not through a bed I need to work. When I must work where ants want to be, I blast them with the hose, which buys me time. But when I find a new trail, I follow it to its source, because ants are a sign of trouble (see Aphids) and I need to know what's what.

If you can place a barrier ants can't get around, that's easy. Barriers I've spread on the ground that work are diatomaceous earth, bonemeal, and ground charcoal.

If you can't make a barrier, and blasting them with a hose doesn't do much, a soapy spray of 1 tablespoon dishwashing liquid per quart of water is effective. Add 1 tablespoon alcohol or kerosene per quart of soapy water and you've got the ultimate solution—but be careful you don't spray it where the kerosene can leave an oily residue.

Wear a hat, gloves, long sleeves, and cover your face as much as possible with a cotton scarf while you spray.

Aphids

$\mathcal{I}$ suppose there must be a place in this country that aphids haven't found. One good thing about winter is there are no aphids. Healthy plants tend not to be attractive to pests, but aphids have an age-old interest in a vast number of plants, healthy or not. Often aphids go unnoticed until it's too late—until the strength is sucked out of a plant. If you see a trail of ants marching to and from a plant, look for aphids. From sap, aphids manufacture a sugary substance called *honeydew*. Ants feed on this honeydew by stroking and tapping the aphids' abdomens. Some ant species even ensure their sweet supply by trundling aphids off to shelter when the weather turns bad.

See the soapy sprays for Ants. I have tried a rhubarb leaf spray, which works very well, but one can quickly run out of rhubarb leaves. The last resort is to spray with an insecticidal soap.

It's important to get rid of aphids at the first sign. However, wait a week or so after their first appearance in spring. Ladybugs may turn up and devour the aphids.

After that, the best weapon against aphids I know is a barrier of floating row cover secured over a vulnerable plant from the moment it's set into the ground or from the moment it shows leaves. Of course if the plant needs to be pollinated, you must remove the cover when blossoms appear and take your chances.

Look for ladybugs, great eaters of aphids. If you live near a pond, often there are vast colonies of them in spring waiting to be scooped into a big paper bag and brought home to your garden. Do this on an afternoon when the garden is moist. If there's ample food for them, they won't fly away.

Autumn Cleanup

There are two reasons why you can't just walk away from the garden after killing frosts and then step back into the garden come spring. Pests winter over in spent foliage. You may not have noticed signs of beetles in late August, but if you leave foliage in place, you'll be sure to see passels of them tumbling out of the ground come spring. The second reason is that digging in spent plants breaks them down over winter, enriching the soil.

So if everything looks good and healthy, chop up those vines and leaves and stalks and turn them into the soil. If there's a hint of trouble, bag them up and send them to the dump. Also, you can rake up fallen leaves and shake them over your beds. Excellent mulch, and they'll have weathered down by spring.

Do bear in mind that when you are looking forward to volunteers from a favorite plant, the ground where it spent the summer should be disturbed as little as possible.

If your climate and timing are right, sow a crop of green manure for the winter.

Autumn Sowing

There is something wonderfully optimistic and redeeming about sowing seeds at season's end. The whole thrust of the gardening year is one great birthing push in spring. Midsummer, we begin to learn what sort of children we've brought forth. Then around the middle of August, it's the true gardener's heart that lifts at the prospect of yet a new round of sowing.

What I've observed about autumn sowing is that these are the delicacies of the garden. With the last rush of summer's sun there will be minuscule greens from thinnings 3 weeks after sowing. And we can pull peas, small snap beans, carrots, beets, turnips, and scallions before—and after—the snow flies. Just the expectation of young chicories and endives makes my mouth water. And there are a dozen more sturdy greens, most of them mustardy and many of them Asian, that will settle themselves for cold weather. We will eat well.

It will take digging, working in the compost and chicken fertilizer. Sifting the carrot and beet beds for stones. Rolling out airy swaths of row covers and tucking the babies into their beds. But it's worth it. When lettuce is a fortune in January, as I pull tender Bibb leaves from the cold frame under the snow, I won't be sorry.

B-1 Solution

A liquid with vitamin B-1 and often several other trace elements that act as a tonic for transplants and plants feeling puny. Mostly, it helps prevent transplant shock.

Bats

Invite these fascinating creatures into your garden by putting up a bat house (many gardeners' catalogs offer them). Bats eat hundreds of insects an hour—and it's fun to watch them dart and dive at twilight.

BEDS

A garden bed is a defined area with plants in it. Several beds can compose a border—with paths or other manner of passage between them.

The trick of laying out workable beds is having them less than twice as wide as you can comfortably reach, so you can weed and thin and harvest in the middle of the bed when kneeling in a path. Four feet is usually ideal, but you can stretch it to 5 if your arms are long and the math of your garden makes it necessary.

Also see Raised Beds.

BIENNIAL

From *Hortus Third:* "Of two seasons' duration, from germination to maturity and death, usually developing vegetative growth the first year, and flowering, fruiting, and dying the second."

BIRDS, DESTRUCTIVE

The bird scare line—plastic tape stretched between poles—netting, silvery tape, and black plastic ribbons that rattle and flap in the wind did nothing. But paper bags over the corn ears a week before harvest work well for us. The big Japanese round yellow balloons with the glowing metallic eyes have worked. With this caution: You must move the scare around every couple of days. If you put up a lifelike plastic owl or lay down a lifelike plastic snake, just keep it moving. Birds keep watch. A bird will think, You know, that thing hasn't moved for days.

BLANCHING VEGETABLES

By shading a vegetable from the sun you create an ivory color and a texture that's more tender than it would have been in green. The flavor will also be more delicate by comparison.

The plant must be blemish free and bone dry at the time you start the process, or soon you'll have a rotted vegetable. Keep the soil as moist as you would normally.

Keep an eye on the plant. Check occasionally to make sure nothing is rotting. Blanching weakens tissue (the chlorophyll that greens it up gives it vigor), so once the plant has reached a pleasing color, harvest as usual, and cook ASAP.

Asparagus. Set a tall flowerpot or box over emerging spears and cover the pot's drainage hole with a rock. Cover the box's openings with duct tape. By the time the stalk is 6 or so inches tall, its color is an ethereal ivory-green, perhaps tinged mauve. The sort of thing one should eat only in the moonlight.

To blanch several spears at once, you can mound 8 to 10 inches of organic mulch over the emerging spears—enough to block out the sun but not water and air.

Cardoon. When stalks reach about 3 feet tall, wrap the plant in something supple and opaque like burlap, thick brown paper, or black planting paper.

In about a month (or whenever you like), release the prisoner. Slice off the stalks—now looking like oversized celery—flush with the ground. If you live where it gets no colder than 10°F, the stalks will regenerate next spring.

Cauliflower.

If the cultivar isn't self-blanching, as soon as the curds are visible, loosely cover them with big leaves, snapping their stalks so the leaves lie flat, and tie with cotton string or secure with a rubber band. Make it loose because air must be able to circulate, raindrops must be able to dry so nothing rots, and there must be space for the curds to grow large.

Celery (including Chinese Celery).

When it's 8 to 12 inches high, wrap the plant in the manner of cardoons. Harvest before frost or whenever you like.

Chicories.

Cover the plant like asparagus. The leaves will be blanched in about 10 days.

Chinese Cabbage, both types.

About 7 to 10 days before the seed packet says the cabbage should be mature, tie a strip of soft fabric around it toward the top. Harvest in about two weeks.

Chinese Chives:

Blanching is begun immediately after a full cut of green leaves and its attendant feeding. Because it's a strain on the plant, blanch just once a season in the north. In the warmest parts of the south, you might try two blanchings after two cuttings and see how the plant responds. Cover with earth or a box or pot as for blanching chicories. Harvest when the leaves are the color of pale daffodils and use at once.

Dandelions, Curly Endive, Escarole, Romaine Lettuce.

To blanch the centers, tie up the bunch as for Chinese cabbage. To blanch the whole head, cover it like asparagus. It will probably be 10 days to harvest.

Endive, Belgian.

Over summer, grow the plants as usual—you can harvest a few of the bitter leaves for salads. After one or two frosts, or when roots are 8 inches long, choose sound, stout roots, at least 1 inch wide at the top. Cut off the stalks at 1 inch, cut back roots to 6 inches. If you don't have frost, set roots in unsealed plastic bags and chill for two to three weeks. You can have a continuous supply of Belgian endive through winter. Store the waiting roots in a bag of moist sand at just above freezing or in the refrigerator.

Use a large, deep pot or sturdy cardboard box with drainage holes a little larger than the roots you'll be putting in it. Pour in about 6 inches of garden soil. Stand the roots upright in the soil like soldiers. Add soil up to the crowns and water thoroughly. There must not be a crack of light, or the leaves will be ultra-bitter. Keep at 50°F to 60°F, and the more humid, the better. Once a week or so feel down to check the soil. When it's dry, use a bulb baster to spurt water at the base of the leaves—wet leaves rot.

In three to six weeks the chicons (blanched sprouts) will be 4 to 6 inches high. Harvest them, cutting just above the crown. The nubbin of a shoot will grow into another chicon—you may even get a third and fourth crop, although the shoots will diminish in vitality.

Leeks and Nebuka Onions.

Three weeks after setting the seedlings in the trench or hole, the roots will have taken hold. Carefully stand each plant upright, tamp the roots gently into the soil, then sprinkle soil around the plant up to where leaves begin. Water in gently. Pat firm. As they grow, add soil or fine compost as needed to keep the earth at the same point. *Be careful not to get soil into the spaces between the leaves*—it will work its way down into the stem. Some grit is inevitable, but you can try.

When the trench or hole is full, keep earthing up as long as the stems continue to be pale. Rather than soil, you can use straw or a mixture of straw and grass clippings or sawdust.

Keep the plants constantly moist and feed with a half-strength solution of manure tea or liquid seaweed or fish emulsion every couple of weeks during the growing season.

To hold the soil in place, you can bank each side with flat stones. The row will look like an onion graveyard. Dig an irrigation ditch along the base of each side. As you bank up the hillock, remove the stones first, of course, add the earth, then put them back. The stones add warmth, keep moisture inside, and help prevent erosion. Leeks and nebukas go right through winter, rain, and snow—but never let the roots dry out.

To harvest, carefully dig down, then scoop back the soil around each stalk with your hands and use scissors to cut the stem off an inch above the roots. The coarse leaves are fit only for flavoring broth. Leave the hole open so the bulblet can see the sky. As a new plant grows, fill in the soil and repeat the blanching process. The root is really good only for a second stalk.

When the plants start to send up flowers, harvest or pull them up. Although the flowers are a big, round, fat cluster of tasty blossoms, their stalk makes a woody center.

Salsify Chicons. Grow a root sown in spring until the following January. If it will need shelter from frost, mulch it with leaves or move to a cold frame. Trim the leaves to an inch above the crown and cover like asparagus. Keep roots moist. See if you can harvest the pale shoots in March—cutting them like Belgian endive—and try for a second harvest.

BLOOD MEAL

An animal by-product used as nitrogen fertilizer. Many small critters will not cross a 3-inch-wide band of it.

BOLTING

When plants go into the seed-making business, they begin to swell in the center, eventually sending up a flowering stalk. At that point the edible portions—usually the leaves and root—turn from tender to tough and from sweet to bitter, since all the plant's energy is going into forming a flower and ultimately seeds. This process is called *bolting* and is triggered by time and/or heat or stress. By cutting out the flowering stalk at the base you can forestall the process for a few days or even weeks—or altogether, according to the time of year.

Some plants—cauliflowers, for example—mature in stages, and stress during a transition of any stage can cause the plant to bolt.

BONEMEAL

Another animal by-product, steamed, used as fertilizer for its phosphorus.

BORDER

Strictly speaking, a border is an ornamental strip bordering a lawn or other established area of planting. I think of a border as a bed—a pleasing mix of flowers, vegetables, herbs, and fruits—not bordering anything in particular.

BORON

A chemical element needed most by broccoli, cauliflower, and celery, then by asparagus, beets, cabbages, carrots, eggplants, horseradish, rutabagas, squashes, sweet corn, tomatoes, and turnips, and to a lesser degree by peppers and sweet potatoes. Soil rich in humus and/or plants fertilized with kelp are rarely deficient in boron. Very alkaline soil (pH above 6.8) can make its boron unavailable to plants. Boron deficiency generally shows as distorted leaves, shortened, hardened stems, and dying growing points. Suspect a boron deficiency when cauliflower turns brown, celery's stems crack, beets have a blackened heart, and turnips are brown inside. The first thing to do is to bring the soil's pH to a more neutral level. Then add rock phosphate and granite dust according to package directions, then more humus. Foliar feed with kelp according to package directions. Studies indicate boron helps regulate the body's ability to absorb calcium, phosphorus, and magnesium.

CABBAGE MAGGOTS

Y ou'll never have these if you cover your brassica and pea seeds or transplants the moment they go into the ground with insect-weight floating row covers, thoroughly weighted. The fly lays her eggs at the base of the plant, and if she can't get there, well then, no eggs, no maggots.

CAGES FOR GROWING PLANTS VERTICALLY

M ade of 4-inch-mesh galvanized wire fencing, these round upright cages support fruiting vines. Because they have thorough air circulation and access to sunshine, vines supported this way at least equal if not outproduce other systems of support. Six cucumbers or one indeterminate (long-vining) tomato plant can be contained in one cage 24 inches wide and 5 to 6 feet high. Determinate tomatoes can have a 4-foot cage. See Tomatoes.

CATALOGS: ORDERING SEEDS AND PLANTS THROUGH THE MAIL

T o me one of the principal pleasures of gardening is that I can grow dreams, not someone's notion of what I ought to grow—or what's economically enriching for a purveyor to offer me.

I want to see what a fluted lavender Violetta di Firenze eggplant looks and tastes like rather than picking up a six-pack of seedlings at the nursery and spending the summer nursing the same eggplants I've seen for years at the market. And, rather than seeds from a rack at the nursery, I have an infinitely greater selection from catalogs since most seedsmen specialize and plumb the range and depth of selection. In most cases the quality of seeds bought through catalogs is fresher and in some cases of higher quality.

But the biggest reason for growing from catalogs is the selection there is for good flavor. That's the first word I look for in cultivar descriptions. I almost always let considerations of appearance, maturity dates, size, shape, disease resistance, and ease of cultivation come after how something will taste.

At this point, even though the trend is toward international megaliths taking over the industry, there are still three sorts of seed companies: the big guys who have been in business for decades, some more than a century; the medium-size guys who have laboriously built their businesses; and the little guys who are crazy about seeds and punishment. There's something to be said for giving your business to each. The big guys have resources and a name to maintain. The medium-size guys are competitive, with inventive breeding, struggling to hang in there. The little guys are passionate and deserve their piece of the pie, too.

The more one reads, the more the names of a few respected companies keep turning up. Still, the way things are going, the quality of seeds and the range of cultivars from a once-trusted company can alter dramatically in one season. Therefore, I make fresh decisions each year, guided by the catalogs. Namely:

The more information in a catalog—solid detailed gardening how-to, even some history and lore—the more, I find, the purveyors care about what happens to their seeds after the shipment leaves the warehouse. They want you to be successful so you'll reorder next season. Don't be gulled by appealing photographs and ebullient copywriting that in fact tell you little about the plant.

The more unusual, varied, and considered the selection of cultivars offered, the more the purveyors are sincerely interested in the gardener's reward. Anybody can ship out bushels of Early Girl tomato seeds. But when somebody's made the effort to find and develop a bright yellow tomato that gives me fruit in two months, is easy to grow, has glorious flavor, bears all season, and is open pollinated (that's Taxi), I think he or she deserves my nickel.

A list of mail-order companies I like is in Sources at the back of the book.

Few of the hundreds of companies that offer seeds for sale produce their own—most are brokers. Recently I was confounded by the appearance of my citron melons. When I queried the seed company—one I esteem—the reply came back that they'd never seen the melons because they couldn't grow them in their climate. A shock. So look for the phrase "in our trials" frequently in the catalog. By that you know the seedsman knows what he or she is sending you.

Mail-order nurseries also fall into three categories: the big seed companies that also ship plants, large nurseries of long standing that offer everything from asparagus to wisteria, and medium to small nurseries that specialize in every imaginable category from heritage fruits to water gardens.

For both seeds and plants I've found the giant old-line companies reliable, but with a few notable exceptions, their offerings are uninspired. When I can, I deal with the companies that specialize. They are usually dedicated and enthusiastic. And I like companies that have one or two real people at the heart of the operation—those people address me in the catalog, and their caring is palpable.

One advantage of ordering catalogs that specialize in climates other than your own is that if you hunger to taste Native American corn, you know to look in catalogs from the Southwest. If you want to try your luck at cauliflower, you can be sure a fine selection will be offered from the moist and cool Northwest. Don't for a moment feel you must stick with cultivars bred for your own backyard. Be adventurous, then set about creating pockets of microclimates in your garden to accommodate what you want to grow and eat (see Microclimate entry).

There's another consideration: it's crucial that we support the people who obtain rare seeds for us and who are concerned with fostering genetic diversity of seeds on this planet. To quote the Seed Savers Exchange's *Garden Seed Inventory, Third Edition* (1992):

> There is a tremendous amount of excellent Oriental and European material currently flowing into the U.S. . . . Often business contacts in the East are shaky, however, and many Oriental varieties are only available for a single year. . . . We can never predict when windows to foreign varieties will close. . . . Several unique seed companies . . . are offering plant material unlike anything the U.S. seed trade has ever seen. . . . In a very real sense, gardeners are voting with their mail-order seed purchases on the survival of these companies. Make your dollars count. If you want these varieties to remain available, buy them.

Why all the concern about genetic preservation of open-pollinated—traditional nonhybrid—plants? Because they're being dropped by seed companies with a thud. To give you an idea why alarm bells are ringing all over the world in horticulturists' chambers, 5,307 cultivars of nonhybrid vegetables were offered in U.S. seed catalogs in 1987. Four years later, 1,263 of them had been dropped in favor of more expensive (read profitable) hybrids. That's almost 24 percent gone.

OPEN-POLLINATED VEGETABLES LOSING GROUND

According to Seed Savers Exchange's *Garden Seed Inventory, Third Edition*, biennials and vegetables that are easily turned into hybrids are in particular peril of being dropped from seed catalogs and thus, essentially, lost. Vegetables with more than 25 percent of their open-pollinated cultivars dropped from seed catalogs since 1981 (those with a star have lost more than 35 percent) are

> broccoli
> *brussels sprouts
> *cabbages, green, red, savoy
> cauliflower
> Chinese cabbage
> kohlrabi
> *mangels and sugar beets
> *onions, yellow
> peppers, sweet bell
> *rhubarb
> *soybeans
> spinach
> *turnips

So, whenever possible, order, grow, and offer friends seeds of open-pollinated cultivars of these vegetables to help save them from extinction.

Hybrid seeds have their place too. Clearly they can have the virtues of the open-pollinated cultivars they combine. They can be immensely productive and have great disease resistance—particularly when grown in an area over time, like those grown by Native Americans in the inhospitable Southwest—and fine flavor and form. As a friend in the seed business has said, hybrids are not inherently evil.

But how will you know in each year who's doing what in seed companies and nurseries and where you will find them? In early spring, look in gardening magazines when they report on what's new—note the names of companies that crop up again and again with innovative cultivars. Most gardening magazines aren't on the newsstand, but perhaps your local library subscribes to one. Certainly someone in the local garden club will lend you magazines and free advice about sources. If your library has no gardening magazine and your town no garden club, look around for a garden you admire, knock on the door, introduce yourself, and ask questions of the gardener within. Most great gardeners, like beekeepers, adore what they do and will chat about it with anyone who will listen.

Order your catalogs in September. When the catalog comes, make your decisions and send in your orders no later than the end of January—early January if what you want is rare.

CATCH CROPS

A bare patch of soil isn't doing anything for your table. If a crop has been harvested and you have four to six weeks before the next can be planted—or before you must close up shop for winter—drop in a fast-maturing crop. Don't worry about crop rotation. The plants are in the soil so brief a time—although it's best not to follow one member of the Mustard family with another.

Some of the best catch crops are arugula, baby beets, baby carrots (Little Finger), sugar loaf chicory, cresses, endive, kohlrabi, dwarf lettuces, green onions, dwarf peas, purslane, radishes, rapini, spinach, and turnips (Tokyo Cross).

CATS

*I*f you have mice, moles, voles, and gophers, get a great big lionhearted cat. Or two or three. Cats can be an enormous help in the organic garden.

And cats can be infuriatingly stubborn once they've found a spot in the garden they fancy for their private matters. Commercial sprays smell as nasty to me as to the cats and can damage plants.

I did two things that broke Teeny and Thistle's cat-box-in-my-best-beds habit. The first was to give them an indoor box, ridiculous in summer with a forest as far as the eye can see, but cats respond to mollycoddling. The second was to lay down sheets of wide-gauge chicken wire on top of the soil in the places they fancied. I figured the wire would make it impossible for them to dig, and digging is an essential part of the ritual. I threw earth over the wire to hide it and seeded the beds with annuals—I wouldn't put a food crop there because cat deposits can carry disease. The flowers came up freely through the mesh, and I left the wire in over the winter, just to make sure the habit was broken. It was. I removed the barrier, and in the two years since, they've never taken up business in another bed. Do they think there's wire under all the earth?

CLASSIFICATION OF PLANTS (TAXONOMY)

*T*aking the cherry tomato as an example, the order goes

> phylum: Spermatophyte
> class: Angiosperm
> subclass: Dicotyledon
> superorder: Asteridae
> order: Polemoniales
> family: Solanaceae (Nightshades)
> genus: *Lycopersicom*
> species: *Lycopersicun*
> subspecies: *cerasiforme*
> cultivar: Gold Nugget
> form: determinate

CLAY/ADOBE SOIL

*S*oil made of very fine particles that, when dry, is so impenetrable it can be turned into brick. Although clay retains nutrients wonderfully, the circulation of water and air is minimal. To gradually make it friable, when the soil is lightly moist but not gummy, work it deeply with a digging fork, and amend it—sometimes half and half in severe cases—with finished compost, gypsum, well-rotted manure, decomposed sawdust, and peat. A mix rather than just one of these is most desirable. If any amendment is not fully rotted, add a handful of blood meal to satisfy the need for nitrogen. Keep plants mulched with humusy materials so the worms will drag it down and loosen the soil. If the problem is severe, consult your county agricultural agent.

CLOCHES

Cloche is French for bell—you know the close-fitting hats by that name so popular during the 1920s. Because of its close-fitting and transparent qualities, *cloche* is used to describe systems protecting plants from the elements.

Glass Jars. In spring, at night, to protect newly transplanted seedlings from frost, I just put wide-mouth quart jars over them. Be sure to remove them in the morning, or the sun will cook the plants.

Glass Panes. If you can secure them against breaking, you can make a tent of panes of glass over a special plant, as long as there's side ventilation. Secure against the wind.

Plastic Milk Jugs. Be sure not to use a container that held something caustic, such as bleach. Cut out the bottom and set these on seedlings the same way as glass jars. Leave the cap in place for the night. In the morning, if it's overcast and cold, you can leave the jug in place as long as you uncap it for ventilation. Otherwise remove it, or sun will cook the plant.

Slitted Row Covers. In very cold regions, sheets of ventilated polyethylene fitted over wire hoops provide greater intensity of light and warmth than floating row covers. Probably the best way of making a tunnel.

COLD FRAMES

Though they're called *cold frames* because they were designed mainly to protect seedlings from low temperatures, these boxes can shelter so much good eating through winter, late fall, and early spring.

Construction. Here we have a simple shallow box, usually rectangular, consisting of four sides and a lid. The back is higher than the front so the lid, hinged on the back, slopes down toward its closure at the front. If the rectangle is broad enough, it's best for the cover to be in sections. Calculate the size in terms of flats, since you'll find you often set seedlings in flats in the cold frame. The frame is sometimes of wood (untreated weathering wood such as redwood or cedar), sometimes of metal. The lid is always clear, either of glass or durable plastic, and sometimes the sides are clear as well. Depending on its construction, the frame can be permanent or lifted and either moved elsewhere in the garden or taken apart in the manner of a child's Tinkertoy set to store. Our cold frame is like the latter. I ordered four of them from a catalog. They're aluminum and plastic, sturdy but light enough to move easily. This is an advantage, because should something you started in the cold frame's soil rapidly grow a lot taller than you expected—it has happened to me a number of times—rather than have to cut the plant back or, worse, pull it up, I just lift the cold frame up and away and the plant grows merrily on. The system we have has been designed so ends can be removed and any number of frames can be connected. I've put all four together one time, two and two together at other times, and three together another time.

It's critical that the frame be solidly anchored against strong winds. Sinking it slightly into the ground not only helps anchor it but also keeps out mice. There should be a prop that can firmly hold the lid open at several positions—about 2 inches, halfway, fully or simply off altogether. Keep the lid clean so ample light and sun can shine through.

You can also make a "pit greenhouse"—very popular in England because the inside is so warm. For taller plants—so their leaves will feel the sun—dig down as much as 4 feet, being sure the bottom slopes for good drainage. Cover with the usual cold-frame top.

Using It. In winter, many greens add their leaves to our salads.

In early spring, with a heating cable laced beneath the soil, I've germinated seeds in flats at a cozy 70°F when the air outside was 28°F. This is called a *hot bed* and can be achieved with a thick layer of fresh (steaming!) horse manure. Dig the bottom 2¹/₂ feet deep, pack in a 1¹/₂-foot layer of fresh manure, then cover it with 6 inches of good soil.

In late spring, with the heating cable disconnected, the cold frame is handy for hardening seedlings before planting them. I don't have to bring the flats indoors at the end of the day, just clap the lids on the frame and cover it with a blanket.

In early summer, after refreshing the soil with old manure and spoiled straw for humus, I use the frame to start seedlings that the mice and birds can't leave alone, such as kohlrabi, orach, and peas. I just lay a fitted cover of hardware cloth over the frame and wait for the seedlings to get larger than the mice.

And in late summer/early autumn, I start the seeds for our winter salad greens.

In every season I water and fertilize what's inside the way I water the same sort of plant outside. I don't fertilize plants in the cold frame over winter—as I don't fertilize other plants in the garden. Growth in the cold is so very slow, and fertilizing encourages tender growth that's particularly vulnerable to frost. Nothing should dry out, but because the plants are so sheltered from desiccating winds, you have to be careful that they don't get soggy.

Placement. Set the frame in a sheltered but sunny place, ideally with the lid sloping to the south. Make sure that, where you stand, you can not only reach but dig in every part of the interior.

The Soil. The frame should be over soil as rich and as well drained as can be mustered.

Keeping What's Inside Warm Enough. We live in zone 8, and it can be 10°F for weeks in winter. When I first had a cold frame, I'd knock myself out running outside at night, throwing blankets over the thing, then dashing out in the frozen morning and pulling them off so the sun could warm the chattering plants.

I've since discovered that 10°F in a cold frame is not hardship for hardy plants. Last winter I didn't even bother to put the lid on the cold frame. There was a wire top to keep the critters out, and it held the snow above the seedlings for a while, but ultimately it fell in of the snow's weight and snow blanketed the plants closely. Now, in April, all the autumn-sown lettuces, mustards, chicories, miner's lettuce, and whatnot are cruising. I lost nothing to the cold.

The plants closest to the back of the cold frame (on the north side) are almost twice the size of those toward the front—the sun against the plastic back warmed them.

If you live where the air is really cold, a couple of layers of floating row covers directly on the plants inside the frame and a covering of rugs and blankets and/or tarps on top should see the tender things through. Experiment.

Ventilation. Don't let too many days go by in even the most inclement weather without opening the frame just an inch for air. On rainy days I open the frame completely to let the seedlings have a good soak. This is crucial to good health. When the sun shines, I open at least one of the lids for ventilation. You can hear the babies oohing and aahing in the crisp sweet air. And when fine weather comes, you needn't cover the frame at all.

Consult Eliot Coleman's *Four-Season Harvest,* a superb work on bringing crops through icy winters.

COLOR IN VEGETABLES AND EDIBLE FLOWERS

*T*his is just a beginning list. Remember, as brilliant as the colors of beets sound in catalogs, don't expect to see more than a flash of their color above ground. Same for radishes, carrots, and turnips.

Purple/Purply Red. Amaranth, any purple leaf; artichoke, Violetto; basil, leaves and flowers, Dark Opal, and many others; beans, purple pods, flowers, and beans; beet (leaves—mostly in winter), Detroit; broccoli, Purple Sprouting; brussels sprouts, Rubine Red; cabbage, any red; cauliflower, Purple Cape; eggplant, Violetta di Fiorenze and many others; Johnny-jump-ups; kale, Red Russian; kohlrabi, Rapid; lettuce, Red Salad Bowl, Red Oak Leaf, and many others; mint flowers; mustard greens, Red Giant; nettles, Purple Stingless; onion, Southport Red and several others; orach, red; pak choi, Flowering Purple; pansies, many; peppers, Purple Beauty; perilla, red; radicchio, Rossa di Verona or any red; radish, Plum Purple; sage, purple; sweet potato flowers; tomatillo, Purple Milpa; turnip, Purple Top; violas, many.

Blue. Violas, many; flowers of blue potatoes, hyssop, rosemary, borage, and chicory; pansies, many.

Pink/Pinky-Lilac. African Blue Basil flowers and leaves; chard, Charlotte and Rhubarb Red; chive flowers; eggplant, Bride/Pink Bride; hyssop flowers; lavender; marjoram flowers; nasturtiums; pansies, many; rosemary flowers; violas, many.

Red. Beans, flowers of scarlet runner; nasturtiums, many; peppers, most mature sweet and chili; pansies, many; sages, flowers of pineapple.

Orange. Calendulas, many; marigolds, especially Tangerine Gem; nasturtiums, many; pansies, many; peppers, Corona; squashes, winter; tomatoes, Caro Rich, Persimmon, and several others; violas, many.

Yellow. Beans, wax; calendulas, many; cucumbers, lemon; dandelion flowers; dill flowers; fennel flowers; marigolds, especially Lemon Gem; marjoram, golden; mustard flowers, all; nasturtiums, many; okra flowers; pansies, many; lovage flowers; sage, golden variegated leaves; squash flowers and many summer squashes; thyme, golden variegated leaves; tomatoes, Taxi and several others, yellow currants, yellow plums, and yellow pears; violas, many.

White/Cream. Arugula flowers; beans, White Dutch runner flowers; nasturtiums, especially Alaska for flowers and cream-marbled leaves; onion and Chinese chives flowers; pansies, many; pea flowers (*not* sweet pea flowers); radish flowers; thyme flowers.

More in Assorted Colors. Cornstalks, hollyhocks, mints, scented geraniums, sunflowers, tomatillos.

COMFREY

This is a big, blowsy leaf of a perennial from succulent roots that love to grow. Just blink at a comfrey plant and it will double in size. Once the leaves were used for tea, but they're now on the carcinogenic list. Curiously, comfrey tea doesn't harm plants at all—being rich in potassium, it's very good for plants and the soil. Fill a big bucket with *wilted* comfrey leaves, cover them with water, and forget about it for a month or so. Dilute 1 pint to a gallon of water. It's a high old smell, but the plants adore it. You can keep the bucket topped off as you do with manure tea.

Then you can also line the potato trench with torn comfrey leaves. Keep a few plants in your utility corner. It sends up pretty little purple bells in summer. But you'll never get rid of it once it's in, so choose the spots carefully.

COMPANION PLANTING

*T*here is a folk tradition in gardening that a given plant has properties that can help other plants grow better than it would on its own or that some plants are bad friends and shouldn't be neighbors.

I was all prepared to give you an exhaustive chart with vegetable companions—what tradition says and what has been proved scientifically. But the truth is, the more I practice companion planting, and the more I read about it, the less solid information there is to go on.

In terms of interplanting vegetables, herbs, and flowers for their mutual benefit, here is what *research* has shown.

The wild mustard referred to is *Brassica nigra,* the source of table mustard.

Information is from Anna Carr's *Companion Planting for Gardeners,* which has a persuasive bibliography (Rodale Press, 1985). The book has both traditional and scientific research in its pages.

Beans. French marigolds do repel Mexican bean beetles, but at the same time they have a detrimental effect on the crop. Potatoes interplanted with beans have helped control Mexican bean beetles to some degree. Corn can help reduce leafhopper damage. Spiny amaranth can draw away black cutworms.

The big thing in intercropping with beans is to create a canopy of leaves so dense that marauders simply can't find the beans. Also see Nettles.

Brussels sprouts. Weeds permitted to grow among them attract hover flies, which reduce aphids. Wild mustard also reduces aphids. Also see Mustard family.

Cabbage. Tomatoes among cabbages can help reduce whitefly. Other nightshade plants inhibit the growth of cabbage flea beetles. A cover crop of clover can significantly reduce cabbage root flies—lettuce did the same in one study. French marigolds reduce cabbage pests considerably—as well as the size of the cabbages. Also see Mustard family.

Celery and Other Members of the Parsley Family. Their flowers attract beneficial wasps.

Collards. Intercropped with beans, collards have more beneficial wasps and thus many fewer aphids, and the harvest is increased. Wild mustard reduces cabbage aphids and flea beetles in collards. Also see Mustard family.

Corn. A few studies have shown higher yields when corn is intercropped with a legume. However, one study found ears of corn were smaller when grown with peas. Alternating strips of soybeans and corn (especially when the strips are narrow) increases the yield of both crops. Soybeans also can control corn earworms by attracting beneficial wasps. Planted with corn, soybeans seem to produce larger nitrogen-fixing nodules. Summer savory seems to attract corn earworms. Peanuts and/or soybeans can reduce corn borers. Peanuts seem to attract spiders to the corn patch, which helps regulate pests. Soybeans or bush beans every 10th row have reduced armyworms. Best results occur when the beans are sown 20 to 30 days before the corn. A cover crop of alfalfa each year where corn will grow can gradually reduce wireworms.

Cucumbers. Broccoli, corn, and radishes seem to discourage striped cucumber beetles. Spiny amaranth helps control black cutworms.

Lettuce. Decaying broccoli plants can inhibit germination and growth. Lettuce is sensitive in the same way to favas and rye, among other plants. *Chrysanthemum × morifolium* inhibits the growth of lettuce.

Mustard Family. Snap beans and wild mustard have helped reduce aphids. Clovers, lettuce, and weeds help camouflage crops so cabbage root flies and aphids can't find them. Red and white clovers draw predatory ground beetles. Tomatoes seem to deter flea beetles and diamondback moths when planted with brassicas.

Nematodes. African, French, and golden marigolds each control particular species of nematodes. At summer's end, pull up the marigolds by the roots and burn them—the nematodes gather on the roots.

Nettles. These greens nurture 11 sorts of beneficial insects that prey on aphids, flea beetles, Mexican bean beetles, and other bean pests.

Peanuts. Planting with a nonlegume crop seems to increase the yield for both.

Peas. In one study tomatoes and peas were mutually beneficial. Root rot in peas seems to be reduced in the presence of the Mustard family. White mustard *(B. hirta)* supports a parasite of pea aphids.

Peppers. Catnip, coriander, marigolds, nasturtiums, onions, and tansy have helped reduce aphids.

Potatoes. In one study coriander reduced Colorado potato beetles—and catnip, coriander, nasturtiums, and tansy reduced the larvae of the beetles to a degree. The scent of dandelions repels Colorado potato beetles. And marigolds mask the scent of potatoes, which fools Colorado potato beetles. Deadly nightshade also helps control the beetles.

Pyrethrum Daisies. These reduce nematodes in the soil.

Soybeans. The remnants of a corn crop can increase yields, but the remains of lamb's-quarters, sunflowers, and soybeans do not. Also see Corn.

Tomatoes. Spiny amaranth draws away black cutworms.

Zucchini. Catnip and tansy seem to keep squash bugs away.

COMPOST

*C*ompost is the gardener's way of making humus, the Hershey's cocoa of dirt. When created in the soil, organic matter (material from the animal and vegetable kingdoms) becomes humus as soil animals and microbes digest and excrete the matter at a leisurely pace: i.e., help it decompose. In the gardener's compost heap a layer cake of organic matter bakes, one way or another, into humus. Sometimes the process gets frenetic as the soil animals and microbes are whipped to a lather to bake fast—compost in two weeks! Mellow gardeners allow these magical creatures to eat and excrete at their own pace, and it can take months if not a year to get compost—humus.

The breakdown is only partial, mind you. There must be more to go. Organic matter is valuable to the soil only in the *process* of decaying, in the excretions of the organisms doing their jobs—earthworm castings, for example.

Compost can get frightfully technical. Much has been written about it, and it's worth reading about in detail. You might begin with Shepherd Ogden's remarks in *Step by Step Organic Vegetable Gardening*, then move on to *Let It Rot!* In the meantime, here's what you *need* to know.

The Heap and Where to Place It.

If you have a casual sort of garden, a need for lots of compost, and space, you might do as we did in the beginning. We set aside an area about 10 feet square, marked with small boulders (it could have been wooden planks). It was on a sloping slab of boulder— good drainage is essential—and a stone's throw from the front door. If the heap isn't convenient to the kitchen, you're not going to carry out the collecting jar cheerfully. We divided the space in half, making adjoining heaps 5 by 10 feet. The idea is that while one heap is working you're building the other. If you plan to make hot compost—compost fast—place the heap where a hose can reach it, because you'll need to water it daily.

Perhaps compost in a tidy container better suits your garden. You can build something of wood, or from catalogs choose something as simple as plastic-coated-wire bins or as elaborate as plastic tumblers on a stand (for mixing hot compost easily). There is never a dearth of articles about compost or ads for compost machinery in gardening magazines.

The Collecting Jar.

The big glass cookie jar by the kitchen sink is the heart of our compost. It fits in a wicker basket so you can't see what's inside, and its top easily lifts off—both valuable attributes for compost gathering. One friend's collector is a covered bin under the sink; another's is a crock right in the sink. Wherever you put it, make sure it's easy to get to and big enough so you're not constantly trotting out to the heap. *Or* have a small tight-closing garbage can by the back door where you can stash a few days' worth of makings.

The Makings.

Every dot of coffee grounds, tea leaves, eggshells, old bananas, wizened fresh ginger, undyed paper, nutshells, spent flowers, and grunge from the refrigerator goes in the jar.

What else goes onto the pile? Almost anything biodegradable. What, that's biodegradable, doesn't go in? Diseased plants or animals, most poisonous plants (foxgloves may be composted), materials impregnated with pesticides or herbicides, ashes of coal and charcoal (excessive sulfur and iron), toxic materials (for example, rags used with chemicals of any sort), colored newspaper pages (the ink is toxic), waxed and glossy paper (too slow to break down), oil and fat (ditto), thorny canes, and most leaves of hardwoods (they affect the pH of the soil).

Theoretically you can compost the excrement of healthy humans. The Chinese have been enriching their soil with the contents of their honey buckets for 40 centuries—that's one reason why so little in traditional Chinese cuisine is eaten raw. The excrement of healthy animals, including feathered and furry pets, is also used in the garden in other parts of the world. I wouldn't, because it can contain very harmful pathogens, and I can't be sure my compost will heat to 150°F and maintain that temperature long enough to destroy them 100 percent.

To kill weed seeds and disease organisms, ideally compost should cook at 150°F (or even 160°F) for the first three or four days—but 130°F will kill many pesky organisms.

One human by-product the compost heap can use happily is urine, which is sterile and rich in minerals. "Urine-impregnated topsoil is particularly valuable," says Rodale.

Because coyotes, raccoons, and other people's dogs and cats live within the sounds of our voices, I don't mix meat, fowl, or fish scraps in our compost. But they would be fine for the soil. And, of course, there's no other part of an animal that, theoretically, can't make fine compost. Our heaps have been vandalized only in the dead of winter when food was scarce. Our black Lab Sam knows the compost heap, like my garden beds, is off-limits. His fur is the closest I get to animal residue (hair is high in nitrogen).

Hot Compost. Hot compost becomes humus in about eight weeks, a standard length of time. Reading about how to do this can make you crazy, because there are so many techniques, and everybody's got a different set of rules. As many ingredients as possible makes the best compost. Try this mix:

2 parts dry vegetation such as softwood shavings and softwood sawdust (a lumber company may let you bag them up free), dried leaves, spoiled hay, dry grass clippings, and shredded newspapers (to provide carbon to the organisms)

1 part soil

1 part fresh horse or cow manure (from nearby stables and dairy farms—some rotted manure can also be added)

2 parts green vegetation such as kitchen wastes and fresh garden trimmings (these plus the manure provide nitrogen)

Each part is about 2 inches high. Each layer is watered until it has the texture of a wrung-out sponge.

Hot compost is so called because there must be heat to move the process of decomposition swiftly along. Nitrogenous materials heat up when they decompose. Fresh manure is considered a compost "starter" because it is high in nitrogen. Alternatives include a little hoof-and-horn or blood or alfalfa meal from sacks from the nursery to get things hot. For the heap to work efficiently, 3 feet is minimal all ways. Placing it on a slight mound gives good drainage, but this is not critical.

Water enough to keep the moist-sponge texture and turn the heap with a hay fork about once a week in warm weather.

For its heat, keep the pile a distance from trees and buildings.

Superfast. Compost was most exciting—and exhausting—when I made it in two weeks by the University of California's method. We chopped and crumbled up everything, added moldy oak leaves, and blessed it all with a sprinkling of ashes. Made a heap about 3 feet high, watered it daily to keep it the right spongy degree of moisture, then tossed it like a salad with a hay fork (top and outsides in, insides out) every day. On the 14th day, as promised, I had gorgeous dark brown compost.

What the UC method demonstrates is that everything breaks down faster if it begins in small pieces. That's why serious composters own shredders. But hand-turned shredders take only smallish items to begin with (no corncobs, tree prunings, or palm fronds, items notoriously slow to break down), and the electric shredders that do take such materials cost a fortune and jam a lot. So we have neither. Instead, my husband spins up most everything bulky from the kitchen in the food processor, and I bash up garden trimmings with a sharp hoe.

Our compost never has an odor because the jar goes out from the kitchen faithfully when it's full. But if yours does, all you have to do is throw $1/2$ inch of dirt on top, and the scent will be buried too. This blanket of earth also keeps flies from compost.

Supereasy. On the heap, we throw the contents of the collecting jar and every scrap of healthy nonweedy refuse from the garden. We chop and cut things in small bits as time permits. If there's manure to spare, on it goes. But that's it. With the rusty old shovel thrust in the ground down there, my husband scoops up dirt and buries the new stuff by a few inches. We don't water; we don't turn. It can take a year. When I need compost, I just burrow down with the shovel to a level where there are shadows of grounds and rinds and delectable sweet brown fluff.

Always in summer the heap is covered with volunteer squashes and melons from seeds that couldn't believe their luck. Since I don't water, the fruit rarely matures, but it's charming to see their vitality.

Leaching of Nutrient Content by Rain. Unless the heap is covered in rain, most nutrients will wash out of the compost. Ideally it should be covered. Ours isn't, however.

Finishing. Sometimes you'll need very fine compost, for covering special seeds that are germinating or when adding it to a potting mix. Then put it through a screen of $1/4$-inch hardware cloth.

Sheet Composting. My favorite way to compost is Rabelaisian. Rather than go down to the heap, I strew compost straight from the kitchen over bare beds. You're supposed to dig it in, but I don't always. Of course conscience seizes me—or a guest is expected—and I throw soil over the skins and peels. They decompose nicely over time. The sun will burn up much of the nutrients, so it's always better to dig stuff in. It's a wise idea not to pile up the makings—too much compost can react like too much fertilizer.

Commercial Compost. You can buy "compost" in bags at the nursery, but the quality varies wildly. Mushroom compost is the material in which mushrooms have grown, and it's uncommonly rich in minerals.

CONTAINER KITCHEN GARDENING

Sometimes there just isn't space in the garden for a cultivar I'm dying to grow. It happened one year with Porter tomatoes and Minnesota Midget muskmelons. So I put each in a 5-gallon tub, and I was amused that the container plants outpaced their brethren in the ground. And sometimes a plant just isn't happy where I've planted it, so I gather it up, put it in a pot, and care for it until it *is* happy. This gives the plant time to collect itself and me time to observe it and figure out where it really wants to be. Sometimes if you're having a devil of a time with disease in the soil and no certain place to rotate a vulnerable crop to, growing the crop in containers for a few seasons can break the cycle. If your garden hasn't the room for or the character conducive to experimental plants such as dippy rocambole garlic or Giant Japanese Red Mustard, containers can be whisked out of sight when necessary.

More important, container plants have the advantage of being given precisely the exposure they need, even if there's no soil in that spot. You have no place hot enough for eggplants, but what about setting them in pots in the reflected warmth of your sunny south wall? It doesn't matter what the containers stand on. They'll be at least as decorative as purple dahlias. And although my corn grown in growing bags wasn't decorative, growing bags were the only place I could put corn one summer when I had hardly any water and space.

What Can Be Grown. Although almost anything can be grown in a container, it makes sense that plants with modest root systems have the best chance of success. Every plant in this book that is suitable for container growing is so noted in its entry.

Timing. All elements being equal, plants grown in the ground and grown in containers mature around the same time.

The Container. Any vessel not made of or treated with a toxic material that can hold soil mix with a plant in it, provide *good* drainage, and last long enough for the crop to mature can be used. Wooden boxes constructed of raw redwood or cedar are best. Sphagnum moss–lined wire and wicker baskets have great drainage in addition to charm. Nongalvanized metal cans, punched on the bottom for drainage holes, make picturesque containers—such as a no. 10 vegetable or gallon-size olive oil or 10-pound cookie can, stamped in brilliant colors. See if you can complement the picture with the plant.

Deep-rooted vegetables grow happily in nursery-sold growing bags or in several thicknesses of plastic garbage bags with drainage holes poked in the bottom. The number of bags depends on the thickness of each bag—just be sure the walls are sturdy enough to bear the pressure of strong roots in damp soil. A cubic foot of soil or soil mix can weigh 25 pounds. Make sure it's a heat-loving plant, too, since dark plastic makes soil *hot*.

A strawberry barrel purchased from the nursery can be filled with potting mix and each cup planted with a different herb instead of strawberries.

Container Materials. Clay is handsomest but dries out fastest. Not only do you have to water more often, but the more you water, the faster the planting mix compacts and nutrients leach out. That's why it's important to use the largest container practicable made of the least porous material. Unfortunately, plastic preserves moisture best, but a close second is metal. Do not, however, use galvanized metal for growing plants because the metal's antirust treatment can be toxic.

Light-colored containers are best. Dark colors can absorb too much heat for the plant—except in the case of a heat-crazy vegetable like eggplant in a cool climate.

Container Size. Depending on how quickly the plant can be expected to grow, the container should be 1 to 2 inches larger on all sides than the volume of the plant's roots. Why can't you immediately set a small tomato seedling into the 5-gallon tub it will eventually occupy—why does it have to be moved up in stages? Because the planting medium not involved with roots can stagnate and become the breeding ground for harmful organisms.

A reason for using the largest reasonable container is ultimately that most gardeners have found that the larger the container, the larger the crop.

Since a small variation in space isn't crucial and since shapes of containers vary wildly, as a reference point, here are volumes for containers *as round as they are deep*—figure yours accordingly:

1 gallon = $6\frac{1}{8}$"; 2 gallons = $8\frac{3}{8}$"; 3 gallons = $9\frac{1}{2}$"; 4 gallons = $10\frac{1}{2}$"; 5 gallons = $11\frac{3}{8}$"; 6 gallons = 12"; 7 gallons = $12\frac{1}{2}$"; 8 gallons = $13\frac{1}{4}$"; 9 gallons = $13\frac{3}{4}$"; 10 gallons = $14\frac{1}{4}$".

Soil Mix. A soilless mixture, whether packaged from the nursery or homemade, is excellent because it carries no disease and its structure is ideal for holding air and water. Packaged planting mixes usually have nutrients added. Soilless mixtures are excellent but expensive, and may be used only one season, because they've been drained of every last bit of nourishment. They're best for smaller containers.

My germinating-through-transplanting mix is fun to put together and gives super results, since it's light enough for germination but sustaining enough to nourish seedlings and beyond. Sift the soil, compost, and peat moss through $\frac{1}{4}$-inch hardware cloth before measuring.

> 1 gallon humusy soil
> 1 gallon garden compost (lacking compost, use 2 gallons soil)
> 1 gallon sphagnum peat moss
> 1 quart fine vermiculite or perlite
> $\frac{1}{2}$ cup agricultural lime or dolomite
> $\frac{1}{2}$ cup fish meal
> $\frac{1}{2}$ cup bonemeal or 1 cup soft rock phosphate
> $\frac{1}{2}$ cup kelp meal

All amendments except kelp meal are generally available at nurseries. If you've got to have some of the mix and the kelp meal is not on hand, make it without. Then you can feed the seedlings as they emerge with a one-quarter-strength seaweed solution. You might think of using wood ashes for potash here, but don't—the ashes are too caustic to put in so intimate a mixture as soil for containers.

The simplest mix, without nutritive amendments but good if you feed the seedlings and plants faithfully, is equal parts sifted humusy soil, compost, sphagnum moss, vermiculite, and sharp sand (from a builder's supply).

For larger pots of perennial vegetables, equal parts sphagnum peat moss, sand, and compost or humusy soil.

Spacing. If you water and feed like crazy, you can crowd plants in a container as much as you would in the ground, perhaps even more. But never let a leaf flag.

The Arrangement. As long as there's ample space for all the roots, good drainage, water, and fertilizer—and you pinch back lanky branches faithfully—you'll be astonished at what delicious combinations you can put together.

Filling the Container. Used to be you were supposed to drop shards of pottery or stones into the container to assure drainage without losing soil mix. But common sense has prevailed. Potting mixes don't fall out enough to worry about. For soilless mixes such as flyaway perlite or vermiculite, cover the bottom hole with one sheet of newspaper, then fill with the potting medium. By the time the paper has dissolved, the mix will have settled in and little will escape through the drainage hole. However, if your pots will be set in places infested by small earth-burrowing pests, such as slugs, a square of fine screening over the hole keeps them out.

Center the plant in the vessel, holding it so its crown (where the stem and roots meet) will be in the same place in the soil as it was before transplanting (unless directions tell you otherwise).

Always leave plenty of room on top for water—1 to 2 inches from the top of the pot to where the soil begins for an 8-inch pot, proportionately more as the pot size and the need for water increase. If you're working with lots of pots, investigate drip systems for containers.

Mulching. It's as important to mulch a plant in a pot as one planted in soil. Because I have an inexhaustible supply, I mulch containers with rocks. I fit them over the top as closely as a jigsaw puzzle. Rocks keep the soil moist, prevent weeds from popping up, and couldn't be more aesthetic. But you can use any mulching material you like.

Saucers. A capacious saucer under your container is recommended. Set on soil, it keeps critters from entering through the drainage hole and rootlets from taking root in the soil. Never allow water to stand in the saucer.

Watering. More potted plants (you've probably heard this) die from overwatering than from underwatering. Unless the plant is a tropical or swamp creature, let the soil dry out between waterings. That way air fills the interstices of the planting medium and welcome oxygen becomes available to the plant. However, mixtures that are made largely of peat moss must never be allowed to dry out completely, because it's hellish saturating them again. Usually you can tell if the soil is damp by looking at it. However, if the pot is covered with mulch it's wise to wiggle a finger in the soil to find out whether it's dry. A better test: stick a slender wooden pencil or smooth stick into the potting medium. If it comes out clean, it's time to water. If it comes out with bits of the medium attached, no need to water yet.

Always water until you see water flowing from the drainage hole on the bottom. In hot weather, water in the morning so the plant is revitalized and can face the day. Sometimes, in suffocating weather, you might have to water two or even three times so as not to stress the plant.

Use a water-breaker nozzle or soft sprinkler at the end of whatever you use to water. It turns the water into a gentle rain that won't compact the soil or mash delicate leaves and roots if misdirected. You can attach it to a long pole, which makes aiming from a hose infinitely easier.

Fertilizing. Because they're planted not in nourishing Mother Earth but in mixes of bark and leaves and peat and such, it's critical to feed potted plants. There are good organic, slow-release, granular feeds, but I prefer to give something liquid that I can spray on their leaves. Plants in pots need lighter but more frequent feeding than ground plants.

When fertilizing with granules or something else solid, use half the recommended dose.

Fertilizing rule of thumb: Every seventh time you water, add water-soluble fertilizer to your water at a third to half strength—the amount depends on the plant's needs. That means if you water once a day you'll fertilize once a week. If you need to water a couple of times a day, you'll need to fertilize a couple of times a week. You can kill potted plants more easily with too much water and food than too little.

Repotting. Every spring, repot perennial plants into the next-larger-size container (an inch wider on all sides). If this proves impractical, every spring remove the top third of the soil mix and replace it with fresh. Depending on how fast the plant grows, every two or three years you may have to pull the plant out and trim back the roots so they'll again fit comfortably in the pot. Then cut back the top part of the plant to be in proportion to its roots.

Repot any time of year when you see roots creeping out from the drainage hole.

In the Landscape. I fill gaps in the border with pots of flowers, particularly the tender lavenders, sages, and geraniums that winter over indoors. Because they're not at ground level, you have greater height with potted flowers—a free couple of years' growth.

How to Keep Container Plants from Rooting in the Earth. When you set plants in the garden, set the container on a saucer or bricks or something else impermeable that lets water through but not the roots. At summer's end, when you want to bring the plant indoors—or move it somewhere else—pulling a season's growth of roots from the soil can be a terrible shock, even fatal, to the plant.

Preparing Containers for Winter. If you know you'll need to bring a large tub indoors to winter over, before you go near it with potting mix, get a caster-mounted base for it. This will make all the difference between a plant that's easy to care for and one you dread dealing with. After a bleak winter in the garage or a dim corner of the house, when fine spring days come, the plant needs to breathe fresh air and warm itself in the sunshine. Until the weather settles, you'll want to slip it out of doors in the morning and bring it in at night. This gradual return to the world helps break dormancy.

To protect a vulnerable plant that you can't bring indoors, see Winter.

COTTONSEED MEAL

*J*ust what it sounds like—ground seeds of cotton. It's fairly high in nitrogen, but the crop may be sprayed with pesticide these days, so check the source to make sure it's been produced organically.

COVER CROPS

*C*rops that cover the soil to nourish it and prevent erosion when it's not planted with a crop meant for harvesting. Most cover crops are planted for overwintering. Instead of letting land lie fallow, you sow seeds of a crop that grows quickly and then till or dig it in and let it decompose. After extensive testing at the Rodale Research Center, the seven favorite cover crops were hairy vetch, yellow blossom sweet clover, Austrian winter pea, Hubam clover, Alsike clover, spring oats, and crimson clover. Except for the oats, all these add nitrogen to the soil because they're legumes. Buckwheat is also good in summer, as are cowpeas.

See the entry Green Manure.

CROP ROTATION

*I*f you want to raise glorious vegetables, the first decision you must make is how you'll rotate crops through your garden. The ancient Chinese and Greeks and Romans did it. After they grew onions in the sunny patch beside the path, several years passed before they set onions in that spot again. Around 765, the first European three-field crop rotation system was described: grains and legumes were sown in two fields, one was left fallow, and each field was given a rest one year in three. Not long after, Charlemagne encouraged farmers in his kingdom to use this system.

There are two main reasons for rotating your crops. First, each growing plant has a particular need for one nutrient of the big three—nitrogen, potassium, phosphorus—and this it takes from the soil. Crop rotation provides an orderly withdrawal of nutrients from the soil as well as an orderly replenishing. Without rotation, you might deplete the soil of potash by planting carrots three years running, then sweet potatoes, then beets. Second, each plant family has a unique susceptibility to pests and diseases, and some are much more vulnerable than others. If a plant is grown in the same place year after year, bacteria, fungi, viruses, and insects will become established in that soil and ultimately cripple if not destroy any plant hoping to grow there. Moving the plants around leaves the mean guys nothing to sustain them and no way to settle in.

Now, I'm not talking about beds all planted to one crop or another. My garden is a mixed bouquet, and I rotate crops in as little as a couple of square feet at a time. Where I love a flash of red in front of the lady apple tree, this year's big Scarlett O'Hara cabbage will next year be a bunch of red-leaved Sweetheart beets, then a velvety Red Wonder okra the following year, a stand of Nepal tomatoes after that, and back again to a ruffly, red-and-green ornamental kale. How to remember which plants went where each year? Take snapshots. Make sketches. Scrawl in your garden notebook—but don't forget to record the year.

There are as many crop rotation schemes as there are thinking gardeners. Some are based on plant families, some on nutrient needs, some on the *degree* of demands on the soil—there are light, moderate, and heavy feeders in the vegetable kingdom. The number of years spun out in rotation varies considerably. After 14 years of rotating crops in this small garden, I can tell you the four-year plan I've devised works beautifully.

Because ultimately all success comes down to the fertility of the soil, my rotation is based on nutrient needs of the plants. But because soil-borne problems particularly plague the brassicas and nightshades, I've gerrymandered districts in my plan to accommodate them. I also try, as much as possible, to balance heavy feeders with light.

So the rotation groups are partly by physical characteristic—leaves, roots, fruits—and partly by family—the legumes.

N.B. Of course radishes, rutabagas, turnips, and kohlrabi are roots, but being brassicas they are susceptible to brassicas' problems and should be rotated with the rest of the clan. Potatoes are susceptible to Nightshades' troubles—best keep them with their family, too. The Goosefoot family can be plagued by leaf miners, but beets can be independently rotated with roots if it helps. I've combined the alliums with roots to even out volume. In terms of need, they belong with leaves—if it's as practical for you to have them there, do so.

So it goes like this:

First Year: Legumes. Peas, beans, soybeans, peanuts, alfalfa, and clover.
Legumes add nitrogen to the soil and thus are heavy givers.

Second Year: Leaves. The brassicas: broccoli, brussels sprouts, cabbage, cauliflower, Chinese
cabbage, collards, kale, mustard greens, radishes, rutabagas, turnips, kohlrabi . . . chard, spinach . . . lettuce . . . New Zealand spinach . . . celery, celeriac.
Leaves particularly need nitrogen and are heavy feeders. Boost nitrogen with aged manure.

Third Year: Roots and Bulbs (the underground group). Sweet potatoes . . . beets . . .
carrots, parsnips, horseradish . . . salsify, scorzonera . . . and the alliums (onion tribe).
Roots particularly need potash and are light feeders. Boost potash with wood ashes or kelp meal. The
alliums particularly need nitrogen and are heavy feeders with their roots close to the surface. Boost nitrogen with aged manure.

Fourth Year: Fruits. Eggplant, peppers, tomatoes, potatoes . . . cucumbers, melons, squash,
pumpkins . . . corn . . . okra . . . artichokes, cardoons.
Fruiting vegetable plants particularly need phosphorus and are heavy feeders. Boost phosphorus
with bonemeal. Potatoes particularly need potash. Line their trenches with comfrey.
If it's feasible, you can slip in a crop of legumes after heavy feeders every couple of years to build up
nitrogen. If there's not enough sun in your garden for even crop rotation, fill containers with vegetables
and put them in the sun that way. Or simply give plants that can manage it fewer hours of sun. Or cheat
with crops that have few soil-borne problems—I've done it with lettuce, spinach, and chard.
Keep root crops from following fruiting ones *since roots split with lots of manure, which the fruiting
crops need.* Unless the fruiting crop has been in the ground long enough to use up the excess nitrogen, it
shouldn't be a problem. If you must follow a light feeder with a heavy one, dig in an extra feeding of compost or aged manure.
Don't forget that, should there be a month or so between crops in good weather, throw out seeds of
a catch crop or green manure as fast as you can.
There are gardeners who don't rotate their crops, who raise beautiful vegetables, and who rarely
have disease. Most of them live in temperate climates where excesses of heat and cold don't debilitate the
plants or foster pests and diseases (although subzero temperatures will kill many diseases). And most of
them live where the soil is naturally superb. These gardeners simply dig in plenty of humus, practice good
garden sanitation, and harvest their crops. If you live under such circumstances, more power to you.
When things start looking puny, you'll know it's time to rotate.

HEAVY GIVERS

legumes:
alfalfa
beans
clover
peanuts
peas
soybeans

HEAVY FEEDERS

Brassicas	*Nightshades*	*Squashes*	*Goosefoot*	*Parsley*	*Miscellaneous*
broccoli	eggplant	cucumbers	chard	celeriac	corn
brussels sprouts	peppers	melons	spinach	celery	New Zealand spinach
cabbage	tomatoes	squash		parsley	okra
cauliflower		pumpkins			cardoons
kale					artichokes
mustard greens					
Chinese cabbage					
collards					

LIGHT FEEDERS

Brassicas	*Nightshades*	*Goosefoot*	*Parsley*	*Miscellaneous*
radishes	potatoes	beets	carrots	shallots
rutabagas			parsnips	onions
turnips				garlic
kohlrabi				leeks
				lettuce
				sweet potatoes

LOW NITROGEN NEEDS

sweet potatoes

peppers

CROWN

*T*he base of a plant where the stem and root meet.

CULTIVAR

*F*rom *culti*vated *vari*ety. Used internationally, *cultivar* replaces *variety* in all languages, according to *Hortus Third*.

CULTIVATE

*B*efore mulching became the way to keep weeds down around plants and the soil in good condition, common practice was to chop up the soil around plants with a hoe or a long-handled pronged tool called a *cultivator*. Some plants very much like their soil ruffled from time to time—roses are one; corn is another. Frankly, I do little of this. Once in a great while I weed with a scuffle (or stirrup or hula) hoe. I'd rather smother the weeds with mulch or solarize them. I'm for doing as much of what I enjoy and as little of what I don't enjoy as possible in the garden.

CUT-AND-COME-AGAIN CROPS

These are the leaves you pick one by one from loose-heading crops. The heads will last a long time in the garden, forming new leaves to enjoy, particularly if you feed them lightly after harvest and if you can keep the plant from sending up a flower.

When you do harvest a whole head of a leafy green plant, if you leave the root intact and six or seven leaves at the base of the stalk, Chinese cabbage, lettuce, corn salad, pak choi, kale, arugula, the mustards, and chicories may send up new leaves. Experiment with this technique—you have leaves to gain and nothing to lose.

CUTWORM COLLARS

At night, cutworms curl around the stem of a seedling, sever it at the base, then move on to the next seedling and do the same. I make impenetrable collars by snipping the bottom out of a small paper cup and slipping it over the seedling, setting it in the soil. End of cutworm problem. The paper is biodegradable, but you can always collect them at the season's end.

DAMPING OFF

Sometimes seedlings inexplicably topple over at the soil level. This is damping off, caused by soil- and airborne fungi. The solution is to germinate seeds in a soilless medium. Since warmth and moisture aid the fungi, keep the surface of the medium as dry as possible and avoid overwatering. Or sprinkle a light veil of sharp sand or pulverized sphagnum moss—which contains an element of fungicide—over the surface. This isn't possible, of course, when tiny seeds are being germinated on top of the soil. Good air circulation and generous spacing are helpful if you can manage.

You can try sprays of chamomile or nettle tea or a minced garlic clove mixed with a quart of lukewarm water over seeds as prevention.

DEADHEAD

To pick off the spent—dead—heads of flowers to keep them from forming seeds. Better to deadhead plants willy-nilly than not at all—flower production will stop when seed production starts. If you can take the time, nip the flower stem at the next place where there's a swelling in the stalk near a leaf—that's where a new flower is forming.

DEER

Deer are browsers. They sample—a tidbit here, a morsel there—just enough to debilitate a plant.

Deer are creatures of habit, and if you plant a garden in their accustomed path, the plants are doomed.

The most intelligent way to coexist with deer is to plant things they don't like. They don't fancy tough grasses, plants with hairy or leathery leaves, or those that release a strong smell when chewed. About the only thing they don't enjoy in the kitchen garden is odoriferous herbs. Among their least favorite are mint, rosemary, lavender, scented geraniums, borage, and thyme.

Then repellents must be used. Our niece had success with a bag of blood meal tied to every plant she didn't want the deer to eat. But another friend tried everything from bags of human hair to dangling bars of soap to lion dung begged from the San Francisco zoo. A hungry doe will ignore all repellents except a fence she cannot leap.

Galvanized hardware cloth barriers 4 to 5 feet high around their favorite treats (set a few feet away from the plant) are helpful. Some say a *solid* 8-foot fence keeps deer out; others say deer can jump that. Some say a see-through 8-foot fence with a 3-foot fence just inside it effectively confuses deer. Bear in mind that a fence on an uphill slope may be a fence deer can leap, but they are timid about jumping down-hill. We've had deer trapped in our garden a couple of times in the past, and it's a terrifying experience for everyone, particularly if there's a challenged dog involved.

I'm told a 4-foot width of chicken wire laid on the ground around the garden will keep deer out, since they don't like the feeling of wire under their delicate hooves.

DIATOMACEOUS EARTH

This grayish powder is the pulverized remains of fossilized aquatic plants. Every grain is razor sharp. Spread it over the garden, and slugs and snails will be . . . you get the idea. It's a *very* effective barrier until it's wet, and then it's no good at all. If you can figure out a way of not watering for long periods where you need it, it's great, and it's not harmful to the soil. But it is to your lungs if you breathe it.

DISEASE IN PLANTS

If you rotate your crops, clean up all debris at the end of the season—composting healthy stuff and bagging up suspicious-looking stuff for the dump, use floating row covers whenever possible *from the beginning* to keep disease-harboring insects from finding homes at the feet of vulnerable plants, and plant disease-resistant cultivars whenever possible, you should have little trouble with disease. In all the years I've been gardening, I've had to pull out only a few potato plants one season.

If disease should appear on something, don't try to save the plant; pull it out and *burn* it or wrap it in a garbage bag and get it to the dump. Be certain you don't grow the same crop in the same place for three or four years, because the offending bacteria and fungi can live in the soil that long.

The subject of plant disease is complex, but there's plenty of help. I especially recommend any of the Rodale books, particularly *Garden Problem Solver,* and *Pests of the Farm and Garden* by the University of California Press.

DOGS

Dogs yearn to please. I've found that all you need to do to keep most dogs out of a bed is to run a physical boundary around it for them to get used to—a string with ribbons that whip in the breeze every few feet just may be enough. Once an intelligent dog gets the idea, you can take the string down. I tell my Lab, "That's my *garden*, Sam!" when he puts a paw into the magic circle. He promptly takes the paw out. There are ghastly-smelling solutions you can daub on rags and hang around the perimeter of a bed if it comes to that. But they'll probably keep *you* out of the garden, too.

Doing their duty anywhere near your border calls for a serious and mortifying scolding.

DOLOMITIC LIMESTONE

A rich source of calcium and magnesium that also neutralizes acid soil. Beds of the limestone are quarried, the stone ground and sold as agricultural lime. It is available at nurseries in some areas but must be sent for in others. It's great for peppers, basils, and melons unless the soil is already high in magnesium.

DORMANT

*J*ust as we must sleep, most plants that live more than one year become somnolent during some part of winter, either losing their leaves or simply not growing. What needs to be done to a plant—dividing it, moving it, pruning it—is always best done when it's dormant.

DOUBLE-DIGGING

*I*f you are putting in a garden on soil that hasn't supported a blade of grass for eons (as we did here in decomposed granite), or if the patch for your garden has been compacted in being built, the only way to have a successful harvest the first year is to double-dig.

This is a matter of loosening the soil, amending it, and fluffing it—then *never walking on it.*

But if your soil has grown anything at all within recent memory and is friable enough so that you can get your spade down into it, when you first start gardening, just find out what it needs by testing it and then amending it. Do this each year, amending as you go. In time you should have excellent soil. *Just never walk on it*—compacted soil can't breathe, can't produce the best for you.

John Jeavons's *Everything You Need to Know* and Shepherd Ogden's *Step by Step Organic Vegetable Gardening* are two books that will give details about double-digging and soil amending. But briefly, this is what you have to do:

After getting the results of your soil test, dig a trench one spade wide along one side of the bed in which you want to garden. Dig down one spade deep—be realistic—throwing the soil onto a tarp or into a wheelbarrow. Add amendments as needed—nitrogen? phosphorus? potassium? humus? sand? peat? Then dig the same sort of trench next to the first one, throwing the soil into the first trench. Amend the second trench, then dig a third trench, throwing the soil into the second . . .

When you've finished, drag the soil from the first trench around to the last, and turn it in.

Take a nap, then lay out your beds and paths.

DROUGHT TOLERANT

*D*rought *tolerant* means a plant can survive on less water than the norm. Most drought-tolerant species are native to deserts and sun- and windswept seasides and mountains. Surviving under adversity is in their genes. Mother Nature has tricks for adapting plants to little moisture. The preponderance of drought-tolerant plants store water somewhere on their persons. Not just in the succulent leaves of purslane and stalks of cardoon, and chard. In the juicy shoots of asparagus. The fleshy tubers of Jerusalem artichokes. Other plants such as daylilies have leaves with a protective finish that seals in moisture. Many plants with gray or silver leaves—clary sage, for example—have a fuzzy covering that not only traps moisture but acts as insulation for the leaf beneath. And there are felted coats, like the leaves of lambs' ears—the weave is at once open and dense, and moisture is absorbed and retained like a sponge. Still other leaves are leathery and laced with oil—rosemaries come to mind. Many plants have tiny leaves—thyme, for example. The scant surface minimizes the evaporation of moisture, the leatheriness keeps what moisture there is from transpiring, and the oil gives triple insurance against water's being released.

Drought-tolerant plants are checked in the Planning Chart.

The crucial thing to remember is that a plant is drought tolerant only after it has developed a full and deep root system. Only then can it cope with the stresses of little water. *Established* is the gardening word.

Once plants are established, I ease my way between waterings until finally I can wait until the soil has completely dried out. To test the soil, I dig down or poke down a stout piece of wire—it slips through moist earth but balks at dry. At every stage of growth I watch for signs of stress. Once fruits and vegetables reach the wilting point, their fruiting ability can be affected. Symptoms of a serious lack of water are dull-looking or yellowed leaves. Sun-scalded leaves are another clue. A halt in the plant's growth is another. All these are symptoms of approaching dormancy or worse. At that point instant shade, deep watering, and a mild dose of vitamin B_1 might revive them.

The plants marked on the Planning Chart can survive on—even flourish in—about 15 inches' moisture annually. That's less than a third of what most flowering and fruiting plants need. However, if rains are not fairly evenly dispensed, you may need to give a deep drink during prolonged dry spells to prevent stress and the resultant vulnerability to insects and disease.

Dry Gardening: Xeriscaping

A dry garden is one composed of drought-tolerant plants—the trademark Xeriscape is from the Greek, *xeros:* dry. The more precious water becomes on our beleaguered planet, the more it behooves us to meet the challenge of dry gardening with resourcefulness and grace.

Exposure has much to do with how thirsty a plot can be. More water will be wanted by plants in an open sun-drenched site than those sheltered or dappled with shade. Too, drying winds and bone-dry air pull an enormous amount of moisture from plants and soil. And heat. A temperate 70°F day in and day out is clearly less dehydrating than a torrid 100°F.

Another drying factor is how plants are placed in the ground. Plants growing shoulder to shoulder create a protective microclimate—the moister it gets, the moister it gets. When leaves touch, they create a cool canopy for the soil, and the soil stays more moist than were it exposed to the elements. Without sunshine under the canopy, few weeds germinate and grow—weeds that would otherwise compete for water.

Of course rainfall is critical. Not only how much but how often. Many parts of this country have plentiful moisture in fall and winter, but then, with the exception of August thundershowers, the plants go begging for water all spring and summer.

Soil is critical too. A water-retentive yet fast-draining soil is what one strives for in building a dry garden. Humusy loam is the ideal. However, the curses of an uncompromising site, harsh climate, little rainfall, and less-than-ideal soil can be mitigated by one magic element: mulch.

Making educated choices of what to plant in a dry garden is the most crucial factor of all. See Drought Tolerant.

Earthworms

Earthworms are one of the most important catalysts in the garden. Earthworms pull humus and compost and organic mulch from the top of the soil down to their level beneath the surface, working it in.

Worms are particularly fond of compost that's not too hot. and multiply in it like crazy, ingesting whatever soil and decaying matter fits in their teeny mouths (they have no teeth), mixing it with calcium carbonate and sending it through their digestive system with its enzymes and gizzardlike pulverizing organ.

Actually there is a system of compost based purely on worms called *vermiculture.* You can create it indoors. Make or find a box about 2 feet deep and as long and wide as you like. I use a heavy cardboard box, usually something around 21 inches tall by 13 by 14 inches. I line it with two large garbage bags—to keep in moisture and make lifting out the finished compost easy. I fill the box with the usual compost makings, the French intensive method three-part mixture because there's no chance it will get too hot and cook the little darlings: $^1/_3$ dry vegetation, $^1/_3$ green vegetation and kitchen waste, and $^1/_3$ soil. Bearing in mind the size of their mouths, I put the kitchen gleanings through the food processor and use thin wood shavings and/or shredded newspaper instead of spoiled hay for the dry stuff. After the earth I add enough water little by little to give the mixture the texture of the wrung-out sponge. Finally I introduce the red worms—100 per cubic foot. For the size box I've described, I use 5 pounds each of vegetable matter, shavings or newspaper, and earth. Fifteen pounds, moistened, comes down to about 2 cubic feet. Then I roll down the tops of the garbage bags to just a few inches above the mix and set the box on the back porch—it should be a fairly dark, well-ventilated place between 40°F and 70°F. And on my calendar every few days I write "Water worms!" because they must be kept moist. I also make a note two months from the day I've put the vermicompost in motion to see if it is done then. It will be, a crumbly, pleasant-smelling, peatlike substance, the best compost imaginable. And some of my worms are happy to do it all over again. Now that's spirit.

What comes out the nether end of worms, called *castings,* is richer in nitrogen, phosphorus, and potassium than what went in and superior to all other animal manures. In 24 hours it is said that an earthworm will deliver itself of its own weight in castings. We cannot believe how rapidly our kitchen leavings strewn on our beds in early spring (see Sheet Composting in the entry on Compost) disappear. For signs of worms, bend down where you can see the surface of the soil closely and look for tiny grayish heaps—or tiny squiggles of grayish brown, like minuscule volcanic eruptions. It's easiest to see them on soil that's smooth and moist. Once you've seen them, you can spot them easily. If there are lots of worm castings on the surface of your soil, you've got fine soil.

Worms are not native to decomposed granite—nary a one was in this soil when we began gardening it. So I sprinkled a dozen pint cartons of red worms in sawdust over the soil in the cool of the evening when I wasn't expecting frost. I covered the worms with a protective veil of sphagnum peat moss, wet it down, and gave them my blessing. By morning they were all in the soil. We've done this every spring since. Now there are beautiful juicy red worms all through our beds. Now when I turn a bucket of compost into the garden, I'm also turning in a family of worms.

If you don't have a fishing store nearby, you can send away for earthworms (see Sources). Actually, they'll probably be an even more efficient bunch for composting.

EGGSHELLS

$\mathcal{I}$'m the sort of gardener who, if I'm in a friend's kitchen and if there is something going on with eggs, packs up the shells and carries them home. Eggshells contain a considerable amount of calcium as well as a little nitrogen and phosphoric acid. Calcium "sweetens" the soil—that is, soil on the acid side becomes more alkaline—and of course eggshells add wonderful humus. If you have lots, eggshells can be sprinkled directly on the soil. The brassicas are particularly fond of them. I give each young plant a shell of its own, the teeny bits speckled in a circle—a bonus: sharp edges discourage creepy crawlers. If there's time, I dry the shells in the sun or the oven to make them sharper.

ESTABLISHED

Established can have different applications, but essentially it always means "thoroughly acclimated." Relating it to drought tolerance, the time it takes to be established comes soonest for annuals because their life span is abbreviated—it might be just past their seedling stage. Perennials can take weeks to become established, shrubs months, and trees years before their roots develop an adequate system that can survive with minimal water.

Families

It's very useful to know who's related to whom since there will be more similarities in growing wants and needs than disparities. It also helps with crop rotation. Here are the major families of the vegetables, herbs, and edible flowers in this book. If it's not among the following, it's a member of a smaller clan.

GOOSEFOOT FAMILY   *Chenopodiaceae*

beets, chard, Good-King-Henry, orach, spinach, spinach beets

So called because the shape of many leaves resembles the splayed foot of a goose. Mostly the goosefeet grow so easily they're considered potherbs at best, weeds at worst.

GOURD FAMILY   *Cucurbitaceae*

melons, cucumbers, gourds (miscellaneous), squashes (summer, winter, pumpkins), watermelons

Mostly tropical or subtropical plants, all but one being tendriled vines.

LILY FAMILY   *Liliaceae*

asparagus, chives, Chinese chives, and all the onion clan

This family flourishes in temperate and subtropical parts of the world, and most are grown from bulbs, corms, rhizomes, or tubers.

MINT FAMILY   *Labiatae*

Anise hyssop, basils, Chinese artichokes, hyssop, lavenders, mints, oreganos, perillas, rosemary, sages, summer savory, sweet marjoram, thymes

$\mathcal{M}$ostly from the Mediterranean, you can tell a member of the Mint family because its stem is roughly square. This family contributes many volatile oils and perfumes and sweet herbs to the world.

MUSTARD FAMILY

Brassicaceae

arugula, broccoli, brussels sprouts, cabbages, cauliflower, Chinese cabbages, Chinese kale, collards, cresses, kale, kohlrabi, komatsuna, mizuna, mustards, radishes, rutabagas, turnips

$\mathcal{N}$ot only are brassicas superior nutritionally, but all in all brassicas are the easiest vegetables to grow. Sow two dozen sorts of seeds in a flat, and the little cabbages and broccolis and kohlrabis will thrust their tiny round green leaves through the soil first.

NIGHTSHADE FAMILY

Solanaceae

eggplants, peppers, potatoes, tomatillos, tomatoes

$\mathcal{F}$ascinating family, this. Largely from Central and South America, here we also have tobacco and deadly nightshade—never mind the name; we know which is the most lethal of the lot.

PARSLEY FAMILY

Umbelliferae

caraway, carrots, celeriac, celery, chervil, coriander, dill, fennel, lovage, parsley, parsnips

$\mathcal{A}$lternately called the Carrot family (and sometimes *Apiaceae*), it's found mostly in temperate and northern climates. Most have lacy, sweet-scented flowers that attract beneficial insects.

PEA FAMILY

Leguminosae

asparagus peas, common beans, cowpeas, fava beans, lima beans, peanuts, peas, runner beans, soybeans, sugar peas, yardlong beans

$\mathcal{T}$he pea family is divided into three subfamilies. One has butterflylike flowers, the flowers of another are irregularly shaped, and one has flowers that are many and small—as in acacias, for example. The family has about 12,000 subspecies. Marvelously wide-ranging, after the family of grains, the Leguminosae provide the most important sources of food for man and lots for birds and beasts.

SUNFLOWER FAMILY

Compositae

artichokes (globe), burdock, calendulas, cardoons, celtuce, chicories, dandelions, endives, garland chrysanthemums, Jerusalem artichokes, lettuces, marigolds, salsify, scorzonera, tarragon

$\mathcal{A}$lso called the Daisy family (and *Asteraceae*). This is an enormous family divided into 12 or 13 tribes, many of which are wonderfully ornamental.

FERTILIZING, THE BASICS

W̶eaving my way through the bewildering world of organic fertilizers takes all the wit I can muster. I read charts; I read opinions—few of them jibe from source to source. Essentially I'm on my own. So are you. All I know is, I gave spindly eggplants a dose of manure tea 10 days ago (a week after transplanting them in late June, much too late, poor things) and they've since trebled in size.

Here are some simple rules for fertilizing that have worked for me.

Some common organic soil amendments (percentages are approximate). The ideal application is to combine both quick- and slow-releasing amendments to the soil: blood and organic cottonseed meals for nitrogen, bonemeal and rock phosphate for phosphorus, kelp meal and granite dust for potash. As you dig and amend, jot down the fertilizers in the amounts you give, then record them somewhere so you don't give too much.

Numbers vary considerably from product to product, but the average nitrogen-phosphorus-potash contents for each element are given: 11-0-0, as in the case of blood meal, means that the product has 11 percent available nitrogen but no phosphorus or potash: the first number is nitrogen, the second phosphorus, the third potash.

N = Nitrogen for green growth

Note: Give less nitrogen to plants grown in some shade than to the same cultivars grown in full sun. Remember that too much nitrogen on plants can lead to soft lush growth that makes aphids and other predators go crazy.

Blood Meal. 11-0-0; quick acting. Dig in well so it won't attract carnivores; lasts three to four months.

Cottonseed Meal. 6-2-1; slow releasing; especially valuable for acid-loving crops. Lasts four to six months. N.B. Check the source to make sure it's been organically produced.

Fish Emulsion. 5-1-1; quick acting; spray in dilute solution on the plant's leaves and stems.

Fish Meal. 5-3-3; quick acting. Dig in well because it's smelly; lasts six to eight months.

Hoof and Horn Meal. Animal by-products. 10-1.5-0; breaks down slowly unless kept moist. Work well into the soil so it won't attract flies; lasts 12 months (results may not be apparent for some weeks).

P = *Phosphorus/phosphate for root, flower, fruit, and vegetable growth and disease resistance*

Rock Phosphate. 0-33-0; very slow—releases over three to four years. Lasts in the soil three to five years or longer.

Steamed Bonemeal. 2-20-0; very slow releasing. Acts more quickly in well-aerated soil and tends to reduce soil acidity; lasts 6 to 12 months. It also contributes a bit of calcium.

K = *Potash/potassium for strong stems, root vigor, and added disease resistance*

Hardwood Ashes. 0-1-4; quick acting. Use only for alkaline-loving plants. Do not leave in the rain, or potash will be leached out; lasts six months.

Granite Dust. 0-0-3; the more finely ground, the quicker the release—very slow releasing over a long period. Contains valuable trace minerals; lasts up to 10 years.

Kelp Meal. 1-0-10; quick acting, with abundant trace minerals. Helps keep plants from becoming leggy, to resist frost, in controlling red spider mites and fusarium wilt; lasts six months to one year. Use sparingly, because it contains growth stimulators.

A balanced liquid organic fertilizer is 1 tablespoon liquid fish emulsion plus 1 tablespoon kelp solution mixed in 1 gallon water. Remember to shake the fish jug well before pouring. This is a once-a-season formula. To apply with each watering, use 1 tablespoon each of fish and kelp to 4 gallons of water.

A balanced organic fertilizing meal is this from Steve Solomon, founder of Territorial Seed Co.: By volume, 4 parts seed or fish meal, 1 part dolomitic lime, 1 part rock phosphate or 1/2 part bonemeal, and 1 part kelp meal. Use about 1/2 cup for 5 square feet.

Standard Feedings. The easiest and surest is, in spring, to dig in compost or slow-release fertilizers as needed according to soil tests. Then every month during the growing season, if needed, give fish emulsion sprayed on the leaves and stems alternating with kelp solution applied to the soil. *Do not apply these fertilizers to fruiting crops after flowering or to leaf crops near harvest time, or they'll taste of the sea!* Apply fish sparingly to root crops since it's high in nitrogen and may cause them to fork. And don't use fish near the end of the season since it can delay flowering.

Minimum Feedings. Dig in compost or one application of slow-release fertilizer in spring.

Heavy Feedings. Apply standard fish and kelp, spraying every two weeks.

Application. The soil should be moist before you apply fertilizer in any form. Granular fertilizers and natural fertilizers, such as manure and meal, will stay where they land better and begin breaking down immediately. Liquid fertilizers will spread more evenly—the damp sponge principle—and be more accessible to roots.

Fertilizer keeps from one season to the next and up to several years.

Also see Manure.

FISH EMULSION

Made from soluble fish canning wastes, this is a quick-acting source of nitrogen, phosphorus, potassium, and magnesium.

FLAT

Shallow square or rectangle, usually of firm black plastic, wood, or pressed fiber, with drainage holes usually punched out on a grid. Used for growing lots of small seedlings in one place.

FLOATING ROW COVER

A blanket of translucent material that rests ever so lightly on the shoulders of plants. The cover lifts as the plants grow. Its purpose: to keep cold and insects out while letting water and sunshine in. Underneath, it's several degrees warmer. The cover also conserves moisture a bit—a conscience salver in drought and a boon when you can't let seeds dry out one minute until they have germinated. However, you must check regularly. Place floating row covers over the beds from the beginning, and tiny marauders simply can't get through. Unless they're slugs.

There are two weights of the material, one for temperature control and one to control insects. The warming row covers also keep insects out, but they can make it suffocating for plants in hot weather. Materials have evolved and will doubtless continue to in terms of durability and efficiency.

The only disadvantage of floating row covers is aesthetic. All those beautiful raised beds you've wrestled out of the ground, all those ruffly rows of greens and feathery tops of carrots aren't visible.

FOLIAR FEEDING

Spraying the leaves, stems, and fruit with fertilizer is the most efficient way to feed; the plant absorbs almost 100 percent of the nutrients immediately. Apply in the early morning in a fine mist so droplets stay on the leaves.

FOX LURE

If you read about raccoons being warned off by the oldest form of territory marking in nature, then you know what fox lure is. Time was you could buy it in vials and sprinkle it around a bed, and no small creature would come near that bed. Someone had the bright idea to package the stuff in plastic disks you can hang in the garden. I blanketed the garden with the disks called Scentfence one summer. They worked incredibly well with everybody except field mice. But the manufacturers had problems, and I haven't seen the disks in catalogs lately.

If you see them, they're worth trying if you're plagued. The next step is to lure a pretty little fox into your garden.

FRENCH INTENSIVE BIODYNAMIC METHOD

The Englishman Alan Chadwick is responsible for popularizing the French intensive method of growing. The results of gardening intensively have shown that a given space can produce up to four times the harvest as that gleaned from traditional methods. The technique begins with loosening the soil by double-digging it, then by amending it with organic fertilizers and compost. Raised beds are *de rigueur*. Plants are set equidistant in beds rather than close together in rows far apart. Rows were created for the convenience of farmers—you notice nothing in nature grows in a row. Plants are spaced in the beds so closely their leaves touch and form a canopy, which shades the soil, conserves moisture, keeps the soil from crusting, and inhibits the growth of weeds. Crop rotation and mulching are other tenets of the method.

My teachers have been John Jeavons in *How to Grow More Vegetables*, John Seymour in *The Self-Sufficient Gardener*, Duane Newcomb in *The Postage Stamp Garden Book*, Joy Larkcom in *Vegetables from Small Gardens*, and Peter Chan in *Better Vegetable Gardens the Chinese Way*.

FROST AS SWEETENER

Frost, whose chilly hand blackens sweet basil and sets tomato vines in a tailspin, sweetens many crops. The blast of icy cold enhances native sugars, and crops like parsnips, turnips, kale, artichokes, pumpkins, and radicchio are improved. If you don't have frost, you can sweeten these crops by keeping them in the refrigerator for a few days before eating.

FRUIT

$\mathcal{B}$otanically speaking, a fruit is the ripened ovary of a flower, together with its seeds and other closely connected parts—squashes, pea pods, tomatoes, peppers, cucumbers, and so on, are fruits.

FUNGICIDE

$\mathcal{W}$hen leaves look as though they're dusty with mildew or have small black spots, use a sulfur spray as directed. Safer's Garden Fungicide is such a product.

GRASS: HOW TO CONVERT IT TO PLANTING BEDS

$\mathcal{J}$ust dig it up to a spade's depth and turn it over, belly up. The sod will decompose, adding humus to the soil, the roots underneath will be smothered so they can't send up new leaves and they'll die, and the roots with their feet in the air will dry out in the sun and die. Couldn't be easier. Just be sure all roots have given up the ghost before planting. Best to do this in very early spring or fall but it's worth doing any time of year.

GRAY WATER

$\mathcal{I}$f you live or plan to live on a septic system and can have your shower, laundry, and kitchen sink vacate to a separate tank, look into using this gray water. If intelligently controlled and directed, this recycled water can be used on *nonedible plants*. Repeat: *nonedible*. Robert Kourik has written a fine tract on the subject that should be available from your library.

GREEN MANURE

$\mathcal{G}$reen manure is a crop grown quickly on vacant soil and turned over. The crop decomposes, thus adding humus to the soil—and, if it was a legume, nitrogen is added.

For example, once the soil is warmish in spring, throwing out buckwheat seeds will produce a crop of green manure in about one month. That means that while the tomatoes and peppers and cucurbits are waiting to go into the ground, you can be growing buckwheat. When it's time to plant, just chop in the buckwheat and you'll be adding invaluable humus.

This is a superb and easy way to build your soil. Each crop has its advantages and limitations, so have a chat with your local agricultural adviser about which is best for your area. Ask about combining seeds for great results.

Sow when it's about to rain if you can—it's important not to let the seeds dry out. Throw out the seeds on moist soil as evenly as you can, perhaps mixing it with sand or fine soil, then rake the soil to cover them. Large seeds such as peas or beans need to be covered with $1/2$ inch of soil. Walk on the seeds to give them good connection with the earth, then scatter grass clippings or loose straw to help keep the seeds from drying. (I know you're not supposed to walk on the soil, but gardening is an art as much as a science.)

You can leave the crop in the ground as long as you like, but usually it's turned under before it sets seed. Don't let vetch or ryegrass go to seed, or you'll have a nuisance on your hands.

Under no circumstances should you sow kudzu *(Pueraria lobata)*. Its roots go down so deep and its vines roll along so merrily that it becomes literally almost impossible to eradicate. Kudzu is the beast that can swallow buildings, trees, and woodlands.

The green-manure technique of adding humus to the soil is a complex subject. Let Eliot Coleman draw the fine points for you in his *The New Organic Grower*.

HARDENING OFF

This process acclimates plants from the warmth of wherever they were born and grew to the chilly world of the garden. This is *crucial* to success.

When setting out plants to harden off after having been produced indoors or a sheltered place *or somewhere other than the conditions of your garden in its present state,* a week before planning to set the plants in the garden, cut back on watering as much as possible without letting the plants wilt (actually you can let tomatoes wilt). Also, don't fertilize. If they were planted in a nourishing mixture and have been fed until then, don't fertilize within two weeks of transplanting.

Take the plants outside in the morning and put them in a sheltered place out of the sunlight. Bring them in before the sun sets. The next morning, set them somewhere that gets morning sun and afternoon shade, then bring them in as before. The next morning, depending on how they look, give them either afternoon sun or full sun, but bring them in before dark. The next day, they're outdoors all day and all night—however, should it turn bitter cold, bring them back in until it's milder. After another two or three days-and-nights outside—a week of the process altogether—they can be transplanted.

This hardening-off procedure makes the plant tougher, better able to withstand the stresses of a new climate, insects, sun, frost, wind, and so on. When you do transplant, water in with a half-strength fertilizing solution.

It's a hassle, but you can lose the plant if you don't follow the regime.

HARDINESS OF VEGETABLES

There's little agreement among authorities regarding the frost-hardiness of plants. For example, some say spinach and parsley are very hardy, some say they're only half-hardy. It's frustrating, but understandable, since so many factors are involved. Some proven hardy crops are in the entry on Winter.

HARDY

Without regard to the whys and wherefores, this means a plant can cope with temperatures well below freezing. Half-hardy generally means it can cope down to 20°F but not much more.

HEATING CABLE

This thin cable covered with plastic warms the seed-germinating mix. You arrange it under the mix, attached to a board or some other waterproof surface. Don't make the mistake I did the first time and let the wires touch—they'll melt together and possibly short out.

When germinating lots of seeds, I cut out the sides of deep flats and tape them together to make one long flat. I lay the superflat on a board carefully positioned so the end of the cable will be near an outlet—this is important, since the darn thing will be unmovable once you start.

I line the bottom with several thicknesses of newspaper. To lay the cable four hands are best, since the cables are thin and tangle infuriatingly. I lay out the cable, setting about 2 inches apart, firmly taping down with duct tape as I go. Next, a layer of sphagnum moss, then the soil mix. Heat at least overnight.

HILLING UP

*D*rawing soil up around a plant enough either to cover it (potatoes) or to stabilize its base (corn).

HORTUS THIRD

*T*his concise dictionary of plants cultivated in the United States and Canada was initially compiled by Liberty Hyde Bailey and Ethel Zoe Bailey. It has since been "revised and expanded by the staff of the Liberty Hyde Bailey Hortorium, a unit of the New York State College of Agriculture and Life Sciences, a statutory college of the State University at Cornell University." For me, it's the bible.

HUMUS

*H*umus is to the soil of an organic garden what yeast is to bread—it gives the soil its texture, its loft.

What *is* humus? I thought humus was all the gorgeous old stuff—the compost, manure, blood-bone-cottonseed-alfalfa-fish-feather-hoof-horn meal, spoiled hay, straw, seaweed, sludge, hulls and shells of beans and grains, corn cobs and stalks, peat moss, grass clippings, sawdust, newspapers, ashes, dusts, and wool and cotton rags laid on as mulch and fertilizer, together with the finished flowers, fruits, nuts, cones, stems, stalks, leaves, needles, twigs, bark, roots, and juices of growing things themselves, plus any shells of creatures complex and simple, great and small that may have ended there—mixed with earth. Earth, in its primeval form, is just tiny fragments of rock.

While it is true that all the above becomes humus after it has been so broken down—enzymes and microorganisms in the soil do the job—that it turns into something dark sweet-smelling fluffy and fine-textured. But on its way to becoming humus, all the above is technically still organic matter. Organic matter may smell less than sweet and it bears hints of its past life.

Humus in the soil functions in two ways—physically and, one might say, spiritually. In sandy soil, humus helps fill the spaces between grains, slowing down the water as it sweeps through, saving nutrients from being leached out, retaining moisture. At the opposite end of the spectrum, the powdery specks of clay soil are so fine they scarcely allow water to penetrate. Humus helps bind specks into crumbs in clay soil, permitting water to flow through as well as be absorbed.

On the spiritual side, the more decaying matter microorganisms in the soil are fed, the happier they are, the more they multiply, and the better able they are to resist disease. Safety in numbers. In addition to contributing to the process of decomposition, some of these microorganisms (bacteria, algae, fungi, acinomycetes) also make nutrients available to plants, change carbon dioxide into organic matter, synthesize organic matter into cell tissue, and alter air relationships in the soil. Thus, soil with lots of humus is also healthier, more nurturing soil.

The earth I'm talking about is called topsoil, the arable two to three feet that lie above inert subsoil, which lies above impenetrable rock. If you'll work three inches of humus six inches deep into denuded subsoil for three years, you'll create topsoil—something it takes Mother Earth a century or more to do.

You can add organic matter to the soil and wait for the soil to decompose it into humus. Or you can make humus yourself as I do—presto!—by making compost.

Hybrid

A hybrid is a plant resulting from cross-fertilization between parents of different species or different cultivars of the same species. The parents may be open pollinated or hybrid themselves, although generally they're open pollinated.

Seeds of hybrids cannot be counted on to breed true. The fruit of a hybrid cross between a yellow pattypan summer squash and a green pattypan may be yellow. The F_1 next to the resulting hybrid's name indicates this is the first generation of the cross. But *its* fruit, the second generation, is as likely to be green as yellow—the genes of the grandparents surfacing.

In this way, an open-pollinated cultivar can be developed from a hybrid. One seed company did this with the lovely hybrid Sunburst pattypan squash. When first offered in 1991, their cross was an F_4 offspring of Sunburst—that is, the plants were three generations removed from the original cross of two hybrid Sunbursts. What Peace Seeds did was keep taking the golden-fruited progeny and crossing them.

I grew the F_4 Sunburst that first year. Of my two plants, one reverted back to a green pattypan, and one was as much a Sunburst as the control F_1 hybrid Sunburst I grew. However, sometimes even after several generations, the cross will turn unstable. Perhaps that's the reason the cultivar is no longer offered. Even so, an experiment in breeding is great fun in the home garden when there's nothing at stake but expectation.

Hybrids Versus Open-Pollinated Cultivars

Rob Johnston of Johnny's Seeds: "While your own open-pollinated . . . varieties will not often have the vigor expressed in hybrids, in the long run it seems more valuable to enjoy the 'constant warmth' of well-maintained varieties than to depend on the short-lived 'fire' of the hybrids."

By saving seeds of open-pollinated plants you like, you can hang on to them. Otherwise they may disappear. In the Thompson & Morgan catalog—a catalog that offers an uncommonly large and unusual assortment of seeds—of two years ago there were six pages of primroses. Now there are $2^1/_2$. Where there were three pages of carrots there are two. No more Winfreda early winter hardy peas, no Hurst Beagle nor Titania wrinkled early spring peas, no Onward nor Multistar wrinkled second early peas. So to be as self-sufficient as possible, choose open-pollinated seeds and increase them for yourself as insurance.

When you do order OP cultivars for your garden, if they're a tricky crop, it's wise to get them from a seed company in your region—and ask whether the seeds were raised in your neck of the woods. Certainly you can order from a seedsman elsewhere, but ask whether the cultivar is adapted to your growing conditions.

A horticulturist at a large commercial seed company who grows heritage flowers and vegetables in his garden and has himself been a member of Seed Savers Exchange, told me that the really important thing about heritage OP plants is their regional selectability. My friend says there isn't an OP plant that grows well everywhere, and one value of a hybrid is its adaptability—many flourish in 90 percent of this country. But the OP plant can become wonderfully adapted to a place. Each year the farmer selects seeds from the finest plants in his crop and sows them the following season. With each generation, the cultivar becomes increasingly adapted to meeting challenges from pests, soil, climate, sunshine, water, or length of growing season. Ultimately, the plant will perform *in that place* as well as any hybrid, but it may be discombobulated when grown elsewhere. For example, O'odham 60 Day white flour corn that has been grown by the Papago in the Arizona desert for generations took 136 days to mature in cool Iowa, and grew rank in the bargain.

Hybrid seeds, on the other hand, can have the virtues of the open-pollinated cultivars they combine. They can be immensely productive, provide crucial disease resistance, have fine flavor and form. There is no protection in the marketplace for an open-pollinated cultivar. A plant can be patented (PVP after its name), but this is costly and rarely practical. OP strains that have been developed by a company can be reproduced and sold by competitors with ease. Only hybrids give a seedsman a modicum of control over his product.

HYDROPONIC GARDENING

*T*his is a system of growing plants in pure water—not a speck of earth. A friend harvests excellent produce from her hydroponic garden. If you have space but no soil and container gardening doesn't appeal—or if a handicap makes working the soil difficult—try this. The tables are waist high, so gardening is easy. The library should have books to get you started.

INOCULANT FOR LEGUMES

*L*egume inoculant is a charcoal-like powder or granules of rhizobium bacteria. The bacteria grab nitrogen from the air and the soil and fix it in the soil so legume seeds have access to it and can grow more easily.

Like most plants, peas, beans, and other fruiting legumes need nitrogen to prosper. As a result, legume plants provide their own nitrogen factory in the form of nodules on their roots. This is called *nodulating* or a *nitrogen-fixing ability*. That's why legumes are so valuable in crop rotation. The nodules they leave behind in the soil are jam-packed with nitrogen, a great tonic for spent soil. Just as sourdough bread needs soured bacteria (a starter) the plant needs a little nitrogen in the vicinity. But not too much, or the plant will be all green leaves and no fruit. That's why it's as important for legumes to be rotated out of their spot to a new one—so they won't be overnitrogenated. In soil where legumes have grown a few years before, there will be a residuum of nitrogen, and the legumes will get off to a fine start, grow well, and form their nodules. But when a leguminous plant has never grown in that soil, unless the soil is rich in organic matter—which harbors bacteria—it needs the starter, the bit of inoculant.

Each legume responds to a specific strain of rhizobium. Clearly peas and beans have grown happily in the wild without their very own fix of bacteria. Or have they? Different cultivars vary considerably in their ability to respond to nitrogen elements in the soil, to form nodules. Some don't respond. Some, like Scarlet Runners, are called *promiscuous nodulators* because they'll use any rhizobium handy. This responsive characteristic seems to be linked to wild Central American beans. So cultivars, not crossed and recrossed as hybrids, seem the best candidates for inoculants.

Living organisms, inoculants are viable for only a few months. Even though *R. phaseoli* is specific for beans, *R. leguminosarum* is meant for peas, and *R. japonicum* is what soybeans like, most companies combine strains in the packet to cover several kitchen garden crops. Because each rhizobium species may come in several strains—one handles wet soil, another tolerates cold soil, another poor soil—a packet of inoculant might easily be a blend of a dozen strains, balanced to give results under a broad spectrum of circumstances.

It beats me why all nurseries don't offer inoculants on the rack with peas and beans. Every seed catalog worth ordering from offers inoculants, although they're not always in the pea section but may be with the beans and may not be named inoculant but have a cute name such as Booster or Nature's Aid. Between sowings, keep the packet closed tightly and dry and cool.

To use, moisten seeds in cool water, then shake in a bag with just enough inoculant to dust each seed.

INSECTICIDAL SOAP

*T*he name on the bottle is Safer's, and it is safer than anything in that army of chemical killers you see lined up on shelves at the nursery. Dilute according to directions. For bad situations, spray every two to three days for two weeks to catch all the emerging young.

You can also use mild dishwashing detergent for mild infestations.

Soap is a contact insecticide, so it must hit the critter. Spray it early in the morning, before it gets hot and the wind comes up. Wear a hat, rubber gloves, long sleeves, and mask as much of your face as you can with a cotton scarf. You need gloves because you must handle the curled-up leaves, opening them up so you can spray—can you believe how many creatures there are inside that cabbage leaf?—and glasses because you'll find that uncurled leaves can curl again with a snap, flinging droplets of the soap into your eyes. Be sure to turn yourself upside down and spray under all leaves—usually bad guys, cowards all, hide on the undersides of leaves.

Adding $\frac{1}{2}$ cup rubbing (isopropyl) alcohol or 1 tablespoon kerosene to every quart of solution increases the insecticidal soap's efficiency enormously. This is the second step—try the soap plain first, because the alcohol can burn plants just the way it stings our skin.

INSECTS, BENEFICIAL

*Q*uoted from *Sunset's Guide to Organic Gardening:* "Around here," the director of a showplace organic garden once said to a journalist, "we don't kill anything until we know what it does."

If you can get an insect book, you can look up these good friends and then, when you see them, welcome them into your garden.

Helpmates include these:

braconid wasps: they lay parasitic eggs on the larvae of pests
true bugs: damsel, wheel-, big-eyed, pirate, and such suck the juices from bad guys
ground beetles: they dine on pests in the ground, even snails and slugs
ichneumon wasps: like braconid wasps, only they parasitize destructive caterpillars
lacewings: they suck juices from aphids and spider mites
ladybird beetles aka ladybugs: they feed on aphids, scale insects, spider mites, and mealybugs
praying mantises: they eat aphids
robber flies: both larvae and adults are hungry predators
spiders: terrific predators
syrphid flies: their larvae feed on aphids
tachinid flies: they feed on cutworms, squash bugs, sawflies, tent caterpillars, and a number of other pests

You can attract and nurture many of these good fellas by growing lots of Queen Anne's Lace, red and white clover, several sorts of daisies, wild buckwheat, buttercups, goldenrod, asters, strawberries, white clover, alfalfa, angelica, morning glories, and yarrows.

Intercropping, Interplanting, Double-cropping, Undercropping, Underseeding, Intersowing, Living Mulch

These are all essentially the practice of growing a mix of crops together, taking advantage of their complementing need for sun/shade, their fast/slow maturing, their light/heavy feeding, and so on.

Intensive gardening is fitting crops together so no soil is barren, so there's no room for weeds to flourish. As you can imagine, combinations of compatible plants are endless, so it behooves you to get out the pencil and scratch pad and fit the pieces of your garden's puzzle together. The charts hold the keys.

Lights, Growing Plants Under

It's amazing how much 16 hours a day of two shop lamps—each fitted with two 4-foot fluorescent tubes—can do for the growth of seedlings being raised indoors. There are lights developed just for plants, with a scientific balance of this ray and that, but I just use the lights from the dime store. The tubes last a couple of seasons; the shop lamps last indefinitely. Hang them on chains with S hooks so the lights are just above the little plants. You'll see how quickly and often you must raise the lamps. Each lamp will accommodate two flats. Every day, rotate the flats or whatever containers you're using to make sure the light is evenly distributed over time.

Be as faithful about the 16 hours as you can, turning them on and off at the same time. And more light isn't better—the teenies need to sleep after the exertion of growing. They can stay under the lights—the lamps going up, up, up—until it's time to harden the plants off.

Most of us have limited places to set up these lights, so give first dibs to peppers, tomatoes, and others that have a craving for warmth and light in their genes.

Manure

Says *The Encyclopedia of Organic Gardening:* "It has been calculated that a farmer by wise management of his animal manures can return to the soil 70 percent of the nitrogen, 75 percent of the phosphorus and 80 percent of the potash which was taken out by the homegrown plants his animals eat. This is a considerable saving when it is realized that a dairy cow gives 27,000 pounds of manure annually and a horse, 18,000."

	Nitrogen	Phosphorus	Potash	Age
	(%)	(%)	(%)	(%)
Rabbit	2.4	1.4	.6	2 months+
Chicken	1.1	.8	.5	2 months+
Horse	.7	.3	.6	2–3 months+
Steer	.7	.3	.4	2 years+

The only time to use fresh manure—the sort that steams in the morning mist—is when you're heating up compost or a hotbed in a frame. Otherwise, the older the manure, the better—it's best when it really has very little scent.

The only manure I've found to be free of weeds is from rabbits raised on pellets. The numbers—

nitrogen, phosphorus, and potassium content—don't tell the whole story. There's something extraordinary there. See if you can find a source; if not, consider raising rabbits. A large doe and her four annual litters (28 to 32 bunnies) will present your garden with 6 to 7 cubic feet of manure each year.

Every bag of composted steer manure I've bought—even those labeled weed free—and even horse manure from stables where there haven't been horses in five years sprouts weeds in my garden. The way around these weeds is to cover the manured soil with mulch, thereby having the benefit of the manure's nourishment and humus but none of its problems.

But steer manure can be high in salt content, so use it sparingly.

Aged manure makes a grand mulch.

Generally, save manure for leaf and fruiting crops more than root—and never give root crops fresh manure, or they'll be hairy and will fork. Annuals love a ton of it—they have a lot of growing and flowering and fruiting to do fast, and manure is a big help. All members of the Nightshade and Cucumber families are crazy about manure; in fact, they'll grow in pure manure, given the chance.

MANURE TEA

$\mathcal{D}$ry manure works its wonders slowly into the soil, but manure tea is a quick fix. Measure aged manure by volume and dump it in a barrel. Add three times the water, cover, and steep for at least a couple of days. Then bucket out the tea and add water to make a light tea-colored brew—too strong, and the tea will work against rather than for you. Wet the soil around sickly plants or plants you need to force, then sprinkle the tea on the soil only, giving a nitrogen pick-me-up. Allow about 1 pint of tea for each plant and serve it no more often than weekly, two or three times. The proper way to make the tea is to have the manure in a burlap sack so you can haul it out of the barrel when the tea is ready, but I leave it in the barrel until the tea's gone. Then I take the cover off and let the manure dry until I can bucket it out and use it as mulch.

MICROCLIMATES

$\mathcal{W}$hen you look at your place on a gardening map and the color key says you have this climate or that, take it with a grain of salt. A complex combination of elements creates microclimates: In addition to nearby bodies of water, physical elements are elevation, orientation, landform, vegetation, and structures—elements of climate are sun, rain, temperature, and wind. You can see why your plot of land is unique in all the world.

You'll get to know which corners of your garden are best for growing this and best for that. Observe and take notes. But bold gardening takes wit. My mother got lilacs to bloom in a subtropical climate with the aid of ice cubes. If you want to try something said to be impossible in your garden, even small variations in one or two aspects of its microclimate can spell success. Consult a hands-on landscaping book like *Nature's Design* (Carol A. Smyser, Rodale Press, 1982) for details.

MOON: SOWING AND PLANTING BY IT

$\mathcal{D}$ue to the pull of the moon on the tides of this planet, many who work the soil feel the magnetic connection between the moon and the tides of the earth make a difference. Here are the rules.

The notion of the biodynamic growing method is that the greatest sum of influences—including gravity, the magnetic field, and light—occurs at the new moon. Therefore, short- and extra-long-germinating seeds should be sown two days before and up to seven days after the new moon. Long-germinating seeds should be sown and seedlings should be transplanted at and up to seven days after the full moon. This all has to do with increasing and decreasing lunar gravitational force. Moonlight is thought to stimulate leaf growth.

Another school of planting by the moon contends that flowering plants and those that bear crops above the ground should be sown or planted by the light of the moon—from the new to the full moon—and plants that bear crops below the ground should be sown or planted by the dark of the moon, the day after it's full to the day before it is new.

I've grown a number of plants using both theories, but I can't be sure they made a difference.

Frost and the Full Moon. According to John Gale, seedsman extraordinary, in spring when there's a full moon and clear sky, watch out: there will be frost. John gardens in a peachy microclimate near Niagara Falls. When he sees there will be a full moon before June 10, he waits until afterward to transplant his peppers.

MULCH

$\mathcal{M}$ulch is what keeps not-by-nature-drought-tolerant plants alive in my dry garden. What *is* mulch? Mulch is a covering over the soil that shelters a plant in many ways. Not only is mulch the natural way to conserve moisture—re-creating the forest floor—but a thick mulch defies weeds to grow through it. The third benefit of organic mulch is that in time earthworms pull it down into the soil, and more humus is effortlessly added.

What to Use. First, my report on black mulches—in this case, black paper and black plastic.

I laid biodegradable black paper (highly recommended by friends in the Northeast) in my tomato patch. On a balmy May day, I cut big Xs in the paper and set out 24 perky tomato seedlings in the ground, then watered them in well with fish emulsion. At dusk I covered them with light insect-weight floating row cover, hoping to keep the critters from nibbling at them overnight. The next morning, with the air at around 70°F, I found six plants completely frizzled. This had never happened to me. I watered the rows deeply, and since I had some backup plants, I set them in the places of their hapless mates. This time I didn't cover them, thinking the fabric had made it just too hot. The next morning, four of the six had frizzled. When we pulled up the black paper, we found the soil beneath was bone dry, even though I thought I'd been watering well. So we turned on the soaker hose for the morning, and everybody revived. A sorry lesson. Unless you live in a frozen clime, that stuff can be lethal.

The same is even truer of the impermeable plastic mulches. I spread it over my herb bed in anticipation of the squashes that were to come. But when I fed the calendulas and petunias I'd transplanted with fish emulsion, the stuff puddled on top of the plastic, the flies went crazy, and so did I. Experimenting with the holey black plastic, I laid it down on my trellised squash and melon patch. It's okay because it breathes and water can go through.

Impermeable black plastic mulch is, however, excellent for simply warming the soil before planting a heat-loving crop. Then you don't have any flies to worry about. See Plastic Mulch.

Of course there are organic mulches such as manure, straw, newspapers, and partially decomposed compost. Usually I just strew around 2 or 3 inches of spoiled straw (rural feed stores sell it cheap). If plants are set close enough, the straw can't be seen beneath their leaves. But when the drought was grave, I laid down first a good inch of newspaper (black-and-white sections only), then 6 inches of straw. The newspaper keeps seeds in the straw from germinating *and* everything wetter. I add more straw as the season advances. I leave at least 6 inches open around the stem of a large plant for breathing room. A bed swathed to its chin in straw isn't elegant (shredded bark is elegant and also expensive), but it works. I like the look of it, though; it's very rustic.

There are paper mulches for sale in catalogs, and I'm sure they're excellent. But why not just use newspaper, a cheaper resource and as biodegradable, instead?

Another useful thing about manure, compost, or ground bark mulch is that it gives a finished look to the garden. Stones, too, make a handsome and marvelous mulch. The heat they've collected during the day is slowly distributed during the night. They're decorative, they give shelter to earthworms from birds, and they allow no weeds to surface.

When to Mulch. The timing depends on its purpose. You mulch some plants with a light material such as straw to keep the roots cool—potatoes, for example. You mulch other plants to prewarm the soil—melons, for example. You mulch eggplants to keep the soil cozy after planting.

In all cases but prewarming the soil, plants must be established before you mulch. If you're bringing seedlings along, it's impossible to mulch. The little ones will have to get big enough. In hot weather this can be very hard on fragile leaves such as lettuces. Unmulched, you must keep an eye on them for wilting and water often. Help the seedlings grow as fast as possible so they'll be big enough to have some mulch under their feet, thus keeping the soil cool and moist, thus helping them grow faster. There *is* that difficult time from birth to youth when they'll be unprotected. Also see Intercropping.

MUSIC IN THE GARDEN

*R*esearch from Madras to Ottawa to Illinois has found that plants respond—one way or another—to sound. Apparently summer squashes are attracted to 18th- and 19th-century European composers (Haydn, Beethoven, Schubert)—the vines bend toward the music's source. While some plants appear disinterested in folk and country-western, they grow toward the jazz of Ellington and Armstrong. Summer squashes scramble from heavy rock, but it's apparently not the atonality, since many plants grow plumper listening to the 12-tone work of Berg and Schoenberg. And some fall all over themselves, drawn toward the strains of the Indian sitar.

There are scientists, of course, who call this nonsense. Before I read about the research, I played classical music from dawn to dark; it makes everyone in the garden feel better, and who can *prove* not the plants?

NO-TILL GARDENING

*D*o read Masanobu Fukuoka's *The One-Straw Revolution*—the exact opposite of French intensive double-digging, but profoundly moving, and a way of gathering you up into the Zen of growing vegetables.

OPEN-POLLINATED

*P*arents of an open-pollinated plant are the same cultivar and species.

ORGANIC GARDENING

*T*his means not applying any material to your soil or to the surfaces of plants that hasn't been part of the soil or some living thing before.

Instead of giving nitrogen in inorganic gray granules, use manure, which once was grass. Or use fish meal, blood meal, hoof and horn meal, organic cottonseed meal—it's clear where they came from. Instead of giving phosphorus in gray granules, give bonemeal. Instead of potassium in gray granules, wood ashes.

But if it's true—and it is—that plants are indifferent to the source of their nutrients, why make the effort to garden organically? If, head to head, you can't absolutely tell the difference between cauliflower nourished with gray granules or with organic meal, what's the point? If malathion gets rid of the aphids, why fuss with soaps made from daisies?

Because we are stewards of the soil. To keep it alive and prospering, we must return to it good things that came from it, not from a chemical process. Because chemicals can pollute the environment in the making and in the breaking down. Organic gardening is about the planet and our bodies and only incidentally about ephemeral things like food.

ORGANIC MATTER

Organic matter—the component in the soil that, most of all, absorbs and retains water—is the likes of rotting compost, manure, peat, straw, and so forth. The ultimate end is humus, organic matter decomposed to a rich, dark fluff.

PAPER POTS

Between paper pots and soil blocks, starting large, fast-growing seeds couldn't be easier, more foolproof, or cheaper. For soil blocks there's a onetime investment for the molding device. With a newspaper you have free paper pots. The pots are amazingly durable no matter how much water and sun they absorb. Tight spacing keeps the pots moist and holds them firm. Roots have ample room to grow from sprouting until transplanting without becoming potbound because there is no bottom to the pot. And there's no transplanting shock because not one rootlet is disturbed—the whole package goes straight into the soil. That means you can start plants that don't like to be transplanted in paper pots and they won't know they've been transplanted. And there's a bonus of a little humus added to the soil with the paper.

I make three sizes: 2½ inches wide for small plants; 3 inches for eggplants, melons, brassicas, tomatoes, and peppers; 4 inches for squash, cucumbers, corn, and other vigorous flowers and vines. Usually I make the pots as tall as they are wide, but if I'm growing plants with a long taproot that mustn't be disturbed, I make the pots twice as tall as they are wide. That's one of the great advantages of paper pots—you can tailor them to the plant. Depth depends on the plants' growth habits and how long they'll have to be in the pots. You never know whether you're going to be able to transplant just when you're supposed to, so it's always better to make the pots deeper rather than shallower.

Now there are molding devices and premade paper pots in catalogs. Paper pots that come in a glued-together honeycomb are awkward to fill, the size they come in doesn't fit a flat, and they don't easily separate into individual pots. As for buying a wooden paper pot mold, that's silly because you can use cans as a mold and make any size you want. Paper pots are quick-as-a-wink to make. Besides the newspaper, the soil mix, sphagnum moss, and a strong flat to contain the pots, all you need is a mold to get you started.

For pots 4 inches deep, fold a single page of newspaper (not tabloid size) from bottom to top. Tucking the two edges of the paper inside, fold in the same direction in thirds—you'll have a band 4 inches wide. Wrap the band around the mold or your hand to make a cylinder as wide as you need. You don't need to be precise. I quickly measure the overlapping ends: 3 inches on either side makes a 3-inch pot (in no time you'll be able to eyeball it and make them rapidly without measuring). I either tape in the middle with a strip of paper tape (something biodegradable, not Scotch tape) or tuck a paper clip on top (which I'll retrieve at planting time). Have a flat or box with drainage lined with enough newspaper to keep the dirt from falling out, plus sphagnum moss if you have some. Fit the tubes cheek by jowl in the flat—it helps when they can prop one another up. Use a trowel to fill them to the top with soil mix, slam the box down on something to settle the soil, then top it off and slam again. Sow seeds in them or set in transplants, then water gently but thoroughly—the earth will settle again, leaving a margin for watering.

You can also transplant tiny seedlings you've started on paper towels or in a soilless mixture into paper pots. Just drop them into the soil mix in the center.

When you're ready to plant your paper pots in the ground, use a broad palette knife or flat trowel to lift the pot gingerly from the flat. Roots will probably hold the earth in place, but I always coddle the bottom of the pot with my hand just to be sure. Before planting, use a small knife to slit the paper on four sides—or gently remove the paper completely. Plant, setting the earth in the pot flush with the ground.

PARTHENOCARPIC

From the Greek *parthenos,* virgin, and *karpos,* fruit: plants with fruits that are self-fertilizing and have few or no seeds (technically only undeveloped seed membrane). That means you can grow the plants under the protection of floating row covers from start to finish and be assured of no insect pests and reduced disease. Since these plants don't have seed making on their minds, they're free to throw their energy into fruit. But even though the point is no seeds, should an insect stray by and pollinate the blossoms with male pollen from a neighbor's plant, nothing disastrous will happen—you may get fruit with seeds. The tomato Oregon Spring is parthenocarpic.

PEAT AND SPHAGNUM PEAT MOSS

These are remains of prehistoric plants that have decayed without air—usually in a watery bog. The moss has been finely ground, and it makes a wonderful addition to sandy soil. It has the ability to absorb up to 20 times its weight in moisture. Although usually sterile, it contains a form of fungicide that inhibits disease when seeds are germinating. Before using it, wet it thoroughly; then never allow it to dry out. Peat moss doesn't make a good mulch by itself because it can dry and blow away so easily, but it's excellent as an ingredient in mulch or as a soil amendment to add organic matter that holds moisture. It is very acid, however, so be careful when adding it to already acid soil.

PERENNIAL

Hortus Third: "Of three or more seasons' duration."

Growing perennial plants from seed is a yea-saying practice, an act of faith that you'll be around the following year when they bloom—although many, if sown early enough, will bloom or crop from seed the first year. Perennials are practical—you only have to sow them once, as opposed to resowing annuals each season. Usually frost-tender perennial vegetables (eggplants, peppers, tomatoes) are grown as annuals. Let them winter over in mild climates or in a pot indoors—they'll grow and produce for you the following season.

PERLITE

These tiny white polystyrenelike beads are actually a mined volcanic material that has been crushed and heat-treated to pop to 20 times its original volume. As with vermiculite, perlite is weed and insect free but also without nutrients. And like vermiculite, it's excellent in a potting mix because it holds up to four times its weight in water. Perlite does not, however, attract molecules of nutrients as does vermiculite. Because of perlite's sparkling whiteness, it's also good for covering seeds germinating in the garden. It marks the place of fine carrot seeds, for example, and helps keep them from drying out.

PESTS

*Y*our library or your local extension adviser will have a pamphlet or book on how to deal organically with hungry insect pests. Mostly it comes down to finding big creatures and picking them off by hand (sometimes I think seeing the disguise is worth the price of admission) and spraying small creatures with the hose or ultimately insecticidal soap. Barriers and traps are helpful, and certainly predatory insects are the best.

pH

*T*he level of acidity or alkalinity in the soil. The letters stand for *potential Hydrogen* and indicate the breakdown of water into the hydrogen ion and an oxygen/hydrogen ion. Soil acidity and alkalinity are determined by the process of this breakdown.

The pH scale ranges from 0 to 14—0 being purely acid soil (termed *sour*), 14 being purely alkaline soil (termed *sweet*), and 7 being neutral. Fortunately, acid and alkaline, in reference to the scale, are in alphabetical order. It's a cinch to remember: 6.5 is on the acid side, and 7.5 is on the alkaline.

It's crucial to know the pH of the soil in your garden because acidity or alkalinity affects the absorption of nutrients by plants. Phosphorus, potassium, calcium, and magnesium are most available with a pH between 6.0 and 7.5. Lower pH—more acid—and these nutrients cannot be taken up by plants. Iron, trace minerals, and some toxic elements are available to plants at a low pH. But above pH 8, when the soil is alkaline, phosphorus, iron, and some trace minerals are rendered unavailable. The absorption of nitrogen is affected indirectly by pH. Much of the nitrogen used by plants is released in a complex process through bacteria in the soil. Below 5.5, the bacteria can't function, and thus the nitrogen is unavailable.

The pH of soil derives from the nature of the rock from which the soil evolved and from the decomposition of vegetable matter on the soil. Perfectly neutral soil has the value of pure water.

In the days before testing equipment (you can buy a pH meter from a garden supply catalog at no great expense), the sourness or sweetness of the soil could be determined by what wild things grew there. Taking the healthiest plants and looking only at communities of plants (not a stray seed or two dropped by the wind), here are some indications of soil:

Acid Soil Plant Indicators. Bracken (eastern), silvery cinquefoil, corn marigold, English daisy, dandelion, docks, hawkweeds, horsetails, knapweeds, prostate knotweed, mayweed, mullein, mustards, stinging nettles, wild pansies, plantains, wild radishes, sorrels, wild strawberries, and sundews.

Alkali Soil Plant Indicators. Bellflowers, campion, wild carrots, hop clover, black henbane, orach, pennycress, salad burnet, salep, and scarlet pimpernel.

You may read in English gardening books about "chalky" soil: that's alkaline. Here's a quick overall view:

H Value	Levels of Acidity or Alkalinity and Locations
4.0–4.5	Extremely acid: humid forests and sometimes areas where there is wet peaty soil
4.5–5.0	Very acid: mainly areas of cold and damp
5.0–5.5	Fairly acid: very wet climates
5.5–6.0	Slightly acid: moderate climates with high rainfall
6.0–6.5	Mildly acid: moderate climates without too much rain
6.5–7.0	Neutral's range: hot, dry climates
7.0–7.5	Mildly alkaline: even hotter, drier climates
7.5–8.0	Slightly alkaline: semideserts of the West

How to Alter Your Soil's pH. *To lower the pH 1 point,* apply 50 pounds of aged manure for every 100 square feet. Acid peat moss and any part of oaks—leaves, sawdust, ground-up bark—also help. So does a *little* borax and manganese or sulfur according to package directions. *To raise the pH 1 point,* spread dolomitic limestone at these rates: for every 100 square feet of sandy soil, 3 pounds; sandy loam, 5 pounds; loam, 7 pounds; heavy clay, 8 pounds. Hardwood ashes not leached by rains are another good corrective. Spread in fall after turning over the soil (do not dig in) and be patient because it will take a year or two to have an effect. Repeat every four or five years if necessary.

OPTIMAL SOIL pH FOR SOME KITCHEN GARDEN PLANTS

5.0.|..|..|..|.5.5.|..|..|..|.6.0.|..|..|..|.6.5.|..|..|..|.7.0.|..|..|..|.7.5.|..|..|..|.8.0

←←←←←peanuts→→→→→

←←chicory, dandelion, endive, escarole, fennel, potatoes→→

←←rhubarb, shallots, sorrel, sweet potatoes, watermelon→→

←←←←←tomatillos→→→→→

←beans, black-eyed peas, brussels sprouts→

←←carrots, chick-peas, collards, corn→→

←←cowpeas, cucumbers, eggplant, garlic→→

←←←←gourds, kale, kohlrabi→→→→

←←←lima beans, mustards, parsley→→→

←←←←peas, peppers, pumpkins→→→→

←←radishes, rutabagas, southern peas→→

←squash, strawberries, tomatoes, turnips→

←←←←←West Indian gherkins→→→→→

←←←←←←lentils, thymes→→→→→→

←←←corn salad→→→

←←←←←caraway→→→→→

←basils, dill→

←←asparagus, beets→→

←←broccoli, cabbages→→

←cauliflower, celeriac→

←celery, celtuce, chard→

←Chinese cabbages, cress→

←←fava beans, leeks→→

←←lettuce, melons→→

New Zealand spinach, okra

←onions, orach, parsnips→

←←salsify, spinach→→

←←←watercress→→→

arugula, chives, lemon verbena, lovage

←mint, sages, scented geraniums→

←←←←←←←←Jerusalem artichokes→→→→→→→→

←←←←←borage→→→→→

←←←←←hyssop→→→→→

←←←←salad burnet→→→→

chervil, marjoram

oregano, rosemary

summer savory

←tarragon→

←←artichoke, cardoon→→

←←←←lavender→→→→

PLANNING THE GARDEN

A plan is absolutely essential for your kitchen garden, and the more detailed, the more helpful it will be. Not only do you need to know where the plants will go, but you'll need to figure the space allotted to each vegetable, herb, flower, and fruit. You must take into account the path of the sun over your garden and the shade cast by tall objects. It's a bore, but otherwise your garden will look like Hodgepodge Lodge, and sometime in mid-July you'll be sorry you didn't think ahead.

Once planned and once planted, though, the garden will take on a life of its own. There will be unexpected volunteers, which technically are weeds, plants out of place—but some will be irresistible and thus ruin your plan. And some plants won't perform as expected—they'll be taller or more sprawling or shorter or the wrong color, or they'll sit on their hands and pout. Maybe you'll leave them in; maybe you won't. But once your garden is in full fig, the only person you need to please is yourself.

Don't forget that you can use potted plants to fill gaps.

Where do you put new plants you've brought home from the nursery or have raised from seedlings while there are still plants in the spaces you had planned for them? Best thing is either to keep them in the container they're in, watching carefully that they don't dry out or get potbound, or find any place in the garden where you can plant them temporarily—a method called *heeling in*. Get them out of their temporary quarters as soon as you can.

PLANTING/TRANSPLANTING

C arelessly done, transplanting can weaken a plant—may even finish it off. But carefully lifting a plant from one situation and placing it in another usually seems to strengthen it, just as adversity can make us strong. Most of the brassicas and onions gain vitality from two or three moves. Usually you move something because it's better for the plant—it's gotten too big for its britches, or it isn't prospering where it is, or you've found a place where it will show to better advantage.

Although you will never stop learning about the fine art of setting a plant in the ground, beginners can do it well. First dig a hole. A square hole: It's less complicated, and roots seem to spread better, heading for the corners. But as you dig it, bear in mind that the plant's roots have to find their way, have to go hunting for water and sustenance; that worms have to be able to wriggle in and out through the roots; that the health and happiness of your plant depends on the tilth, on that home of a hole.

If you need to add anything to the hole to make it friable, do so with a light hand. If you're a baker or a salad maker, when you add amendments to the soil, do it with the same light hand that you whip the eggs and toss the salad. Air is all, in a cake and a hole.

Water the hole to make sure there's good drainage. If there's not, get a pick and whack away until the water disappears in at least an hour. If the plant is in a container, set the pot in the place where it will be growing and let the plant become accustomed to its new circumstances for a day or two—or a week if the weather has been cold (see Hardening Off). The sun's pattern, the shadows, the wind, the insects, the new neighbors all should be familiar when the time comes for the jolt of being pulled from a cozy old pot and thrust into unfamiliar new ground. So many times I've lost things because I've been too eager to finish putting in a bed. The plant won't have up and died the next morning—it will linger, looking droopy and miserable for days. There are plants and cultivars, of course, that are as tough as nails, and you can change your mind and move them three times in a day and they'll be perky as jaybirds the next morning (purslane, geraniums, lavender for example), but they are few and far between.

Try to wait for an overcast day to transplant. If none are in view, always transplant in the evening so harsh sunshine won't sap the plant's strength and send it further—perhaps irretrievably—into shock.

If you take home nursery stock that's badly rootbound or in full blossom and nearly spent, take it out of the pot and set the whole root ball in a bucket of vitamin B$_1$ solution or a weak solution of liquid fertilizer such as fish or kelp for 6 to 8 hours.

At planting time, always loosen the root ball by pulling it apart a bit. If the roots are tangled cut down about one-fifth the depth of the ball with a knife or sharp spade, around the sides in four to six places. This gives the roots a breather and lets new ones start. If the roots are threaded through the drainage hole, loosen them, too.

If the plant is flowering, you have to assess the situation: How strong is the plant, how long will its life be (annual or perennial), how hot will tomorrow be, and such. The plant is going to be asked to grow roots like crazy to become established. You may have to cut off the flowers.

When you set the plant in its new home, you will either set it slightly lower than the surrounding soil so it will have a basin around it for watering or, if the plant's crown and roots are easily rotted, you'll want to spread the roots on a mound of soil and raise the plant slightly higher than the surrounding earth—you can make a watering basin around it still. If a basin is not part of your watering method, still you have to make sure there's something to catch and hold water for the plant—it may be a shallow ditch on one side.

Now the fun part. If the plant is large enough, you can stomp around it as though you were treading grapes. You want to make firm contact between the roots and the soil—most brassicas love this. There are some plants—lettuces, for example—that hate being manhandled—directions that come with the plant will probably tell you. Still, the plant will probably recover if you stomp when you shouldn't.

If the plant is small, just pat the soil firmly with your hands. Watering in will settle the soil.

Be prepared with transplanting solution. You'll need to feed the plant a good dose of antishock something after it has been moved. Vitamin B$_1$ is perhaps the best (it comes in a jug), or old-fashioned Superthrive, a super product (you give just a few drops of it). You can also use a weak fish emulsion or kelp solution.

In most places in very early spring the protection of a floating row cover is advised until the plant becomes established, but if you want to set out plants extra-early, the protection of something heavier such as glass jars or plastic milk jugs is recommended. See Cloches.

Keep a close eye on the plant for at least 10 days, never letting it dry out and providing more shelter if it looks wilted. Most plants will come back nicely after transplanting if you give them tender loving care.

PLASTIC IN THE GARDEN

*R*ecycle it. Take the pots and flats back to the nursery so they can be reused. Write on plastic markers with pencil, then erase and use them again. Reuse plastic mulch as much as you can, but be careful not to get to the point where it starts dropping plastic shreds into the soil.

PLASTIC MULCH

*F*rom 1 to 3 mils thick, plastic mulch comes in rolls, usually from 4 to 6 feet wide. Cover the edges with earth or rocks to keep the sheet in place. Black and clear plastics are used to warm the soil for heat-loving crops in cool climates—they can warm the soil as much as 20°F above uncovered soil. Now I slash or stab it at least every few inches to achieve this end. This is crucial! There are perforated mulches available—they're comparatively expensive, but they work very well.

Even many organic gardeners with strong environmental concerns feel the advantages of plastic as mulch and as floating row covers outweigh its aesthetic and environmental shortcomings. For inhospitable short-season climates, the two combined—plastic above and below—can so enhance growth that cucumbers and melons have been demonstrated to fruit three weeks earlier than uncovered crops and to bear double or triple the yield. When mulched with clear plastic, eggplants have yielded 3 times their traditional amount of fruit and peppers 2½ times. That means several crops can be brought to fruition in areas where once they were out of the question.

As water grows increasingly precious, plastic mulch can be used to retain moisture in the soil—up to nearly 20 percent longer than uncovered soil. This is a boon in droughty areas and for gardens anywhere with raised beds or naturally good drainage. Plastic mulch also acts as a physical barrier to weeds, thus eliminating the temptation to use herbicides. Black plastic, which blocks light, is particularly effective in keeping weeds down. Heavy clear plastic can solarize the soil, baking many seeds of weeds—and seeds you want, as well.

There are, in fact, many sorts of plastic mulches for the garden. Dark green infrared transmitting (IRT) plastic excludes weeds better than clear and permits more light than black plastic mulch. Light-sensitive (photodegradable) mulches are designed to break down in place quickly. In trials in the South, black plastic mulch painted red grew tomatoes faster, larger, and more abundantly than those unmulched and mulched with other plastics. Bicolor mulches are black on the bottom, for blocking weeds and retaining moisture, and white on the top, for reflecting the sun back up to the plant, thus giving it a double dose of heat.

All these products are available through catalogs, but rarely at the local nursery.

To camouflage the plastic, to keep it from decomposing in the sun, and to weight it down, throw straw or bark chips on top. Walk on the plastic as little as possible to maintain its integrity.

But as with so much in this world, the virtues of these plastics can quickly turn to disadvantages. Too much heat in the ground, and roots sizzle. For all the good it does, the plastic cover drives earthworms deep and inhibits the natural give-and-take among soil, air, and sky.

POLLINATION

The only certain way to keep seed pure is to wrap the plant completely—it's called *caging* in pollinese. If the plant is insect pollinated, build something that will support screening. If wind pollinated, wrap the plant in well-secured insect-weight floating row cover or cheesecloth. Otherwise the following basic rules should help prevent mistakes. Details of instructions involving pollination are in *The New Seed Starters Handbook* and Suzanne Ashworth's *Seed to Seed*.

Hand-Pollinating. The beginning gardener can easily help the bees and the wind. Essentially you remove the petals from a male flower and press its central parts into those of a female flower. Often then you cover up the female flower so no unwanted pollen will be added to the mix. It's most frequently done with corn and squashes. The two books just mentioned will instruct you.

Insect Pollinated (Principally by Honeybees). Asparagus, basils, beans (lima, fava, and runners), broccoli, brussels sprouts, cabbage, carrots, cauliflower, celeriac, celery, Chinese cabbages and all mustards, collards, cucumbers, gourds, kale, kohlrabi, leeks, muskmelons, onions, parsley, parsnips, pumpkins/squashes, radishes, rutabagas, turnips. Note: Crosses will occur among and between varieties of celeriac and celery, broccoli and cauliflower, squashes and gourds, melons and cucumbers—for starters.

For saving seed of these plants, raise only one cultivar at a time or early and late so they will flower at different times. Otherwise separate similar cultivars by a tall barrier crop or 200 feet to prevent most cross-pollination—¼ mile for purity, 5 or more miles with some crops for absolute purity. So be aware of what your neighbors are growing!

Self-Pollinated (Will Usually Produce True Seeds). Beans (common snap and soy), eggplant, endive, lettuce, okra, peas, peppers, potatoes, salsify, scorzonera, tomatoes.

Insects and wind can cross-pollinate up to 20 percent of these plants, so for absolute purity of seed there must be a separation of 1 mile between okra varieties; ¹/₈ mile for eggplants and peppers; a tall barrier crop and 30 feet for peas; 10 feet for beans, lettuces, salsify, and scorzonera; 6 feet for tomatoes; and a few yards for endive. Or, before the blossoms open, thoroughly wrap the plants whose seeds you want to save in floating row cover, throw in a few flies (not bees; they would starve) to ensure pollination, then staple it closed and bury the edges. Remove the cover after fruits have set.

Will Cross with Wild Things—Caution! Carrots, lettuce, radishes, sunflowers. Remove the flowers of wild relatives within at least 200 feet—1,000 feet for sunflowers.

With beans, even when seeds of different cultivars may be placed reasonably close together, never plant two adjacent cultivars with seeds that look alike—plant black seeds next to white, small round next to large oval, and so forth. That way, should crossing occur, you'll see it. Don't plant two varieties of pole beans where they can intertwine, or the seeds will surely mix.

Corn and beans are among the few crops in which you can see changes in cross-pollinated seeds the first year. Changes generally show up in the fruit of the next generation.

Remember that it isn't just your garden you must take into consideration when you're trying to save pure seed. Unless you live a mile away from the nearest garden, insects and the wind will cross-pollinate your neighbors' seeds with yours as though they were your own. Ask what's being grown around you.

Wind Pollinated. Beets, corn, sorrel, spinach, Swiss chard. N.B. Chard will cross with beets; however, crosses between the two—for your own use—may not be objectionable.

For saving seed, raise only one cultivar of these plants at a time or early and late cultivars so they will flower at different times. With corn you can grow early and late cultivars if pollen formation on the early sort doesn't overlap with silk formation on the late. Because pollen grains of beets, sorrel, spinach, and chard are so fine, for absolute purity similar varieties must be separated by 1 mile—it can be ¹/₄ mile for the heavier pollen grains of corn. Or, before the blossoms open or the silks emerge, tightly wrap the flowers or ears of plants whose seeds you want to save in muslin or sturdy brown paper bags and hand-pollinate, then remove the cover after seeds have set.

QUAIL AND OTHER SKITTERING BIRDS

To keep out the heartless ravaging quail, a barrier of 1-inch chicken wire 3 feet high is best, with a cover on it, *well anchored in the soil so no one can dig under it.* For more, see Rabbits.

RABBITS

Watership Down will never allow the rabbit to be my enemy. Still. A barrier of floating row covers is too flimsy for a hungry rabbit. So I've cut big squares and rectangles of chicken wire, shaped them into boxy lids, and set them over all tender greens. A tedious business, but the wire can be flattened at summer's end, stored easily, then set out again in spring.

Do *not* spread used cat litter around the perimeter of your patch of lettuce or other vegetables to ward off rabbits. Cat litter may contain disease highly toxic to pregnant women. Who knows how long this might live in the soil? And rain and raking and hoeing could slop it over into where you grow food.

RACCOONS

*I*f you're tempted to catch a raccoon in one of the no-harm-done traps, thinking to relocate the critter, understand that raccoons are very social creatures, living together in families. In spring you might be taking a parent away from helpless offspring. No matter how destructive the raccoon may be, them's hard lines. If you decide to wait until autumn when the babies have been raised, thinking you could trap the whole family and move them, be aware that a trapped raccoon can go crazy. It might make a dreadful mess, it might scream bloody murder nonstop until released, and until then, with its intelligence and sharp claws, it might be extremely dangerous—and possibly rabid. Better to let the family live peaceably in your neighborhood and just be resourceful in beating the raccoons at their own game.

I've had 100 percent luck with *prickly* barriers. For several years now, corn grown surrounded by a thicket of great big scratchy leaves of pepo squash plants has never been touched. Tempting melons are covered with boughs of airy (so the sun and rain can reach them) thorny branches, and they're not bothered either. Simple as that.

But there's a more ancient solution: marking territory. Remembering that urine is sterile and contains valuable minerals for the soil may make it easier to embrace this solution. A spray bottle works perfectly. You can neutralize the acid on the ground with a cleansing spray of the hose. This method solved our most vexing raccoon problem, and it's worked for friends perfectly. I've since read letters in a gardening magazine that other gardeners have struck upon the same solution. Native Americans marked their territory against critters the same way.

RAISED BEDS

*B*uilding up your beds even a few inches above the surrounding pathways gives the plants better drainage, and the soil warms earlier in spring than it otherwise might. Root crops such as carrots and beets are partial to raised beds.

REPELLENTS

I could give you a laundry list of repellents steeped in garden tradition—not to mention kerosene, ammonia, and garlic juice. But none of them is foolproof. Which is to say that one day you'll come out and spray your sweet pepper seedlings with Tabasco and dishwashing soap (1 tablespoon each in a quart of water), and the plants will be beaming in the sun. But a day or two later you'll go into the garden and look around for your sweet peppers, and they'll be gone. I have bitter experience with this. Cage or fence what you want to harvest.

RODENTS

A chipmunk ran past me and dived into the unfurling curled mallow. Unlike the ground squirrels, they're charming. Chipmunks are the first to find what's best to eat.

Suddenly I found myself on the phone to our mountain park's biologist. What do these guys do in nature anyway? She said in the chain of life rodents mostly distribute seeds. Some, by churning up the soil, can check runoff. Others burrow under the soil; they help aerate it and increase fertility. And of course rodents are food for larger animals and birds of prey.

The family of cats dates back only 600,000 years, but the family of squirrels and mice, rats, and voles dates back 25 million years. Pocket gophers have been burrowing for 35 million years. Foxes, coyotes, hawks, and many of the owls have lived on this planet for 55 million years. This dance of life and death has been going on a breathtakingly long time.

A neighbor puts out poisoned grain to protect his crops from all the rodents that make their home near his garden. A question, long suppressed, asked itself in my head.

The answer was yes. A hawk eats a mouse fed the grain, and the poison stays in the bird's fatty tissue. Enough poisoned mice and it's good-bye, hawk. The hawk might have lived for 14 years. Owls can live for 68. Coyotes can live to be 10 years old, foxes 12 to 14 years, and mountain lions 19.

A chipmunk could get to be 8.

Oh, no, I thought. So we fence the plants I want to keep. Tree squirrels can leap 6 feet. Once they develop a taste for something, the plants must be caged in such small circles that the squirrel has no landing room and no launching room, and you hope he/she won't chance it. Mice can slip through all but ½-inch fencing. Against woodchucks, you'll need to bury fencing about 10 inches, bending it toward you, so they'll hit the fence when they dig.

When I have no choice but to dispatch something above ground, I use a trap since it's the most humane and that's the start and finish of the matter. I bait and set the trap with gloved hands so I don't foul it with my human scent. With gophers and voles, after many tries, we've had success burning cylinders of gas (from the hardware store) in their runs. This harms no one above ground, and I'm told the scent of one dead critter in the run can send others flying.

Ultimately, good hunting cats are the best control. They help protect not only what I grow but the world I live in.

ROOTBOUND/POTBOUND

Roots in a pot or other confined space go around the ball of earth in circles because they've no place else to go. Not good. When you're at the nursery and a plant looks disproportionately well developed for its container, check to see whether roots are growing out of the drainage hole. If not and you're still suspicious, be as bold as brass and lift the plant out of the pot just enough to see whether roots are wound around the soil. If they are and you don't have to buy the plant, don't. If they are and you do, take it home and plant it as soon as possible.

At planting time, try to gently unwind the roots. If that's impossible, use a sharp knife to cut three or four slashes down the length of the ball. Cut about an eighth as deep as the diameter—⅓ inch deep in a 3-inch pot. This seems drastic, but it will save the plant. At the same time, trim off some from the top of the plant about in proportion to the severity of binding of the roots. Thus energy can go into critical root making instead of more flowers or leaves or whatnot, which will come once the roots are again healthy.

RUST

Rust is a fungus. Beans are susceptible to it. Symptoms are small reddish to brown spots, then yellowing leaves that dry up and drop—sometimes it appears on the stem. Treat the moment symptoms appear. Dust with a sulfur fungicide (wear protective garb and wash all exposed skin thoroughly afterward). Repeat every seven to ten days until under control or three to four weeks before harvest. To help prevent rust, try not to wet the plants when watering—irrigate instead. If you must water overhead, do so before noon so the plants can dry before the cool of evening and do not handle the plants, which would spread the disease. Thoroughly wash anything you're going to eat that has been treated.

Salt-Tolerant Vegetables

*I*f you garden near the sea or in the desert or where soil is salty, moderately tolerant vegetables are zucchini and beets. Moderately sensitive vegetables (from least to most) are scallop summer squash, broccoli, tomatoes, cucumbers, spinach, celery, cabbage, potatoes, corn, fava beans, sweet potatoes, peppers, lettuce, radishes, and turnips. Sensitive vegetables (from least to most) are onions, carrots, and beans.

Sand, Sharp

*W*hen mixing it into soil for draining, this is the clean sand you'd buy for a child's sandbox, not sand from the beach, which would be salty. A builder's supply store can direct you to a source.

Seedlings, Care of

*I*f you're sprouting them indoors (which could be outdoors in fine weather, for that matter), after your seeds germinate, you'll either let them stay in their germinating medium until they have two true leaves or lift them out into something in which this can happen. The first true leaves are the second pair—you'll see the difference (the first pair are called *seed leaves*).

The reason to move a seedling from one container to the next is either the medium isn't nourishing enough (a soilless medium isn't) or the vessel isn't large enough or both. Always handle the seedling by its leaves, and gingerly. A chopstick is a splendid tool for all seedling operations. It can gently wriggle the roots free; it can support its bottom; it can make a hole for the roots to slip into in the new pot; it can tamp down the soil to force out any air pockets and to make good contact between roots and soil mix.

Now all you have to do is keep the mix lightly moist but never wet (tomatoes can be kept on the dry side). Use a light spray and water with tepid water if you can so it's less of a shock to the small plants. Give the seedlings bright light but not direct sunlight as much as possible all day or light from shop lamps. Give a splash of one-quarter strength solution of liquid kelp or seaweed once a week, then be faithful about hardening them off before planting.

Seeds, Germinating Indoors

I write this in February with packets in the oven with the pilot light and the door propped open and others under a lamp above the trash masher. What never ceases to surprise me are the few seedlings that invariably germinate way ahead of their siblings. For seed saving—the next generation—plants from these seeds must be tagged because they carry especially vigorous genes. Then it's interesting to watch the plants—*are* they more vigorous than everybody else? Wait and see.

Many seed packets give the percentage of germination; that way you can sow as many more as you'll need to make sure you have what you want.

In Styrofoam trays. These have small pyramidal cells sloping from wide at the top to narrow at the bottom so the soil mix won't fall out. They are open at the bottom, and so it's easy to push a finger up at transplanting time and scoot the little seedling out. Roots can grow as long as they please. These trays come in varying sizes, last for years, are lightweight, and enormously useful. The trays usually are fitted with bottoms and plastic lids, but if you ever see a product called Speedlings—no fussy bottoms or tops—buy those.

In a bubbling water bath. This is by far the easiest and most fascinating method of germinating seeds

As Soon as the Soil Can Be Worked . . .

How do you know when the soil can be worked? Here's the test (this is applicable straight through the season): Scoop up a handful of earth and squeeze it, then open your hand. If the earth stays compressed, the soil's too wet. Try again the next day. If the soil crumbles—like chocolate cake—put on your sweater and your gardening shoes.

Preparing the soil in spring for planting is one of the most important things you can do for your garden. No matter how humusy, friable, and loamy (i.e., perfect) your soil may be, it will always need attention. Most of us will want to dig in enriching amendments, such as manure and compost and rotted straw, and maybe bonemeal and some form of phosphorus, but even if you just need to wiggle the digging fork back and forth, loosening the soil, timing is everything. If you try to work wet soil, you'll compact it and your good intentions will be harmful.

This is also the time to sow or transplant the hardiest crops that need cool weather.

I've found. In the language of a botanist I consulted, it's called *imbibing* seeds. In a warm aerated bath, seeds absorb water and swell, thus enhancing the process of germination. I find it accelerates germination amazingly. Onion seeds sprouted in one day instead of ten.

The setup comes from the tropical fish store: one cheapest pump, one 25W thermostatic fish tank heater, one airstone, and as much tubing as you need to connect the airstone to the pump. My tank is a 2-gallon clear glass jar. The setup is a onetime purchase and costs about as much as one night for two of hamburgers and the movies.

Set the thermostatic heater to keep the water between 70°F and 72°F. Change the water every two days so bad bacteria and fungi won't have a chance to become so dominant that they could harm the seeds after they've been sown. You can use this water to moisten seedlings since it contains some encouraging growth elements emitted by the germinating seeds. *Be very careful that the replacing water is at the same temperature, or you'll break the heater (ask how I know).*

If you live in an area where power can fail, set the pump on a shelf above the bath—when power goes off and then comes back on (sometimes in the flicker of an eye), water can get sucked back into the pump and ruin it. Wrap the pump in a sound-absorbing cloth.

I tie the seeds in fine tulle netting from the dime store or in nylon stocking squares, secured with a rubber band that holds the plastic marking label with the seeds' name written on it in pencil.

I check for germination once a day, although some seeds germinate in hours. Usually it does no harm for the little tails to drift and dream in the water for an extra day if you're pressed for time—unless they're fast growing. Then the root threads will grow long through the netting, and you can have a devil of a time getting them out without breaking them off. When a rootlet does get caught in the mesh, use tweezers to coax it back through. If it breaks off, plant the seed anyway and hope the root will regenerate—some plants will (onions, corn); some won't (radishes).

But be sure you set the sprouted seeds in a growing container the day they've germinated. If the tails get too long, they'll be impossible to set correctly in the growing medium.

Unfortunately, you shouldn't germinate legumes with this method; they can emit elements that are inhibiting to the germination process—their own and everybody else's in the same water.

There's not as much oxygen in this bubbling bath as in the air, so if you find you've reached the time generally allowed and nothing's happening—I found this with marigolds—set them in soil and let them proceed on their own.

Here are times from seeds I've germinated this way. When I'm germinating a lot of seeds, I always sow the first to germinate, leaving the rest in the water bath. After another couple of days, when most have germinated, I remove the lot and sow them all, sprouted and unsprouted. Some numbers I can't give you, because nobody's written the standard germinating time. If the "Average Time" column is blank, it's because once I had a few seeds germinate I sowed everybody out. The eggplant, by the way, wasn't happy in the tub.

Plant	Shortest Time	Average Time	Traditional Time
	(Days)	(Days)	(Days)
basil	2	4	5–10
beets	3	4	5–10
celery, Chinese	6	8	21
celtuce		2	7–10
eggplant	9	12	5–10
fennel		3	10–14
garland chrysanthemum	2	10–14	10
kale	2		7–10
kohlrabi	2		10–14
leek, Chinese	2	13	10–14
mustards	1		9–14
nettles	6		12
onions	3		10
pak choi	2		7–10
parsley	6		12
peppers, hot	3	4	8
peppers, sweet	5	6	8–21
radish, autumn/winter		1	3–10
salsify	3	5	21
tomatoes	1	3	6–10

On a paper towel. An excellent method for medium to large seeds, especially those that need heat, because they can easily be kept in an oven with the pilot light (and door ajar), on top of the refrigerator or water heater, or in another toasty place. With an indelible marker, write the name of the cultivar at the top of a dry paper towel. Moisten the towel. Sprinkle seeds across the center, then fold the towel in thirds (two layers over them). Pat the layers so the seeds are firmed into place. Set in a zippered plastic bag, force out air, and seal. You can slip three or four packets into a quart-size bag. Write the contents on top of each bag. Every day, check for moisture. When the toweling seems dry, sprinkle with warm water, then reseal until sprouted. Do not leave damp paper towels over tiny germinating seeds for more than a few days—or they'll pop right through the moist paper and you'll lose them. They also can get moldy or light starved and leggy.

N.B. A 10X hand lens is most helpful. It's important to be able to tell whether what appears to be a sprout is a sprout or mold—mold can spread to nearby seeds and ruin the lot. A hand lens also will show when the seed coat has broken and it's time to turn the seed into a growing medium.

For seeds that may not be as fresh as they ought to be, a trick is to soak them in cool water for 24 hours and then germinate them as above.

On a saucer. An almost infallible method for tiny and/or temperamental seeds. Lay two thicknesses of barely moist paper towels over a saucer—it must not be wet, or the seeds will molder. Sprinkle on the seeds, giving each elbow room. Cover the saucer tightly with plastic wrap and set the dish in clear light—not direct sunshine, or the seeds will cook. Keep the towel moist. When your eye or hand lens tells you the seeds have germinated, sow them out at once—I touch the tip of a toothpick to my tongue and gingerly lift up each seed. Set tiny seeds on moistened soil mix, but do not cover them. Protect with plastic film or a sheet of glass. Mist the seeds and soil so they don't dry out—watering the container from beneath is the best method. Soon the roots will work down into the soil as if they'd always been there.

In flats or similar broad containers. Lay down ½ to 1 inch of sphagnum moss or spoiled straw or one or two thicknesses of newspaper lining the bottom. If you have and need one, arrange a heating cable on it.

The mix in the vessels must be soilless—pure, fine-grade vermiculite is ideal. Organic matter is busy decomposing and in the process can emit substances that inhibit the germination of seeds. Further, vermiculite is sterile, so it brings no inherent problems such as damping off. Half fine vermiculite and half peat is the choice of many gardeners.

When sowing in broad spaces, I've found it most intelligent to sow in rows. When it's important to keep cultivars from mixing (as when you're sowing five sorts of chili peppers in one flat), hold a length of cardboard on either side of the row you're sowing (a few blithe seeds will skip away no matter what you do). Overall, rows should be no closer than 2 inches apart. And although you can place small seeds as close as ⅛ inch apart in the row, the more I work with seeds, the farther apart I sow them. When the time comes to lift the seedlings out, unless each seedling's rootlets are free and clear, you risk drying out—if not damaging—*somebody's* threads every time you must untangle. Thinly sowing is also less wasteful, and seeds are becoming more and more expensive. Of course it depends on how much space you have and how many seeds you wish to germinate and on the size and dexterity of your fingers. But I would say the ideal distance between seedlings in a row is a minimum of 1 inch.

Never let the germinating medium dry out!

Temperature. When you're germinating seeds, whether outdoors in the ground or indoors in flats, what's important to understand about temperature and germination is that *temperature* refers to the germinating medium, not the air. Now it's early March as I write and I'm germinating dozens of sorts of seeds in my unheated cold frame. Inside it at night, the air temperature can dip as low as 30°F. Most seeds want to be kept around 70°F. Everything is germinating wonderfully despite the numbers in the air. A soil heating cable keeps them at 70°F or thereabouts. Seventy is a good average for most seeds, but optimum temperatures are given in the Sowing Chart.

All germinating seeds are either wrapped in plastic or covered with a sheet of glass to keep moisture in. With such a magnifying cover, they're kept out of direct sunlight, *very important*—an empty flat set on top of the seeds gives nice speckled shade. Direct sun would solarize them. At night I insulate the cold frame's soil with a double layer of wool blanket—those who want more heat first get layers of newspaper and then the blanket for extra warmth. Flats with seeds that like it cooler just get a few layers of row cover.

Now that I've done seeds in the cold frame essentially at 30°F air temperature, I would feel safe germinating seeds on the front stoop the same way—as long as I had that warming cable under the flats. So you can germinate seeds on the fire escape if that's the only place you've got.

For the next step, see Seedlings, Care of.

SEEDS: INSURANCE

*T*hompson's First Rule of Seed Insurance: If you expect to grow only one plant of a cultivar, begin by germinating six to eight seeds. Not only do some seeds not germinate, you'll also lose some in the growing process, or some will be spindly, and so forth. Lift out the four most splendid into soil blocks, Speedling cells, or small pots, transplant the noblest three of these into larger paper pots, harden them off, *then* see if you can plant two of the remaining. One of the two may well disappoint or be eaten, which leaves you with the single plant you'd planned for.

Thompson's Second Rule of Seed Insurance: Try to give at least one seedling of something you value to a friend who would be happy to add it to his/her garden. That way, should the unexpected happen, at least you'll be able to taste the corn or smell the basil you'd looked forward to.

A chipmunk once ate half a dozen of my tomato seedlings, but later a friend was able to give me samples of every one I'd lost grown from the seedlings I'd given him.

SEEDS, SAVING

*T*his is a meticulous matter, and you need guidance as to how to isolate, harvest, and treat your precious seeds. You might begin with the pamphlet written by Rob Johnston from Johnny's, *Growing Garden Seeds*. Nancy Bubel's *The New Seed Starter's Handbook* and Marc Rogers' *Saving Seeds* will contribute more excellent information, and Suzanne Ashworth's remarkable work, *Seed to Seed*, is the last word on the subject.

To give you an idea of how it's done, from open-pollinated cultivars, decide on the healthiest plant or plants as early in the season as you can. Let's use tomatoes as an example, which don't cross-pollinate and need only about 10 feet between plants for pure seed.

Tag tomatoes with the qualities you value most—the first tomato to ripen, an uncommonly tasty or fruitful plant, or a plant that's still fruiting well into October. When ripe, crush the fruit in a glass, freeing the seeds. Keep at around 70°F and stir twice daily while the pulp ferments. (Clearly, if you're saving seed from assorted tomatoes, dip the stirrer in water each time and make absolutely sure it doesn't drop seeds from one glass into the next. And be sure to identify the seeds in each glass so there'll be no mix-up.) In three days (if the temperature is 80°F—less desirable—process after two days), add a few inches of water, stir, then let the viable seeds settle to the bottom while the no-good seeds float to the top. Pour off the liquid with its top seeds and pulp and repeat until the remaining good seeds are clean. Dry on paper towels; when they're bone dry, wrap them to store.

SEEDS: SOWING DEPTH

*T*he basic rule is to plant seeds to a depth of three times their thickness. Very tiny seeds usually should not be covered but pressed into the soil to make contact with it.

SEEDS, STORING

Wrap seeds in paper towels in a zippered plastic bag. Drop some powdered milk or silica gel from a camera shop in the bag as a dessicant. Close, forcing out air. Tuck in a jar, close tightly, label, and keep in a cool, dark, dry place.

SEEDS, WINNOWING

Essentially a matter of letting the wind take the chaff while your seeds stay in place. Try lots of blowing on them or a hair dryer set at no heat.

SHADE, BRIGHT/HIGH

Our black oak is 100 feet tall, but the first branches start 25 feet off the ground. The oak leaves are airily set on the branches, and the branches are airily set on the tree, nothing like a dense conifer. So even though the onions and lettuces growing at the foot of the tree aren't in full sun, there's nurturing light for their needs. With many crops (see the box on Bright Shade) bright light is a good substitute for full sun, and in a pinch you can rotate crops under it and they will grow decently. Or at least try.

SHADE TOLERANT

The term is elusive, but I reckon it between full shade and half-day sun. All you can do is try plants there and see what flourishes—probably more than you'd imagine.

SHELTERED PLACE

Shelter is the same for a plant as for us—respite from stress. Some plants can't deal with wind, so you shelter them with windbreaks with taller plants or a screen of some sort. Shelter can mean a warm wall at a frail plant's back or a cool place in a torrid garden.

SLUGS AND SNAILS

First thing is to check every plant you bring into the garden for slugs and snails. I had none until I brought home a six-pack of zinnias with slugs hiding in it.

In beds where you can, lay planks down near anything tender and succulent. You can also set empty turned-over berry boxes. Toward sunrise, the slugs will seek the shelter of the underside of the board or the boxes. Then turn these traps over and plop! Don't mash slugs in place, since eggs might be dispersed.

Physical barriers, such as ashes, crushed eggshells, sand, diatomaceous earth, and bonemeal, are a good idea—anything that makes it uncomfortable or lethal for the bodies to glide over. The trouble is, once wet, the irritating factor in these barriers is largely diminished. I've read that salt (which dissolves the creatures) sprinkled on petroleum jelly slathered on a plank (placed as just described) is a one-two knock-out punch. There are also copper strips that you can set into the ground around a slug-free area—the slugs' surface reacts with the copper, and they die.

What I do, mostly, is patrol places that have signs of having been nibbled—irregular holes in tender leaves and silvery trails leading up to the plant. I carry a jar of soapy water and simply scoop the critter off the leaf with a spoon and drop it into the jar, telling it I hope it will come back as a butterfly. Mostly, slugs and snails emerge in the dark of the night, so going out with a flashlight is very efficient. By day they can often be found close to their feeding ground in a shelter of thick cool growth—mine congregate beneath the catmint.

A saucer of ¹/₂ inch of beer—either lager or nonalcoholic—is an old-fashioned bait. Set the top level with the ground. The creatures are attracted to it, and then they drown, not an unhappy end.

If you're desperate, you may have to resort to covered bait holders (available at the nursery). Fill them with metaldehyde—I've found the product That's It works best. It's not organic, but if it doesn't get into the soil, it's safe. You must keep it from pets, of course, and children. A good time to deslug and desnail the garden is in early spring or whenever you don't have edible plants in the ground yet. Set the traps close to thickets of underbrush. Just throwing the bait onto the ground will leach the poison into the soil, so never do that.

SOIL

Lean and rich. Occasionally you'll read about rich and lean soils. What are they?

I just happened to be looking at a photograph of an enormous field of lavender in France. The flowers are healthy as can be and intensely royal purple. The soil between rows is rosy crushed rock. Hills rise behind the field, so we know that the rock wasn't carried in as a mulch; the field is made of crushed rock that has been sloughed off the hills over the millennia. In this case, the word *soil* is used generically as the planting medium—there's very little earth in this soil. But lavender has a Spartan heart—it grows most fervently in lean, hot, dry, rocky soil in full sun.

Lean soil, by definition, is relatively infertile—retains a small amount of nutrients. Clearly plants like lavender, being lean machines themselves, thrive in such soil. Lean soil is usually on the rocky or sandy side, since water leaches out the nutrients as it flows through the spaces—and the water itself rushes through, so little lasts. The densely packed particles of clay soils, by contrast, cling to their nutrients and don't let go. So clay soils are more often liable to be rich.

However, in cold winter climates, an advantage of rocky soil is that each little rock is a solar collector. Gravelly soil can warm up dramatically in spring and bring crops to fruition considerably faster than clay soil. Bear this in mind if your soil is gravelly. Of course you don't have to let your rocky soil stay lean; you can always amend it with organic matter.

The quintessential rich soil is fertile soil—where the millennia have gently laid down layer upon layer of decomposed matter, rain and wind have sifted soil between the layers, and what is offered the gardener is soil that's humusy, nurturing, and friable. Many plants need this to thrive, but there are some who will pour their energy into making leaves rather than concentrating on fruits if the soil is too rich.

Fertile soil is not necessarily on the acid or alkali side, nor is one side of the pH scale more nurturing than the other. It all depends on what a given plant needs.

Loam. The nirvana one wants one's soil to achieve is called *loam.* Loam is part clay, part sand, part

Bright Shade

Vegetables grown for their fruits must be given priority in the sun. Vegetables and herbs grown for their leaves and roots can be grown in bright shade.

I have had experience growing all of these with a maximum of three hours' sun—some in just high shade. As you'll read in the entries on beets and celtuce, for example, the crop wasn't as vigorous as it would have been with more sun. But I'd rather have a smaller version of something than none at all, which is the option when space is limited.

Vegetables:

arugula	*cresses*	*miner's lettuce*
beets	*endive (spring sown)*	*mizuna*
burdock	*escarole*	*mustard greens*
cabbage	*fennel*	*nettles*
carrots	*garland chrysanthemum*	*New Zealand spinach*
celery (leaf)	*green-in-the-snow mustard*	*pak choi*
celtuce	*Jerusalem artichoke*	*perpetual beets*
chard	*kale (all sorts)*	*radishes*
chicory (red	*kohlrabi*	*sorrel*
sugarloaf)	*leeks*	*spinach*
Chinese cabbages	*lettuce*	*tendergreen*
collards	*Malabar spinach*	*turnips*
corn salad	*mallow*	

Herbs:

anise hyssop	*hyssop*	*rosemary*
borage	*lovage*	*salad burnet*
chervil	*marjoram*	*savory (summer and*
Chinese chives	*mints*	*winter)*
chives	*parsley*	*tarragon*
ginger	*perilla*	*thyme*

Fruits:

rhubarb	*strawberry (alpine)*

Edible Flowers:

calendula	*pansies*	*violets*
Johnny-jump-ups	*sunflower (common)*	
nasturtium	*violas*	

silt (mineral material whose particles, larger than clay and smaller than sand, cling to moisture), and part organic matter.

Sandy loam is half to three-quarters sand, the balance clay and silt. Sandy loam is fertile soil and has the advantage of warming quickly—invaluable where it's essential to get crops in the ground early in spring.

Clay loam has 20 to 30 percent clay and proportions of the balance determine how easy it is to cultivate the soil. In retaining moisture and nutrients, clay loams can be fine soil for growing, although they may be difficult to work.

SOIL BLOCKS

*S*oil blocks and paper pots are two of a kitchen gardener's most valuable tools. A soil blocker takes a moist soil mix and compresses it into a small, sturdy block. Set a seed (or two or three or six) in the small indentation in the center of the block, and for some reason the seed will grow uncommonly happily. In fact, if you set six onion seeds or four beet seeds into the dimple, you'll have more vigorous onions and beets than were you to plant them separately. The roots of soil-block-grown seedlings seem to be maximally strong—the roots hold the block together. And when you transplant, there's no shock to the roots because they aren't aware of having been transplanted.

Send for a $1^3/_4$- by $1^3/_4$-inch soil blocker through a catalog. This size makes four blocks of a universally useful size, considered the equivalent of 2-inch pots.

The thing to do is to cadge a few deep flats from the nursery, then line the bottoms with a couple of thicknesses of newspaper. Mix the soil for the blocks in a dishpan or wheelbarrow. The pamphlet that comes with the blocker will give you a mix, but every gardener who knows better has his or her own. I use one part garden soil, one part sifted compost (or two parts good soil if I'm out of compost), one part commercial potting mix, one part fine vermiculite, and for every cubic foot of this mixture I stir in a handful of Kellogg's all-purpose organic fertilizer. Then add water: the mix must be wet enough so you could turn it into a mud pie.

I germinate small batches of seeds in the soil blocks, and the booklet will tell you how to do that. But with large amounts I germinate them in the water bath, then I use tweezers to set germinated seeds into the dimple in the center of the block, sprout side down. I sprinkle over just enough potting mix to cover the seeds, mist with water from a spray bottle, and cover the flat with plastic film. I set the flat on a sheet of heavy foil in a bright spot next to a window that gets a few hours of sun each day. Watering must be done daily by a spray bottle to keep the blocks intact until roots can bind the soil together. After the first week, add just enough fish emulsion to the water to color it—by then the plants will need more nourishment than they receive from the soil.

Transplant your soil-block seedlings into the ground or into a larger paper pot when the appropriate size for the plant. They can, however, hang around in the blocks for weeks and weeks, as long as you nourish them with half-strength fish emulsion.

When you place multiseeded blocks in the garden, you must allow each plant as much space as if it were planted separately.

SOIL, WELL-DRAINED

*I*t seems that everywhere you look in this book, the plant requires "well-drained soil." If, after a rain, there are no lakelets in your beds that take days to percolate into the soil, your soil is well drained. If, on the other hand, not only is the water slow to go away but your plants never seem to be truly vigorous and fruitful even after it does—if you have dense clay soil or you hit water when you dig a foot down—you must address the problem.

If it's the soil, wait until it's dry enough to work, then dig in a mort of humus—compost, packaged soil amendments from the nursery, old straw, whatever you can throw in that will add porosity. Add earthworms by the barrelful. If it's a rocky subsoil that plagues you, you'll have to put in a drain or two or three. Your garden won't be the only one with the problem, so ask the local nursery or hardware store to recommend someone who can advise you what works.

Plants in waterlogged soil must feel desperate to breathe sweetly.

SOLARIZING THE SOIL

While seeds are germinating indoors, it's always a good idea to create a misty, moist atmosphere by enclosing the flat or milk carton or pot in light plastic—as long as air can get in so you don't risk damping off. By extension, it would seem intelligent to do the same for seeds germinating in the ground. In fact this spring, when I read somewhere that one should cover germinating seeds with plastic, I bought a roll of clear 4-mil plastic—beautiful heavy stuff that, with care, would last a few seasons. I laid a sheet out over my bed of mixed potherbs, over my bed of mixed radishes, beets, and carrots, over the sweet corn interplanted with corn salad, over some Burgundian mustard, and over some Hopi lima beans.

Nothing came up.

Yes, the plastic kept the earth moist longer than earth exposed. And yes, when the vibrant spring sunshine emerged, all the seeds, little and big, baked in their plastic-covered ovens.

I imagine what I read was a reference to a light film of kitchen wrap or an airy tunnel or cloche of plastic. I lost a fortune in seeds and time to my stupidity.

However, that's how I stumbled on the simple method of killing weed seeds called *solarization*. In spring, do just what I did with soil containing pesky weeds. You won't have any volunteer calendulas come back in the patch, but you won't have any weeds either. Just remember that weeds *away from plants* can attract beneficial insects, so don't sterilize your whole garden!

SUCCESSION SOWING

This is principally for vegetables that don't store for any length of time or that taste their best fresh. The idea is to sow the crop over the season at intervals, just enough so the vegetable is harvested at its peak, with no waste.

Succession sowing has changed somewhat now that there are, in many perishable vegetables, cultivars that mature extra-early, midseason, and late. You can sow the three sorts of seeds all at once in spring and pick until frost.

TILLING (ROTOTILLING) THE SOIL

I have a small rototiller, which is marvelous when I want to break new ground. But Peter Chan makes an interesting point in *Better Vegetable Gardens the Chinese Way* (Garden Way Publishing, 1985): "The tiller works the ground very fast, but it throws insects and fungus and weed roots all over the garden." It also goes only about 4 inches deep, whereas 8 inches is what's needed. On the other hand, when you are doing the gardening yourself and *must* get the soil turned over to some degree, a small light rototiller is a godsend. It also works in crop residues easily in autumn.

Still, the goal is to establish permanent beds that can be turned over quickly with a spade each spring.

TOADS

Toads are magnificent creatures and they eat thousands of bad bugs. If I could have a bevy of them, I would, but they must come to you. To welcome them, have a watering hole and a sheltered place for them to snooze out of the sun.

VERMICULITE

Inflated mica that's sterile, this product is useful for germinating seeds because it weighs next to nothing—like perlite, a bag as big as a child can be hoisted by that child. It's a very nurturing medium for tender seeds, and vermiculite holds water well.

VERTICAL GROWING

Of course pole beans, peas, cucumbers, and tomatoes are routinely grown upward. But if your space is limited—even if it's not—experiment with growing melons and vining squashes on trellises or fences or poles. It's airy up there—less problem with mildew—and the sun can strike the fruits more evenly than when they're on the ground. Make slings of soft cotton rags to support the fruit.

Just be sure the netting is strong enough that it doesn't collapse under the weight of the vines once the fruit is in full fig. Get netting that has large enough spaces so you can put your hand through to the other side.

Do watch out that the vines don't get *too* warm against a wall that reflects light and heat—leaves can burn, and fruit can shrivel, not what you had in mind.

WATER

All things being equal (which they never are), non-drought-tolerant plants in the warm growing season need to be given a weekly average of 1 inch of water. That much will seep down about 4 to 6 inches in clay soil and 12 inches in sandy soil, with loams somewhere in between. But sandy soils cannot accept more than ¾ inch of water at one time before nutrients start leaching out, so you have to water them more often. One inch of water is 4½ gallons per square yard of surface area. To find out how much that is from your garden hose, turn the hose into a bucket with the flow you usually use, time 1 minute, then measure the water. With a sprinkler, set a few jars around, time 15 minutes, then measure. Drip emitters usually give 1 gallon per hour. Calculated for soil that still contains moisture (not too wet, not too dry), 1 inch of water should moisten to a depth of several inches, and 1½ inches will go down about as deep as most feeder roots.

GALLONS OF WATER

AMOUNT OF WATER	PLANTS SET INCHES APART								
	9	10	12	14	16	24	30	36	42
1 inch	1 ⅛	1 ¼	1 ½	1 ¾	2	3	3 ¾	4 ½	5 ¼

The following measures are scant:

1 ½ inches	1 ⅔	2	2 ¼	2 ⅔	3	4 ½	5 ⅔	6 ¾	8

Sending water down a foot or more even when plants are young isn't as harebrained as it sounds. Although roots aren't there yet, they'll quickly start diving for the water. That's why digging in organic matter a couple of shovelfuls deep is of such enormous benefit. Well-aerated, well-drained soil uses water to best advantage, and the deeper the soil, the deeper the roots, the less the roots are at the mercy of drying influences on the surface. In the stony Médoc, I've read, roots of the vines go down 30 feet, and whether there are showers or dry spells up above, the roots placidly, continually, send up everything the legendary wine grapes need.

A drip system is the most economical way to water. It directs the water precisely where it's needed, and evaporation and runoff are nil. But in drought years hereabouts, our drip system becomes a nightmare because every thirsty critter—from bluebird to coyote—nips into the line. I finally put out pans of water for them, which cut down on the drip-nipping substantially. Old-fashioned hose irrigation is the next most saving of water. But last year, with the drip system in tatters, I had no time to dig trenches, so I attached a sprinkler head on a stake to the garden hose and watered early in the morning. The sprinkler had merits. Even though water was lost through evaporation, parched leaves got relief, and the mist created a mini-climate that was respite for plants under stress.

Critical periods of watering. Although most cropping plants need an even supply of water from start to finish, many only need consistent watering during certain periods of growth.

Beans: pollination, then pod development
Broccoli: as seedlings, then head formation through enlargement
Cabbage: head formation through enlargement
Carrots: the first three-fourths of life
Corn: tasseling through ear filling
Eggplant: flowering through harvest
Onions: bulb enlargement
Peas: flowering, then pod development
Potatoes: from formation of tubers
Squashes, summer and winter: bud development through flowering
Tomatoes: pollination through enlargement
Turnips: root development through enlargement

WEEDS

Never throw weeds into the compost unless you're sure they haven't gone to seed. Never let weeds go to seed if you can possibly help it.

It's best to pull weeds after watering—or after a rain—and in the heat of the day. The earth will be soft and will surrender the roots gracefully. Get in the habit of pulling weeds the moment you first see them. I've learned from painful experience that you can't let weeds go, or they'll take over the garden. Pull weeds in the heat of the day so the roots will wither, or the roots might reconnect with the soil.

The best tool I've found for weeding, based on the Dutch hoe, is the so-called hula or scuffle hoe. Although some weeds must be pulled up by their roots, many weeds are done in by cutting them off below the soil. It's worth running the hoe through your weeds a few times—you'll find out soon enough which those are.

Mulch, remember, saves most weeding problems. Also read about Solarizing the soil.

WINDBREAKS

I've gardened in windy places, and it was as frustrating as gardening with too little water. Besides keeping the wind under control, windbreaks are also helpful in preserving moisture in plants and in the soil. The wind must be able to sift through the break—if it hits a solid wall, it may break up into countercurrents that can be more damaging than before.

In its catalog, Northwoods Nursery recommends three rows as the most effective windbreak, using both evergreen and deciduous plants. Its suggestion for the first row against the prevailing wind is a dense 6- to 8-foot shrub. Next comes a medium or tall deciduous tree. The third row can be taller evergreen trees. Ideally the three rows should be about 16 feet apart—the first two rows 3 feet apart and the second and third rows 9 to 10 feet apart.

In a smaller space, bamboo or smaller deciduous shrubs are best. For a single row, plant shrubs 2 feet apart.

WINTER

*I*f you live where the ground freezes and where plants go dormant in winter, don't encourage succulent new growth that will get zapped with the first killing frost. Stop fertilizing and water sparingly a good month before frost is expected in your garden—partly because the stress of little water hastens the ripening and concentrates the flavor of almost-ripe vegetables and melons, and partly because water makes tissues succulent and therefore vulnerable to frost.

As nights get colder and colder and the traditional date of autumn's first frost approaches, have coverings ready for the beans, tomatoes, peppers, eggplants, potatoes, basils, and anything else tender: floating row covers, portable cloches, sheets, thermal blankets, cardboard boxes, whatever.

Many annual vegetable crops are so hardy they can be sheltered in a cold frame and harvested through winter when the air is as cold as −20°F. Usually seeds of hardy crops are sown between late August and mid-September. Of course in frigid climates, you should always experiment with overwintering, trying now this sheltered spot, now that.

The surest winter crops in cold climates are arugula, baby beets, baby carrots, Chinese celery, chard, Chinese artichokes, loose-headed Chinese cabbages, Sugar Loaf chicory, corn salad, collards (if they don't get too tall), dandelions, endive, escarole, garlic, green-in-the-snow mustard, kales (including ornamental), kohlrabi, komatsuna, leeks, lettuces, miner's lettuce, mizuna, scallions, rosette pak choi, parsley, baby parsnips, radishes, sorrel, spinach, and baby turnips. Don't forget there's thyme and sage for picking from under the snow.

If you find you can't harvest these crops, then be assured that although growth will slow or stop, come spring they'll put on the steam and you can harvest them early.

Our great ally in a frozen winter is snow, which blankets the garden with its sheltering warmth. Depending of course on how hard the ground has frozen, a garden covered in snow all winter will be perky come spring. Straw and salt hay (more common to the East) and autumn leaves are great mulches. They provide a cover that lets air and rain through, but they blunt the effect of killing cold. As soon as the soil starts to freeze in autumn, lay on a foot or two of this loose mulch wherever it's critical—wet leaves down well. Flakes of hay can be used to insulate the cold frame, sides and even the top, though it's a nuisance to pull them on and off.

Where the ground isn't frozen all winter, you can have fun with sheet composting.

Watering in winter? In the Midwest, they worry about being waterlogged. On our dry mountain, we need to amend the rainfall. Some plants will need a little water; some will want to curl up and rest. You must watch closely and see who needs water when. Plants usually protect themselves by going dormant when it's very cold. In the cold frame plants need little or no water from November through January, but feel the soil from time to time. Don't let friends grow weak because they're not "supposed" to need water.

To protect a vulnerable plant that you can't bring indoors, surround it with hay bales if that's practical and lay some sort of old window arrangement on top to let light in. Or you can swathe it in a floating row cover—I do that with our fig tree. A cage of 1-inch chicken wire with at least 6 inches to spare on all sides and above it works well—how much space you'll need around the plant depends on how cold it's going to get and how vulnerable the plant is. Fill the sides with straw or leaves. If it's going to get bitter cold, wrap the package in something waterproof like tar paper. On fine days, take off the wrapping and let air in, but don't forget to put it back.

If a plant appears to have been leveled by hard frost, very often the roots are still viable, even when the leaves are dead. Don't toss the plant out until you've given it a chance to revive—at least a month after it's unwrapped in spring.

For more about winter growing, Eliot Coleman lives and gardens in Maine, and his *Four-Season Harvest* is inspiring. Anne Halpin offers another view of winter in *The Year-Round Vegetable Gardener*. Binda Colebrook's *Winter Gardening in the Maritime Northwest* is excellent for that cool, moist part of the world. *The Harrowsmith Northern Gardener* by Jennifer Bennett is rich in information about winter gardening particularly in Alaska and Canada.

WINTERING INDOORS

Around the middle of October, I gently dug up my musky-scented Cleveland sage and put it in a 10-inch pot to winter over indoors. As vigorous as sages are, this poor fellow had the vapors every day in the warm Indian summer weather, but at night he'd perk up and feel better. I set him in the coolest, shadiest spot in the greenhouse, kept him refreshed with spritzing when I could, gave him a comforting dose of kelp solution a few days into his ordeal, and inside of a week he was his old upright self day *and* night. The basils, lavenders, and geraniums I potted up never skipped a beat, but I still kept them out of direct sun for a few days so they could catch their breath. It's the reverse of hardening off. A watchword of the garden is *gradual*.

WOOD ASHES

Ashes of hardwoods are preferred as a good source of potash/potassium for your garden. Just be sure not to let them get rained on, or the potassium will be leached away. And don't use too much—a light veil will suffice.

ZONES, HARDINESS

*D*on't forget there are microclimates everywhere—you live in one. But generally speaking, these zones are immensely helpful in determining what will and what won't grow in your garden.

USDA PLANT HARDINESS ZONES

ZONE	AVERAGE ANNUAL MINIMUM TEMPERATURE (°F)
1	Below $-50°$
2	$-50°$ to $-40°$
3	$-40°$ to $-30°$
4	$-30°$ to $-20°$
5	$-20°$ to $-10°$
6	$-10°$ to $0°$
7	$0°$ to $10°$
8	$10°$ to $20°$
9	$20°$ to $30°$
10	$30°$ to $40°$
11	$40°$ and above

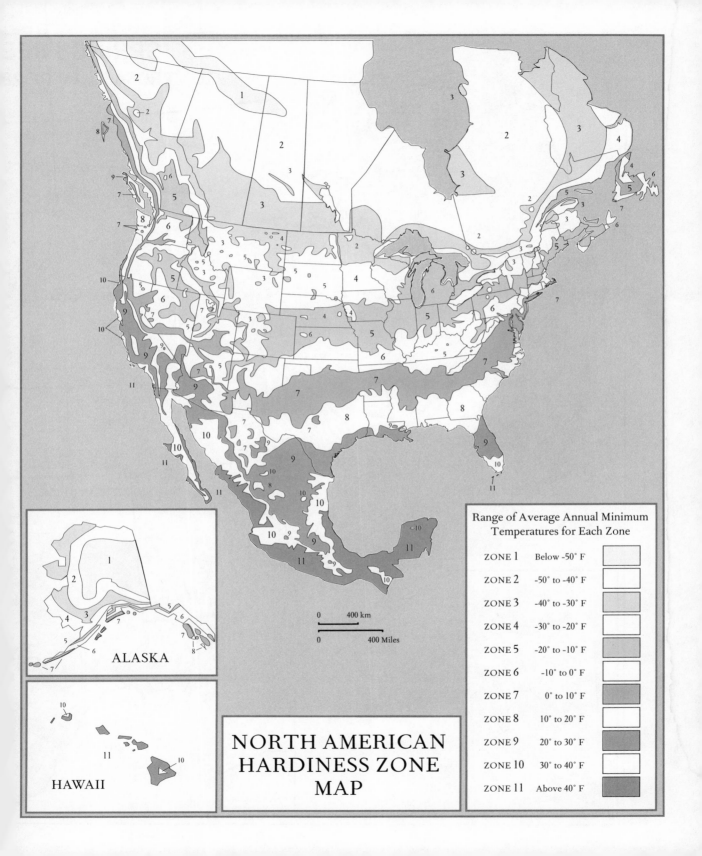

NORTH AMERICAN
HARDINESS ZONE
MAP

ALASKA

HAWAII

Range of Average Annual Minimum
Temperatures for Each Zone

ZONE 1   Below -50° F

ZONE 2   -50° to -40° F

ZONE 3   -40° to -30° F

ZONE 4   -30° to -20° F

ZONE 5   -20° to -10° F

ZONE 6   -10° to 0° F

ZONE 7   0° to 10° F

ZONE 8   10° to 20° F

ZONE 9   20° to 30° F

ZONE 10   30° to 40° F

ZONE 11   Above 40° F

0   400 km

0   400 Miles

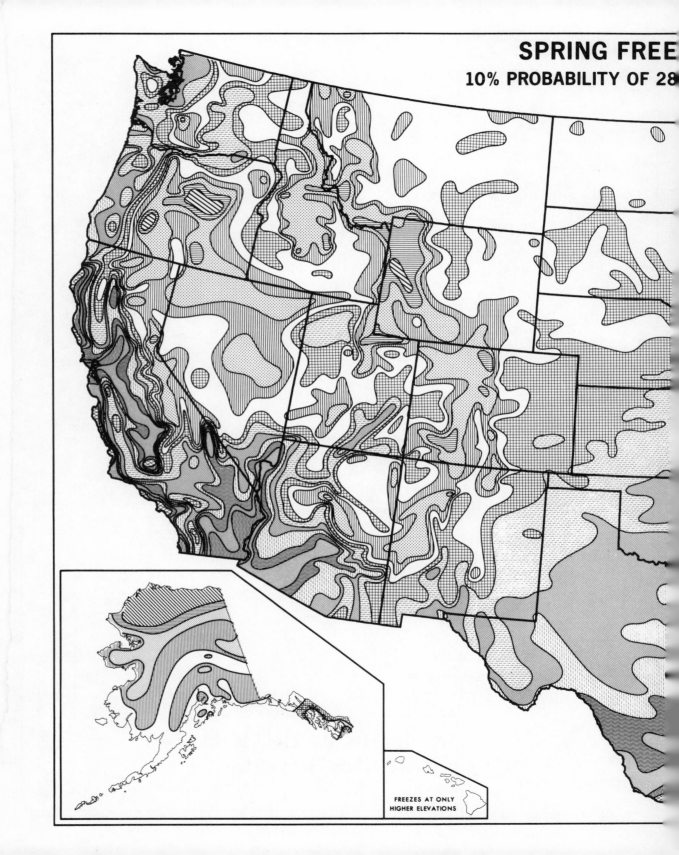

SPRING FREE

10% PROBABILITY OF 28

FREEZES AT ONLY
HIGHER ELEVATIONS

OCCURRENCE
R LESS ON A LATER DATE

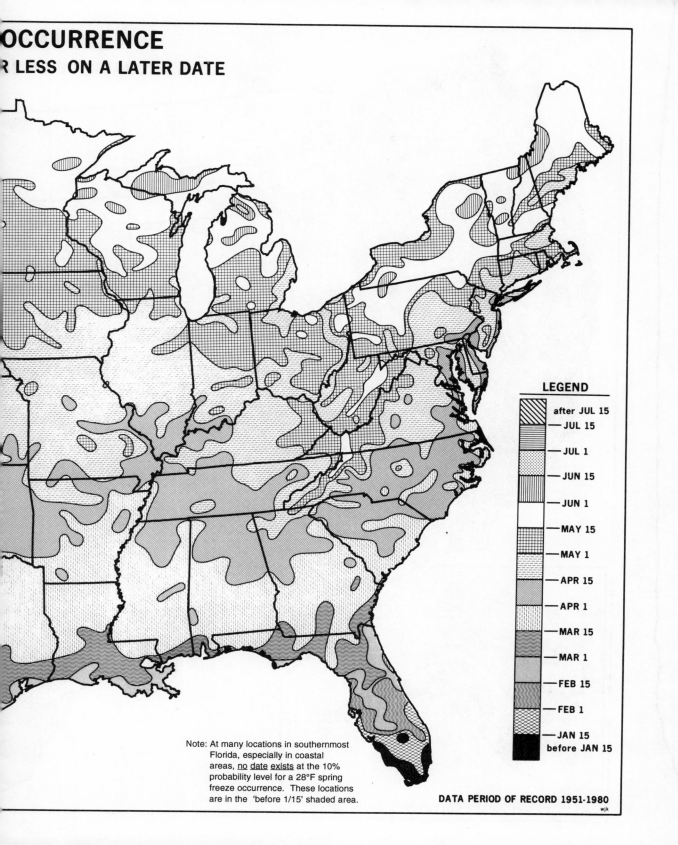

LEGEND

- after JUL 15
- JUL 15
- JUL 1
- JUN 15
- JUN 1
- MAY 15
- MAY 1
- APR 15
- APR 1
- MAR 15
- MAR 1
- FEB 15
- FEB 1
- JAN 15
- before JAN 15

Note: At many locations in southernmost Florida, especially in coastal areas, no date exists at the 10% probability level for a 28°F spring freeze occurrence. These locations are in the 'before 1/15' shaded area.

DATA PERIOD OF RECORD 1951-1980

wjk

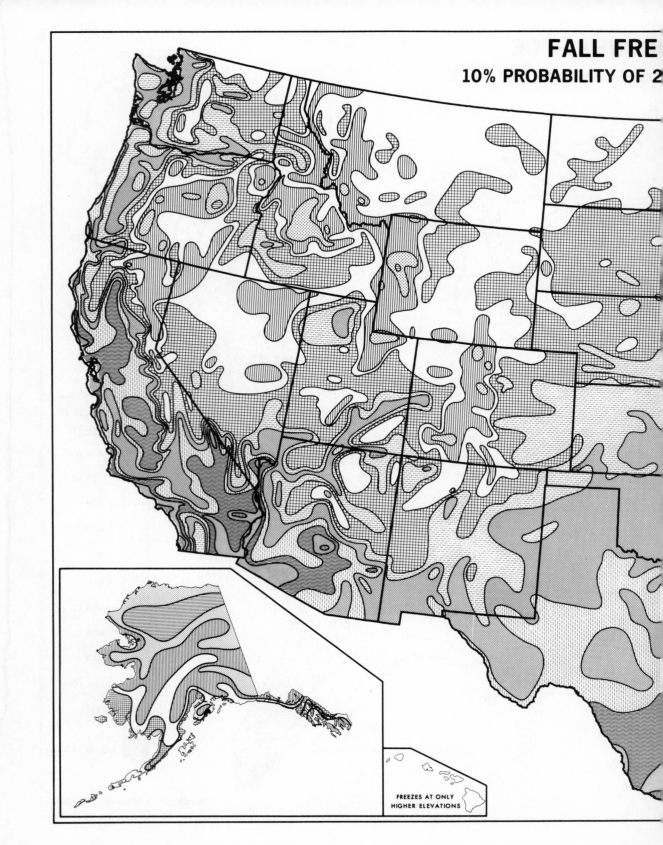

FALL FRE

10% PROBABILITY OF 2

FREEZES AT ONLY
HIGHER ELEVATIONS

OCCURRENCE

R LESS ON AN EARLIER DATE

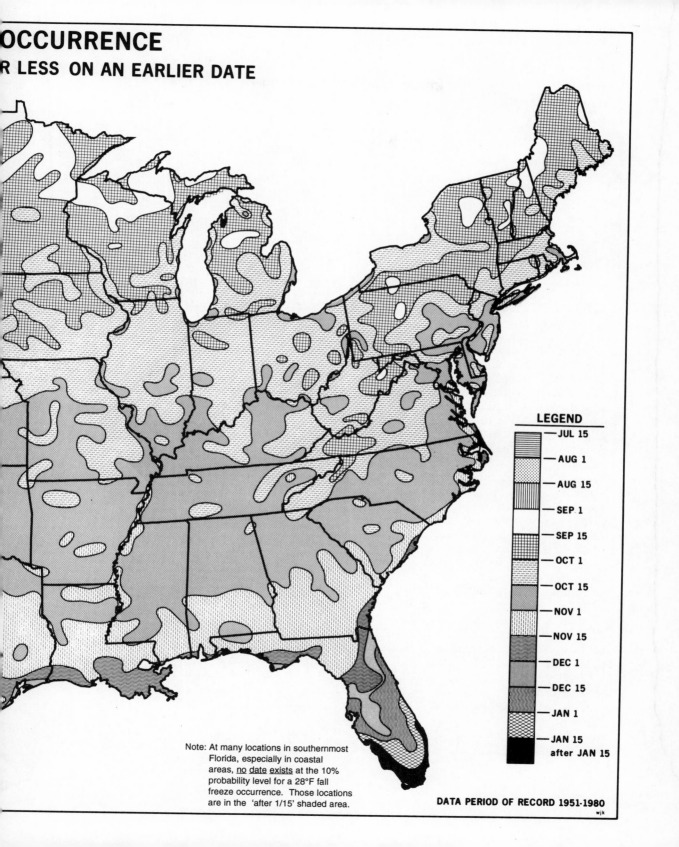

LEGEND

- JUL 15
- AUG 1
- AUG 15
- SEP 1
- SEP 15
- OCT 1
- OCT 15
- NOV 1
- NOV 15
- DEC 1
- DEC 15
- JAN 1
- JAN 15
  after JAN 15

Note: At many locations in southernmost
Florida, especially in coastal
areas, no date exists at the 10%
probability level for a 28°F fall
freeze occurrence. Those locations
are in the 'after 1/15' shaded area.

DATA PERIOD OF RECORD 1951-1980

wjk

CHART 1: PLANNING

C=some cultivars; H=half-hardy;
S=in hot, sunny climates; V=vine

PLANT NAME	THE PLANT: hardy	Tolerates: drought	poor soil¹	heat	shade	Optimal soil: rich	moist	Optimal sun: ◑	○	Height: under 12"	12–24"	24–36"	over 36"	Flower color: greenish	white to yellow	pink to crimson	orange to red	blue to purple
Artichoke	H					•	•		•				•					•
Cardoon	H	•	•	•		•	•		•				•					•
Asian Greens																		
Chinese cabbage, headed	H			•		•	•		•		•				•			
Chinese cabbage, loose-headed	H			•		•	•	•	•		•				•			
Chinese kale	H			•		•	•		•		•				•			
Choy sum/purple flowering						•	•		•		•				•			•
Garland chrysanthemum	H	•		•		•	•	S	•			•			•			
Komatsuna	•			•		•	•		•		•				•			
Mizuna	•			•	•	•	•		•	•					•			
Pak choi/Flowering pak choi	H			•		•	•	•	•		•				•			
Rosette pak choi	•					•	•	•	•	•					•			
Tendergreen	H	•				•	•		•		•				•			
Asparagus	•	•				•			•				•					
Beans																		
Adzuki		•	•			•			•		•				•			
Butter/Lima/Sieva bush			•			•			•		•				•			
Butter/Lima/Sieva pole			•			•			•				V		•			
Chick-Pea/Tepary		•	•			•			•		•				•			•
Common/Flageolet/Hort. bush		C		C		•	•		•		•				•			•
Common pole				C		•	•		•				V		•			•
Cowpea/Blk-Eye/South. pea bush		•	•	•	•	•		•	•	•	•				•			•
Favas	H	•				•		S	•						•			•
Lentils	•	•				•			•	•					•		•	•
Runner						•		•	•				V		•	•		
Soybeans			•	•		•			•		•						•	•
Winged peas	H					•			•		•						•	
Yardlong			•	•		•			•				V					
Beets/Mangel	•	C			•	•	•		•		•			•				
Broccoli, Romanesco/Sprouting	H	C			•	•	•	•	•			•			•			
Brussels Sprouts	•						•		•			•			•			
Burdock, Great	•				•	•	•		•				•	•				
Cabbage, early	H	C			•		•		•		•				•			

C=some cultivars; H=half-hardy;
S=in hot, sunny climates; V=vine

| | THE PLANT | | | | | THE LANDSCAPE | | | | | | | | | | | | |
| | Tolerates | | | | | Optimal soil | | Optimal sun | | Height | | | | Flower color | | | | |
PLANT NAME	hardy	drought	poor soil¹	heat	shade	rich	moist	◑	○	under 12"	12–24"	24–36"	over 36"	greenish	white to yellow	pink to crimson	orange to red	blue to purple
Late cabbage	H				•		•		•	•					•			
Ornamental cabbage/Kale	H				•	•	•	•	•	•	•				•			
Carrots	H	C			•		•		•	•					•			
Cauliflower	H				•		•		•	•					•			
Celeriac	H				•		•		•	•					•			
Celery, Chinese/Trenching	H			•	•	•	•	•	•			•			•			
Leaf celery	H			•	•	•	•	•	•						•			
Celtuce	H				•		•	•	•						•			
Chard	•				•	•	•	•	•					•				
Chinese artichoke	•		•	•			•		•								•	
Collards	•				•	•	•		•	•	•				•			
Corn for drying (incl. popcorn)		C		•		•			•			•						
Sweet corn, milk stage		C		•		•			•			•						
Cucumbers		C		•					•				V		•			
West Indian Gherkin		•		•					•			•			•			
Eggplant, Asian/European				•		•			•			•						•
Fennel, Florence/Common	H	•						S	•			•			•			
Herbs																		
Anise hyssop	H		•					•	•			•						•
Basils						•			•	•					•	•		
Borage	H	•	•		•			•	•			•			•	•		•
Burnet, salad	•	•	•		•			•	•			•			•			
Caraway	•	•							•			•	•		•	•		
Chervil	•	•		•		•	•	•	•		•					•		
Chives/Chinese chives	•	C		•	•	•	•	•	•		•				•	•		
Coriander	•	•							•		•				•			
Dill	H	•	•				•		•			•			•			
Ginger				•	S	•	•		•			•			•	•		
Hyssop	•	•	•	•	•				•		•					•		•
Lavender	•	•	•	•					•		•			•	•	•	•	•
Lemon verbena	H	•				•			•				•		•			
Lovage	•			•		•	•	•	•				•	•	•			
Marjoram, sweet	H	•							•		•				•			

CHART 1: PLANNING

C=some cultivars; H=half-hardy;
S=in hot, sunny climates; V=vine

PLANT NAME	THE PLANT — Tolerates					THE LANDSCAPE — Optimal soil		Optimal sun		Height				Flower color				
	hardy	drought	poor soil[1]	heat	shade	rich	moist	◑	○	under 12"	12–24"	24–36"	over 36"	greenish	white to yellow	pink to crimson	orange to red	blue to purple
Mints	•	•			•		•	•	•	•					•	•		
Oreganos	•	•	•				•	•		•					•	•		
Parsleys	H			•	•		•	•	•	•					•			
Perillas	H		•	•			•	•	•			•			•			
Rosemary	H	•	•						•			•				•		
Sages	•	•	•						•			•				•	•	•
Savory, summer	•	•	•						•	•						•	•	•
Tarragon, French	•	•						S		•								
Thymes	•	•	•					•	•	•						•	•	
Flowers																		
Calendulas	•	•			•	•			•	•					•		•	
Hollyhocks	•						•		•				•		•	•	•	•
Marigolds	H	C	•				•		•	•	•	•			•		•	
Nasturtiums		•	•						•				V		•	•	•	
Pansies et al.	•						•	•	•	•					•	•	•	•
Scented geraniums	H		•	•					•	•	•	•	•		•	•	•	•
Sunflowers	•	•	•			•			•	•	•	•	•		•	•	•	
Jerusalem Artichoke	•	•	•					•	•				•		•			
Kale	•				•		•	•	•	•					•			
Kohlrabi	H		•	•			•		•	•					•			
Melons		C	•			•	•		•				V		•			
Watermelon/Citron melon			•			•			•				V		•			
Mustard Greens	•				•		•		•	•	•	•			•			
Broccoli Raab	H				•	•	•	•	•	•					•			
Green-in-the-Snow Mustard	•				•		•	•	•	•					•			
Rapini/Turnip Greens	•						•	•	•	•					•			
New Zealand Spinach	H	•		•	•			•	•	•					•			
Okra			•						•		•	•			•		•	
Onion Clan																		
Garlic, cured	•							S	•		•				•	•		
Elephant garlic	H							S	•	•					•			•
Green garlic	•	•	•					S	•	•					•	•		
Rocambole	•	•	•					S	•	•								

CHART 1: PLANNING

C=some cultivars; H=half-hardy;
S=in hot, sunny climates; V=vine

PLANT NAME	THE PLANT — hardy	Tolerates — drought	poor soil	heat	shade	THE LANDSCAPE — Optimal soil: rich	moist	Optimal sun: ◐	○	Height: under 12"	12–24"	24–36"	over 36"	Flower color: greenish	white to yellow	pink to crimson	orange to red	blue to purple
Leeks	H	C		•		•		S	•		•			•				
Onions, bunching	H	•		•		•	•		•		•				•			
Common onions, cured	H	•		C	•	•	•		•		•				•			
Sets	H	•		•			•		•		•				•			
Pearls/Picklers/Boilers	H	•	•	•		•	•		•		•				•			
Potatoes/Multipliers	•	•		•		•	•		•		•				•			
Scallions	H	•		C	•	•	•		•		•	•			•			
Shallots	•								•		•	•			•			
Parsnips	H			•			•		•		•		•		•		•	
Peanuts		•							•		•			•	•	•		
Peas, garden/Soup bush	H				•	•		•			•			•				
Snap/Shoots/Snow peas	H	•		•					•				V	•				
Peppers, chili		C		•					•		•	•		•				•
Sweet peppers				C					•		•	•		•				•
Potatoes	H								•		•				•			
Potherbs																		
Amaranth greens		•		•	•		•		•		•	•	•		•		•	
Good-King-Henry	•	•				•	•		•		•			•				
Nettles, stinging	•				•		•	•		•		•						
Orachs	•				•		•		•			•	•	•	•			
Sorrel, garden	•				•	•	•	•	•	•	•					•		
Spinach beets	•				•	•	•		•		•							
Radishes, Sum/Aut/Win/Rat-tailed	•		•	•					•	•				•			
Radishes, spring	H	C	•	•					•	•				•			
Rhubarb	•						•		•		•	•	•					
Rutabaga	•					•			•	•				•			
Salad Greens																		
Ambrosia	H		•						•	•				•			
Arugula	H	•		•		•	•	•		•				•			
Buck's-horn plantain	•						•	•			•			•			
Chicories, leaf	•			•		•		•	•								•
Witloof/Belgian endive	•			•					•								•
Corn Salad	•					•		•	•				•	•			•

CHART 1: PLANNING

C=some cultivars; H=half-hardy;
S=in hot, sunny climates; V=vine

PLANT NAME	THE PLANT — Tolerates					THE LANDSCAPE — Optimal soil		Optimal sun		Height				Flower color				
	hardy	drought	poor soil[1]	heat	shade	rich	moist	◑	○	under 12"	12–24"	24–36"	over 36"	greenish	white to yellow	pink to crimson	orange to red	blue to purple
Cress, garden/Pink/Upland[2]	•				•	•	•	•		•					•	•		
Watercress	•				•		•			•						•		
Curled mallow	•						•		•						•			•
Dandelion	•			•		•	•	•	•		•				•			
Endive/Escarole	•		•		•	•	•	•	•	•								•
Lettuces																		
Batavia/Butterhead/Romaine	H	C		C	•	•	•	•	•	•					•			
Crisphead	H	•	•		•	•	•	•	•	•					•			
Looseleaf	H			C	•	•	•	•	•	•					•			
Malabar spinach		•			•		•	S	•				V		•			
Miner's lettuce					•	•	•	•	•		•				•	•		
Purslane							•		•		•				•			
Samphire	•	•					•		•		•					•		
Shepherd's purse	•	•	•						•		•				•			
Salsify/Scorzonera	•				•		•		•		•				•			•
Spinach	•	C			•	•			•	•					•			
Squashes, gourds, pumpkins																		
Gourds																		
Angled luffa			•			•	•		•				V		•			
Bitter melon			•			•	•		•				V		•			
Chinese fuzzy gourd			•			•	•		•				V		•			
Cucuzzi/Lagenaria			•			•	•		•				V		•			
Squashes, summer		C	•			•	•		•			•			•			
Squashes, winter/Pumpkins		C	•			•	•		•			•	V		•			
Strawberry, alpine	•						•		•		•				•	•		
Strawberry, garden	•								•		•				•	•		
Sweet potatoes		•		•		•	•		•			•						•
Tomatillos		•							•			•						
Tomatoes		C		C		•	•		•			•	•	V	•			
Turnips	•			R			•	•				•			•			
For the Garden																		
Black mustard	•								•					•	•			
Comfrey	•	•	•	•	•		•	•	•	•			•				•	•

CHART 1: PLANNING

PLANT NAME	THE PLANT — Tolerates					THE LANDSCAPE — Optimal soil		Optimal sun		Height				Flower color				
	hardy	drought	poor soil[1]	heat	shade	rich	moist	◐	○	under 12"	12–24"	24–36"	over 36"	greenish	white to yellow	pink to crimson	orange to red	blue to purple
Green Manures/Cover Crops[3]																		
Legumes																		
Austrian winter peas	H	•							•		•				•		•	•
Clover, crimson	•		•		•				•		•	•				•		
Cowpeas		•	•	•	•	•		•	•		•		•		•		•	•
Fava beans	H		•		•			S	•		•		•		•			•
Soybeans		•	•		•				•		•				•			•
Sweetclover, Hubam	•								•				•		•			•
Vetch, hairy	•	•	•		•				•				•		•	•		•
Nonlegumes																		
Buckwheat		•	•	•					•		•	•	•		•			
Mustard, white	•		•		•				•		•				•			
Oats									•	•				•				
Rape		•							•		•				•			
Rye grass, annual	•								•					•				
Rye, winter	•	•	•						•				•					

1. The plant won't perform as well as if the soil was fertile, but when you're creating a garden, slim pickings are better than none. Make sure the drainage is good.
2. Upland cress is half-hardy.
3. The Green Manures/Cover Crops are all annuals.

CHART 2: SOWING

*=chip the seeds; **=soak the seeds in warm water 8 hours; ***=seeds germinate irregularly

t=start in a container for transplanting later; d=start directly in the ground

D=needs complete dark, cover; L=needs light, sow on surface and press in

Plant Name	seed/tuber life (years, minimum 50% germination)	for transplanting/ starting directly	Shorter: spring	Shorter: summer	Shorter: autumn	Longer: spring	Longer: summer	Longer: autumn	Longer: winter	cold: 55–65°F	cool: 70–75°F	warm: 80–85°F	very warm: 90–95°F	just cover	¼–½"	3 × width or...	days to germination/sprouting
Artichoke*/**	7	t	•			•				•						1"	13
Cardoon*	7	t	•				•			•						2"	15
Asian Greens																	
Chinese cabbage, headed	5	td		•	•	•	•			•						•	3
Chinese cabbage, loose-headed	5	td	•	•	•	•	•	•		•						•	8
Chinese Kale	4	d	•	•	•	•	•	•				•	•				4
Choy Sum/Purple flowering		td		•	•		•					•	•				4/7
Garland chrysanthemum		td		•	•		•			•				•			10
Komatsuna	5	d	•	•	•	•	•	•								•	7
Mizuna	5	td	•	•	•	•	•	•								•	
Pak choi/Flowering pak choi	5	td	•	•	•	•	•	•								•	8
Rosette pak choi	5	d		•	•		•									•	8
Tendergreen	5	d	•	•	•	•	•	•		•						•	
Asparagus (seeds*, crowns)	3	td	•			•	•			•						1"	10
Beans																	
Adzuki	3	d	•			•				•						•	7
Butter/Lima/Sieva bush	3	d		•		•	•					•				•	7
Butter/Lima/Sieva pole	3	d		•		•						•				•	7
Chick-Pea/Tepary	3	d	•			•	•	•	•				•			•	9
Common/Flageolet/Hort.	4	d		•		•	•	•				•				•	6
Common pole	4	d		•		•	•					•				•	6
Cowpea/Blk-eye/ South. pea	7	d		•		•	•						•			•	8
Favas	6	d	•		•		•			•						•	10
Lentils	4	d	•			•				•					•		12
Runners*	6	d	•			•						•				•	10
Soybeans	6	d		•		•						•				•	10

Chart 2: Sowing

*=chip the seeds; **=soak the seeds in warm water 8 hours; ***=seeds germinate irregularly

t=start in a container for transplanting later; d=start directly in the ground

D=needs complete dark, cover; L=needs light, sow on surface and press in

Plant Name	seed/tuber life (years), minimum 50% germination	for transplanting/ starting directly	Shorter: spring	Shorter: summer	Shorter: autumn	Longer: spring	Longer: summer	Longer: autumn	Longer: winter	cold: 55–65°F	cool: 70–75°F	warm: 80–85°F	very warm: 90–95°F	just cover	1/4–1/2"	3 × width or...	days to germination/sprouting
Winged peas	5	d	•			•				•						•	7
Yardlong	3	d		•		•									•		10
Beets/Mangel*/***	6	td	•	•	•	•	•	•	•		•				•		5
Broccoli, Romanesco/Sprouting	5	td	•			•	•	•			•				•		12
Brussels sprouts	4	t					•	•	•	•	•				•		12
Burdock, great*/**	5	d	•		•	•	•				•			L			14
Cabbage, early	4	t	•			•					•				•		4
Late cabbage	4	t		•		•					•				•		4
Ornamental cabbage/Kale	3	t		•		•	•	•		•				L			17
Carrots	3	d	•	•		•	•			•					•		6
Cauliflower	5	t	•	•		•				•					•		5
Celeriac	8	t	•			•					•			•			15
Celery, Chinese/Trenching	8	t	•	•	•	•				•				L			21
Leaf celery	8	t	•			•	•			•				•			15
Celtuce	3	td	•	•		•				•					•		7
Chard	4	d	•			•	•		•		•				•		8
Chinese artichoke (tubers)	1/3	d	•			•				•						1"	
Collards	4	td	•	•	•	•	•	•		•					•		12
Corn for drying (incl. popcorn)	3+	td	•	•		•	•						•	•		1"	3
Sweet corn, milk stage	3+	td	•	•		•	•					•	•	•		1"	3
Cucumbers	10	td	•	•		•	•						•	•	•		8
West Indian gherkin	5	td	•	•			•						•	•	•		10
Eggplant, Asian/European	7	t	•	•		•						•	•	•			5
Fennel, Florence/Common	4	d	•	•		•		•		•				D			12
Herbs[1]*																	
Anise hyssop		t	•			•	•		•						•		7
Basils	8	td	•	•		•			•		•				•		5

*=chip the seeds; **=soak the seeds in warm water 8 hours; ***=seeds germinate irregularly

t=start in a container for transplanting later; d=start directly in the ground

D=needs complete dark, cover; L=needs light, sow on surface and press in

Plant Name	seed/tuber life (years, minimum 50% germination)	for transplanting / starting directly	Shorter growing season, cold to icy winter — spring	summer	autumn	Longer growing season, moderate to warm winter — spring	summer	autumn	winter	Optimal temperature of soil/soil mix — cold: 55–65°F	cool: 70–75°F	warm: 80–85°F	very warm: 90–95°F	Sowing depth — just cover	1/4–1/2"	3 × width or...	days to germination/sprouting
Borage*	8	d	•	•		•					•			D			5
Burnet, salad	3	d	•		•	•		•			•			•			9
Caraway	3	d	•				•	•			•			•			14
Chervil	2	d	•	•	•	•	•	•		•				•			10
Chives/Chinese chives	2	td	•	•	•	•		•			•			•	•		12
Coriander	6	d	•	•	•	•		•		•						•	10
Dill	5	d	•	•	•	•		•		•					•		23
Ginger (rhizome)	2 mo	t				•		•			•				•		30
Hyssop	3	td	•				•	•			•			•			17
Lavender (plants)		d									•						
Lemon verbena (plants)		d								•							
Lovage (plants)		d									•						
Marjoram, sweet (plants)		d									•						
Mints (plants)		d									•						
Oregano, Greek (plants)		d								•							
Parsleys**	3	td	•	•	•			•	•		•			•		•	12
Perillas	5	td	•	•			•	•			•			L			18
Rosemary (plants)		d										•					
Sages		td	•			•					•					•	12
Savory, summer	1	d	•				•	•		•	•			L			13
Tarragon, French (plants)		d									•						
Thymes (plants)		d								•							
Flowers																	
Calendula	3	td	•					•			•			•	D		12
Hollyhock		td	•	•				•			•			L			12
Marigold		td	•					•			•			•		•	9
Nasturtium*	5	d	•	•		•				•				D			10

Chart 2: Sowing

Plant Name	seed/tuber life (years, min 50% germination)	for transplanting/ starting directly	Sowing Seasons Shorter: spring	summer	autumn	Longer: spring	summer	autumn	winter	cold: 55–65°F	cool: 70–75°F	warm: 80–85°F	very warm: 90–95°F	just cover	1/4–1/2"	3 × width or...	days to germination/sprouting
Pansies et al.		td	•	•	•	•		•	•	•				D			24
Scented geraniums (plants)		d								•	•						
Jerusalem artichoke (tubers)	1/6	d	•			•										4"	14
Kale	4	td	•	•		•	•				•					•	7
Kohlrabi	3	td	•	•		•	•		•		•					•	14
Melons, dessert	5	td	•	•		•						•				•	3
Watermelon, citron melon	6	td	•	•		•							•			•	3
Mustard Greens	4	d		•	•	•		•			•					•	9
Broccoli raab	5	d	•					•			•					•	9
Green-in-the-snow mustard	4	d		•	•			•			•					•	9
Rapini/Turnip greens	5	d		•	•			•			•					•	7
New Zealand spinach*/***	5	td	•			•						•				•	8
Okra**	5	td	•			•	•						•			•	6
Onion clan																	
Garlic, cured (cloves)	1/2	d	•		•			•	•	•						1"	
Elephant garlic (cloves)	1/4	d	•		•			•	•	•						1"	
Green garlic (cloves)	1/3+	d	•		•		•	•	•	•						1"	
Rocambole (cloves)	1/4	d	•		•		•	•	•	•						1"	
Leeks	3	td	•					•			•					•	10
Onions, bunching	1	td	•	•		•					•					•	10
Common onions, cured	1	td	•			•					•					•	10
Sets (bulbs)	1/3	d	•					•	•	•						*	
Pearls/Picklers/Boilers	1	td	•				•				•						10
Pot./Mult./(bulbs)	1/3	d	•	•	•			•	•	•							10
Scallions	1	d	•	•		•					•					•	10
Shallots (bulbs)	1/4	d	•				•			•	•					2"	
Parsnips	1	d	•			•					•					•	15

*=chip the seeds; **=soak the seeds in warm water 8 hours; ***=seeds germinate irregularly

t=start in a container for transplanting later; d=start directly in the ground

D=needs complete dark, cover; L=needs light, sow on surface and press in

Plant Name	Seed/tuber life (years), minimum [50% germination]	For transplanting/ starting directly	Spring (shorter)	Summer (shorter)	Autumn (shorter)	Spring (longer)	Summer (longer)	Autumn (longer)	Winter (longer)	Cold: 55–65°F	Cool: 70–75°F	Warm: 80–85°F	Very warm: 90–95°F	Just cover	¼–½"	3 × width or…	Days to germination/sprouting
Peanuts	4	td	•	•		•							•			1"	10
Peas, Garden/Shoots/Snow bush	3	d	•		•		•	•		•						•	7
Snap peas	3	d	•	•		•		•		•						•	7
Peppers, chili	3	t	•			•						•				•	8
Sweet peppers	3	t	•			•						•				•	8
Potatoes (sprouted tubers)	1/2	d	•	•		•		•		•							12
Potherbs																	
Amaranth greens		d		•		•							•	•	•		12
Good-King-Henry	3	d	•			•				•						•	12
Nettles, stinging		td	•	•		•				•						•	12
Orachs	6	d	•	•				•		•						•	9
Sorrel, garden	4	d	•		•	•		•	•	•						1"	10
Spinach beets	5	td	•					•		•						•	9
Radishes, Sum/Aut/Win/Rat-tailed	5	td		•	•		•					•				•	3
Radishes, spring	5	d	•	•	•	•		•				•				•	3
Rhubarb (crowns)			•		•							•				5"	
Rutabaga	5	d	•	•			•					•				•	8
Salad Greens										•	•			L			14
Ambrosia		d	•			•						•		L			21
Arugula	2	d	•	•		•		•	•			•				•	6
Buck's-horn plantain		d	•	•			•		•	•		•				•	
Chicories, leaf	8	d	•	•		•	•	•	•	•						•	9
Witloof/Belgian endive	8	td	•			•		•		•						•	9
Corn salad	5	d	•	•	•	•	•	•	•	•						•	8
Cress, garden/Pink/Upland	9	d	•	•		•		•		•						•	7
Watercress	9	d	•		•		•	•		•				L			7

CHART 2: SOWING

*=chip the seeds; **=soak the seeds in warm water 8 hours; ***=seeds germinate irregularly

t=start in a container for transplanting later; d=start directly in the ground

D=needs complete dark, cover; L=needs light, sow on surface and press in

Plant Name	seed/tuber life (years, minimum 50% germination)	for transplanting/ starting directly	Sowing Seasons — Shorter growing season, cold to icy winter: spring	summer	autumn	Longer growing season, moderate to warm winter: spring	summer	autumn	winter	Optimal temperature of soil/soil mix — cold: 55–65°F	cool: 70–75°F	warm: 80–85°F	very warm: 90–95°F	Sowing depth — just cover	¼–½"	3 × width or...	days to germination/sprouting
Curled mallow	5	d	•			•				•					•		7
Dandelion	5	d	•				•	•		•					•		7
Endive/Escarole	8	td		•	•		•	•		•					•		7
Lettuce																	
Batavia, butterhead, romaine	6	td	•	•		•		•		•				•			3
Crisphead	6	td	•			•		•		•				•			3
Looseleaf	6	td	•	•	•	•		•		•				•			3
Malabar spinach*	5	td	•				•			•						•	12
Miner's lettuce	5	d	•				•			•				•			
Purslane	7	d	•			•				•				L			6
Samphire	3	td	•					•	•	•					•		18
Shepherd's purse	1	d	•		•			•		•					•		
Salsify/Scorzonera	4	d	•	•	•	•						•			•		21
Spinach	5	td	•			•		•		•					•		6
Squashes, gourds, pumpkins																	
Gourds																	
Angled luffa	6	td	•			•	•						•			•	12
Bitter melon	6	td	•			•	•						•			•	2
Chinese fuzzy gourd	6	td	•			•	•						•			•	3
Cucuzzi/Lagenaria	6	td	•			•	•						•			•	3
Squashes, summer	6	td	•			•	•	•					•			•	
Squashes, winter/Pumpkins	6	td	•			•							•			•	
Strawberry, alp. (seeds, crowns)	3	t	•				•	•	•					L			18
Strawberry, garden (crowns)	3	d	•				•	•		•					•		30
Sweet potatoes (slips)	1/4	d		•		•						•				3"	12
Tomatillos	3	td	•			•						•			•		6
Tomatoes	4+	td	•			•	•					•			•		6

CHART 2: SOWING

*=chip the seeds; **=soak the seeds in warm water 8 hours; ***=seeds germinate irregularly

t=start in a container for transplanting later; d=start directly in the ground

D=needs complete dark, cover; L=needs light, sow on surface and press in

Plant Name	seed/tuber life (years, minimum 50% germination)	for transplanting/starting directly	Sowing Seasons							Germination/Sprouting							days to germination/sprouting
			Shorter growing season, cold to icy winter			Longer growing season, moderate to warm winter				Optimal temperature of soil/soil mix				Sowing depth			
			spring	summer	autumn	spring	summer	autumn	winter	cold: 55–65°F	cool: 70–75°F	warm: 80–85°F	very warm: 90–95°F	just cover	¹/₄–¹/₂"	3 × width or…	
Turnips	5	td	•	•	•	•	•	•			•				•		1
For the Garden																	
Black mustard	5	d	•	•		•						•		•			9
Comfrey (roots)		d	•				•				•					3"	
Green manures/Cover crops																	
Legumes																	
Austrian winter peas		d		•	•		•	•		•						•	4
Clover, crimson		d	•		•	•	•							•			
Cowpeas	7	d		•		•						•		•			
Fava beans	6	d	•	•		•						•		•			
Soybeans	6	d	•	•	•	•						•		•			
Sweetclover, hubam		d	•			•						•		•			
Vetch, hairy		d		•	•		•	•	•					•			
Nonlegumes																	
Buckwheat		d	•	•		•	•					•		•			
Mustard, white		d	•	•	•	•	•	•				•		•			
Oats		d	•	•		•	•			•				•			
Rape		d	•	•		•	•					•		•			
Ryegrass, annual		d	•			•				•				•			
Rye, winter		d		•	•		•	•		•				•			

CHART 3: PLANTING, GROWING, HARVESTING

TS=when the starter plant has tripled in size;
U=to save space, grow it on a support

Plant Name	minimum weeks seed to transplanting size[3]	PLANTING SEASONS[1] — Shorter growing season cold to icy winter[4]: spring[3]	summer	autumn	winters over	Longer growing season moderate to warm winter[5]: spring[3]	summer	autumn	winter	Growing[6]: intensive spacing in bed (inches)	optimal water weekly (inches)[7]	needs extra fertilizer[8]	Harvesting: minimum days earth to table[9]	long harvest season
Artichoke	4		•	•					•	24	1½		120	
Cardoon	8		•	•					•	24	1+		110	
Asian greens														
Chinese cabbage, headed	4	•	•	•				•	•	12	1+		60	•
Chinese cabbage, loose-headed	4	•	•	•	•		•	•	•	8	1+		50	•
Chinese kale		•	•	•		•		•		10	1		30	•
Choy sum			•	•			•	•		6	1		40	•
Garland chrysanthemum		•	•	•		•	•	•		3	1+		40	•
Komatsuna		•	•	•		•	•	•	•	8	1		30	•
Mizuna		•	•	•	•	•	•	•	•	8	1		40	•
Pak choi/Flowering pak choi		•	•	•		•	•	•		7	1		30	•
Rosette pak choi			•	•	•		•	•		12	1		30	•
Tendergreen		•	•	•		•	•	•		6	1		20	•
Asparagus		•						•		21	1		3yr	•
Beans[2]*														
Adzuki, dried		•				•	•			7	1		118	•
Butter/Lima/Sieva bush, shell			•			•	•			4	1		85	
Butter/Lima/Sieva pole, dried			•			•	•			12	1		95	
Chick-pea/Tepary, dried		•	•			•	•			4	1		95/75	•
Common flag./Hort. bush, shell			•	•			•	•		4	1		68	
Common pole, dried			•			•	•			24	1		110	•
Cowpea/Blk-eye/So. pea bush, shell			•				•			6	1		60	
Favas, shell		•		•	•		•			4	1		98	•
Lentils, dried			•				•			4	1		90	
Runners, snap		•	•			•	•			13	1		84	•
Soy, shell			•				•			8	1		75	
Yardlong, snap			•				•			4	1		75	•
Winged peas			•				•			4	1		50	
Beets/Mangel	4	•	•		•	•				4	1		50	

Chart 3: Planting, Growing, Harvesting

TS=when the starter plant has tripled in size;
U=to save space, grow it on a support

Plant Name	minimum weeks seed to transplanting size[3]	Planting Seasons[1] Shorter growing season cold to icy winter[4]				Longer growing season moderate to warm winter[5]				Growing[6] intensive spacing in bed (inches)	optimal water weekly (inches)[7]	needs extra fertilizer[8]	Harvesting minimum days earth to table[9]	long harvest season
		spring[3]	summer	autumn	winters over	spring[3]	summer	autumn	winter					
Broccoli, romanesco/Sprouting	5	•			•	•	•			16	1+		68	•
Brussels sprouts	4		•		•	•				18	1	•	110	•
Burdock, great		•		•	•	•		•		18	1		120	
Cabbage, early	5	•	•			•			•	16	2		74	•
Late cabbage				•	•			•	•	20	1		109	•
Ornamental cabbage/Kale	5			•	•	•	•	•		16	1		60	•
Carrots			•		•	•	•			3	1		50	•
Cauliflower	5		•			•	•			16	1		70	
Celeriac	9	•	•			•				9	1½		170	
Celery, Chinese/Trenching	9		•		•	•		•		9	1½	•	85	•
Leaf celery	4		•		•	•				9	1	•	85	•
Celtuce	4	•	•						•	12	1		80	
Chard			•		•	•	•			12	1		50	•
Chinese artichoke		•				•				12	1		240	
Collards	4		•			•				24	1	•	56	•
Corn, drying (incl. popcorn)	4		•	•		•	•	•		12	1		100	
Sweet corn, milk stage	4		•			•				12	1		64	•
Cucumbers	3		•			•				18	1½		48	•
West Indian gherkin	3		•			•				18	1		60	•
Eggplant, Asian/European	6		•			•				12	1½		100	•
Fennel, Florence		•				•		•		6	1		120	•
Herbs														
Anise hyssop	4	•	•	•	•	•			•	10	1½		50	•
Basils	4		•			•				6	1		30	•
Borage			•			•				12	1		40	•
Burnet, salad		•	•	•	•	•		•		12	1		40	•
Caraway (for seeds)		•	•	•	•	•		•		12	1		1 yr	•
Chervil			•		•	•	•			6	1		40	•
Chives/Chinese chives	4	•	•	•	•	•				12	1		40	•

CHART 3: PLANTING, GROWING, HARVESTING

TS=when the starter plant has tripled in size;
U=to save space, grow it on a support

Plant Name	minimum weeks seed to transplanting size[2]	Planting Seasons[1] Shorter growing season cold to icy winter[4] — spring[3]	summer	autumn	winters over	Longer growing season moderate to warm winter[5] — spring[3]	summer	autumn	winter	Growing[6] — intensive spacing in bed (inches)	optimal water weekly (inches)[7]	needs extra fertilizer[8]	Harvesting — minimum days earth to table[9]	long harvest season
Coriander		•	•	•		•	•			10	1		35	•
Dill		•	•	•		•	•	•		4	1		46	•
Ginger		•				•				5	2		90	•
Hyssop	4	•	•	•	•	•	•			12	1		40	•
Lavender			•	•	•	•	•			48	1		TS	•
Lemon verbena			•			•				24	1		TS	•
Lovage		•	•	•	•	•	•	•		12	1		TS	•
Marjoram, sweet	5	•		•		•				8	1		TS	•
Mints		•	•	•	•	•		•		12	1		TS	•
Oreganos	5	•	•	•	•	•		•		18	1		TS	•
Parsleys	8	•	•	•	•	•				8	1		75	•
Perillas	4	•	•			•	•			10	1		40	•
Rosemary	5	•	•	•	•	•				18	1		TS	•
Sages		•	•	•	•	•				20	1		35	•
Savory, summer		•				•				10	1		42	•
Tarragon, French		•	•	•	•	•		•		20	1		TS	•
Thymes		•	•	•	•	•		•		12	1		TS	•
Flowers														
Calendulas	4	•					•			12	1		60	•
Hollyhocks	6	•	•	•	•	•		•		18	1+		150	•
Marigolds	6	•					•			8	1		70	•
Nasturtiums		•					•			12	1		70	•
Pansies et al.	8	•				•	•		•	6	1		90	•
Scented geraniums		•	•	•	•					18	1		TS	•
Sunflowers		•					•			24	1		70	•
Jerusalem artichoke		•					•			12	1		90	•
Kale	4	•		•		•	•			20	1		50	•
Kohlrabi	5	•	•		•	•	•			6	1		38	•
Melons	3	•				•				18	1		78	•

CHART 3: PLANTING, GROWING, HARVESTING

TS=when the starter plant has tripled in size;
U=to save space, grow it on a support

PLANT NAME	minimum weeks seed to transplanting size[3]	Shorter growing season cold to icy winter[4]				Longer growing season moderate to warm winter[5]				intensive spacing in bed (inches)	optimal water weekly (inches)[7]	needs extra fertilizer[8]	minimum days earth to table[9]	long harvest season
		spring[3]	summer	autumn	winters over[3]	spring[3]	summer	autumn	winter					
Watermelon, Citron melon	3		•			•				18	1		75	•
Mustard Greens		•		•		•		•		6	1		35	•
Broccoli Raab		•		•	•	•		•		6	1		42	•
Green-in-the-Snow mustard		•		•	•	•		•		6	1		50	•
Rapini/Turnip greens		•		•	•	•		•		3	1		40	•
New Zealand spinach			•	•		•	•			12	1		55	•
Okra	8		•			•				24	1		48	•
Onion clan														
Garlic, cured		•		•				•		12	1		90	•
Elephant garlic				•				•		6	1		90	
Green garlic		•	•	•	•	•	•	•	•	2	1		50	
Rocambole garlic				•	•					6	1		90	
Leeks	7		•					•		6	1¹⁄₂		60	
Onions, bunching	7	•		•	•	•				1	1	•	50	
Common onions, cured	7	•		•		•				3	1	•	80	
Sets		•				•				1/2	1	•	95	
Pearls/Picklers/Boilers	7	•		•		•				3	1		60	•
Potatoes/Multipliers		•		•	•			•	•	10	1+		95	
Scallions		•		•		•		•	•	1	1		57	•
Shallots		•		•	•	•				6	1		90	•
Parsnips		•			•	•				4	1	•	100	•
Peanuts	6		•			•				8	1		110	
Peas, Garden/Shoots/Snow bush		•	•					•	•	2	1		52/35	•
Snap peas		•	•					•	•	2	1		52	•
Peppers, chili			•			•				12	1		96	•
Sweet peppers			•			•				15	1		112	•
Potatoes		•					•	•		10	1¹⁄₂		91	•
Potherbs														
Amaranth greens		•				•				10	1+		28	•

CHART 3: PLANTING, GROWING, HARVESTING

TS=when the starter plant has tripled in size;
U=to save space, grow it on a support

Plant Name	minimum weeks seed to transplanting size[3]	Shorter growing season cold to icy winter[4]				Longer growing season moderate to warm winter[5]				Growing[6] intensive spacing in bed (inches)	optimal water weekly (inches)[7]	needs extra fertilizer[8]	Harvesting minimum days earth to table[9]	long harvest season
		spring[3]	summer	autumn	winters over	spring[3]	summer	autumn	winter					
Good-King-Henry	•				•	•				12	1	•	60	•
Malabar spinach	6		•					•		12	1		70	
Nettles, stinging			•		•	•				18	1		60	
Orach			•					•		18	1		60	
Sorrel, garden		•		•	•	•		•	•	12	1		60	
Spinach beets		•			•				•	6	1		50	
Radishes, S/W/A/Rat-Tailed			•	•	•			•		4	1		70	
Radishes, Spring/Summer		•	•	•		•		•	•	2	1		55	
Rhubarb		•								36	1		1 yr	•
Rutabaga		•	•		•		•			6	1		90	•
Salad Greens														
Ambrosia		•				•				6	1		50	•
Arugula		•		•	•					6	1		30	•
Buck's-horn plantain		•	•			•		•		8	1		50	•
Chicories, leaf		•			•	•	•	•		10	1		65	•
Witloof (for forcing)	4	•					•			10	1		124	•
Corn salad		•	•	•	•	•	•	•	•	4	1½		40	•
Cress, garden/pink		•	•		•	•				4	3		50	•
Watercress		•		•	•			•	•	4	2		50	•
Curled mallow		•		•	•					10	1		75	•
Dandelion		•		•			•	•	•	8	1		75	•
Endive/Escarole	4		•		•			•	•	10	1		57/74	•
Lettuce														
Batavia, butterhead, romaine	4	•	•		•	•			•	8	1	•	55	•
Crisphead	4	•	•			•			•	12	1	•	70	•
Looseleaf	4	•	•	•		•			•	12	1	•	40	•
Miner's lettuce		•			•			•		6	1	•	45	•
Purslane		•				•				6	1		60	•
Samphire		•							•	2	1		60	•

CHART 3: PLANTING, GROWING, HARVESTING

TS=when the starter plant has tripled in size;
U=to save space, grow it on a support

Plant Name	minimum weeks seed to transplanting size[3]	Shorter growing season cold to icy winter[4]				Longer growing season moderate to warm winter[5]				Growing[6] intensive spacing in bed (inches)	optimal water weekly (inches)[7]	needs extra fertilizer[8]	Harvesting minimum days earth to table[9]	long harvest season
		spring[3]	summer	autumn	winters over	spring[3]	summer	autumn	winter					
Shepherd's purse		•		•	•				•	6	1		45	•
Salsify/Scorzonera		•	•		•			•		4	1		110	
Spinach	4	•			•		•	•		4	1		34	•
Squashes, gourds, pumpkins														
Gourds														
Angled luffa	3	•				•	•			24U	1½	•	70	•
Bitter melon	3	•				•	•			24U	1½	•	75	•
Chinese fuzzy gourd	3	•				•	•			18U	1½	•	80	•
Cucuzzi/Lagenaria	3	•				•	•			24U	1½	•	65	•
Squashes, summer	3	•				•	•	•		24	1½	•	50	•
Squashes, winter/Pumpkins	3	•				•	•			24U	1½	•	75	•
Strawberry, alpine	16	•		•				•	•	12	1½		1yr	
Strawberry, garden		•						•	•	12	1½		60	
Sweet potatoes	4		•			•				12	1		90	•
Tomatillos	7		•				•			18	1		100	•
Tomatoes	5		•				•	•		18	1½		90	•
Turnips	4	•	•	•	•	•	•	•		4	1		30	
For the Garden														
Black mustard			•	•		•		•		6	1		35	•
Comfrey roots		•	•	•	•	•	•			18	1		60	•

1. This is when to transplant your own seedlings or set plants you've purchased into the garden.
2. Beans: As examples, beans are given at various stages of development—randomly. You'll see in their entries that nearly every bean can be harvested at nearly every stage.
3. Hardy plants can go into the soil as soon as it can be worked. For the rest, wait until all danger of frost has passed.
4. Roughly zones 3–6.
5. Roughly zones 7–10.
6. In cold weather, remember to harden off the plant before planting. At any time, remember to water the plant regularly until it is established.
7. Consult the Water/Watering entry.
8. Consult the Fertilizing entry.
9. Generally based on fairly temperate growing conditions.

For a description of the suggested controls, please see p. 359.

CHART 4: GARDEN PESTS AND DISEASES

Pest / Disease	Urine, human	Urine, fox	Terror-eyes balloon	Tangletrap paste	Summer oil sprays	Sulfur	Sticky traps	Smoke bombs	Semaspore (Nosema locustae)	Sabadilla	Ryania	Rotenone	Pyrethrum	Lime-sulfur	Japanese beetle trap	Insecticidal soap/ soapy water	Insect-weight floating row cover	Hinder repellent	Hand picking	Dormant oil sprays	Diatomaceous earth	Copper	Colorado potato beetle beater	Beneficial nematodes (Biosafe)	Beneficial insects	Bacillus thuringiensis (Dipel)
Ants					•			•					•								•					
Aphids				•	•	•	•			•		•	•			•					•	•				
Army worms																•				•				•		•
Birds			•														•									
Blister beetles										•		•							•							
Cabbage loopers										•		•	•			•										•
Cabbage worms										•	•	•				•										•
Colorado potato beetles												•	•			•			•				•			•
Corn earworms											•					•			•							•
Corn borers										•		•				•			•							•
Crickets									•															•		
Cucumber beetles										•		•	•			•			•					•		
Cutworms																								•	•	•
Deer																		•								
Downey mildew					•																	•				
Early blight																						•				
Earwigs												•									•			•		
Flea beetles										•		•	•			•					•			•		
Flies							•					•														
Gophers, moles								•																		
Grasshoppers									•							•					•					
Groundhogs	?	?						?										•								
Gypsy moth larvae				•				•											•	•					•	•
Japanese beetles												•	•		•				•					•		
Leafhoppers					•	•	•			•		•	•			•					•			•		
Leaf spots														•								•				
Mealy bugs					•		•					•				•								•		
Mexican bean beetles												•	•			•			•		•			•		
Mites					•							•	•	•		•				•				•		
Powdery mildew						•								•								•				
Rabbits		?																•								
Raccoons	•																									

	Urine, human	Urine, fox	Terror-eyes balloon	Tangletrap paste	Summer oil sprays	Sulfur	Sticky traps	Smoke bombs	Semaspore (Nosema locustae)	Sabadilla	Ryania	Rotenone	Pyrethrum	Lime-sulfur	Japanese beetle trap	Insecticidal soap	Insect weight floating row cover	Hinder repellent	Hand picking	Dormant oil sprays	Diatomaceous earth	Copper	Colorado Potato Beetle Beater	Beneficial nematodes (Biosafe)	Beneficial Insects	Bacillus Thuringiensis (Dipel)
Red spider mites					•							•				•									•	
Rodents	•																•									
Root maggots																	•							•		
Root weevils																	•				•			•		
Scales					•											•				•					•	
Slugs, snails							•										•				•				•	
Squash bugs										•		•	•			•			•						•	
Squash vine borers												•				•			•						•	•
Tent caterpillars												•				•			•						•	
Thrips					•	•				•		•	•			•					•				•	
Tomato hornworms												•	•			•			•						•	•
White flies				•	•		•				•	•	•			•									•	
Wireworms																								•	•	

Suggested Controls

 ased on the chart from Johnny's Selected Seeds. After identifying the culprit, give an organic control a chance. Many of these formulae are as lethal as any pesticide—to the victim, but not the environment. You'll feel good about your choice, and the planet will too. A=adult stage, L=larval stage.

Bacillus thuringiensis (Dipel): Group of bacteria harmless to all but pests—apply as soon as first caterpillars appear.

Beneficial insects: The likes of green lacewings, ladybugs, trichogramma, and such gobble up or parasitize dozens of bad guys. The only difficulty is making sure they stay put after they arrive—grow lots of members of the Parsley family to feed them.

Beneficial nematodes (Biosafe): Parasites on our side—apply yearly when needed.

Colorado potato beetle beater: Contains a variety of Bacillus thuringiensis that affects only this beetle—apply early.

Copper: Fungicide that comes in liquid form for spraying and dust for powdering.

Diatomaceous earth: Ground fossilized remains of diatoms, single-cell aquatic plants.

Dormant oil sprays: Spray only on woody plants while dormant—they act by smothering.

Hand picking: A flashlight, gloves and/or a spoon, and a bucket of soapy water are the best tools against pickable pests.

Hinder repellent: Contains ammonium soaps of fatty acids.

Insect-weight floating row cover: Ultra-light material that barely raises the temperature underneath, but keeps pests out. Not only insects, but well secured all around, it's protection against the small hit-and-run rodents who don't have time to stop and nibble through. Some do, but it's saved most of the seedlings like peas, lettuces, and basils in our garden. Given juicy squashes underneath, however, bigger rodents like ground squirrels do stop and chew their way through to the feast.

Insecticidal soap: Fatty acid salts, safe to apply to vegetables and ornamentals—but first try 1 tablespoon dishwashing liquid per quart of water, *then* 1 tablespoon kerosene per soapy quart.

Japanese beetle trap: Set out before beetles emerge—contain lures for both males and females.

Lime-sulfur: Fungicide-bactericide and insecticide—it also helps improve drainage in clay soil.

Pyrethrum: Extract of the blossoms of the Dalmatian daisy—sunlight breaks down the compound within a day, so spraying may need to be repeated.

Rotenone: From the roots of a South American plant, wait 3 days after applying to harvest an edible crop.

Ryania: An extract from the stems of a woody South American shrub.

Sabadilla: Pulverized seeds from a lily-like Caribbean plant. Use in rotation with rotenone or pyrethrum.

Semaspore (Nosema locustae): Developed by the USDA, these are live protozoa deadly to grasshoppers and some crickets. They take a year to have optimum effect, but they do work.

Smoke bombs: Light the fuse, slip the bomb down into a main gopher run, cover the entry with earth—if smoke curls up from the ground somewhere else, dash over and shovel dirt onto that place, too. Bombs may need to be repeated. I understand the deceased in the tunnel warns off others of his ilk.

Sticky traps: Lures attract insects and they stick—hang them up near an infestation.

Sulfur: A trace element that is an old-time, highly effective pest fighter.

Summer oil sprays: Distilled mineral oils that are lighter than those for dormant plant use—also work by smothering.

Tangletrap paste: Apply to a band of leakproof material as a barrier—it stops ant trails. Material will stain.

Terror-eyes balloon: 15-inch bright yellow balloon with shiny eyes that would scare me if *I* were a bird. Dangle from a string about 1 foot above the crop, and put in a new place every week or two. Growers use 6 to 8 per acre, so order accordingly.

Urine, fox: Impregnated disks with the stuff kept chipmunks, ground squirrels, and squirrels out of our garden all summer. Aka foxlure.

Urine, human: Mark your territory the way other large animals do, and larger animals will respect the boundary. Apply at night against raccoons, then rinse off in the morning since the material can be acid.

Sources

Over the years, I've gotten to know most of the people behind the names on these pages. They are dedicated seedsmen. For each plant, I've tried to choose the companies with the best cultivars, and when there are a number of equal value, I've been even-handed. In most cases, there are four sources. In a few cases, there may be just one or two companies offering the plant or specializing in it. When there's a string of listings, it's because none of the collections can be omitted.

Few seed catalogs are free, some are costly. Every season, cultivars I've recommended will be dropped from catalogs, and every season, seed companies will drop from the fray. When you write for a catalog, inquire whether the cultivar you have in mind is available—and if not, what's in its place. I'll always be glad to hear of your experience with sources, seeds, and plants.

This list is organized to mirror the order of the book, so you can browse through Salad Greens, for example, without having to skip around. The Index will remind you where a plant is listed.

Plants are listed with alternative names used by one or another of the seedsmen. Sources are listed not in order of merit, but alphabetically. *Et al.* means there are many companies offering the plant.

As I've mentioned in the text regarding the wealth of Asian seeds available, names and descriptions don't always match up with what I've written. It can make you crazy. Fortunately, no matter what plant comes in the packet, it will be delicious.

Here's an invaluable resource: *Garden Seed Inventory: An Inventory of Seed Catalogs Listing All Non-Hybrid Vegetable Seeds Still Available in the United States and Canada*. This book tells you where to find the likes of Black Diamond Yellow Flesh watermelon, Alabama No. 1 Purple Pod pole beans, Triple Curled Parsley, and Abruzzese o di Galatina chicory. Designed as a preservation tool to save endangered commercial cultivars, the inventory not only lists what is available, but counts open-pollinated cultivars dropped from catalogs each year. The book is published every three years by Seed Saver Publications, Rural Route 3, Box 239, Decorah, Iowa 52101. They also publish a similar inventory on fruits, nuts, and berries. Write them directly.

VEGETABLES

Amaranth. See Potherbs.

Ambrosia. See Salad Greens.

Artichokes: PGS, PKS, SGS, RN; cardoons, CG, GCS, LS, NGN, VBS

Arugula. See Salad Greens.

Asian greens

    Chinese cabbage: heading (napa, michihili), EE, GS, KS, SE, VBS; nonheading/pe tsai/Tokyo Behana/miniato santo/santoh, CS, EE, NGN, SE, VBS

    Chinese kale/gai lon/kailaan: EE, NGN, SGS, VBS

    flowering brassicas: choy sum/Chinese tsai shim, EE, SE; purple-flowered choy sum/hon tsai tai, CS, EE, JSS, SE

    garland chrysanthemum: CG, EE, GS, SE

    komatsuna, komatsuna crosses: EE, PGS, RC, VBS

    mizuna: EE, JSS, NGN, SE, SGS

pak choi/pok choy: EE, NGN StS, SE, TS, et al.; flowering/Chinese tsai shim, CS, NGN, PGS, SE; rosette/Chinese flat cabbage/tah tsai/tatsoi, EE, SE, SGS, StS, TS

Asparagus: In asparagus-growing territory, I suggest you order whatever cultivar Shepherd's offers for your area. Everywhere else, order what Park's Seed or its sister nursery, Wayside Gardens, offers. Also from B, JSS, LS, NF, StS.

Beans

beans for drying: adzuki beans, DD, GSC, JLH, PGS; black beans, AL, FH, SGS, VLH; chick-peas/garbanzos, AL, DG, JLH, PS (black, AL, DD, GS, SC; kala chana, AL, JLH); cowpea relatives, moth, RC; mung, rice, urd, DD; for growing on restricted water, DD, NSS, PS, SW; kidney beans (red, HF, LSC, StS, VBS; white/cannellini beans, CG, SB, JSS, PGS); lentils, DD, GCS, JLH, NSS; tepary, Virus Free White and Virus Free Yellow from NSS, others from DD, RC, SC; yankee shell and dried beans, FH, FM, JSS, SB, SC, SGS, VGS, et al.; fresh beans: butter/sieva, dwarf butter/sieva, DD, GSN, PGS, VBS; cowpeas/southern peas, DD (offers Sunapee), HF, P&S, SB, SS, TwS (black-eyed peas, HG, P&S, NSS; yardlong/asparagus beans, EE, NGN, RC, SE); fava (for temperate climates, AL, DD, SC, TS; for colder climates, FM, GS, StS, TM; for unusual favas: The Aprovecho Institute, 80574 Hazelton Rd., Cottage Grove, OR 97424); lima, bush, P&S, SC, StS, VBS; pole, DD, NSS, RC, StS, VBS, et al.; Dr. Martin: Fern Hill Farm, P.O. Box 185, Clarksboro, NJ 08020; cornfield beans, PGS, RHS, SES, VBS; runner beans (black seeded, DD, GM, PkS, SC; scarlet and mauve, PkS, SC, SS, TJ, TM; White Dutch, SGS, SS, VBS); snap beans, bush and pole, every vegetable catalog offers snap beans; for my part, I *start* with B, BG, CGC, HrS, JSS, PkS, SGS, StS, TS, VBS, WD; filet beans, CG, GCS, JG, JSS, SGS, StS; Italian/Roma beans, CG, HrS, JSS, SGS, StS; purple pod beans, BG, CG, SGS, TS, et al.; wax beans, CG, SGS, JSS, StS, VBS, et al.); shell/horticultural beans, PGS, JSS, StS, VBS (flageolet beans, DD, JG, NGN, SGS); soybeans, AL, DD, GS, JSS, PGS, SE; winged peas/asparagus peas, TM

Beets

garden: CG, SC, SGS, StS, TwS, et al.

greens: CG, JSS, PGS, StS

mangel: JLH, SB

Broad-leaf mustards. See Mustard Greens.

Broccoli: JSS, SGS, StS, TS, TwS

romanesco: JSS, PkS, SB, SES

sprouting: BG, DG, FM, RC

Broccoli raab/rabe. See Mustard Greens.

Brussels sprouts: CG, HrS, SGS, TS

Buck's-horn plantain. See Salad Greens.

Bunching onions. See The Onion Clan.

Burdock, great: BG, EE, KS, SE

Cabbages: green/red, GSN, OL, StS, SES, et al.; savoy, JSS, PGS, SGS, StS, TS, WD; sauerkraut type, LS, PGS, SB, StS; overwintering, StS, TM, TS, V

Cardoons. See Artichokes.

Carrots: BG, PkS, StS, TS, TM, et al.

Cauliflower: JSS, NGN, StS, TS, et al.; green, JSS, PkS, StS, V; purple, JSS, SB, StS, VBS, WD

Celeriac: JG, SGS, TS, WD

Celeries: Chinese, AL, EE, SE; leaf/par-cel, WD, R, SB, SGS, TM; trenching, GS, PkS, SB, StS, TM

Celtuce: BG, NGN, SE, WD

Chao chow. See Mustard Greens.

Chard: CG, FM, PkS, SGS

Chick-peas. See Beans for Drying.

Chicories. See Salad Greens.

Chinese artichokes: DD, SB, SE

Chinese cabbage. See Asian Greens.

Chinese chives. See Herbs.

Chinese kale. See Asian Greens.

Citron melon. See Watermelon.

Collards: B, HrS, SES, TwS

Comfrey roots: AL

Common or leaf mustards. See Mustard Greens.

Corn: baby, EE, NG; dent, NSS, SB, SC, SES; flint, LS, LSC, OL; flour, GCS, GS, NSS, SC; flour-flint, NSS, RC; flour/flint/dent, NSS; for growing on restricted water, NSS, PS, SC, SW; gourdseed, SES; popcorn, JLH, JSS, SC, SES; sweet, LSC, JSS, SC, TS, TwS, et al.

Corn salad. See Salad Greens.

Cowpeas. See Beans, fresh.

Cresses. See Salad Greens.

Cucumbers: apple/lemon, BG, DD, GS, GSN; cornichon/gherkin, GG, JG, NGS, SGS; pickling, GS, HF, LSC, RHS; slicing, JSS, PkS, SB, SES, StS, et al.; West Indian gherkin, GS, GSN, PGS, RC

Curled mallow. See Salad Greens.

Curled mustards. See Mustard Greens.

Dandelion. See Salad Greens.

Eggplant: Asian, EE, RC, SE, StS; European, PkS, SB, SGS, TJ; for growing on restricted water, NSS, PS, SC, SW

Elephant garlic. See The Onion Clan.

Endive and escarole. See Salad Greens.

Fennel: bronze, CG, GCS, R; Florence, CG, RC, SGS, TM

Flowers. See page 105.

Flowering brassicas. See Asian Greens.

Flowering pak choi. See Asian Greens.

Garland chrysanthemum. See Asian Greens.

Garlic. See The Onion Clan.

Good-King-Henry. See Potherbs.

Gourds. See Squashes and Pumpkins.

Green-in-the-snow mustard. See Mustard Greens.

Herbs. See page 91.

Jerusalem artichokes: GCS, PGS, RSP, SB

Kale: BG, FM, HA, SB, SES, TS; ornamental cabbage/kale, HrS, NGN, PkS, SGS, StS

Kohlrabi: B, LSC, SGS, TS

Komatsuna. See Asian Greens.

Lagenaria. See Squashes and Pumpkins.

Leeks. See The Onion Clan.

Lentils. See Beans for Drying.

Lettuce. See Salad Greens.

Malabar spinach. See Salad Greens.

Melons, dessert: cantaloupe (true)/Charentais, CG, JG, PkS, StS, WD, et al.; netted/muskmelon (nutmeg, Persian, etc.), AL, GS, JF, LS, et al.; Oriental crisp melon, EE, GS, NGN, PkS; smooth/winter melon (honeydew, crenshaw, casaba, etc.), LS, PkS, TwS, WD, et al.; Mediterranean/tropical, AL, CG, StS, TM; watermelon, DD, GS, LS, SES, SS, WS, et al.; citron melon, DD, GS, JG, SB; for growing on restricted water, NSS, PS, SC, SW; for edible seeds, GS

Miner's lettuce. See Salad Greens.

Mizuna. See Asian Greens.

Mustard greens

    bau sin/Chao Chow: EE, GS, SC

    broad-leaf: EE, SE, TS, VBS

    broccoli/spring raab: CF, JSS, SGS, StS; rapini/fall raab/turnip greens, OL, StS

    common or leaf/India: PkS, LS, SE, TwS

    curled/green wave: HA, LS, PkS, P&S

    green-in-the-snow/hsush li hung: NGN, SB, SE, TS

    wild *(B. nigra):* AL, JLH

Nettles. See Potherbs.

New Zealand spinach: GCS, PGS, RC, SES

Okra: P&S, SES, SS, TwS; red, DD, DG, GS, NGN

Onions

    bunching onions: Japanese/Nebuka, DG, EE, KS, SE, StS; Welsh, NGN, SB, SES, R, VBS

    cooking/slicing: seeds, B, BG, CG, JSS, LS, et al.; sets, B, GSN, PGS, SGS, WD

    elephant garlic: FF, HF, KF, NGN

    garlic: FF, GS, KF, RSP, SES; rocambole/hardneck/topsetting, FF, JG, KG, SES, NGN

    leeks: JSS, SGS, StS, TS

    potato and multiplier onions: KF, RSP, SES

    scallions: B, HrS, SB

    shallots, sets: JG, KF, SES, SGS

Orach. See Potherbs.

Ornamental cabbage and kale. See Kale.

Pak choi/pok choy. See Asian Greens.

Parsnips: FS, HrS, TM, TS

Peanuts: B, PkS, SS, StS

Peas, garden: CS, JSS, StS, TM, VBS, WD, et al.

    snap peas: GSN, SGS, StS, WD

    snow peas: AL, GSN, SGS, StS, WD

    snow pea shoots/seedlings: EE, SE

    soup peas: DD, WD

Peppers

    chili: HE, JLH, PG, PJ, PS, RC, NSS, et al.; for growing on restricted water: NSS, PS, SC, SW

    sweet: HE, JSS, PG, SGS, SS, StS, SW, et al.

    tabasco and squash peppers: PG, SB

Potatoes: RSP et al.

Potato and multiplier onions. See The Onion Clan.

Potherbs

      amaranth/tampala: GCS, NSS, RC, SB, SC

      Good-King-Henry: CG, FH, FM, SB

      nettles, stinging: DD, R, SB

      orach, green, yellow, or red: BG, CG, GCS, SB

      sorrel: garden, CG, JSS, PGS, R

      spinach beet/perpetual spinach: BG, CG, CS, TM

Pumpkins. See Squashes and Pumpkins.

Purple-flowered choy sum. See Asian Greens.

Purslane. See Salad Greens.

Radishes: leaf, EE; podding/rat-tailed, BG, PGS, SC; spring, HrS, PkS, SGS, StS, TS, et al.;
      summer/autumn/winter/Oriental, EE, GS, KS, NSS, RC, SE, et al.

Rhubarb: seeds, BG, FS, PGS, RHS; plants, NF, LSC, PkS, SGS

Rocambole garlic. See The Onion Clan.

Rosette pak choi. See Asian Greens.

Rutabagas: GCS, OL, StS, TS

Salad greens

      ambrosia/Jerusalem oak: AL, DD, NGN, R

      arugula/rocket: CG, GCS, JS, SGS, et al.

      buck's-horn plantain: CG

      chicories (including Witloof): CG, JSS, SGS, StS, WD

      corn salad: CG, GG, TS, WD

      cresses: garden/broadleaf/curly/peppergrass, CG, NGN, SGS, V; pink, SB; upland, FH, OL, SB,
         VBS; watercress, CG, OL, R, SGS

      dandelion: DD, JG, SC, SGS

      endive/escarole: GC, JSS, NGN, SGS, StS

      lettuce, garden: AL, BG, CG, JSS, PkS, SGS, StS, et al.; Batavian, CG, PGS, SGS, WD

      Malabar spinach: GS, P&S, PkS, SS

      mallow, curled: CS, FB, FP, GCS

      miner's lettuce/claytonia: CG, CS, RC, R

      purslane: BG, CG, SGS, TS

      salsify: NGN, OL, PGS, RHS

      samphire: NGN

      scorzonera: CS, JG, JSS, WD

      shepherd's purse: DD, R, SC

Samphire. See Salad Greens.

Shallots. See The Onion Clan.

Shepherd's purse. See Salad Greens.

Sorrel. See Potherbs.

Soybeans. See Beans, fresh.

Spinach: P&S, SGS, StS, V, WD, et al.; Asian/megaton, EE, SE, StS

Spinach beets. See Potherbs.

Squashes and Pumpkins

      gourds: lagenaria, GS, NGS, SB, SS

squashes: for growing on restricted water, NSS, PS, SC, SW; squashes for seeds, DD, NSS; summer squashes (cocozelle summer squash, GCS, HA, SGS, StS; crookneck summer squash, B, HrS, SES, StS, et al.; pattypan/scallop summer squash, BG, LS, P&S, SES; zucchini, JSS, LS, PGS, SC, SGS, SES, et al.); winter squashes and pumpkins: acorn, GS, GCS, JSS, StS, et al.; banana, GS, GSN, SB, SS; buttercup, GCS, JSS, RHS, SES; butternut, JSS, NSS, SES, StS; cheese, GS, JLH, NSS, SES; cushaw, GS, GSN, PS, NSS; Hubbard, AL, JSS, NSS, StS; kabocha/Japanese, EE, JSS, KS, LS, NGN, StS; maximas—more, AL, JSS, LS, RHS, StS, TS, et al.; moschatas— more, AL, NGN, RHS, SES; pepos—more, JSS, LSC, SES, StS; pumpkins, BG, CG, GG, GS, JSS, SES, SGS, et al.; vegetable spaghetti, EH, HF, PkS, StS, TwS, et al.

Strawberries, garden: seeds, B, CG, JSS, PkS, SGS, SES, et al.; plants, B, FT, NF, RN, SGS; alpine: seeds, JSS, PkS, SB; plants, LG, PGS, R, WG

Sweet potatoes: B, FPF, GSN, PkS

Tomatillos: HE, NSS, PS, SS

Tomatoes: slicing/salad, GG, GS, HA, HrS, JSS, RC, SB, SC, SGS, StS, TG, TSC, TT, et al.; cherry, SB, SCS, SW, TG, TSC, TT, et al.; currant, JLH, JSS, SB, TG; for growing on restricted water, NSS, PS, SC, SW; pear/plum, SB, StS, SW, TG, TSC, TT, et al.

Turnips: BG, SES, SGS, VBS.

Winged peas/asparagus peas. See Beans, fresh.

HERBS

Anise hyssop: seeds/plants—CP, NGN, R, SM

Basils: CG, FRF, R, SGS, WD; blue: plants—CG, CP, FB, R, et al.

Borage: CP, FP, FRF, WD

Burnet, salad: FRF, PkS, R

Caraway: FRF, R, TS, WD

Chervil: R, SGS, TS, WD

Chinese chives: CG, R, WD, WG

Chives: CG, FRF, R, WD

Coriander: FRF, PkS, SGS, WD

Dill: FRF, PkS, SGS, WD

Ginger: rhizomes, CP, GSN, R

Hyssop: CG, FRF, SM, WD

Lavender: plants—CP, FRF, R, SM, WG

Lemon verbena: plants—CP, FRF, R, SM

Lovage: seeds/plants—FRF, R, SM, WD

Marjoram, sweet: seeds/plants—FRF, PkS, R, SGS

Mint: plants—FRF, R, SGS, WG

Oregano, Greek: plants—CG, CP, PkS, SM

Parsley: CG, CP, R, SGS, TT

Perilla: EE, NGN, R, SE

Rosemary: plants—CG, PkS, SM, WG

Sages, garden: plants—CP, FRF, R, SM

Savory, summer: FRF, PkS, R, WD

Tarragon, French: plants—CG, PkS, R, WG

Thymes: plants—FRF, IAT, LG, R, SM, WG

FLOWERS

For annual and perennial flower seeds, I turn first to Burpee, Harris, Park, Stokes, Territorial Seeds, and
Thompson & Morgan. For perennial plants, Logee's Greenhouses, Richters, Wayside Gardens, and
White Flower Farm. Most vegetable seedsmen offer flower seeds, and the quality matches that of
their vegetables. Investigate.

SUPPLIES AND RESOURCES

Bat houses: GA, GCS, GSp, PGS, PV
Bean towers, A-frame trellis: PS (trellis also from GSp, M)
Beneficial insects: R, BG, PS, NG, M
Books: AL, BG, JSS, PGS, SES
Cloches, cold frames, greenhouse film and clips: M, PV, TS
Cold frames, portable: M, PS, PV, StS
Compost supplies: GSp, M, PGS, PV
Diatomaceous earth: GA, GSC, M, PS (from pool supplies, be sure it doesn't contain piperonyl butoxide)
Drip/soaker irrigation systems: GSp, M, NG, TS
Earthworms and castings: CCW, GA, RRW, WW
Floating row covers: GSp, JSS, M, PV (JSS and PV also have wire for hoops)
Fluorescent growing lights: GSp, JSS, M, WW
Green guide resource: list of resource organizations: GCS
Gro-bags: M, PV
Heating cables: CG, GSp, RHS, TS
Inoculants for legumes: JSS, PGS, PV, VBS
Mulch, plastic/paper: CG, GSp, JSS, PGS
Organic fertilizers and pest controls: GA, NG, NS, PV, WW
Pots, plastic: M, PV
Repellents, mechanical, and traps: B, BG, GSp, PGS, PV
Seedling trays (Styrofoam, plastic): CG, GSp, RHS, TS
Seed saving, pollinating supplies: SES
Shade cloth: PV, TS
Slug/snail bait .13 percent metaldehyde (others contain 4 percent): NS
Soil blockers: GSN, GSp, PV, TS
Soil-testing kits: GCS, GSp, JSS, PGS
Terror-eyes balloons: HP, JSS, PGS, PV
Tools, quality: AML, BC, GSp, L, M, SH

KEY TO SOURCES

AL=Abundant Life Seed Foundation
P.O. Box 772 / 1029 Lawrence Street
Port Townsend, WA 98368

AML=A.M. Leonard, Inc.
P.O. Box 816 / 6665 Spiker Road
Piqua, OH 45356-0816

B=W. Atlee Burpee Company
300 Park Avenue
Warminster, PA 18974

BC=Brookstone
5 Vose Farm Road
Peterborough, NH 03458

BG=Bountiful Gardens
18001 Shafer Ranch Road
Willits, CA 95490

CCW=Cape Cod Worm Farm
30 Center Way
Buzzards Bay, MA 02532

CF=Comstock Ferre & Company
P.O. Box 125 / 263 Main Street
Wethersfield, CT 06109

CG=The Cook's Garden
P.O. Box 535 / Moffits Bridge
Londonderry, VT 05148

CP=Companion Plants
7247 N. Coolville Ridge Road
Athens, OH 45701

CS=Chiltern Seeds
Bortree Stile
Ulverston,
Cumbria, England LA 127PB

DD=Deep Diversity
P.O. Box 190
Gila, NM 88038

DG=DeGiorgi Seed Company
6011 N Street
Omaha, NE 68117-1634

EE=Evergreen Y.H. Enterprises
P.O. Box 17538
Anaheim, CA 92817-7538

FB=Flowery Branch Seed Company
P.O. Box 1330
Flowery Branch, GA 30542

FF=Filaree Farm Route 2, Box 162
Okanogan, WA 98840-9774

FH=Fox Hollow Herbs and Heirloom Seed
Company
P.O. Box 148
McGrann, PA 16236

FM=Floating Mountain Seeds
P.O. Box 1275
Port Angeles, WA 98362-1275

FP=The Fragrant Path
P.O. Box 328
Ft. Calhoun, NE 68023

FPF=Fred's Plant Farm
P.O. Box 707
Dresden, TN 38225

FRF=Fragrant Fields
128 Front Street
Dongola, IL 62926

FS=Farmer Seed & Nursery
P.O. Box 129 / 818 N.W. 4th Street
Faribault, MN 55021

FT=New York State Fruit Testing
Association Coop
P.O. Box 462
Geneva, NY 14456-0462

GA=Gardens Alive!
5100 Schenley Place
Lawrenceburg, IN 47025

GCS=Garden City Seeds
1324 Red Crow Road
Victor, MT 59875

GG=The Gourmet Gardener
4000 West 126th Street
Leawood, KS 66209

GS=Gleckler Seedmen
Metamora, OH 43540

GSC=Good Seed Company
Star Route, Box 73A
Oroville, WA 98844

GSN=Gurney's Seed & Nursery Co.
110 Capital Street
Yankton, SD 57079

GSp=Gardener's Supply Company
128 Intervale Road
Burlington, VT 05401

HA=High Altitude Gardens
P.O. Box 1048 / 308 S. River
Hailey, ID 83333

HE=Horticultural Enterprises
P.O. Box 81002
Dallas, TX 75381-0082

HF=Henry Field Seed & Nursery
415 North Burnett
Shenandoah, IA 51602

HP=Hartmann's Plantation, Inc.
   310 - 60th Street
   Grand Junction, MI 49056
HrS=Harris Seeds/Garden Trends, Inc.
   60 Saginaw Drive
   Rochester, NY 14623
IAT=It's About Thyme
   11726 Manchaca Road
   Austin, TX 78748
JG=Le Jardin du Gourmet
   P.O. Box 75
   St. Johnsbury Center, VT 05863
JLH=J.L. Hudson, Seedsman
   P.O. Box 1058
   Redwood City, CA 94064
JSS=Johnny's Selected Seeds
   Foss Hill Road
   Albion, ME 04910-9731
KF=Kalmia Farm
   Route 1, Box 149
   Esmont, VA 22937
KS=Kitazawa Seed Company
   1111 Chapman Street
   San Jose, CA 95126
L=Langenbach Fine Tool Co.
   Dept 4200 / P.O. Box 453
   Blairstown, NJ 07825-0453
LG=Logee's Greenhouses
   141 North Street
   Danielson, CT 06239
LS=Lockhart Seeds
   P.O. Box 1361 / 3 North Wilson Way
   Stockton, CA 95201
LSC=Liberty Seed Company
   P.O. Box 806 / 128 1st Drive S.E.
   New Philadelphia, OH 44663
M=Mellinger's Inc.
   2310 W. South Range Road
   North Lima, OH 44452
NF=Nourse Farms, Inc.
   RFD, Box 485 / River Road (Whately)
   South Deerfield, MA 01373
NG=Natural Gardening Company
   217 San Anselmo Avenue
   San Anselmo, CA 94960
NGN=Nichols Garden Nursery, Inc.
   1190 N. Pacific Highway
   Albany, OR 97321
NS=Naturally Scientific
   P.O. Box 500335
   Atlanta, GA 31150

NSS=Native Seeds/SEARCH
   2509 N. Campbell Avenue, 325
   Tucson, AZ 85719
OL=Orol Ledden & Sons
   P.O. Box 7 / Center & Atlantic Avenues
   Sewel, NJ 08080-0007
P&S=Porter & Son
   P.O. Box 104 / 1510 E. Washington Street
   Stephenville, TX 76401-0104
PG=The Pepper Gal
   P.O. Box 23006
   Fort Lauderdale, FL 33307-3006
PGS=Pinetree Garden Seeds
   Box 300
   New Gloucester, ME 04260
PJ=Pepper Joe's, Inc.
   1650 Pembrooke Road
   Norristown, PA 19403
PkS=Park Seed Company, Inc.
   P.O. Box 46 / Highway 254 North
   Greenwood, SC 29648-0046
PS=Plants of the Southwest
   Route 6, Box 11A, Agua Fria
   Santa Fe, NM 87501
PV=Peaceful Valley Farm Supply
   P.O. Box 2209
   Grass Valley, CA 95945
R=Richters Herbs
   357 Highway 47
   Goodwood, ON, Canada LOC 1AO
RC=Redwood City Seed Company
   P.O. Box 361
   Redwood City, CA 94064
RHS=R.H. Shumway Seedsman
   P.O. Box 1 / Route 1, Whaley Pond Road
   Graniteville, SC 29829
RN=Raintree Nursery
   391 Butts Road
   Morton, WA 98356
RRW=Rainbow Red Worms
   P.O. Box 278
   Lake Elsinor, CA 92531-0278
RSP=Ronniger's Seed Potatoes
   Star Route, Road 73
   Moyie Springs, ID 83845
SB=Seeds Blüm
   Idaho City Stage
   Boise, ID 83706
SC=Seeds of Change
   621 Old Santa Fe Trail, #10
   Santa Fe, NM 87501

SE=Sunrise Oriental Seed Company
    P.O. Box 330058
    West Hartford, CT 06133-0058
SES=Southern Exposure Seed Exchange
    P.O. Box 158
    North Garden, VA 22959
SGS=Shepherd's Garden Seeds
    6116 Highway 9
    Felton, CA 95018
SH=Smith & Hawken
    117 East Strawberry Dr.
    Mill Valley, CA 94941
SM=Sandy Mush Herb Nursery
    Route 2, Surrett Cove Road
    Leicester, NC 28748
SS=Southern Seeds
    P.O. Box 2091
    Melbourne, FL 32902-2091
StS=Stokes Seed Company
    P.O. Box 548
    Buffalo, NY 14240
SW=Seeds West Garden Seeds
    P.O. Box 1739
    El Prado, NM 87529
TG=Tomato Growers Supply Company
    P.O. Box 2237
    Fort Myers, FL 33902
TJ=The Thomas Jefferson Center For Historical
    Plants
    Monticello / P.O. Box 316
    Charlottesville, VA 22902
TM=Thompson & Morgan
    P.O. Box 1308 / Farraday & Gramme
    Avenues
    Jackson, NJ 08527-0308
TS=Territorial Seed Company
    P.O. Box 157
    Cottage Grove, OR 97424
TSC=The Tomato Seed Company
    P.O. Box 1400
    Tryon, NC 28782

TT=Totally Tomatoes
    P.O. Box 1626
    Augusta, GA 30903
TwS=The Otis S. Twilley Seed Co., Inc.
    P.O. Box 65
    Trevose, PA 19053-0065
V=Vesey's Seeds, Ltd.
    P.O. Box 9000, York
    Charlottetown, PEI, Canada C1A 8K6
VBS=Vermont Bean Seed Company
    Garden Lane
    Fair Haven, VT 05743
WD=William Dam Seeds
    P.O. Box 8400 / 279 Highway 8
    (Flamborough)
    Dundas, ON, Canada L9H 6M1
WFF=White Flower Farm
    Route 63
    Litchfield, CT 06759-0050
WG=Wayside Gardens
    P.O. Box 11
    Hodges, SC 29695-0001
WSH=Well-Sweep Herb Farm
    317 Mt. Bethel Road
    Port Murray, NJ 07865
WS=Willhite Seed Company
    P.O. Box 23
    Poolville, TX 76487
WW=Worm's Way
    3151 S Highway 446
    Bloomington, IN 47401-9111

About These Companies

Companies offering rare or unusual material are starred (*). Those focusing on genetic preservation are double-starred (**).

With particular attention to flavor: *The Cook's Garden, *Nichols Garden Nursery, *Shepherd's Garden Seeds
North: Gurney's Seed & Nursery Co., *Johnny's Selected Seeds, Stokes Seeds Inc.
North Pacific Rim: **Abundant Life Seed Foundation
Northern Rockies and Great Plains: **Garden City Seeds
Northwest (Maritime): *Territorial Seed Company

Mid-Atlantic region: **Southern Exposure Seed Exchange
South: Porter & Son, Southern Seeds
Southwest: *Plants of the Southwest, **Native Seeds/SEARCH
West: Seeds West Garden Seeds
California: Lockhart Seeds, Inc.
High altitudes: *High Altitude Gardens
Short seasons: Stokes Seeds Inc., Vesey's
Broad range of heritage and non-hybrid cultivars: **Abundant Life Seed Foundation, **Bountiful Gardens,
    **Seeds Blüm, **Seeds of Change, **Southern Exposure Seed Exchange
Specialists in one or two vegetables: Garlic: *Filaree Farm, *Kalmia Farms; Peppers: Horticultural
    Enterprises, The Pepper Gal, Pepper Joe's, Inc.; Potatoes: *Ronniger's Seed Potatoes; Tomatoes:
    *Tomato Growers Supply Company, The Tomato Seed Company, Totally Tomatoes.
Broad range of unusual seeds: **Deep Diversity, *The Flowery Branch, **J.L. Hudson, *Pinetree Garden
    Seeds, **Seeds Blüm, *Thompson & Morgan
Offering a few unusual vegetable seeds: *Gleckler's Seedmen
Asian seeds: *Evergreen Y.H. Enterprises, *Kitazawa Seed Company, *Sunrise Oriental Seed
Unusual herb plants and seeds: *Companion Plants, *It's About Thyme, *Richters, *Sandy Mush Herb
    Nursery, *Well-Sweep Herb Farm
Unusual perennial plants, some herbs: *Logee's Greenhouses, *Wayside Gardens, *White Flower Farm
Unusual perennial and herb seeds: *The Seed Source
Gardening supplies: Brookstone (tools), Gardens Alive!, Garden Supply Company, Langenbach (tools),
    Mellinger's, The Natural Gardening Company, Naturally Scientific, Peaceful Valley Farm Supply,
    Smith & Hawken, Worm's Way
Very small companies which should be supported offering fewer but excellent general seeds: *Fox Hollow,
    *Gleckler's, **Good Seed, **Redwood City
Best-quality reliable general seeds and basics: Burpee, Harris Seeds, Johnny's, Park Seed, Stokes Seeds

If you're eager to be informed about all the seed and plant sources, garden suppliers and services, plant societies, magazines and newsletters, libraries, books available, and a state-by-state index of seedsmen and nurseries, I recommend Barbara Barton's *Gardening by Mail*—a source book for gardeners in the United States and Canada. It is revised every few years, and in the interim, you can subscribe to the updates in frequent newsletters.

A grass roots organization dedicated to preserving genetic diversity in edible plants—that is, saving open-pollinated cultivars from extinction—is the Seed Savers Exchange. A recipient of a grant from the McArthur Foundation, SSE is a crucial cause in the hands of remarkable people. I urge you to join their ranks. Write Seed Savers Exchange, Rural Route 3, Box 239, Decorah, Iowa 52101.

Cooperative Extension Services

A plus sign (+) before an entry indicates the agency is one of many in the state. Ask about county services near you.

ALABAMA

Alabama A & M University
Normal, AL 35762
(205)851-5710

Auburn University
Auburn, AL 36849
(205)844-5323

Tuskegee University Cooperative Extension
    Program
Extension Building Room 208
Tuskegee, AL 36088
(205)727-8806

ALASKA

University of Alaska
Fairbanks, AK 99775
(907)474-7246

ARIZONA

Extension Garden Center
4210 North Campbell
Tucson, AZ 85719
(602)624-8632

University of Arizona Cooperative Extension
Forbes 301
Tucson, AZ 85721
(602)621-7205

ARKANSAS

Extension Administration
P.O. Box 391
Little Rock, AR 72203

University of Arkansas
Fayetteville, AR 72701
(501)444-1755

CALIFORNIA

University of California Cooperative Extension -
    North and North Central
1333 Research Park Drive
UC Davis Campus
Davis, CA 95616
(916)757-8777

University of California Cooperative Extension -
    South
9240 South Riverbend Avenue
Parlier, CA 93648
(209)891-2500

University of California Cooperative Extension -
    Southern
UC Riverside Campus
Riverside, CA 92521
(909)787-3321

COLORADO

+Colorado State University Cooperative
   Extension
1 Administrative Building
Fort Collins, CO 80523
(303)491-6281 -6282 -6283

Tri-River Extension
619 Main Street
Grand Junction, CO 81501
(303)244-1836

CONNECTICUT

Connecticut Agricultural Experiment Station
P.O. Box 1106
New Haven, CT 06504
(203)789-7272

University of Connecticut
Storrs, CT 06268
(203)486-4125

DELAWARE

Delaware Cooperative Extension
032 Townsend Hall
Newark, DE 19717-1303
(302)831-2506

Delaware State University Cooperative Extension
1200 North DuPont Highway
Dover, DE 19901-2277
(302)739-5205

DISTRICT OF COLUMBIA

University of the District of Columbia
Washington, DC 20005
(202)274-6900

FLORIDA

Florida A & M University
Tallahassee, FL 32307
(904)599-3546

University of Florida
College of Agriculture
Gainesville, FL 32611
(904)392-1961 -1761 (Coop Ext.)

GEORGIA

+Fort Valley State College
School of Agriculture
Fort Valley, GA 31030
(912)825-6297

University of Georgia Cooperative Extension
111 Conner Hall
Athens, GA 30602
(706)542-3824

IDAHO

Latah County Extension Office
P.O. Box 8068 / 522 South Adams
Moscow, ID 83843
(208)882-8580

ILLINOIS

University of Illinois
College of Agriculture
Shelbyville, IL 61801
(217)774-9546

INDIANA

Purdue University Cooperative Extension
   Services
Room 104, AGAD
West Lafayette, IN 47907-1140
(317)494-8489

IOWA

Iowa State University Horticulture Extension
105 Horticulture
Ames, IA 50011
(515)294-1870; (515)294-3011; (515)294-6616

KANSAS

+Kansas State Cooperative Extension Services
123 Umberger Hall
Manhattan, KS 66506-3401
(913)532-5820

KENTUCKY

Fayette County Extension Office
1145 Red Mile Road
Lexington, KY 40504-1172
(606)257-5582

Kentucky State University
Frankfort, KY 40601
(502)227-6861

LOUISIANA

Cooperative Extension Services
Louisiana State University
Baton Rouge, LA 70893
(504)388-4141

Southern University A & M College
Baton Rouge, LA 70813
(504)771-4090

MAINE

University of Maine Cooperative Extension
5741 Libby Hall
Orono, ME 04469-5741
(207)581-3188

MARYLAND

University of Maryland
College of Agriculture
College Park, MD 20742
(301)405-2882; 1-(800)342-2507

University of Maryland
Department of Agriculture
Princess Anne, MD 21853
(410)651-6206

MASSACHUSETTS

University of Massachusetts
College of Agriculture
Amherst, MA 01003
(413)545-2715

MICHIGAN

Michigan State University
College of Agriculture
East Lansing, MI 48824
(517)355-2308

MINNESOTA

University of Minnesota
College of Agriculture & Natural Resources
St. Paul, MN 55108
(612)625-1915

MISSISSIPPI

Alcorn State College
Lorman, MS 39096
(601)877-6125

Mississippi State University
College of Agriculture
Mississippi State, MS 39762
(601)325-3036

MISSOURI

Lincoln University Department of Agriculture
207 Foster Hall
Jefferson City, MO 65102-0029
(314)681-5547

University of Missouri
College of Agriculture
Columbia, MO 65211
(314)882-7754

MONTANA

Montana State University General Extension
Office
Culbertson Hall - MSU Room 204
Bozeman, MT 59717
(406)994-6647

NEBRASKA

Nebraska Cooperative Extension Publication
Distribution Center

105 Agriculture Communication Building - Box
83918
Lincoln, NE 68583-0918
(402)472-9713

NEVADA

University of Nevada
College of Agriculture
Reno, NV 89557
(702)784-1660

NEW HAMPSHIRE

University of New Hampshire
College of Agriculture
Durham, NH 03824
(603)862-1520

NEW JERSEY

Rutgers Cooperative Extension Cook College
Marin Hall, Room 111
P.O. Box 231
New Brunswick, NJ 08903-0231
(908)932-9306

NEW MEXICO

New Mexico State University
College of Agriculture
Las Cruces, NM 88003
(505)646-3015

NEW YORK

+Cornell University Cooperative Extension
276 Roberts Hall
Ithaca, NY 14853-4203
(607)255-2237

New York State Agriculture Experiment Station
Geneva, NY 14456
(315)787-2011

NORTH CAROLINA

+North Carolina State University
College of Agriculture
Raleigh, NC 27695
(919)515-2811

NORTH DAKOTA

State University of Agriculture
State University Station
Fargo, ND 58105
(701)237-8944

OHIO

Ohio State University
College of Agriculture
Columbus, OH 43210
(614)292-6181

OKLAHOMA

Langston University
Research & Extension Program
P.O. Box 730
Langston, OK 73050
(405)466-3836

Oklahoma State University
Department of Horticulture and L.A.
Stillwater, OK 74078
(405)744-5406

OREGON

Agricultural Communications
Administrative Services A422
Corvallis, OR 97331-2119
(503)737-2713

PENNSYLVANIA

+Pennsylvania State University
College of Agriculture
University Park, PA 16802
(814)863-0331

RHODE ISLAND

University of Rhode Island
Kingston, RI 02881
(401)792-2900

SOUTH CAROLINA

+Clemson University
College of Agriculture
Clemson, SC 29631
(803)656-3381

SOUTH DAKOTA

South Dakota Cooperative Extension Service
Agriculture Hall 154
South Dakota State University, Box 2207D
Brookings, SD 57007
(605)692-6268

TENNESSEE

Tennessee State University
School of Agriculture
Nashville, TN 37203
(615)320-3423

University of Tennessee
Institute of Agriculture
Knoxville, TN 37901
(615)521-2340

TEXAS

Texas A & M University
College of Agriculture
College Station, TX 77843
(409)845-7800

UTAH

Utah State University
Department of Plants, Soils & Biometeorology
Logan, UT 84322-4820
(801)797-2258

VERMONT

University of Vermont
College of Agriculture Extension System
501 Main Street
Burlington, VT 05401-3439
(802)656-2990

VIRGINIA

Virginia Tech School of Agriculture and Life
    Sciences
Blacksburg, VA 24061
(703)231-6636

WASHINGTON

Washington State University Cooperative
    Extension
411 Hulbert Hall
Pullman, WA 99164-6230
(509)335-2933

WEST VIRGINIA

West Virginia University
College of Agriculture
Morgantown, WV 26506
(304)293-5691

WISCONSIN

+University of Wisconsin
Extension Building 601
432 Lake Street
Madison, WI 53706-1498
(608)263-6260

WYOMING

University of Wyoming
College of Agriculture
Laramie, WY 82071
(307)766-5124

Selected References

Of the garden books I consulted to give mine depth and breadth, the following are a drop in the bucket—and none of the background sources on history, lore, nature, landscaping, ecology, and design are here. These are the books I used constantly, and I recommend them to you.

All About Vegetables by the Editorial Staff of Ortho Books. San Ramon, CA: Ortho Books, 1990.

Cooking from the Garden by Rosalind Creasy. San Francisco: Sierra Club Books, 1988.

Crockett's Victory Garden by James Underwood Crockett. Boston: Little, Brown and Company, 1977.

Edible Landscaping by Rosalind Creasy. San Francisco: Sierra Club Books, 1982.

Encyclopedia of Organic Gardening by the Staff of *Organic Gardening* Magazine. Emmaus, PA: Rodale Press, 1978.

Garden Seed Inventory, Third Edition. Decorah, IA: Seed Saver Publications, 1992.

Good Neighbors: Companion Planting for Gardeners by Anna Carr. Emmaus, PA: Rodale Press, 1985.

Growing Fruits & Vegetables Organically. Edited by Jean M. A. Nick and Fern Marshall Bradley. Emmaus, PA: Rodale Press, 1994.

Growing Organic Vegetables West of the Cascades by Steve Solomon. Seattle: Pacific Search Press, 1985.

Handbook of Southern Vegetable Gardening by Barbara Pleasant. Atlanta, GA: Peachtree Publishers, Ltd., 1984.

Harrowsmith Illustrated Book of Herbs by Patrick Lima. Camden East, Ontario: Camden House Publishing, 1986.

Harrowsmith Northern Gardener by Jennifer Bennett. Camden East, Ontario: Camden House Publishing, 1982.

High-Yield Gardening by Marjorie B. Hunt and Brenda Bortz. Emmaus, PA: Rodale Press, 1986.

Hortus Third. The Staff of the Liberty Hyde Bailey Hortorium. New York: Macmillan Publishing Co., Inc., 1976.

How To Grow More Vegetables by John Jeavons. Berkeley: Ten-Speed Press, 1982.

Illustrated Guide to Organic Gardening by the Editors of Sunset Books and Sunset Magazine. Menlo Park, CA: Sunset Publishing Corporation, 1991.

Knott's Handbook for Vegetable Growers by Oscar A. Lorenz & Donald N. Maynard. Third Edition. New York: John Wiley & Sons, Inc., 1988.

Making Vegetables Grow by Thalassa Cruso. New York: Van Nostrand Reinhold Company, 1981.

New Organic Grower's Four-Season Harvest by Eliot Coleman. Post Mills, VT: Chelsea Green Publishing Company, 1992.

New Seed-Starters Handbook by Nancy Bubel. Emmaus, PA: Rodale Press, 1988.

Oriental Vegetables by Joy Larkcom. Tokyo: Kodansha International, 1991.

Random House Book of Vegetables by Roger Phillips and Martyn Rix. New York: Random House, 1993.

Rodale's Garden Problem Solver by Jeff Ball. Emmaus, PA: Rodale Press, 1988.

Rodale's Illustrated Encyclopedia of Herbs, Claire Kowalchik and William H. Hylton, Editors. Emmaus, PA: Rodale Press, 1987.

Salad Garden by Joy Larkcom. New York: The Viking Press, 1984.

Seed to Seed by Suzanne Ashworth. Decorah, IA: Seed Savers Exchange, Inc., 1991.

Self-Sufficient Gardener by John Seymour. Garden City, NY: Dolphin Books, 1980.

Step by Step Organic Vegetable Gardening by Shepherd Ogden. New York: HarperCollins Publishers, 1992.

Sturtevant's Edible Plants of the World. Edited by U.P. Hedrick. New York: Dover Publications Inc., 1972.

Sunset Western Garden Book. Menlo Park, CA: Sunset Publishing Corporation, 1992.

Taylor's Encyclopedia of Gardening. Edited by Norman Taylor. Boston: Houghton Mifflin Company, 1961.

Taylor's Guide to Vegetables & Herbs. Boston: Houghton Mifflin Company, 1987.

Vegetable Expert by Dr. D. G. Hessayon. Waltham Cross, Herts., England: pbi Publications, 1985.

Vegetables from Small Gardens by Joy Larkcom. London: Faber and Faber, 1976.

Wise Garden Encyclopedia. New York: HarperCollins Publishers, 1990.

Index

Notes

Notes

Notes

Notes

Notes

Notes

Notes

Notes

Notes